# THE ERA OF EDUCATION

T0287760

# The Era of Education

*The Presidents and the Schools,*
*1965–2001*

LAWRENCE J. McANDREWS

UNIVERSITY OF ILLINOIS PRESS
URBANA AND CHICAGO

First Illinois paperback, 2008
© 2006 by the Board of Trustees
of the University of Illinois
All rights reserved
Manufactured in the United States of America
1 2 3 4 5 C P 5 4 3 2 1
⊗ This book is printed on acid-free paper.

The Library of Congress cataloged the cloth edition as follows:

McAndrews, Lawrence J. (Lawrence John)
The era of education : the presidents and the schools, 1965–2001 /
    Lawrence J. McAndrews.
p.  cm.
Includes bibliographical references and index.
ISBN-13: 978-0-252-03080-2 (cloth : alk. paper)
ISBN-10: 0-252-03080-x (cloth : alk. paper)
1. Education and state—United States—History.   2. Federal aid to
education—United States—History.   3. United States—Politics and
government.   I. Title.
LA217.2.M392        2006
379.73—dc22   2006003051

PAPERBACK ISBN 978-0-252-07579-7

*To Mary Ellen, Kevin, Brian, and Chris*

# CONTENTS

# ACKNOWLEDGMENTS

The St. Norbert College Faculty Personnel Committee, Faculty Development Committee, History Discipline, and associate deans Dr. John Neary and Dr. Howard Ebert deserve my thanks for their moral and financial support of this endeavor. I would like to thank Dr. Susan Poulson of the University of Scranton, Dr. Andrew Kersten of the University of Wisconsin–Green Bay, and Dr. Douglas Egerton of LeMoyne College for their valuable contributions to this project. I am grateful to Susan Sorenson, Magdalen Kellogg, Brooke Van Lanen, Valerie Thiel, and Lisa Lee for typing and proofreading this manuscript. Finally, I greatly appreciate the assistance of Laurie Matheson of the University of Illinois Press and Carol Bifulco of BookComp in bringing this manuscript to publication.

# Introduction

When President Thomas Jefferson spoke in 1802 of a "wall of separation," he was alluding to the invisible barrier that the First Amendment had created between government and organized religion. The founder of the University of Virginia could just as easily have been talking about education. The nation's founders viewed it as private, elitist, and virtually absent from the four-month, five-thousand-word debates that produced the U.S. Constitution.[1]

Today in the United States, elementary and secondary education is public as well as private, required of all Americans, and cherished by most. Politicians at every level of government mention education at least as often as they invoke the nation's founders. While paying homage to the tradition of local control of elementary and secondary schools that has rarely permitted more than a dime of every education dollar to come from the federal government, the U.S. Supreme Court, Congress, and the presidents have done more to raise the national profile of education issues in the past three decades than their predecessors did in the previous two centuries. Public opinion polls repeatedly put education at or near the top of national concerns. Presidents routinely cite education as their first domestic priority. Only historians seem to have overlooked the significance of schools to the children who attend them, the parents who send their children to them, the employees who staff them, and the taxpayers who finance them—in other words, just about *everyone*.[2]

## Public School Aid

If a national consciousness toward elementary and secondary education is relatively new, a federal role is not. In British North America, since education was primarily a family and religious function, colonial governments were largely absent from the schools. The American Revolution helped transform education into an instrument for developing and improving society. As private academics encouraged dissent and practical skills, and as "common schools" preached and practiced equality of opportunity, local and state governments began to regulate the schools. The national government's Land Ordinance of 1785 divided public lands in the northwestern United States into townships comprising thirty-six sections of 640 acres each, with the revenue from the sale of section sixteen of each township allocated for public education. The Northwest Ordinance of 1787, which Jefferson authored, established a government for the territory north of the Ohio River, where "the means of education shall forever be encouraged." When Ohio became a state in 1802, the federal government adapted the Northwest Ordinance policy to the region's new states, providing land for common schools.[3]

The first national statistics on education and illiteracy were part of the census of 1840. The Morrill Act of 1862 set aside land in "each loyal state" for the construction of an agricultural college. The first federal Department of Education arrived in 1867 to gather "such statistics and facts as shall show the condition and progress of education in the several states and territories." Two years later, the department lost its cabinet-level status but survived as the Bureau of Education in the Department of the Interior. In 1929, it became the Office of Education (OE).

Two years later, President Herbert Hoover's National Advisory Committee on Education completed the first study of the federal role in education, finding virtually every federal agency "concerned directly or indirectly with education" and calling for the restoration of the Department of Education. President Franklin Roosevelt's Public Works Administration, launched in 1933, issued loans and grants for school and college construction; his Civilian Conservation Corps (1933) and National Youth Administration (1935) provided jobs and job training for high school and college youth; and his Advisory Commission on Federal Aid to Education (1937) advocated temporary federal aid to public schools. During World War II, the Lanham Act (1941) funded school services and construction for soldiers and their children. The Servicemen's Readjustment Act, or GI Bill of Rights (1944), offered a free college education to returning veterans. The Housing Act of 1950 included loans for construction of college residence halls, while Public Laws 815 and 870, enacted in the same year, created impact aid for school construction and operating expenses in the vicinity of naval and military bases. In 1953, the OE joined the new Department of Health, Education, and Welfare. Two years later, President Dwight Eisenhower convened the first White House Conference on Education, which called for federal aid for public school construction. In 1958, in the wake of the Soviet launch of Sputnik I, an anxious Congress overwhelmingly passed the National Defense Education Act, which combined research and development monies for colleges and universities with funds for mathematics, science, and foreign language instruction in elementary and secondary schools.

These federal forays into the national schools, however, were exceptional. The Tenth Amendment—which reserves "the powers not delegated" to the federal government for "the States . . . , or . . . the people"—filled the void left by the Constitution's exclusion of education. Each of these small steps toward federal involvement preceded a giant step back to the states. Though Washington spent 62 percent of all the funds expended by all governments (local, state, and federal) in 1958, it spent only 5 percent of all educational monies.[4]

In 1960, as the post–World War II baby boomers entered high school in record numbers, education for the first time was a major issue in a presidential campaign, with both major candidates and their party platforms supporting some form of federal aid. When John Kennedy entered the White House, he pronounced education his primary domestic objective, only to fail to enact "general" federal aid for public elementary and secondary school construction and teachers' salaries. Less than three weeks after Kennedy's death, however, President Lyndon Johnson signed the Higher Education Facilities Act of 1963, the first major federal aid for college construction. Within two years, Johnson would sign the first comprehensive federal aid to primary and high schools, the Elementary and Secondary Education Act (ESEA) of 1965.[5]

## School Desegregation

The century that followed the Civil War repeatedly raised and then dashed the expectations of the nation's minority schoolchildren. The Thirteenth Amendment of 1865 freed slaves and thus ended legally enforced illiteracy; the Black Codes of 1866 doomed ex-slaves to inferior schools. The Fourteenth Amendment of 1868 promised former slaves "equal protection of the laws" in their quest for educational advancement; the Supreme Court's *Plessy v. Ferguson* decision in 1896 postponed that protection for another six decades. The unanimous rejection of "separate but equal" schools by the Court in the 1954 and 1955 *Brown v. Topeka Board of Education* decisions nonetheless authorized the dismantling of Jim Crow education "with all deliberate speed." After President Dwight Eisenhower sent federal troops to protect the first nine African American students at Central High School in Little Rock, Arkansas, in 1957, Governor Orval Faubus closed all of the state's public schools in 1958. When President Kennedy ordered federal troops to Oxford, Mississippi, to ensure the registration of the University of Mississippi's first black student, James Meredith, they encountered violent resistance.

Finally, after a decade of civil disobedience and in the aftermath of the Kennedy assassination, President Johnson signed the Civil Rights Act of 1964. Title IV of the act empowered the Justice Department to litigate school desegregation cases, and Title VI permitted the Department of Health, Education, and Welfare to withdraw monies from segregated schools. At the time of its enactment, however, only 1 percent of African American children in the South were attending desegregated schools.[6]

## Nonpublic School Aid

Like civil rights advocates, nonpublic school interests, especially Roman Catholic ones, had to wait a long time for assistance from the federal government. But unlike the proponents of racial desegregation, Catholic school representatives were not sure they wanted it. In 1884, early in a wave of immigration that brought more than a million Catholics in each of the decades between 1880 and 1920, U.S. Catholic bishops at the Third Plenary Council in Baltimore ordered a parochial school built for every church. Yet the National Catholic War Council (later the National Catholic Welfare Conference), founded by the American bishops in 1917, opposed federal aid to nonpublic education, deeming it an invitation for a Protestant government to control parochial school curriculum and administration.

The National Catholic Welfare Conference (NCWC) won its first major victory in 1925 when the Supreme Court, in *Pierce v. Society of Sisters,* ruled unanimously against an Oregon law prohibiting attendance at nonpublic schools during school hours. By the end of World War II, political and economic progress as well as the enactment of the GI Bill had brought Catholics into the American mainstream, causing a reversal of the NCWC's opposition to federal aid to education in 1944. Three years later, in *Everson v. Board of Education,* the Supreme Court offered the bishops a powerful rationale for their new position: that public aid to nonpublic schools does not violate the First Amendment's separation of church and state if the tax monies benefit the children rather than the schools. This "child benefit theory," the Court ruled, justified a New Jersey statute permitting the state to reimburse parents for their children's transportation to and from nonpublic schools.[7]

The next year, in *Illinois ex rel McCollum v. Board of Education,* the Court ruled unconstitutional a Champaign, Illinois, released-time religious education program in the public schools sponsored by a council of Catholic, Jewish, and Protestant groups. Justice Hugo Black argued in his majority opinion that the use of tax-supported property and the release of students from their mandatory attendance in secular classes violated the First Amendment's separation of church and state as well as the Fourteenth Amendment's equal protection under the law. In 1952, however, the Court upheld a New York plan that allowed public schools to release pupils during the school day to receive instruction at religious centers. Justice William Douglas, in the majority opinion in *Zorach v. Clauson,* distinguished between the on-campus Champaign and off-campus New York programs. Over the dissent of Justice Black and two others, Douglas explained that unlike *McCollum,* the Zorach case involved neither the use of tax-supported property nor the release of students from public school classes.[8]

The National Defense Education Act (NDEA) of 1958, which aided nonpublic as well as public schools, was the first significant legislative victory for the NCWC. The election of the first Catholic president in 1960 did not improve the climate for nonpublic school aid, however, as two Kennedy administration efforts to expand the NDEA failed to reach the floor of either house of Congress in 1961. By the time Lyndon Johnson ascended to the Presidency in November 1963, the Supreme Court had outlawed official prayers and Bible readings in public schools. Within two years, however, negotiations among the NCWC's Monsignor Francis Hurley, the National Education Association's Robert Wyatt, and Commissioner of Education Francis Keppel produced the church-state compromises that helped pass the Elementary and Secondary Education Act of 1965.[9]

With the passage of the ESEA, a new national consensus thus emerged in favor of comprehensive federal aid to elementary and secondary public schools, the end of de jure school segregation, and the beginning of incremental nonpublic school assistance. By the end of the twentieth century—through many sessions of Congress and the Supreme Court and through the presidencies of Lyndon Johnson, Richard Nixon, Gerald Ford, Jimmy Carter, Ronald Reagan, George Bush, and Bill Clinton—this national consensus remained largely intact, but only after considerable conflict over the effectiveness of public school aid, the gravity of de facto school segregation, and the scope of nonpublic school assistance.

This volume explores the transformation of the federal role in elementary and secondary education through the words and actions of seven administrations, their adversaries, and their allies, underscoring that change, which entered this "era of education" as a hopeful possibility, exited the twentieth century as a formidable challenge.

CHAPTER 1

# Public School Aid
## 1965–81

### Lyndon Johnson

> The taxes of the American people now help support most of those
> people who cannot support themselves, because they haven't the basic
> education to do so. This is why education is our number one priority.
> —Lyndon Johnson (1965)

Lyndon Johnson would be an unlikely revolutionary.[1] An aging New Dealer
with a Southern drawl, Johnson seemed more a career politician than a social
crusader when tragedy thrust him into the Oval Office. But while he spoke
slowly, he would act quickly. "Look, we've got to do this in a hurry," the president said of his school bill in February 1965. "I want to see this coonskin on the
wall." Two months later, when Johnson signed the Elementary and Secondary
Education Act (ESEA) of 1965, he virtually undid two hundred years of history.
Four years later when he left office, he had ensured another three decades of
conflict over the scope and direction of his considerable achievement.[2]

### Johnson and Education

Except for a summer at San Marcos Normal School and two months at Georgetown University Law School, Lyndon Johnson's formal education occurred
exclusively at public schools. After working his way through Southwest State
Teachers' College at San Marcos, Johnson taught at a Mexican school in Cotulla,
Texas, and then at public high schools in Pearsall and Houston.[3]

The authenticity of Johnson's experience as a public school student and
teacher would overshadow his lack of expertise on education issues as a congressman (1937–49), senator (1949–61), and vice president (1961–63). In his
twenty-four years in Congress, Johnson introduced only one education bill, to
provide insurance for federal loans to college students, and gave only one
speech on the subject, in support of a school construction measure that had just
passed the Senate.[4]

## The Elementary and Secondary Education Act of 1965

Contemporary observers and most subsequent analyses have marveled at the political dexterity with which the Johnson administration navigated the treacherous currents of religion, race, and rules that had postponed for three decades the arrival of such broad federal aid. The National Education Association (NEA), which had grown since 1857 from a congressionally chartered study group of college officials, public school superintendents, and public school teachers to the nation's largest teachers' union, strongly opposed federal aid to nonpublic schools. Its leading rival, the American Federation of Teachers (AFT), chartered in 1897 by the American Federation of Labor, was less politically effective than the NEA but equally opposed to nonpublic school aid. The National Catholic Welfare Conference, which continued to represent the country's Catholic bishops on Capitol Hill, had since 1944 just as firmly resisted federal aid without provisions for nonpublic schools.[5]

In November 1963, Democrat John Brademas of Indiana initiated a series of meetings among Commissioner of Education Francis Keppel, NEA president Robert Wyatt, and National Catholic Welfare Conference representatives William Consedine and Monsignor Francis Hurley. The talks led to the administration's abandonment of traditional "general aid" (public school construction and teachers' salaries) in favor of "categorical" assistance to children.[6]

Similarly, the passage of the Civil Rights Act in July of 1964 appeared to preclude racial issues from blocking the ESEA the following year. The act stated that "No person in the United States shall, on the grounds of race, color, or national origin, be excluded from participation in, be denied the benefits of, or be subjected to discrimination under any program or activity receiving federal assistance." Title VI of the act permitted the federal government to withhold funds in the event of such discrimination. No longer would the National Association for the Advancement of Colored People (NAACP), the nation's leading civil rights organization since 1909, deploy its congressional standard-bearer, New York Democrat Adam Clayton Powell, to burden education legislation with Title VI–type amendments. And no longer would the NEA countenance racial segregation policies by its affiliates.

Finally, congressional reform removed procedural barriers that had impeded previous school aid bills. In January 1965, the Eighty-ninth Congress adopted the twenty-one-day rule, allowing the Speaker of the House to move a bill to the floor within twenty-one days of the House receiving a rule from the Rules Committee. The committee's Republican–Southern Democrat alliance could no longer obstruct school aid, as it had done most recently in 1961, when an 8–7 vote prevented a Kennedy school bill from reaching the House floor.

While these obstacles deserve the attention that scholars have accorded them, a far more important reason for the Johnson breakthrough was the 1964 Democratic electoral landslide, which provided Johnson a 295–140 advantage in the House and a 62–38 margin in the Senate—the largest legislative majority since World War II. Johnson administration Assistant Commissioner of Education Samuel Halperin wrote to Frank Munger, one of the scholars who stressed the ESEA's church-state compromises, "If you touch base with reporters, White House aides, Congressmen, lobbyists, HEW [Department of Health, Education, and Welfare] officials, Congressional staff, etc.—as I did in an informal poll in 1965—you will find that the Congressional elections of 1964 far exceeded any other factor" in the passage of the ESEA. The president himself attributed his rush to pass such legislation (over the futile protests of the Republican minority on the congressional education committees) to the realization that "we got in with the majority in Congress."[7]

Although Johnson's legislative majority dwarfed religious, racial, and rules considerations, it did not guarantee the passage of legislation that had eluded his four immediate predecessors. While Congress offered Johnson the necessary consensus, the president would have to contribute the requisite clarity and commitment. A leading critic of the ESEA, Oregon Democratic representative Edith Green, nonetheless applauded the "high priority" that President Johnson placed on education. Johnson's poverty argument furnished the compelling rationale absent from previous school aid proposals.[8]

Thirty-five Republican representatives and eighteen Republican senators joined Democratic majorities in both houses of Congress in supporting the legislation. On April 9, alongside his third-grade teacher in the one-room schoolhouse he had once attended, Johnson enacted what he called "the most significant step in this century to provide widespread help to all of America's schoolchildren."[9]

Title I of the ESEA allocated $1.06 billion to be distributed by state education officials to assist local school district projects directed at "educationally-deprived children." The funds were not to finance either construction or teachers' salaries but could pay for "shared-time" programs by which nonpublic school pupils could attend classes at public schools. Title II provided $100 million for the purchase of textbooks and other materials and for the expansion of school libraries for nonpublic and public school children through public agencies. Title III earmarked $100 million for "supplemental services and centers" open to children in nonpublic as well as public schools. Title IV allocated $100 million to modernize and coordinate federal educational research, and Title V assigned $100 million to improve state education agencies.[10]

Whatever the primacy of causes, the ESEA was a remarkable triumph for the nation's first self-proclaimed "Education President." Johnson and the Eighty-ninth Congress had all but rewritten the Constitution, elevating elementary and secondary schools to a permanent place at the table of Washington politics and policy. But the haste in enacting the historic legislation could not forestall the gradual erosion of its foundations. The remaining four years of the administration would expose cracks in the consensus, clarity, and even the commitment that had effected this landmark law.

## The Elementary and Secondary Education Act Amendments of 1967

Federal aid to education had increased over the previous decade from $294 to $533 in total local, state, and federal per-pupil expenditures; from 4.6 percent to 7.8 percent in the federal share of the revenue; and 120 percent in the Office of Education (OE). Yet calls for more federal aid continued to reach the White House. In January 1967 Sidney Marland, superintendent of Pittsburgh schools, wrote Budget Director William Cannon, "If we are really going to get to the deep problems of poverty and social sickness through education, we must be prepared to spend larger sums than we are now spending." At its February 10–11 meeting, Johnson's Education Task Force considered the proposition that general aid "be given to all city schools, not just schools for the poor," as long as "it [was] spent effectively." On February 13, House Education Subcommittee Chairman Carl Perkins informed Rep. Edith Green that he "wanted [jurisdiction over] ESEA permanently," ensuring continued comfort for the advocates of increased education expenditures.[11]

The president appeared to be listening. In his second Annual Message on Education and Health, Johnson requested a 36 percent increase in funds for Title I and the ESEA. In the House Education and Labor Committee hearings on HR 6230, school superintendents from New York, Chicago, Philadelphia, Detroit, St. Louis, Cleveland, Milwaukee, Memphis, Baltimore, and Buffalo applauded the administration's bill.[12]

But Congress was not so agreeable. Perkins said that the Johnson plan "would set back education in this country by ten or fifteen years," and he called for double the funding requested by the White House. New York Democratic representative Hugh Carey lamented that the "Administration is talking like Midas but is funding like Oliver Twist." Utah Democratic senator Frank Moss urged his colleagues on the Labor and Public Welfare Committee to increase the administration's funding request.[13]

More ominously for the White House, many Republicans vowed to move beyond "opposition to the Great Society" to a policy of "constructive alternatives." All but two of the House Education and Labor Committee's Republicans supported a substitute for the ESEA, sponsored by Albert Quie of Minnesota. Quie, a pilot who during his college days had performed stunts such as flying upside down, proposed a reversal of the ESEA from categorical federal aid to "block grants" for the states. The only restriction on each state's funds would be that (1) at least 50 percent *must* be used for the education of disadvantaged children, as opposed to 80 percent under the administration's bill; (2) at least 7 percent *must* be used to purchase instructional material and equipment; (3) none may be used for general classroom construction; and (4) none may be used for teacher salaries. "It is perfectly feasible to achieve the advantages of general aid through block grants for a broad range of education programs, leaving state and local school agencies to establish their own priorities," explained the House Education and Labor Committee's Minority Report on HR 6230, "and to devise patterns for using the funds which best fit both their needs and their structure of education finance." House minority leader Gerald Ford of Michigan called the Quie substitute "a far better way to improve education in this country than the method now dictated and closely controlled by Washington bureaucrats."[14]

Fearing that it would, in the words of special assistant to the president Joseph Califano, "tear apart the coalition we were able to put together three years ago," the administration launched a major offensive against the Quie substitute. On April 24, Commissioner of Education Harold Howe called it a "backward step" that would transfer funds from poorer to wealthier states and would "delete specific provisions from programs that are operating successfully and deserve to live—among them, the Teacher Corps and special education programs in state institutions for the handicapped, neglected, and delinquent." Three days later, Johnson declared that "four years ago the Office of Education was spending only $700 million to support education. In the coming year it will spend $4.2 billion—six times as much. Now some so-called 'friends of education' want to go back where we started." The supporters of the Quie substitute, the president concluded, "are raising the same roadblocks which halted federal aid to education for twenty years."[15]

Administration representatives conducted massive mailings to Capitol Hill, contacted congresspersons from southern and larger northern states, and met frequently with John Lumley of the NEA, Carl Megel of the AFT, Roy Wilkins of the NAACP, and William Consedine of the United States Catholic Conference (formerly the National Catholic Welfare Conference). Johnson lobbied 130 big-city school superintendents, state school officers, religious school officials, and education interest group representatives at the May conference sponsored by the OE. They counted 174 Democrats and 16 Republicans opposed, 44 Democrats and 124 Republicans in favor, and 26 Democrats and 47 Republicans undecided. "I think the Quie substitute is dead," White House aide Charles Roche predicted, "and that the major problem will come from other amendments."[16]

The most troublesome of the "other amendments" to be offered to the House floor were those sponsored by Representative Green—to "block grant" money for federal "innovation" in Title III of the ESEA, to eliminate the commissioner of education's 15 percent discretionary fund in Title V of the ESEA, and to standardize school desegregation guidelines in Title VI of the Civil Rights Act. "I had come to the conclusion," Green would explain, "that that tremendous bureaucracy that we had in Washington . . . was not what we needed." The administration opposed the Green amendments as jeopardizing the provisions for nonpublic schools in

Title III and the opportunities for federal experiments in Title V. These differences widened a personal and political rift between the representative and the president opened by Green's lukewarm support for Johnson's pet program, the Teacher Corps. "Congresswoman Green is coming to lunch with me at 1 p.m. today," aide Douglas Cater wrote to Johnson on May 1. "Do you wish to shake hands with her when she is here? I can't find it in my heart to recommend that you do."[17]

Green would prove a potent adversary for the president. On May 24, after the Quie amendment failed, 197–168, the House passed the Green amendments before adopting a one-year extension of the ESEA by a 294–122 vote. After the Senate overwhelmingly passed a three-year ESEA extension by 71–7 on December 11, the conference report adopted a two-year extension that compromised the Green amendment by allowing 75 percent of Title III funds to be converted to block grants in FY 1969 and 100 percent block grants in FY 1970, while permitting the commissioner of education to distribute 5 percent of Title V monies in each year. On December 15, the House approved the conference report 286–73 and the Senate concurred 63–3. No Republicans spoke against the bill on the House floor, and Quie pronounced it a "good compromise." In the Senate, South Carolina's conservative Strom Thurmond furnished the only Republican voice against the conference report, deeming it an invitation to federal control of education, while liberal Democrat Morse called it "one of the most important of the landmark education bills we have passed."[18]

The president agreed. Praising the measure for providing "every child in America a better chance to touch his outermost limits," Johnson signed the thirty-ninth education law of his presidency on January 2, 1968. "As late as last spring . . . the forecasters had all but buried" the ESEA extension, Johnson remembered. "The press, citing our loss of 47 House seats in 1966, predicted we just wouldn't be able to muster the votes. And the Republicans, believing what they read, prepared to scatter the program to the winds. And how wrong they were!"[19]

## The Johnson Record

After meetings with the National School Boards Association, the Education Commission of the States, and the Conference of National Organizations, Associate Commissioner of Education for Federal-State Relations Wayne Reed concluded in May 1967 that "if public opinion was fairly represented at the three meetings I attended . . . , then it is safe to conclude that there are very few people who now question the need for massive federal aid. What people are debating now has to do with form, degree, and timing." Not only had the Johnson administration's enactment and extensions of the ESEA institutionalized "massive federal aid" to education, but its exploration of other education issues presaged a thirty-year national debate.[20]

Commissioner Keppel floated the idea of national student testing. While acknowledging that "many educators, perhaps even the majority," opposed national tests as discriminating against disadvantaged students, creating unfair comparisons among schools and inviting federal curricular control, Keppel lamented that "evidence on what is being learned by students in schools and colleges is sorely lacking." Cater foreshadowed the national focus on "excellence" by unsuccessfully urging the president to conduct regional conferences to follow up the July 1965 White House Conference on Education and "wake up the regions . . . to their responsibilities in achieving goals of excellence in education." Johnson inaugurated a limited form of national service, the National Teacher Corps, contained in the Higher Education Act of 1965. Based on "an indication of possible interest in such a program on the part of the President," Peter Muirhead, assistant commissioner of education for legislation, explored the feasibility of free public education two years beyond high school. Howe proposed a partial federal takeover of the District of Columbia schools. The administration launched a two-year "Books for Children" project, and adult education programs became part of the ESEA.[21]

Yet Johnson's enormous success in transforming the federal role and the national debate in elementary and secondary education could not obscure two disturbing effects of the ESEA. First, in many ways, far from pacifying the public education interests and their liberal Democratic allies, passage of the ESEA of 1965 seemed to embolden them. *Scholastic Teacher* noted that Johnson's February 1967 education and health message "incorporates all or part of the seventeen points recently proposed by a delegation comprising the NEA, Parents and Teachers Association, American Association of School Administrators, Council of Chief State Officers, National Association of State Boards of Education, and National School Boards Association." In June 1967 the president told the Baltimore Junior Chamber of Commerce that for "our education program, when I became President a little over four years ago, we were spending four billion dollars a year. This year our budget is twelve billion dollars, three times as much for education in three years, and we're still doing our duty in Vietnam."[22]

The response of the public education community to the president appeared to be "yes, but." Writing in *School and Society* in February 1967, AFT president Charles Cogen and his assistant David Selden complained that "*not nearly enough* funds have been provided, and . . . as long as federal aid is increased, priority must be given to solving the basic problems of American education." In July, former North Carolina Democratic governor Terry Sanford, chair of the Education Commission for the States, urged Johnson to "make aid to the states more general aid, less categorical." In the same month, the NEA at its convention resolved "that further expansion related to federal support of education be general in nature." In August, Cogen called upon Johnson to "convene a national education strategy conference" to "give an honest evaluation of what good education would cost."[23]

The administration reacted to such criticisms with a mixture of detail and disdain. In July 1967 Howe replied to Sanford that general aid would not adequately address the needs of disadvantaged pupils in public and nonpublic schools. In August, the White House prematurely leaked to the *New York Times* the unanimous rejection of general aid by its Advisory Panel on Education, appointed by Johnson in October 1966 and chaired by President William Friday of the University of North Carolina. Howe wrote the AFT's Cogen in October that his opposition to federal aid for teachers' salaries "was not, as you suggested, motivated by the desire to placate school board members' fears of Federal domination" but was "said out of my deep conviction that the states and local boards of education do indeed bear that responsibility." Johnson's FY 1969 budget, while adding dollars to Title I, the Teacher Corps, education for handicapped children, bilingual education, and research and development, nonetheless proposed reductions in school construction and equipment. Privately, the president expressed disappointment with the "critical attitude of educators" toward the administration, despite the tremendous forward steps he had taken on federal aid.[24]

A second negative ramification of the Johnson victory was the absence of careful evaluation of the new federal commitment to elementary and secondary education. In August 1965 Keppel identified the "top priority" of his office: "We need to assess where we are in education and where we propose to go," so he advocated "a steady drumfire of Presidential statements stressing the need for goals and assessment in education." The report of the House Education and Labor Committee on the ESEA Amendments of 1966 claimed "substantial evidence that the Title I program has had and will continue to have beneficial and significant impact upon the entire spectrum of elementary and secondary education." While acknowledging that "most of our education programs have been operating too short a time to provide conclusive judgement about their effectiveness," Johnson nonetheless called for "careful analysis of new programs" in March 1967.[25]

Several observers inside and outside the administration, however, questioned the House Democrats' assertions and the president's intentions in the first full year of the ESEA. The first report of the National Advisory Council on Disadvantaged Children (created under the ESEA) concluded that Title I suffered from "an alarming lack of personnel" to serve underprivileged children in public and nonpublic schools. In *Equality of Educational Opportunity* (1966), sociologist James Coleman contended that the social class of the students was a greater predictor of educational achievement than access to federally funded facilities. Henry Dyer of the Educational Testing Service added that a well-planned evaluation system "for federal aid to education was essential." When asked "how does one measure the effects of spending money on education—in other words, how do we know we're doing the right thing?" Howe replied, "I don't think we have planned, as yet, the kind of broad answer that the question suggests." In February 1967 Johnson's Task Force on Education privately criticized Titles I and II as "too fragmented" to be effective. In *Toward Equality as a Fact and as a Result,* a 1967 study commissioned by the Carnegie Corporation,

Johnson administration Assistant Secretary of Labor Daniel Patrick Moynihan concluded, "If Coleman is right, it is necessary to ask whether Title I is a potential disaster." And in a speech before the Women's Democratic Club, Moynihan went further, saying that Title I "may turn out to be a very bad idea." Writing in *School and Society* in February 1967, Joseph Justman, director of teacher education at Brooklyn College, observed that "Considering the changes wrought by the massive intervention of the Federal government in education, there has been little debate on the subject, itself a departure from our tradition and a symptom of the transformation of our national climate."[26]

If federal aid to elementary and secondary schools was here to stay, however, so too were pleas for more or less of it from different sides of the political spectrum. In helping to end three decades of debate over whether there should be a substantial federal role in education, Lyndon Johnson had begun three decades of debate over how substantial that role should be. By the end of the century, the visibility and intensity of the latter debate would make Johnson's achievement all the more remarkable.

## Richard Nixon

> I have always felt that education should be at the top of our list of domestic priorities.
> —Richard Nixon (1969)

As a presidential aspirant in 1968, Richard Nixon said the right things to the right people about elementary and secondary education.[27] He told liberals that he would spend more federal money on the nation's public schools. He told conservatives that he would return control of education to the states. He assured the education establishment that he would care deeply about students and teachers. He heartened education reformers by pledging greater federal research and accountability.

As president, Nixon fulfilled the letter of all of these promises. Federal spending for elementary and secondary education increased, and federal-state revenue sharing began. Nixon devoted considerable time to education issues, and his administration spoke the language of reform. But Nixon betrayed their spirit. Congress, education interest groups, the economy, ideological inconsistency, political maneuvering, and ultimately scandal contributed to the president's uneven performance on elementary and secondary education. In the end, however, the failures of his policies were the failures of Richard Nixon.

### Nixon and Education

Richard Milhous Nixon was born in Whittier, California, in 1913. "Three words describe my life in Whittier," Nixon recalls, "family, church and school." Nixon graduated third in his high school class and attended Whittier College, where he "continued to plug away at [his] studies." He went on to Duke University Law School, a brief stint in the U.S. Navy, and his first congressional campaign in 1946.[28]

After defeating Democrat Jerry Voorhis, the new congressman from the Twelfth District of California took his seat on the House Education and Labor Committee, his second choice for a committee assignment. Nixon did not serve, however, on the Subcommittee on Education, which considered thirteen federal aid proposals in 1947 alone. (None of these proposals came to a vote in the Eightieth Congress.) Following his reelection in 1948, Nixon signed a resolution that prevented the House Education and Labor Committee from reporting a federal aid bill until it received from President Harry Truman "a statement . . . clarifying the authority and redefining the duties of the United States Commissioner of Education" so as to preclude federal control of schools. Nixon then cast the deciding committee vote against reporting a Senate federal aid bill, assailing the measure's expense and extension of "federal control."[29]

No major education legislation would emerge from the Senate during Nixon's two years (1951–53) of service there. As Dwight Eisenhower's loyal vice president from 1953 to 1961, Nixon defended the president's unsuccessful school construction proposals. In his losing 1960 presidential campaign against his former colleague on the House Education and Labor Committee, John Kennedy, Nixon supported temporary federal aid for school construction but opposed permanent federal support of school construction and teachers' salaries.[30]

## The Education Budget

"Seeing to it that young Americans are the best educated in the world . . . [and] that education is available to all our people so that those who don't have an equal chance at the starting line are being helped up to the starting line—this is the primary American objective," said candidate Richard Nixon in October 1968. "At budget cutting time this is one area that must *not* be shortchanged." President Nixon's Task Force on Education agreed in January 1969, urging the incoming administration to increase federal education expenditures by about $1 billion.[31]

But Nixon disagreed. His nondefense budget, submitted to Congress on April 14, included dramatic reductions in the ESEA. After Congress restored the monies, Nixon would wait almost a year before signing the legislation extending the ESEA because of its "excessive" cost. Nixon was even more frugal toward the overall education budget. After the House of Representatives voted to add $900 million to Nixon's FY 1970 school aid request, Nixon told his Council for Urban Affairs, "I've never assumed that education is the sacred cow some believe it is. It is so goddamn ridiculous to assume everyone should go to college. As soon as HEW gets off that kick, the better we are. I'm willing to put a lot of money in some education programs, but we have to be selective."[32]

NEA president George Fischer decried the "nonprogram" of the Nixon administration. "Not content with the cuts in education proposed by the Johnson Administration budget," said Fischer, "the Nixon Administration has proceeded to slash programs to the extent that some would be wiped out entirely." Citing the Fischer attack, domestic affairs advisor Daniel Patrick Moynihan warned Nixon, "Even as local school board issues go down to defeat, Congress is obviously of a mind to spend more on education, and we are clearly emerging as education skinflints. Following as we do an administration that gave more attention to education than any in history, this Administration risks a domestic crisis of confidence." Chester Finn told the president, "We've been getting branded in the press as anti-education. I don't think we want to aggravate that situation."[33]

But Nixon, while conceding that a balanced budget would be "no political plus," was "looking for something to veto" in HEW. On January 26, 1970, he found it: a $19.7 billion bill containing funds for education, health, and antipoverty programs. The next day Congress sustained the Nixon veto, and the next week Nixon vowed to "fight the NEA."[34]

He would have to fight the AFT as well. When Nixon's March 3, 1970, education message contained no provisions for massive school aid, the AFT Executive Council concluded that "Mr. Nixon has told us that he is going to do nothing about education." The council demanded that Commissioner of Education James Allen resign and urged that letters of protest flood the White House. But Allen refused to resign as long as "the serious financial difficulties facing our schools and colleges are well-known to me." Allen wrote to the AFT Executive Council that "I believe that my efforts in this position can make a contribution to the improvement of American education."[35]

Nixon also refused to yield. At its July 1970 convention, the NEA Representative Assembly raised its request of the federal share of elementary and secondary education funds from one-fourth to one-third, while the AFT continued to call for 39 percent by 1977. In August 1970, Congress passed FY 1971 education appropriations that authorized $500 million of additional spending. At an August 5 meeting, after White House aide Bryce Harlow told Nixon that a presidential veto would bring a "certain override," Finch urged Nixon to sign the legislation to buy "time to mobilize public opinion for the next three budgets." Nixon opened an August 11 gathering of the Republican congressional leadership by asking, "Who's in favor of a veto?" Patrick Buchanan of the White House staff wrote, "The general consensus of just about everyone at the table was opposed to a veto of the education bill." Yet by the end of the meeting, the president's economic concerns had changed virtually everyone's mind, and by the end of the day Nixon had again vetoed an education bill. Two days later Congress overrode the veto.[36]

AFT President Selden's response to the second veto was that "Once again President Nixon has indicated the low priority he attaches to the education of children in this country." NEA president-elect Catherine Barrett promised "a massive political movement the likes of which this nation has never seen. . . . Teachers will develop the political muscle, the money, the campaign workers, and the vote to reshuffle an indifferent or hostile Congress, to defeat an under-achieving President." By July 1971 Nixon had grown weary of such attacks, so in an admittedly "defensive move" he signed a FY 1972 appropriation $375 million over his request. He promised cuts in other areas of the budget to offset the education increases.[37]

But Nixon's truce with Congress and the education interests was short-lived. In June 1972 the president vowed to veto "any appropriations bill that exceeded the budget by $1 billion." Looking ahead to his reelection, the president added, "If we win, we will have a real chance, perhaps our only chance to change our direction of spending."[38]

For now, however, the veto pen would have to suffice. In August, Nixon rejected a Labor-HEW appropriation bill $2 billion over his request. And when the House sustained this third veto, NEA president Barrett, condemning Nixon's opposition to "urgently needed Federal funds for education," announced that, for the first time, her organization would endorse and campaign for congressional candidates who supported its agenda. While it stopped short of endorsing Democratic presidential candidate George McGovern, the NEA announced that it would oppose Nixon's reelection. In an "unprecedented volunteer effort," former NEA president Donald Morrison, NEA Executive Committee member Esther Wilfong, AFT president Selden, and AFT secretary treasurer Robert Porter joined forces to "urge the nation's 3.5 million teachers and other education workers to work and vote for the McGovern-Shriver ticket."[39]

Nixon did not seek simply to restrain elementary and secondary education revenues at the federal level, but he hoped to transfer some of them to state and local governments. "Let us have a federal program that will turn back to the states without any strings the money the states can use to upgrade their education standards at the local level," said candidate Nixon in 1968. "Not only will education be handled more efficiently at that level but we will also avoid making mistakes as big as could be made by a single system administered from the top in Washington, DC." In November 1970 Nixon's second HEW secretary, Elliot Richardson, announced the administration's plans to consolidate federal education programs into block grants to the states. In his FY 1972 budget message in February 1971, Nixon noted that this "new and expanded program of special revenue-sharing for elementary and secondary education" would "draw together the wide array of overlapping and bewildering authorities for categorical grants into four broad areas of national interest, and provide additional funds ($192 million) during 1972." He proposed that four block grants supplant approximately seventy categorical aid programs in the areas of compensatory education for the disadvantaged, education of the handicapped, vocational education, and impact aid.[40]

But Congress had more grandiose revenue-sharing ideas. In January 1972 Nixon legislative liaison Roy Morey offered the administration a "synopsis of the Democratic response to Educational Revenue-Sharing." The opposition suggested two sets of block grants: one to enhance education quality and another to expand educational facilities. The projected cost was $10.6 billion for the first year. "This is just one of several massive aid-to-education proposals floating on the Hill this year," wrote Morey. "It will keep us on our toes." It would also help ensure that while general revenue sharing would become law during the Nixon administration, special revenue sharing for education would not. Congress passed the State and Local Fiscal Assistance Act of 1972, which limited the use of revenue-sharing funds to "priority expenditures," defined as: "1) ordinary and necessary maintenance and operating expenses for public safety, environmental protection, public transportation, recreation, libraries, social services for the poor and aged, and financial administration and 2) ordinary and necessary capital expenditures authorized by law."[41]

## The Education Reforms

"We are the hope of tomorrow in the youth of today," said Richard Nixon in his first inaugural address. "I know America's youth. We can be proud that they are better educated . . . than any other generation in our history." He went on to cite "excellence in education" as a goal toward which "we will and must press urgently forward." And they did. "The early days of the Nixon Administration were a time of excitement and ferment in many areas of domestic and social policy," Chester Finn of Nixon's Working Group on Education would write. "There were fresh looks at old programs, old policies and old assumptions, tough-minded assessments and open-minded attempts at renewal and reform." Elementary and secondary education offered several inviting targets for such creativity.[42]

The first target was the OE. Nixon's Task Force on Education had urged a higher profile for the agency, and the president quickly obliged. His appointment of James Allen to the same post in the federal government that he had held in the state of New York elicited virtually universal acclaim from the education community, including the NEA and the AFT. But lamenting the "tendency down here to get money out fast with a minimum amount of planning and complain later that it won't work," Allen promised to be beholden to no special interest. Allen's top reform priority was the OE itself. A staff that had tripled since the 1960s and a budget that approached $4 billion required a major reorganization, the commissioner explained in August 1969. So he added deputy assistant commissioners for Planning, Research, and Evaluation; Intradepartmental Educational Affairs; School Systems; Higher Education and the Institute of International Studies; and Instructional Resources. He also appointed special assistants for urban education and community colleges.[43]

Another major target of Allen's and the administration's reform would be the ESEA. At the House hearings on HR 514 in February 1969, Finch argued that because of the "growing need to assess the large volume of complex legislation enacted during the past decades," Congress should extend the ESEA for two rather than five years. In March, domestic affairs advisor Daniel Patrick Moynihan reminded Finch of the 1966 Coleman Report's conclusion that "none of the programs [of the ESEA] appear to have raised significantly the achievement of participating pupils, as a group, within the period evaluated by the Commission." In August, Burns informed Nixon that in his recent *New York Times Magazine* article, the "well-known liberal" Christopher Jencks of Harvard University had found that "variations in schools' fiscal and human resources have very little effect on student achievement, probably even less than the Coleman Report originally implied." In October, Finn related to Moynihan an OE study that found a "nineteen percent improvement, a thirteen percent decline, and a sixty-eight percent the same" reading performance among pupils served by Title I. In the same month, at an OE staff retreat, Allen urged a federal "Right to Read" program to combat "failures with respect to the education of the disadvantaged—those who suffer from lack of motivation, physical and mental handicaps, discrimination, poverty, and other environmental deficiencies." Budget Director Sam Hughes and White House aides Bryce Harlow and Bud Wilkinson added their voices to the chorus of ESEA reform.[44]

In November an interagency task force chaired by Deputy Assistant Secretary of Education for Intradepartmental Affairs Timothy Wirth began its review of Title I programs. Citing an NAACP study that showed that Title I funds were not reaching the disadvantaged, the usually unfriendly *Washington Post* cheered news of the administration task force: "That approach offers the hope of reform [that] is urgently needed." In January 1970 the HEW Task Force on Urban Education, chaired by Wilson Riles, weighed in with its recommendations for revision of the ESEA. It called for greater flexibility for states to target funds to disadvantaged children; multiyear, rather than annual, grants and evaluations to ensure program continuity and stability; and public HEW audits of the ESEA. The next month the HEW Task Force on Title I concluded that "there is still confusion" over Title I's efforts to desegregate school districts and target school populations. The task force would issue no final report, Wirth and Richard Fairley of HEW explained, but "implementation will be immediate."[45]

The problems identified by the Riles and Wirth task forces reinforced calls for even more research. "The big city school systems and the Catholic schools systems are everywhere on the brink of financial disaster, and in general the financing of elementary and secondary education in the United States is a chaotic, inefficient, and often unjust process," Finch and Moynihan wrote to Nixon. "The essential fact about elementary and secondary education is that very little is known about what doesn't work, and why." They recommended creation of a commission to "establish the facts and propose a more orderly, dependable, and equitable system."[46]

The federal government not only had to do more research, the administration believed—it had to do better research. As Finn would recall, Nixon's Working Group on Education reasoned that "if what presently goes on in the nation's schools, insofar as we are able to measure it, has little effect on student learning, then we had better find out what does have an effect and how to alter it." During the campaign Nixon had proposed a "National Institute for the Educational Future" to assess the federal performance in education. In October 1969, Finn suggested that the prospective agency, renamed "The National Institute of Education [NIE]," should subsume the former Bureau of Research, the new National Center for Educational Research and Development, varied functions of the Office of Program Planning and Evaluation, Experimental Schools, Bureau of Education Personnel Development, and the Bureau of Library and Educational Technology of the OE; consume about 11 percent of the OE budget; and reside within HEW but outside the OE. The OE, Finn added, "would become in effect, a check-writing operation administering support grants."[47]

The culmination of these efforts came on March 3, 1970, in Nixon's "Special Message to Congress on Education Reform," which proposed a "Right to Read" program, a President's Commission on School Finance, and the NIE. Citing the Coleman report, Nixon asserted that federal programs had been especially unsuccessful in assisting the poor, urged a cost-benefit analysis of federal education monies, and called for a reform of federal education policies. Nixon would return to these themes in his "Special Message to Congress on Special Revenue Sharing for Education" in April 1971 and his State of the Union address in January 1972.[48]

The leading education lobbies were not impressed. The AFT's Executive Council called the Nixon reforms "bitter nonsense"; without adequate funding, the Right-to-Read program "can be little more than an educational wraith in anyone's school," and the NIE is "a dash of sugar [that] fools no one." The NEA's president considered the Nixon proposals "gimmicks"; without adequate funding, the Nixon programs showed "no recognition of education as a top government priority."[49]

The opposition of the AFT, the NEA, and their allies in Congress delayed the Nixon reform agenda. Finn would recall that "there was never a chance that the package would be considered on its merits in the spring of 1970. Preceded by the HEW appropriation veto, it was followed within two months by the bombing of Cambodia. Soon the Commissioner of Education was dismissed [ostensibly for protesting the bombing]. A few months later, Finch moved to the White House. Not long thereafter, Moynihan moved to academia."[50]

"It is already clear that the NEA legislative program will deal primarily with economic questions," the organization's journal announced in January 1971. In

July the Full Funding Committee, comprised of some thirty national organizations including the NEA and the AFT, claimed credit for Nixon's decision to sign the FY 1972 education appropriations, over budget and without the reforms. But delay did not presage defeat. In early 1971 Democrat John Brademas of Indiana, chairman of the Subcommittee on Education of the House Education and Labor Committee, held hearings on the NIE. In March, Neal McElroy presented Nixon with the report of the Commission on School Finance that he had chaired. Its recommendations included greater state and local control of school funding and better mechanisms to evaluate federal programs. In June the two-year ESEA extension, Right-to-Read program, and NIE were part of an omnibus bill signed by Nixon.[51]

The enactment of the reforms, however, was easier than their implementation. In his June 11, 1970, statement the day after his dismissal, Allen deplored the "serious difficulty in carrying out the responsibilities of the Office [because of] the frequent and often lengthy delays in securing from higher levels the action necessary for proceeding expeditiously" with reorganization. Finch, Chief of Staff H. R. Haldeman, and Nixon agreed, promising more access to the White House for Allen's successor, Sidney Marland. Yet as of October 1970, Nixon had not filled more than one-fourth of the positions in the OE. In November 1970 Moynihan, in a letter to Richardson, lamented that "no one [has] a very clear idea just what a National Institute of Education would look like if we had one." Five years later, in a letter to President Gerald Ford, Moynihan argued that the staff of a proposed commission on school desegregation "could be provided by the NIE—and should be. It is a chance to show what . . . the Institute can do." In the same year Finn painted an equally dismal portrait: "The Senate voted to kill it. . . . The first Director and the Chairman of the Advisory Board have both resigned, staff morale is low, new ideas are scarce, enthusiasm within the [Ford] Administration seems less, and numerous Congressmen have taken to delivering lectures on the sins and shortcomings of the Institute." In 1977 a National Council on Education Research–National Academy of Education study determined that the NIE "has not made significant progress toward fulfilling its mandate to strengthen the scientific and technological foundations of education."[52]

The extension of the ESEA with virtually no changes came in the same year that Jencks's article became a highly acclaimed book. When the OE launched the Right-to Read program in 1972, there were seven million elementary and secondary school students with severe reading problems, almost half of whom lived in large cities. Right-to-Read directed $500 million to provide information and technical assistance in reading-related OE programs such as bilingual education and library services. The primary objective of Right-to-Read was to ensure that by 1990, 99 percent of those under age sixteen "will have the skills to read to the full limits of their desires." Yet three years later, Moynihan noted that reading achievement continued to decline, and the Ford administration inaugurated its own Reading Improvement Program.[53]

When the McElroy Commission began its deliberations in 1971, Nixon had hailed "the historic inquiry" into a "national agenda [for] how to make an education system work." When he met with the commissioners in early 1972, he assured them that "if the preferred solution [to school finance] required revenues which could not be met out of the present revenue system, then the commission should say so." But when the commission finished its deliberations and called for "the provision of emergency financial aid to assist large central city public and nonpublic schools" and "the expansion of programs of early childhood education commencing at age four," the president promised to "give it every consideration" but then largely ignored it.[54]

## The Nixon Record

Richard Nixon could credibly claim that he had fulfilled all of his major promises on elementary and secondary education policy. First, he could say that he had increased federal spending on public schools, from $3.2 billion in 1969–70 to $4.9 billion in 1973–74 and from 8 percent of all public primary and secondary education expenditures to 8.5 percent. Second, he could note that he had sought to transfer some of the burden of education spending from the federal government to state and local governments, as part of the extension of the ESEA in 1972. Third, as evidence of his commitment to the public schools, he could point to his mention of education in his first inaugural address and two State of the Union addresses; five annual messages on education; 1971 White House meeting with educators; and the evolution of an education strategy. Finally, he could cite the reorganization of the OE, the Right-to-Read program, the Riles and Wirth task forces, the NIE, and the McElroy Commission as fruits of his administration's reform efforts. He could conclude, as he did at a January 1971 congressional breakfast meeting, that on education and other domestic policies, "Republicans have for the first time in my political career something to be for. We can be for something, instead of against something."[55]

Yet somehow that message could not penetrate the American consciousness, and Nixon failed more than he succeeded in public school policy. The first reason was the economy. Nixon entered office in January 1969 with 4 percent inflation and 3 percent unemployment. He departed in August 1974 with 12 percent inflation and 12 percent unemployment. So Nixon, who a year earlier had written Finch that "I have always felt that education should be at the top of our list of national priorities," told his staff in January 1970 that "the primary national objective now [is to] stop the rise in prices"—even if the pursuit of that goal was politically risky. "We'll do all the 'wrong' political things—kick the teachers, the sick, etc.," the president added, "but I won't have some gnome at the Fed do the

monetary thing all wrong, too." A year later, Nixon's preoccupation with inflation caused him to betray his free-market instincts by imposing wage and price
controls, which would remain in some form until January 1973. Weinberger
would recall that "budget limitations" largely forced Nixon's hand in elementary
and secondary education.[56]

The second cause of Nixon's education failures was the alliance of liberal congressional Democrats, the NEA, and the AFT. In early 1969 the House Education
and Labor Committee sent a questionnaire to more than twenty thousand
school superintendents asking, "In general, have the recent enactments of Congress furnishing support for elementary and secondary education been of great,
substantial, moderate, or little value?" Seventy-four percent answered "great,"
"substantial," or "moderate," and 70 percent said that the ESEA was "underfunded" in their districts. In the committee's hearings on the extension of the
ESEA, representatives of the NEA and the AFT testified against any revision of
the law, as did virtually everyone else. When Rep. Henry Ruth, the committee's
ranking Republican, called for evaluation and potential streamlining of the
ESEA, he complained that he heard "no evidence in testimony that this is a concern" and that "practically all" of the testimony in the "five-volume report" of
the hearings "was in unanimous support of ESEA legislation with a frequent
extension." Burns lamented to Nixon in August 1969 that in the debate over the
FY 1970 education appropriations add-on, "extending over 180 pages in the *Congressional Record*, the proponents argued that not enough money is being spent
on education, while the opponents argued that the budgetary situation and
inflationary pressures do not permit such a large increase at this time, desirable
though it be. No speaker seemed to question whether the quality of education
would be improved by spending more dollars."[57]

The consensus of leading educational researchers who met at the OE in February 1970 was that "the conventional view on how to make public schooling
more effective," explicitly embraced by the education establishment's legislative
allies and implicitly conceded by its legislative adversaries, was "to provide more
money." The Coleman study, however, by rejecting previous findings that
"schools bring [significant] . . . influences to bear upon a child's achievement that
is independent of his background," had undertaken "an agonizing reappraisal" of
the traditional approach for improving pupil achievement. As the NEA, the AFT,
and most congresspersons of both parties continued to speak in "cost-quality"
terms, the reformers within the Nixon administration were adopting Coleman's
"social context" diagnosis. The best formula, the researchers contended, was a
combination of the "cost-quality" and "social context" analyses. The Riles Task
Force report quoted educator Alan Campbell: "There is much uncertainty about
how educational disadvantage can be overcome. One thing, however, is clear. It
cannot be done cheaply. To substitute educational experimentation and innovation for increased resources is to sentence those experiments and innovations to

failure." Former commissioner of education Francis Keppel was more blunt: "To say that compensatory education doesn't work when it is demonstrable that poor children have not usually received the impact of the intended money is like blaming a man for starving when you have deprived him of food."[58]

Yet rather than help compose such a hybrid, Nixon at various times embraced either approach. His allegiance to the "cost-quality" school produced three vetoes of "excessive" education appropriations. His openness to the "social context" viewpoint fueled the conviction that there is "no correlation between expenditures and results" that underlay his reform agenda. "Let's not put the President in the position of opposing education expenditures one week," Finn warned in October 1969, "then proposing them the next." But Nixon would veto the FY 1970 appropriation at the end of January 1970 and then ask Congress for education reforms at the beginning of March. In March 1970 Moynihan gave Nixon and the Republican congressional leadership a "social context" review of the Coleman Report: "The only way to measure a good school is to determine what the children have been learning in it—not how much teachers get paid, or the quality of the books or the teacher-pupil ratio." But the next year he offered the House Education and Labor Committee a "cost-quality" conclusion: "The premises on which we based the ESEA ... were wrong, and it would take a long time, a lot of patience, and even, probably, a lot of money before anything nearer to 'right' would be discovered."[59]

The Nixon presidency had begun with a decidedly "social context" outlook articulated in Finn's educational goals for the administration in December 1969: "1) Bring about educational equality; 2) Improve educational quality through research, experimentation, evaluation, and development; 3) Foster fiscal and educational reform; and 4) Encourage relevance and participation." But it would end with a largely "cost-quality" emphasis, embodied in James Cavanaugh's goals for the OE in January 1973: "1) To provide financial assistance directly to [college] students in the forms of scholarships and loans; 2) To emphasize programs of support to primary and secondary schools as compared to institutions of higher education; 3) To provide financial assistance to black colleges; and 4) To protect programs that provide education to handicapped individuals."[60]

The administration never reconciled these contradictions. In October 1969 Allen urged the "development of a nationwide strategy for maintaining a continuing process of improvement and relevance in American education." In May 1970 Allen wrote Nixon that "I fully endorse our themes of reform and have been carrying a heavy schedule of appearances before Congressional Committees and urging support for the proposals which the messages contain." The commissioner then requested more monies because "reform cannot be achieved in a vacuum." Yet he would depart in June 1970 "frustrated" and "discouraged" by his inability to "obtain a priority for education at the federal level commensurate with its importance and urgent needs." Upon taking office Allen's successor, Sidney Marland, expressed the need to "persuade the President of our ability to reorder priorities." In a memo to Nixon six months later, Marland saluted "our commitment to education renewal" but requested more funds because "educational leaders, both lay and professional, in our big cities are close to the edge of despair."[61]

Nixon appeared unwilling and felt unable to resolve this confusion. His only television address on education was his first veto message. His only radio speech on the subject waited until two weeks before his reelection. His only response to Cavanaugh's September 1973 request for "an event which associates the President with actively working on the education program" was to publicize a meeting with Weinberger a week later. As late as June 1974, the OE felt compelled to urge the administration to "continue to work with the media, constantly reminding them that the President is not a Johnny-come-lately on Federal education assistance." Lamenting that "domestic reforms [are] unsexy," Nixon privately conceded that "We're not effective in putting things out with concepts, slogans, numbers, goals"; so he really didn't try very hard. Education was "one of a number of issues in which he was basically interested," Weinberger would remember, "but it wasn't his greatest concern."[62]

Politics provided another explanation for Nixon's missteps on public school aid. Finn observed in September 1969 that "Allen is not really liked around here. He is having trouble getting some of his staff cleared through the White House. His choices are good, but they are not Republicans." In November, Morgan described the set of recommendations from Allen's staff retreat as "merely a broad statement issued a month ago," adding that "I wouldn't bother the President with it at this time." In December, in urging Morgan to solicit Allen's input into the president's first education message, Finn reminded him that "We still have a Commissioner of Education." Yet the administration needed a new commissioner in June 1970, when Allen's "resignation" letter decried the "inordinate influence of partisan political considerations in the matter of appointments to positions in the Office of Education."[63]

Nixon himself allowed politics to influence his education decisions. Finn would recall that while Nixon helped reduce the ESEA extension from five to two years, the president "did not say 'stop what you're doing,' nor did he try to eliminate the existing compensatory programs or even severely cut them back. No one was sufficiently certain of the new [social context] analysis, and the programs were too popular."[64]

Although his appropriations vetoes were largely unpopular, they were not entirely apolitical. At the January 1970 staff meeting, the president allowed that he "didn't care" if his first veto were overridden, because "the issue is framed." In July, Nixon observed that "getting rolled on education" would be "not too bad," because he could "pass the blame for higher prices" to Congress. Three weeks later, at the Republican congressional leadership meeting, Republican senator John Tower of Texas assured the president that a second education appropriation veto would not jeopardize a higher priority—the imminent Senate vote on the Anti-Ballistic Missile Treaty with the Soviet Union. The legislators helped persuade Nixon not to veto a veterans' assistance bill, which was $218 million over Nixon's request, because it would alienate "friends of the Administration." They accurately predicted, however, that a veto of the school bill simply would engender "the ill will of the people who already have ill will" toward Nixon.[65]

"Ill will" is putting it mildly. If the administration's preoccupation with the economy, its mixed message, and its political machinations were not enough to undermine its public school policies, Nixon's personality furnished a final explanation. For this president, antipathy toward his critics was the natural state of affairs, and paranoia toward his enemies became his undoing. The Watergate scandal, of course, was the outbreak that wrote his political epitaph, but the symptoms long preceded Nixon's demise. And they were especially evident in his relations with the NEA and the AFT.

Nixon did not just disagree with the NEA and the AFT; he shunned them. The president did not meet with any leader of an education organization in the first year and a half of his administration. He would never meet with NEA president George Fischer or his successor, Helen Bain. Fischer recalled virtually ghostwriting a statement from Nixon to the nation's teachers published in the October 1968 *NEA Journal.* Upon Nixon's election, Fischer continued, the "Nixon tune changed," as did the tone—Fischer claimed that after domestic affairs advisor John Ehrlichman threatened him with "fellow" union leader Jimmy Hoffa's fate (Hoffa was presumably murdered), Fischer refused to answer the president's telephone calls. In June 1971, White House aide John Evans attributed Bain's "vociferous" opposition to revenue sharing to "the fact that [she] has been seeking an appointment with the President for five months." He added that to meet with Bain at that time, at the completion of her one-year term, "would be a direct slap in her face and would cause her to be more enraged than she now is." Had Nixon met with her, Bain would remember, she "probably would not have lambasted him" in July 1971. Since the administration had chosen to ignore the NEA, she added, "We thought we might as well go for broke" and endorse congressional candidates in 1972.[66]

After NEA president-elect Catherine Barrett sent the White House a copy of her prospective acceptance speech in which she promised an all-out effort to prevent Nixon's reelection, the administration fired back. White House staffer Charles Colson wrote in August 1971 that "Obviously they [the NEA] have been exploiting their tax-free status. This [the Barrett telegram] is a clear declaration of political activities. . . . I would think that if this gal is elected, we would have something to crack the NEA with." Two days later, staffer Richard Howard added that the Barrett telegram "clearly shows that if there is any thought of having a

representative group of members of the NEA in to see the President it will hopefully be scrubbed. This is clearly a bad outfit." Nixon's defeat of the NEA's unoffi-
cial presidential candidate in 1972 heightened the antagonism between the
administration and the nation's largest teachers' union. "The blood is ankle deep
over there," said an NEA lobbyist in January 1973, pointing to the OE.[67]

The administration was equally dismissive, if not as openly hostile, toward
the AFT. When the AFT opposed the nomination of Marland, the former Pittsburgh superintendent of schools, partly because he had fired striking teachers
there, Nixon told Ehrlichman, "Teachers have no right to strike. Marland must
have that position, or I won't support him." When Nixon invited educators to
the White House in September 1971, it was his first meeting with the NEA or the
AFT. Following the meeting, Nixon solicited ideas from the educators that he
hoped would become part of his State of the Union address and of a "national
education policy"—steps at least two years overdue.[68]

The AFT and the NEA could have made such collaboration more attractive,
however. While both groups promised to give Nixon a chance, neither really did.
Ostensibly nonpartisan organizations, the AFT and NEA leaderships' Democratic leanings were open secrets from the outset of the administration. AFT president Selden endorsed Nixon's opponent, Hubert Humphrey, for president in
1968, and he would later write to the former vice president that "I am happy to
say that I received very few complaints about my unauthorized action." Democratic senator Wayne Morse of Oregon and Democratic representative Arnold
Olsen of Montana cosponsored the NEA's $6 billion general aid bill in the last
year of the Johnson administration, and the group's legislative commission
promised in December 1968 to reintroduce the bill, even before the group had
heard from president-elect Nixon. The NEA's first official foray into national
partisan politics was to publicly oppose Nixon's Supreme Court nominees
Clement Haynsworth (November 11, 1969) and Harold Carswell (February 11,
1970) because of their school desegregation stands. Fischer, a Republican, felt
proud "to appear on Nixon's 'enemies list'" alongside self-proclaimed "yellow-
dog Democrat" Bain and Executive Director Sam Lambert. Lambert's successor,
Terry Herndon, would recall two major rifts within the NEA during the Nixon
era: between the liberal Democratic leadership and the conservative Republican
rank and file, and, more significantly, between supporters and opponents of the
organization's nonpartisan tradition. The Nixon education record, Herndon
concluded, was the "high-level and effective catalyst" in helping the NEA overcome these divisions.[69]

If Nixon's fiscal conservatism was an unreasonable companion to his reform
agenda, the fiscal generosity of the teachers' unions was an unrealistic response
to the nation's economic climate. Within four months, AFT president David
Selden criticized the Riles Urban Affairs Task Force for preferring "revolutionary reforms" to "spending money," then chastised Nixon for not spending the

"many billions of additional dollars" that the Task Force authorized. Within two years, the NEA raised its demand of a federal share of all elementary and secondary education expenditures from 25 to 33 percent, even though it had never reached 9 percent since the enactment of the ESEA in 1965. When asked during the deliberations of the Wirth Task Force, "Do you feel comfortable in not having any data on which you might conceivably come out for proposing, say, that the large influxes of federal dollars in certain programs are to what end?" Herndon replied, "I ask myself in regards to what public policy issue, if any, would my conclusion be affected by those data, and I can't think of one."[70]

The Nixon administration was hardly alone in raising the volume of the White House rift with the NEA and the AFT. When Allen espoused a national literacy campaign in November 1969, Fischer countered, "I just frankly resent anyone, especially the President of the United States, assuming that you can sell platitudes about the elimination of illiteracy and at the same time wiping out money for the purchase of reading materials." When Nixon vetoed the second education appropriation bill in August 1970, Selden replied, "It is difficult for us to understand this strange anti-child behavior of the President of the United States." The AFT's parent organization, the AFL-CIO, branded Marland a "reactionary, anti-teacher union administrator" at the Senate hearings on his nomination in December 1970. There were limits to the bombast, however, even for the education interests. After Director Greg Humphrey labeled Nixon "Public Enemy Number One of every school-age child and teacher in the United States," Selden rebuked his fellow lobbyist: "I question the effectiveness of calling Nixon 'public enemy number one' when it comes to children. Nixon may be what he is; he certainly is no friend. However, extreme statements of that kind tend to lose people rather than attract them."[71]

Because of their wide policy differences, there was little hope that Nixon, the NEA, and the AFT would ever be "friends." But more willingness to talk by the president and a greater openness to listen by the education interests might have produced an atmosphere more conducive to compromise and consensus. Nixon seemed to recognize these imperatives when he praised the "cooperative approach" of public and nonpublic school educators in his statement to their November 1971 conference. The input that Nixon solicited from the education interests for his 1972 State of the Union address predictably requested more money for their schools, but according to Marland, "closely following finance as an issue was recognition of the need for reform." Weinberger would recall that some members of the administration urged a greater "politics of inclusion" toward the NEA and the AFT, if for no other reason than that the unions were "intense and heavily organized."[72]

"Inclusion," however, was one of those concepts at which Nixon just wasn't very good. The president who taught Americans that their foreign enemies in the Soviet Union and China were not always as they appeared tried to teach them that their domestic friends in Congress and the education lobbies were not always who they claimed to be. But the effectiveness of a lesson relies largely on the enthusiasm of the teacher. If the teacher loses interest, the students are sure to follow. The Nixon administration began auspiciously by promising a synthesis of old and new in public elementary and secondary education policy. But it ended disappointingly by depending almost exclusively on the old. The teacher had lost interest.

## Gerald Ford

> Throughout my public life I believed and still believe—that education
> is one of the foundation stones of our republic.
> —Gerald Ford (1975)

For Gerald Ford, his presidency would be, above all, a "time to heal."[73] Any account of the Ford administration must acknowledge the unprecedented circumstances in which an unelected chief executive replaced a discredited one. Next to Watergate, on August 9, 1974, everything else seemed beside the point.[74]

Within a month, Ford had pardoned Nixon, announcing, however wishfully, that the country had moved beyond Watergate. But if Ford shared none of his predecessor's fatal flaws, he did inherit many of Nixon's advisors and most of his policies. So Ford's became a hyphenated presidency, the afterthought of the "Nixon-Ford" years. If this shorthand was not always appropriate in other areas of domestic and foreign policy, it largely rang true in elementary and secondary education. As Ford entered the White House, the question was not whether he would emulate Nixon in public elementary and secondary education policy but rather which Nixon he would emulate. Would he retrench or reform? Would his bottom line be expense or excellence? In many ways Ford adopted both Nixon models but in the reverse order: unlike his predecessor, he began with a "cost-quality" vision of education and ended with a "social context" outlook. Like his predecessor, he never really found an effective combination of both.

### Ford and Education

According to confidant and Chief of Staff Robert Hartmann, Ford considered his education at "neighborhood schools" in Grand Rapids, Michigan, "a very positive experience that all American children should have." After attending the University of Michigan and Yale Law School, Ford entered the House of Representatives in 1949 with a genuine interest in ensuring educational opportunity—as long as the cost was not too great. So while he voted for a successful vocational education bill in 1963 and the two-year extension of the ESEA in 1969, he opposed school construction bills in 1956 and 1961 and voted against the original ESEA in 1965.[75]

## The Education Budget

The first major piece of school legislation that Ford inherited from Nixon was HR 69, the three-year extension of the ESEA. Just three days into the Ford administration, aide Roger Semerad offered his analysis of the bill. Although it modified Title I to "more accurately reflect need" and "provide for better distribution of funds," it contained the "administratively burdensome" bypass provision for nonpublic school pupils and incentive grants for "concentration" of poor children. While it reformed impact aid to eliminate funds for children whose parents work on federal property in another state and to add monies for handicapped or learning disabled children of military personnel, it expanded the program to children of families living in public housing, thus distorting the purpose of impact aid as a way "to finance compensatory education." It established a deputy commissioner for education of the handicapped, but it gave him too much money to spend. It created a new federal policy to "establish equal educational opportunity for children of limited English-speaking ability," but the program cost too much to administer. It consolidated libraries and instructional resources on the one hand and support and innovation on the other but fell short of the massive block grants sought by the Nixon administration. And it contained several "unacceptable" and possibly "unconstitutional" encroachments by the Congress on the responsibilities of the executive branch, such as "a prohibition on decentralization, organizational specifications and requirements for submission of various plans and regulations to the Congress." Although "H.R. 69 falls short of the Administration's objectives for education legislation," Semerad recommended that Ford sign the bill because "the political history regarding elements of the House and Senate versions and the final conference versions suggest the unlikelihood of a better bill." While acknowledging the bill's shortcomings, Ford nonetheless signed it later that day.[76]

"Your Administration could not begin on a better note," the AFT's David Selden wrote to the president the following day. In May 1975 Ford told representatives of the NEA that he was "proud that the first piece of legislation" that he signed as president was HR 69. NEA president James Harris invited Ford to speak at the organization's convention in July.[77]

Ford's accommodation toward Congress and the education interests was short-lived. In July 1975 HEW secretary Caspar Weinberger advised the president to veto the FY 1976 education appropriation. "At a time when most indicators show that we are beginning to make some headway against inflation," wrote the former budget director, "the Congress has just passed a bill for education totaling $7.5 billion in budget authority, or twenty-three percent over your 1976 budget request." Ford took the advice a week later, with the fourth presidential veto of an education appropriation in six years and his thirty-fifth veto of any legislation in less than a year. "Earlier this year, I drew a line on the budget deficit for Fiscal Year 1976 at $60 billion. . . . On May 14, Congress drew its own line at $69 billion," the president explained. "But now, the Congress' own July 21 budget scorekeeping report estimates a possible deficit this year of $83.6 billion."[78]

Others did not see it that way. NEA president Harris called the veto a "national disgrace," and Selden's successor as AFT president, Albert Shanker, warned that "This [veto] is going to make education an issue in next year's Presidential race." Senator Edward Brooke of Massachusetts, the ranking Republican on the HEW Subcommittee of the Labor and Public Welfare Committee, said that he was "deeply disappointed. Our bill was over the budget only because the Administration's request was so inadequate to begin with." After only twenty minutes of debate, the Senate voted 88–12 to override the Ford veto on September 10, one day after a similarly lopsided 379–41 House vote. It was the sixth veto overridden since Ford took office, "a record for overriding the vetoes of Republican Presidents in this century," according to the House Democratic Party leadership.[79]

Ford's other major budget priority, like Nixon's, was to consolidate federal education programs into a more efficient structure. Any such combination would have to answer four major questions: (1) What form should it take? (2) How flexible should it be? (3) Should it encourage states to equalize expenditures? (4) How much should it cost?

As to the first question, the Office of Management and Budget (OMB) favored a "major and mandatory" single block grant that would combine Title I of the ESEA; innovative and supportive services; education for the handicapped; educational broadcasting; occupational, adult, and vocational education; and TRIO (Upward Bound, Talent Search, and Special Services for Disadvantaged Students); and library resources. Such an approach would maximize state choices and minimize federal regulations. HEW and the Domestic Council preferred a performance-based consolidation that would distribute federal dollars in a block grant only if states met federal standards in the critical categories of vocational education, discrimination, children in areas of low property wealth, and children requiring special services. This alternative would preserve national goals as well as state choices.[80]

To the second question, the OMB answered that 75 percent of the funds under either proposal pass through local educational agencies to populations with special needs (the disadvantaged and handicapped). They believed that both of these groups would be justly served. HEW sought to require states to set aside monies (not necessarily federal) for the disadvantaged and to earmark vocational education funds for special needs populations. HEW worried that under the OMB–Domestic Council plan, states would shift money for compensatory education to the handicapped to avoid litigation.

To the third question, HEW and the Domestic Council favored exploration of a method of financially rewarding states for moving toward equalization. This approach would curry favor with Congress. The OMB viewed this idea as unnecessary because many states were seeking equalization without federal incentives and unwise because it would invite congressional demands for even more lucrative rewards. Despite their disagreements on the previous three questions, HEW, the OMB, and the Domestic Council answered the fourth question the same way: to secure congressional acquiescence in elementary and secondary education consolidation, the Ford administration would have to offer more money than without such a revision.[81]

The president arrived at his own answers in March 1976, when he sent to Congress a special message proposing the Financial Assistance for Elementary and Secondary Education Act. Asserting that "education needs can be met most effectively by giving people at the local level the tools to do the job well," Ford chose the "major mandatory" merger of twenty-seven education programs into a single block grant. Seventy-five percent of the funds would serve special needs populations, with no financial rewards for state equalization efforts. And there would be more money for education than the $3.3 billion which Ford had budgeted two months earlier.[82]

The education interests shared neither Ford's enthusiasm for consolidation nor his estimate of its cost. "We urge this Committee to once again ignore the budget requests that have been submitted," AFT codirector of legislation Greg Humphrey told the House Education and Labor Committee in April 1976. "The President's budget is a cut of more than $1 billion below what was appropriated in the current fiscal year. In fact, the president's budget has almost no relation to the needs of education. Simply to reestablish the level of support that existed in 1971 [in inflation-adjusted dollars], $1 billion for elementary and secondary education is necessary." NEA director of government relations Stanley MacFarland, in a June meeting with Ford aide James Reichley, continued to press for one-third federal funding. Congress heeded Humphrey's advice and largely ignored the Ford proposal. "Ford's block grant proposals are going nowhere fast in Congress," wrote Joel Havemann in the April 17 *National Journal.* When members of Congress attacked the single block grant of twenty-seven programs, Ford added two block grants and subtracted three programs from the package. But when the FY 1977 education appropriation emerged from Capitol Hill well above Ford's budget, the president vetoed and the Congress overrode.[83]

## The Education Reforms

"We cannot buy quick miracles in education by spending more money," said Gerald Ford, sounding an awful lot like Richard Nixon. "It would be easier if we could measure education quality in dollars and cents, but we cannot." Like Nixon's, Ford's public elementary and secondary education policy moved beyond arguing dollars and cents with Congress and the education interests. Only five days into the Ford presidency, Semerad outlined three major directions of school reform efforts in the administration: "We should assist the States and localities, who have primary responsibility for education, while striving to insure that equality of educational opportunity is available to everyone. The Federal government should also support and direct research and development designed to accelerate reform and innovation. It should provide leadership in the process of reform in education designed to broaden education alternatives and to create an education system that is more responsive to a rapidly changing society."[84]

Like Nixon, Ford believed that Title I of the ESEA was not achieving the first goal—the equality of educational opportunity it was intended to provide. "Findings from large-scale evaluations of Title I offer little evidence of a positive overall impact on eligible and participating children," Daniel Patrick Moynihan, now ambassador to the United Nations, wrote after meeting with the president in October 1975. Citing the Coleman and Jencks studies, Moynihan added, "There is unmistakable evidence that [public education] has worsened in the past ten years—in the sense that there are more terribly disadvantaged children coming along." Ford concurred: "Too often we have found ourselves asking whether Federal forms have been properly filled out, not whether children have been properly educated."[85]

To attack the reading deficiencies that Title I was not adequately addressing, Ford authorized a Reading Improvement Program for 1975–78. With the ESEA extended until 1977, however, and the education interests and Congress firmly behind it, there was little the president could do to reform Title I. Like Nixon, Ford pursued the second objective—a greater federal role in educational research and development. "What we have learned recently is that much of what we once thought we knew about the impact on education of more dollars, more facilities, etc. may not be true," David Lissy, executive secretary to HEW, wrote in April 1976. To help discover more effective remedies for the country's educational ills, Ford sought $130 million in the FY 1975 budget for the NIE.[86]

But the Ford administration would do little research. Congress did not seem interested; the House voted only $80 million for the NIE, while the Senate voted nothing (and compromised at $70 million). The OE did not seem capable; when Commissioner Terrel Bell resigned in July 1976 to return to the University of Utah, he left behind what Lissy called "a management disaster area." So the research community was not impressed; a two-year study by the National Council on Educational Research, completed in July 1977, concluded that "basic research on the processes of education is today assigned very low priority in Federal agencies charged with the management of educational research and development."[87]

The third goal advanced by Semerad—helping education keep pace with a changing society—evoked the most noteworthy initiative from the Ford administration. In an August 30, 1974, speech at Ohio State University, Ford beckoned educators, students, and business and labor leaders to form a new "community of learning" in the United States. "The time has come for a fusion of the realities of the work-a-day life," said the president, "with the teaching of academic institutions."[88]

The public response to Ford's proposal, according to James Cavanaugh, deputy director of Ford's Domestic Council, was "most encouraging." The administration then moved to transform Ford's general prescription into specific programs. In a December meeting with the president, Weinberger, Secretary of Labor Peter Brennan, and Secretary of Commerce Philip Dent recommended the creation of a Cabinet Committee and President's Council on Education and Work; new funding for cooperative education for students in academic and general as well as vocational secondary school tracks; new monies for research and development into "competency-based" education involving a "closer orientation to the real world of practically every facet of society"; application of existing HEW resources to finance career education programs at the junior high school level; new dollars to train elementary and secondary instructors to teach economic education; use of existing HEW and Corporation for Public Broadcasting money to finance television programs linking education and work; and new funds for technical assistance from the HEW, the Department of Labor, and Department of Commerce in disseminating occupational education information and from the federal Employment Service in establishing job placement offices in secondary schools. Weinberger added $2.4 million to the NIE and $3 million to the Fund for the Improvement of Postsecondary Education for new education and work efforts.[89]

"If you can devise a sensible linkage between . . . education and the 'world of work,' I salute you," Chester Finn wrote to Semerad in April 1975, recalling the Nixon administration's career education initiatives. "We never could, and despite a lot of rhetoric and wasted Federal dollars, no one to my knowledge has yet figured out a workable arrangement." The Ford administration never could, either. Domestic Council director Ken Cole believed that career education needed more study, current occupational information was inadequate, and new job placement offices were unnecessary. Robert Goldwin of the White House staff questioned the initiative's emphasis on elementary and secondary, rather than higher, education. Ford found the recommendations "too general."[90]

## The Ford Record

Gerald Ford's defeat in the 1976 election assured that he would never completely exorcise the ghost of scandal and economic distress that afflicted his presidency. Any judgment of the president thus becomes as tentative as his presidency.

In his public elementary and secondary education policy, a clear picture nonetheless emerged. He was at least as vigorous as his predecessor in battling the education groups and Congress on cost-quality terms. Ford relied on numbers to defend his FY 1976 budget in a May 1975 speech to the NEA, claiming a "fifty percent increase over the 1969 budget." Two months later, when Congress exceeded his budget, Ford again selected quantitative language to explain his veto: "The real issue is whether we are going to impose fiscal discipline on ourselves or whether we are going to spend ourselves into fiscal solvency."[91]

Ford's verbal and legislative sparring over budgets with the education groups and Congress was at least as counterproductive as Nixon's. "Education again was the extra guest at the dinner table," the AFT's Megel complained of the FY 1976 Ford budget, "given what was left over after the invited guests had left." When asked about Ford's commitment to education, NEA president John Ryor snapped, "What commitment?" Weinberger advised Ford not to plan a 1977 White House Conference on Education (as authorized but not required by the 1974 Education Act Amendments) because it would likely provide "a visible platform for demands by interest groups, for more and larger spending programs." When the time arrived in 1976 for the AFT to endorse its second presidential candidate and the NEA its first, neither chose Gerald Ford.[92]

Congress also returned Ford's volleys. "In response to the confrontationalist nature of both presidents [Nixon and Ford], Congress took several steps, both offensive and defensive, to strengthen its capabilities," recalled John Brademas, Indiana Democrat and veteran member of the House Education and Labor Committee. "Increased staff, the Congressional budget process, the War Powers Resolution, the legislative veto, limits on presidential impounding of funds already appropriated by Congress . . . were the weapons with which . . . Capitol Hill armed itself" against the White House's fiscal assault. In this spirit, Congress would override two Nixon and two Ford vetoes of education appropriations.[93]

Like Nixon, Ford was largely unsuccessful in transferring federal school programs to the states. Despite broad public support for the concept and Ford's repeated pleas to "get moving" on revenue sharing, Congress was reluctant to relinquish its newly won control of eight cents of every education dollar. If he "is going to take tax money from the taxpayers in Minnesota, and distribute those funds around the nation," explained former block grant proponent Rep. Albert Quie, ranking Republican on the House Education and Labor Committee, then he should "give some directions as to how those monies are to be spent."[94]

Like Nixon, Ford invested few words and fewer dollars into his "social context" critique of federal school aid. "Basic problems of morale and commitment to quality [in public schools] seem unusually recalcitrant these days, despite a host of visible efforts and very widespread public concern," wrote Mathews in September 1975. "I think it is clear that the President wants to exert such leadership without the Federal Government attempting to buy control of the education enterprise." In April 1976 Lissy called for a "comprehensive statement of the President's philosophy and concerns rather than a program-by-program review." Yet the leadership was lacking, and the statement never came.[95]

For Ford as well as Nixon, there were legal and political boundaries that they refused to cross. In 1974, in *Lau v. Nichols,* the Supreme Court ruled that California schools must provide adequate English instruction to Chinese-speaking pupils. So the Education Act of 1974 provided two new vocational education categorical authorities concerned with bilingual education. The Education for All Handicapped Children Act (AHCA), authored by Brademas and Quie in the House and New Jersey Democrat Harrison Williams in the Senate, provided special education and related services to handicapped children. "The President has said repeatedly that he will continue to veto each and every financially irresponsible act of Congress," and the AHCA "obviously, fall[s] in this category," Terry O'Connell warned in November 1975, but "we are going to have to be smart or we are going to get killed." Ford signed the legislation.[96]

Despite these similarities, the Ford administration was not simply the completion of the second Nixon term. First, the circumstances under which Nixon and Ford entered the White House were radically different. Elected on a platform of more education spending, Nixon arrived in Washington with a balanced budget and a commitment to education reform. Within a year he had vetoed education spending, presided over a budget deficit, and pursued welfare reform. "During his first year in office, Nixon made no serious attempt to take over Lyndon Johnson's self-awarded title of 'The Education President,'" Finn would remember. "So his Special Message on Education Reform in March 1970 looked to many educators like another trick of Nixon's, the anti-education President who had recently vetoed a whopping HEW appropriation chiefly because it earmarked too many billions for the nation's schools."[97]

Ford began with neither an electoral mandate, a balanced budget, nor a reform agenda. So after Nixon squandered the opportunity for reform, Ford postponed it. "Once the economy gets back on the track," Ford told the NEA in May 1975, he would support "new and major initiatives in education at the federal level." The economy never fully recovered, so Ford never really tried. "In the 1974 [congressional] campaign that Ford had entered by the time he became President, he had been making the economy his main pitch and identifying inflation as public enemy number one, which he blamed on the Democratic Congress," Hartmann would recall. "In his first State of the Union address, he dealt exclusively with the economy and energy," while he devoted his second and last State of the Union address to the economy, energy, and defense.[98]

There would be no second Ford term, of course; President Shouldn't Have Been became President Might Have Been. In Ford's last full year in office, he marked the country's bicentennial. In elementary and secondary education, the president, the Congress, and the education interests could celebrate two hundred years of predominantly local control of public schools. There was little else on which to agree.

# Jimmy Carter

> The noblest task of government is education.
> —Jimmy Carter (1979)

"A Great Society," said President Lyndon Johnson in 1964, "asks not only how much, but how good; not only how fast we are moving, but where we are headed."[99] Yet in the decade that followed, "how much" remained the primary question in the federal aid to education wars between Republican presidents and Democratic Congresses. Richard Nixon and Gerald Ford, seeking to reduce federal social spending during inflationary times, had vetoed five education appropriations in eight years. As the White House returned to Democratic rule in 1977, Jimmy Carter assumed Johnson's mantle as a champion of federal aid to public elementary and secondary schools.[100]

President Carter appeared well prepared not only to enlarge the federal presence in elementary and secondary public education but also to reform it. There was indeed much work to be done: standardized test scores were falling, urban schools were failing, and public confidence was flagging. But in the end, despite his celebrated immersion in policy and aversion to politics, Carter did not find the new answers sought by Lyndon Johnson in 1964. And, in large part, he was still asking the old questions.

## Carter and Education

A graduate of the Naval Academy, Carter had served seven years on his county school board before running for the Georgia Senate because "I was concerned about the threats to our system of education." As a state senator, he sat on the education committee, and as governor, he "served as an active member of a commission that studied long-term educational needs for the state, and the recommendations made by the group made their way into new legislative initiatives."[101]

## The Education Department

Almost from its birth in 1857 as a congressionally chartered organization of public school administrators and teachers, the NEA worked toward a greater role for the federal government in public elementary and secondary education. Despite its intensive legislative lobbying efforts, however, the NEA had remained officially nonpartisan. As late as 1970, the NEA Legislative Commission rejected the creation of a political action committee (PAC).

Two years later, however, the NEA inaugurated a national PAC that endorsed, funded, and campaigned for congressional candidates. In October 1975, the NEA issued a statement entitled "Needed: A Cabinet Department of Education." In that same month in Iowa, site of the first presidential caucuses the following year, candidate Jimmy Carter told a group of teachers, "The only department I would consider creating would be a separate Department of Education. I spelled out this position when I met with the leadership of the National Education Association a year ago." In 1976, the NEA endorsed its first presidential candidate—Jimmy Carter.[102]

In March 1977, only two months into the Carter presidency, NEA executive director Terry Herndon reminded the new president of his campaign promise. A month later, after Budget Director Bert Lance assured the president that it "does not conflict with the possibility of creating a new Department of Education," Carter approved Commissioner Ernest Boyer's reorganization of HEW. At the same time, Elizabeth Abramowitz, education specialist on Carter's domestic policy staff, met with a group of public school lobbyists, including the NEA's James Green. "Although the tone of the meeting was cordial," Abramowitz wrote to Carter, "the group is obviously concerned that the President will abandon his campaign promise to create a Department of Education." She recommended that Carter form a task force to study the issue so as not to "automatically lock the administration into a Department of Education as the only way to improve efficiency in education programs."[103]

But the NEA did not wait for the president to act. After helping Connecticut Democratic senator Abraham Ribicoff secure thirty-three cosponsors of a bill creating a Department of Education, the organization's chief officers met with Carter on April 27. The president, forsaking domestic policy advisor Stuart Eizenstat's advice that the matter receive his "immediate personal attention," promised only that he would pursue various options for education reorganization, including a cabinet-level department. The next month he rejected Vice President Walter Mondale's suggestion that Carter address the NEA Convention in Minneapolis in July; Carter sent Mondale instead.[104]

Carter's backtracking worried Eizenstat's deputy, Bert Carp, who warned on June 15, "I think the chances are excellent that we will wind up politically with the worst of all worlds—open alienation of the NEA and a major hassle with the Congress next year." Noting that "the prime objective of the NEA . . . is a massive increase in federal aid to education," Carp concluded that support for a separate Department of Education would minimize potential NEA discord over the budget. While Mondale shared Carp's concerns, he nonetheless endorsed a six-month evaluation of a separate department within the administration. Carter approved the study on June 22.[105]

The study would divide the administration into three camps. HEW secretary Joseph Califano and Council of Economic Advisers chairman Charles Schultze proposed a simple reorganization of the education functions within HEW. Abramowitz, Assistant to the President for Reorganization Richard Pettigrew, and Deputy Budget Director James McIntyre argued for a broadly based Department of Human Development comprising the HEW education division, the Department of Agriculture school nutrition programs, the Endowments for the Arts and Humanities, the National Science Foundation, youth training programs in the Department of Labor, and others. Carp, Lance, and the deputy congressional liaison Les Francis advocated a narrowly based separate Department of Education, incorporating only the education functions of HEW.[106]

Carter reached his decision on December 2. At Eizenstat's urging, he chose to endorse "the general concept of a separate Department of Education, not including social services, early next year." Carter decided that "education needed an advocate in the upper policy levels of the Executive Branch." The next month, he included a call for a separate Department of Education in his first State of the Union address.[107]

By April 1978, when he submitted it to Congress, Carter's proposal had evolved from "general concept" to finished product. In the end, Carter chose a broad-based department including the Agriculture Department's school lunch program and graduate school, the Department of Housing and Urban Development's college housing program, the Interior Department's Indian schools, selected science programs of the National Science Foundation, the Defense Department's schools for overseas dependents, and all of the education programs of HEW, including Head Start and its civil rights office. The Department of Education would include 164 existing programs, with a budget of $17.5 billion. Except for its exclusion of the Endowments for the Arts and Humanities, the administration plan was identical to the Ribicoff bill, which now had fifty-seven cosponsors.[108]

At a May meeting, administration representatives discussed legislative strategy for the plan. The OMB argued for an "all-out" effort in 1978 because such a bill would not pass in 1979. Francis concurred, predicting that "more Republicans" would arrive in 1979. The vice president's office favored "doing nothing" until 1979 because of the "formidable" list of major bills in the current session. Abramowitz counseled a middle ground—passage in 1978, but only after June, when "action may have been taken on [nonpublic school] tuition tax credits." She explained that "the Department issue divides the coalition" that shared the administration's opposition to such credits; once the tuition tax credit legislation had lost, the administration should recruit "a strong person to lead the education reorganization effort." Abramowitz concluded that "The whole thing is a political mess which will be politically damaging if it continues much longer."[109]

Carter sided with Abramowitz, choosing Indiana's Democratic whip John Brademas as his "strong person" to lead the fight for a separate department in the House of Representatives after the defeat of tuition tax credits. But after passing overwhelmingly in the Senate, the proposal died in the House. "Interest group vote counts of the full House indicated that [the bill] would have received over 300 votes if it had been brought to a final vote in the House," McIntyre concluded in January 1979. Reminding Carter that in his February 1978 education message he had pledged his administration's determination "to reestablish education in the forefront of our domestic priorities," McIntyre urged an early, intensive legislative effort in 1979. Such a campaign would counter the two major reasons for the 1978 failure: "first, that the bill was not a high priority of the Administration, and second, that the only group that actively supported the Department was the NEA."[110]

The *New York Times,* in a January 16, 1979, editorial, suggested that Carter give up on the idea altogether. After all, the *Times* wrote, Carter "supported a department for education only to fulfill a campaign pledge to the NEA." A month later, Abramowitz warned that congressional opposition to a separate Department of Education in 1979 would rest on three pillars: "control of the Department by the NEA, state-local responsibility, and civil rights guarantees."[111]

But the president pressed the fight. On February 13, while conceding that "the primary responsibility for education in our Nation lies with state and local government," Carter nonetheless offered a separate Department of Education to fill "a compelling need for the increased national attention . . . to education issues." In submitting his proposal, he wrote that such a department could help "to ensure equal educational opportunities; increase access to postsecondary education by low and middle income students; generate research and provide information to help our educational systems meet special needs; prepare students for employment; and encourage improvements in the quality of education."[112]

The administration then followed McIntyre's counsel in its aggressive campaign for passage of the legislation. S.210, sponsored by Ribicoff, passed the Senate, 72–21, on April 30, and HR 2444, sponsored by Democrat Jack Brooks of Texas, won in the House, 210–206, on July 11. Both bills had removed the three most controversial transfers: Head Start, Indian education, and child nutrition. The inclusion of antiabortion, antiracial quota, and proschool prayer amendments in the House bill, however, as well as strong lobbying by opponents such as the AFL-CIO, the AFT, and several university presidents, jeopardized the final passage.

After the conference report deleted these amendments, the Senate voted for the department, 69–22, on September 24. But a September 26 White House vote count showed the bill losing in the House by 208–215, with eleven undecided Democratic representatives. "In as thorough a lobbying job as I've ever seen," according to one congressional staffer, Carter summoned these wavering Democrats to the White House, where, with a "heavily partisan appeal," he sold the department as a fiscally conservative bulwark against federal control of education. "The bill mandates that five hundred positions be sliced from the Department immediately. This will save more than $20 million annually. . . . The conference committee has reaffirmed the central purpose of the legislation: improved management. . . . The legislation asserts the primacy of local responsibility for education."[113]

The next day, the House voted 215–201 for the conference report, which included 131 programs from the Education Division of HEW; 6 from the Rehabilitative Services Administration; 2 from the National Science Foundation, the Department of Justice, and the Department of Labor; and 1 each from the Departments of Defense, Housing and Urban Development, and Agriculture. It also created Offices of Elementary and Secondary Education, Vocational and Adult Education, Postsecondary Schools, Overseas Schools, Special Education and Rehabilitative Services, Bilingual Education, Educational Research and Improvements, and Civil Rights. Opposing the bill was a peculiar alliance of most Republicans, who feared federal (and NEA) control of education, and several Democrats, who worried that a single-issue, single-interest group department would splinter the traditional education, health, labor, and civil rights liberal coalition.[114]

The *Washington Post* observed that White House staffers joined NEA lobbyists in "noisily applauding" the outcome in the House chamber. The *New York Times* proclaimed Vice President Mondale, a former senator whose brother Mort was an NEA staffer, the "unsung hero" of the administration's legislative effort. The day after passage of the conference report, the NEA endorsed Carter and Mondale for reelection.[115]

Twelve days after signing the measure creating a separate Department of Education, however, Carter resisted NEA pressure to nominate an educator as the department's first secretary. Instead, on October 29 Carter selected Shirley Hufstedler, a liberal judge who had been appointed by President Johnson to the Ninth Circuit of the U.S. Court of Appeals. Hufstedler's only professional education credentials were her memberships on the boards of trustees of the California Institute of Technology, Occidental College, and the Aspen Institute for Humanistic Studies.[116]

## Politics versus Policy

Candidate Carter had promised to reduce the number of governmental agencies from nineteen hundred to two hundred. Candidate Carter had also envisioned a Department of Education that would "consolidate the grant programs, job training, early childhood education, literacy training, and many other functions currently scattered throughout the government." All of President Carter's key education appointees opposed a narrowly defined Department of Education, yet he essentially created such a department.[117]

Why did Carter pursue such a paradoxical course? As White House chief of staff Hamilton Jordan explained, "The teachers' organizations, particularly the National Education Association, are the fastest-growing, most active, and by many standards, the most effective political organizations in the country." Reminding Carter that his promise to create a Department of Education had been "complete, unequivocal, . . . [and] stated repeatedly in the campaign," Jordan concluded that "establishing the department is one of the few things we can do for the teachers' organizations in the next few years, as additional funds for education will be difficult with our goal of balancing the budget."[118]

So when asked to choose between creating a cabinet department or increasing federal education expenditures from 9 percent to 33 percent of all education monies (as the NEA was also advocating), the decision was really quite easy—and early. The appearance of policy making could not disguise the reality of politics. During the administration's elaborate study of a possible Department of Education, Carp scribbled to Eizenstat, "Stu, as you probably know, the decision on Dept. has really been made (or so Ham indicated to me). I think JC [Carter] probably told Ham [Jordan] OK on his memo, but let's go through the motions of receiving the OMB product and giving Joe [Califano] a chance."[119]

## The Education Budget

On February 10, 1977, HEW secretary Joseph Califano submitted his department's first budget to President Carter. It called for a $3 billion increase over the Ford education budget and a $1 billion addition to the OMB proposal. It requested a $150 million increase for Title I of the ESEA and a $70 million reduction in impact aid.[120]

Two months later Abramowitz lamented that the education budget did not adequately reflect Carter's campaign promises. Administratively, Carter had pledged to "establish a comprehensive program, create a separate Cabinet-level Department of Education, [and] consolidate categorical programs." Fiscally, he had promised to "increase federal support to local education administration with 'inadequate' tax base," and to "increase federal aid to education beyond ten percent of budget." She and Eizenstat urged Carter to appoint a cabinet-level task force to adopt a comprehensive education policy and to make a formal statement to underscore the visibility and importance of education in the administration.[121]

In June the task force arrived with Carter's activation of the Federal Interagency Committee of Education (FICE), which had been created by President Johnson in 1964 but had never subsequently worked for the White House. In July the formal statement came, but from the vice president. Mondale told the NEA Convention that Carter's education budget constituted a "fifteen percent increase in total spending for next year."[122]

As the administration quarreled with its critics over how much it had increased education's budget, Abramowitz continued to press the administration to increase education's profile. But her suggestion of a fall address by the president "on his four-year plan and philosophy for federal aid to education" met opposition from Eizenstat and Carp, who preferred that such a speech await the legislative outcomes of the education budget and Department of Education proposals.[123]

While waiting for Congress, the White House continued on the defensive. On September 1 Abramowitz assured the nation's governors that "federal policy in education does exist." On September 27 she wrote that "on the Hill, the general feeling is that the White House is not concerned about education." On October 6 she observed that "HEW is very late (one month) in its scheduled delivery of several important pieces of education legislation," including the expiring ESEA and the overdue Comprehensive Educational Policy.[124]

"Your legislative proposals in this area will set the Administration's elementary and secondary education agenda for at least your first term," Califano reminded Carter in December. "And they will be your first major statement about education generally and about the Federal role. After eight years of Nixon-Ford neglect, the education community is looking to you for leadership." Califano urged Carter to be "the President who focused on quality in elementary and secondary education [and] the relationship of the school to the family, the job, and the community."[125]

Yet Carter's handwritten underlining and notes in the margins of Califano's memorandum seemed to convey a lack of enthusiasm for federally directed educational innovation and an overriding concern for a cost-benefit analysis of education programs. Presidential question marks followed Califano's call for "Support and Innovation Grants" of $197 million, his advocacy of "effective teacher training," and his identification of "global perspectives (new)" as a "special skill" area, to be addressed by a new Educational Quality Act; the Educational Quality Act itself; a requirement that states describe their efforts to "ensure equitable services for public school children" under Title I of the ESEA; and his contention that "Title I has not actively encouraged . . . new testing ideas." The secretary's assertion that "school districts often fail to experiment with a variety of approaches" prompted Carter to write that "some do too much experimenting and not enough teaching."

Where Califano proposed "research and teacher training" because "little is known about how children acquire a second language," Carter appeared to suggest that the children should "speak only other [the English] language." Where Califano proclaimed that "a major change in our package is to move toward a new Federal-State partnership in serving the needy and/or special groups identified in most Federal programs," Carter wrote, "Try to consolidate programs," "teach basics (reading)," "test programs," and "total use of school facilities."

Carter underlined the total enrollment in the public schools (50 million in 1976–77), the total cost of public elementary and secondary education ($73 billion in 1976–77), the percentage of federal money invested in the public elementary and secondary schools (9 percent), the per-pupil expenditures in public elementary and secondary schools ($11,390 in 1975–76), the number of children served by Title I of the ESEA (5.6 million of 9 million eligible), and the average cost per child of Title I's aid to handicapped children ($553). Where Califano proposed to "add a new part to Title I, which would target supplemental funds on school districts with large absolute numbers (5000) or large proportions (20%) of poverty children," Carter asked, "How well, though, are funds utilized" and what is the "best factor?"

Where Califano proposed federal matching money for state compensatory programs in Title I, Carter underlined "new federal program." Where Califano suggested "a concentrated Federal effort . . . for achieving State school finance reform," Carter wrote, "Find way to free states to act." And where Califano offered savings in impact aid, Carter added, "Go further."[126]

At the same time Carter continued to support voluntary local adoption of a national student achievement examination. When Califano informed the president of NEA opposition to such a test, Carter replied, "Teachers just don't want people judging their performance. That's why the teacher unions oppose this."[127]

Carter's private skepticism about the efficacy of federal aid to primary and secondary public schools was well founded. Califano's own department, in its 1978 assessment of the "broad trends affecting educational policy," would identify declining birth rates, "white flight" from cities to suburbs, and Mexican American immigration to the Southwest. It would cite new "programmatic and fiscal challenges" such as addressing the needs of disabled, underprivileged, and language-limited students; redistributing education spending from rich to poor school districts; responding to state and local taxpayer revolts and federal budget constraints; and reacting to the proliferation of federal programs and court decisions affecting education.

It would note positive trends: 74.5 percent of eighteen-year-olds graduating from high school in 1977, and college enrollments of blacks and Hispanics in 1977 exceeding those for whites in 1975 (22 percent and 21 percent compared to 20 percent). But it would spot negative trends as well: deficiencies in basic reading, writing, and mathematics among many seventeen-year-olds and average Scholastic Aptitude Test scores dropping among all students, including prospective teachers. The downward tendencies had led more than thirty states to adopt minimum competency examinations for students, had caused the AFT to propose competency testing for teachers, and had provoked a national "back-to-basics" movement at the elementary, secondary, and higher education levels.[128]

A four-year Rand Corporation study for the OE, released in 1978, would conclude that the federal government had failed to significantly improve the nation's public schools in the first twelve years of the ESEA of 1965. "The net return to the federal investment," the report stated, "was the adoption of many innovations, the successful implementation of few, and the long-range continuation of still fewer." The report, while advocating a continuation of the federal role in public elementary and secondary education, recommended that the federal government do less dictating and more facilitating of reform. "More money supplied by federal funds did not necessarily purchase those things that really mattered," the report contended, "for example, more committed teachers, more effective project directors, [and] more concerned principals."[129]

Califano's response to Carter's written comments came on February 14, 1978, in his department's final legislative proposals for FY 1979. "As you requested in December," Califano wrote, "the primary emphasis in the reauthorization package is in achieving basic skills, and, where possible, attaining educational excellence." He added that "many of the legislative changes are mirrored by administrative changes to streamline and simplify Federal programs so that they can perform their historically limited function—to serve as catalysts and complements to State and locally controlled elementary and secondary education." At the same time, McIntyre and Eizenstat advised Carter that the HEW package "when combined with the unprecedented budget increases in Fiscal 1978 and 1979, clearly establish education as one of your most successful priorities."[130]

Carter's notes moved from outside to inside the margins when he sent his second education message to Congress on February 18. His proposals would "enhance the primary roles of the states and local communities, strengthen our commitment to basic skills education in Title I of the Elementary and Secondary Education Act," and "strengthen the bilingual education program with primary emphasis on teaching English." He promised to "give education a more prominent and visible role in the federal government."[131]

But for Carter, education reform was more rhetorical than real. In the same speech, he proposed a 24 percent increase in federal education spending, promised to "concentrate a major share of increased Title I funding on those school systems most in need," approved a "research and demonstration effort in the area of basic skills," and permitted "flexibility in the use of the first language and culturally sensitive approaches to achieve this goal." And he was silent on the subject of a national student achievement test. In other words, more of the same. "The President's message struck two basic themes," wrote Martin Tolchin of the *New York Times*, "increasing the funds spent on education and giving those funds to areas with greatest need."[132]

After seventy-five days of hearings, the longest deliberation on an education bill since the passage of the ESEA in 1965, the Education Amendments of 1978 passed the Senate 86–7 and the House 350–20. HEW assistant secretary Mary Berry praised the law's "provisions which give local officials greater opportunities to initiate the development of programs to initiate student achievement."[133]

But supporter Carl Perkins, chairman of the House Committee on Education and Labor, admitted, "This is not a revolutionary measure. The impact of these amendments will not come in departing from old patterns, but in building on the fourteen years of experience we have had in forging a national partnership to improve education." Citing an NIE study that observed gains of twelve months in reading and eleven months in math for first-graders covered by

Title I compensatory education programs, Perkins maintained that "these programs are beginning to work. Now is not the time for radical change."[134]

Calling it "a major achievement of your administration in education" that "includes all of the major provisions" proposed by the president, Abramowitz and Eizenstat urged Carter to sign the legislation. The president signed the five-year, $50 billion extension of the ESEA on November 1.[135]

Even as the Carter administration publicly touted the $800 million increase in Title I funds for FY 1979 provided by the new law, its OMB, citing inflation and the budget deficit, planned zero growth in Title I monies for FY 1980. Abramowitz condemned the mixed message: "OMB budget proposals . . . create a credibility gap between what the President says is important in education and what he is to propose for funding." And even before she "had an opportunity to review all education programs" in her new department, Hufstedler decided that "the OMB mark is at least $1.7 billion below the amount required" for education.[136]

Despite soaring inflation and a rising budget deficit, the president sided with his new secretary. His FY 1980 budget, after approval by Congress and the addition of "uncontrollable" HEW supplemental requests, would spend almost $14.5 billion on education, up for the third consecutive year.[137]

In January 1980, in the midst of his presidential primary campaign against Senator Edward Kennedy of Massachusetts, Carter proposed a 7 percent increase in education spending as part of an otherwise austere federal budget. Carter allocated $1.2 billion between the Education and Labor Departments to fund his first new education program, the Youth Act of 1980. The result of a ten-month study by a task force headed by Vice President Mondale, it would provide job training for black and Hispanic teenagers, whose unemployment rate had reached 50 percent in some cities.[138]

But in March, after two consecutive months of 18 percent inflation, Carter revised his budget downward, calling for $1 billion less than he had previously requested. But the president had sufficiently replenished the federal education coffers to declare victory at the NEA Convention in July. "We have increased Title I fifty-five percent. For the handicapped Americans we have tripled state grants. For bilingual education we have doubled funding," said Carter. "The 1981 budget will have increased federal funds for education by seventy-three percent in four years."[139]

## The Carter Record

This was not the policy maker who waged war on inflation and expected a balanced budget. This was the politician who promised to spend more money on education than his predecessors. This was not the policy maker who sought to streamline the federal role in education. This was the politician who proposed to expand it. This was not the policy maker who questioned existing federal innovations. This was the politician who accepted them. This was not the policy maker who dissected the change wrought by the ESEA. This was the politician who conserved it.

The triumph of politician over policy maker was the product of three major factors. First, aside from creating the Department of Education, education was not a major priority in the Carter administration. Hufstedler would recall that in domestic policy, "education was at the top of the President's agenda." While Carter's record in Georgia buttressed such an assertion, his performance in Washington did not. Although uncontrollable influences—the intractability of inflation, the persistence of unemployment, and the imperatives of foreign policy (especially the Iran hostage crisis of November 4, 1979–January 20, 1981, and the Soviet occupation of Afghanistan beginning in December 1979)—helped relegate education to a lesser status, Carter himself did little to elevate it.[140]

In his first State of the Union address in January 1978, Carter cited energy, the economy, and the Panama Canal treaties as his major priorities. He mentioned education in passing only twice in his 1979 State of the Union speech and once in his 1980 address. While Hufstedler would argue that "it is extremely important to have education at the Cabinet table," the new secretary arrived at the table after infrequent cabinet meetings had replaced weekly ones. Elementary and secondary education was virtually invisible during Carter's first year, despite a considerable record of domestic legislative achievements, and during his last year, because of his revised budget. As late as March 1979, Eizenstat was prodding Carter to deliver his first public speech on education, which he would finally deliver in July 1980 to the NEA. In his memoir, the subject receives barely two pages.[141]

Second, despite his "planner engineer mentality" and his disdain for those Democrats "to whom the phrase 'balanced budget' coming from a Democratic President was almost blasphemous," Carter chose to join the liberals of the NEA and the congressional majority rather than fight them. Where Republicans Nixon and Ford had resisted congressional add-ons to education appropriations, Democrat Carter reluctantly acquiesced. While Nixon and Ford chose education to help verify their conservatism (while spending more freely elsewhere), Carter permitted education to help certify his liberalism (while acting more frugally elsewhere). "It wasn't a question of making ceremonial speeches written by someone else," Hufstedler stated, explaining Carter's approach to education. "Dollar signs speak much louder."[142]

Proud of his "progressive philosophy" at a time when "liberal" was not yet an epithet, Carter chose a liberal vice president and liberal cabinet secretaries to lead his education effort. "A lot of people who voted for him [were] thinking he was conservative," recalled Attorney General Griffin Bell, "and then he goes and gets all these people in government from another direction." Eizenstat added, "Although Carter was a more moderately conservative Democrat than many of those against whom he ran in 1976, he was no less a Democrat who felt that the federal government did have certain responsibilities," including education.

Carter was "far more liberal than conservative," Hufstedler agreed. "The money has been good. . . . The policies have been right," Abramowitz concluded when she resigned in 1980. "They have been liberal."[143]

Third, and most significantly, Carter could not overcome history. "The Speaker [Thomas O'Neill of Massachusetts] and [majority leader] Jim Wright [of Texas] have told us that they strongly oppose any effort to oppose the Labor/HEW appropriation," McIntyre, Eizenstat, and Moore wrote to the president on June 2, 1978. They argued that failure to oppose the bill, to which Congress had added $887 million, would undermine the "credibility of the Administration's anti-inflation effort" and "make strong efforts against other appropriations more difficult." But they conceded that "it is far from certain we would secure adoption of a major reduction in the Labor/HEW bill even with an all-out effort." Five days later, Frank Moore wrote the president that the Speaker considered Carter's concern over excessive spending "a hopeless cause and one on which you should not risk enemies. . . . You and the Congress are arguing over priorities and not over amounts of money, and . . . Labor/HEW is a Democratic priority." So Carter signed the legislation.[144]

Unwilling to veto appropriations passed by his own party, Carter allowed Congress to strengthen its hold on federal aid to elementary and secondary public education. From 1969 to 1977, annual appropriations for HEW education programs averaged about 14 percent over requests. "As a result," Califano wrote to Carter in December 1977, "the Executive Branch is usually in a defensive position with respect to the education budget. Thus our legislative package . . . must reflect a serious commitment to elementary and secondary education." So when Carter anticipated congressional add-ons in his FY 1979 education budget, majority whip Brademas observed that "unlike his two predecessors," Carter had indeed demonstrated that he "takes education seriously."[145]

Califano would recall that he entered the administration in January 1977 "determined to step up federal funding [of education] sharply." But he left the administration in July 1979 "alarmed over the deterioration of public education in America and troubled by [a] federal role enlarged and shaped by special interests." Donald Orlich, professor of education at Washington State University, argued in *Educational Researcher* in July 1979 that the "failure" of "federal social engineering in education" was the consequence of too much faith in technology, too much reliance on politicians, and too little attention to research. Writing in *The New Republic* in April 1981, associate editor David Savage of *Education U.S.A.* asked about the ESEA, "How could the Federal government add so much money to education and come up with nothing to show for it?" He answered that Title I had stigmatized remedial learners, spawned bureaucrats, and mimicked educational fads. Califano, Orlich, and Savage argued not for abandoning the federal role in elementary and secondary public schools but for reforming it.[146]

Rather than play defense against Congress and special interests (especially the NEA), Carter played offense and claimed victory. "Within the controllable part of the nondefense budget during my term," Carter would recall in his memoir, "I was able to double the portion going to education." By the terms of the debate over federal aid to primary and secondary public education from 1965 to 1981, from Johnson to Carter, that was all that really mattered.[147]

# CHAPTER 2

# School Desegregation
## 1965–81

## Lyndon Johnson

A conservative, goes the old joke, is a liberal who has been mugged. Lyndon Johnson's seizure of the political center on the Elementary and Secondary Education Act (ESEA) from 1965 to 1967 offered a variation on that theme. A moderate, one could add, is a liberal who has been elected. Nowhere did the Johnson administration more noticeably seek to govern from the middle than in the area of school desegregation. Yet unlike in his implementation of the ESEA, it was not always easy to find the middle—or the president. As a result, a presidency that restored hope in the midst of tragedy ultimately practiced caution in the midst of change.

### De Jure School Desegregation

From the enactment of the Civil Rights Act in July 1964 to the signing of the ESEA in April 1965, about five hundred southern school districts had submitted desegregation plans to the Office of Education (OE). Because most of those plans were "unacceptable," the Civil Rights Act dictated that Commissioner Francis Keppel withhold ESEA monies from those districts. Fearing a "crisis in the making," the Justice Department and the Department of Health, Education, and Welfare (HEW) devised specific guidelines to help ensure greater compliance. The guidelines set the fall of 1967 as the "target date for extension of desegregation to all grades of school systems. . . . However, the Commissioner may modify the target date on or before January 31, 1966, for the purpose of determ[in]ing continued eligibility for federal assistance." They defined a "good faith start" toward compliance as the desegregation of at least four grades for the 1965–66 school year; movement toward faculty desegregation, such as mixed faculty meetings and teacher training sessions; desegregated pupil transportation; genuine "freedom of choice" plans for minority parents; assignment to the nearest school if freedom of choice plans led to overcrowding; abolition of racially discriminatory attendance zones; and public notice of desegregation plans. The commissioner thus placed himself in the forefront of the school desegregation controversy. "Undoubtedly," a White House memo accurately predicted in April 1965, "these guidelines are going to be greeted as too stiff by Southerners and too lenient by civil rights leaders."[1]

And where would the president be? "The question was raised whether to issue the 'new rules' as 'regulations' which would have to be approved by the President or simply as guidelines bearing only the authority of HEW," the memo continued. "Secretary [Anthony] Celebrezze decided that HEW should bear the political burden and issue them as guidelines." In May, when a group of Southern governors met to register their opposition to the new guidelines, Arnold Aronson, secretary of the Leadership Conference on Civil Rights, complained to the president. But top White House aide Douglass Cater advised Johnson, "There is nothing to be done [by the president] in a direct way to influence this meeting."[2]

Members of his administration publicly extolled the guidelines. In June, in *Singleton v. Jackson Municipal Separate School District*, the Justice Department successfully defended the guidelines in a case brought by civil rights groups against the Jackson, Mississippi, school district's delayed compliance. In August, Keppel called the fact that 98 percent of the affected districts had filed compliance documents a "remarkable achievement."[3]

Privately, however, the administration was less sanguine. With 92 percent of Southern black children still in segregated schools, a December meeting between civil rights groups and the OE yielded a consensus that "present desegregation measures were not adequate and that more rigorous steps might be necessary." Citing a U.S. Civil Rights Commission report that criticized the guidelines' allowance of "freedom of choice" plans as unfairly burdening the victims of school segregation, HEW secretary John Gardner concluded that "it is absolutely necessary to toughen the guidelines." So on March 7, 1966, Keppel's successor Harold Howe announced new guidelines, which added detailed provisions for faculty desegregation, the closing of inferior (usually African American) school facilities, and the careful monitoring of freedom-of-choice plans to show progress toward desegregation.[4]

Johnson was still conspicuously absent. "There is some discussion about the form in which these new standards should be issued," wrote Gardner's special assistant for civil rights Peter Libassi. "Should they be departmental regulations signed by the President, Departmental guidelines issued by the Secretary, or Office of Education guidelines issued by the Commissioner of Education? My off-handed thought is that they should be issued by the Commissioner."[5]

The new rules did little to appease critics on either side of the school segregation divide. Lillie Jackson, president emeritus of the Maryland branch of the National Association for the Advancement of Colored People (NAACP), telegraphed the White House to call for an "investigation of the failure of the U.S. Office of Education and the Department of Health, Education, and Welfare to enforce Title VI" in Maryland. The NAACP Washington bureau sought to accelerate school desegregation by amending Title IV of the Civil Rights Act. Noting that the new guidelines "say nothing about proceedings to terminate funds" beyond "judicial enforcement of the compliance agreement," G. W. Foster asked in the *Saturday Review,* "Who Pulled the Teeth from Title VI?"[6]

On the other side, West Virginia Democratic senator Robert Byrd telegraphed Johnson to protest the new guidelines for going "beyond mere school desegregation" to "intrude into the area of busing in order to achieve a degree of racial balance." Seventeen other Southern senators wrote to Johnson urging him "to revoke the 'revised guidelines of 1966' and restore freedom of choice." After the House passed an amendment to the ESEA extension, sponsored by Democrat L. H. Fountain of North Carolina, that would prohibit the OE from withholding funds before a hearing on alleged Title VI violations, both houses passed a modified version giving the OE ninety days to hold a hearing and issue a report before it could withhold funds. A report by the Senate Appropriations Committee charged that "the revised guidelines contravene and violate the legislative intent of Congress." South Carolina Democratic senator Mendel Rivers called Howe the "Commissar of Education" because he "talks like a communist," and North Carolina Democratic representative Walter Johnson demanded Howe's resignation. A Gallup Poll found that 52 percent of Americans believed that the administration was moving "too fast" on school desegregation.[7]

The administration weighed the political merits of both sides. Agreeing with those who advocated strengthening the guidelines, Howe privately called the rules "worthless." Speaking for those who favored weakening the guidelines, White House aide Charles Roche wrote that "It is difficult to see how we can get any more of the Negro vote." He added, "Of . . . vital concern among many members of Congress is the feeling that all-out civil rights enforcement . . . will be fatal at the polls." Despite their preference for weaker rules, several Southern Democratic senators and governors privately counseled the White House to stay the course. "I'm not in sympathy with the guidelines, but off the record, I don't see how you can do anything but stay with them," advised Florida senator George Smathers. "If you change in either direction, you'll catch hell. You'd better just squat." Others with similar advice were Senators Richard Russell of Georgia, Samuel Gibbons of Florida, and John McClellan of Arkansas as well as Governors Mills Godwin of Virginia, Dan Moore of West Virginia, and Robert McNair of North Carolina.[8]

The administration squatted. "There should be no defensiveness" about the guidelines, HEW assistant secretary for legislation Ralph Huitt counseled members of the administration. "We should say boldly that 'freedom of choice' works as a desegregation tool." Gardner insisted that the guidelines "are not designed to compel desegregation beyond that inherent in a fairly working free choice plan, to strike down freedom of choice, or to achieve 'racial balance.'" The Justice

Department successfully defended the guidelines in the Fifth Circuit Court in New Orleans in December, in a suit brought by four Louisiana school districts. Two days later, Howe issued essentially the same guidelines, including the controversial "freedom of choice" and faculty desegregation provisions. "If we had modified the guidelines," Libassi explained, "we could probably never have written another guideline and made it stick."[9]

While his education commissioner and HEW secretary weathered the attacks on the administration's policies toward de jure segregation, Johnson remained above the fray. When he received Senator Byrd's letter in March 1966, Johnson passed it to Cater, who replied to Byrd by quoting Howe. When the House Education Subcommittee reduced Title VI enforcement money in June, Cater said, "It is unlikely that Senator [Lister] Hill [chairman of the Labor and Public Welfare Committee] will restore cuts made by Congressman [John] Fogarty [of Rhode Island]. It is difficult to see how the President can appeal to the Hill on a matter such as this." And Johnson did not make that appeal. After a public defense of the guidelines by Howe, Cater asked Gardner if the president had seen the speech in advance; he had not. Next to yet another allusion to Johnson's teaching career in one of Howe's staff-written speeches, the commissioner penciled, "Well, now I've heard about that episode once too often and besides, I'm not wearing my uniform tonight." In an answer to a question at his October 6, 1966, press conference, Johnson clung tenaciously to both sides of the issue. "The policy of our Administration [is] to continue to promote and expedite the observance of the law of the land, and to see that all citizens of this country are treated equally without discrimination," the president told desegregation proponents. "I realize that in some instances there has been some harassment, some mistakes perhaps have been made, some people have been enthusiastic, and differences have developed," he told desegregation opponents.[10]

Although Johnson privately supported the guidelines as "a wise approach to equal education opportunity" and publicly pledged to enforce the "1964 Civil Rights Act and its prohibition against the use of federal funds to support racial bias," he largely continued to avoid the subject. "To involve the President, without legal necessity, in so controversial an arena as school desegregation has seemed to us administratively and politically unwise," Libassi conceded in February 1967. "We feel that the President should remain above the battle . . . and that the Commissioner rather than the President should defend school desegregation policies."[11]

For the time being, anyway. In May 1967, Howe announced that in the interest of "administrative efficiency," school desegregation policy would move across the street to Libassi's Office of Civil Rights. Libassi then dispatched aides Michael Burla and Richard Warden to Capitol Hill to improve relations with Southern congressmen. Within a month, however, Georgia Democratic senator Herman Talmadge was charging that "Mr. Libassi's incompetence is already apparent, and he should be fired unless his incompetence can be explained." Fountain attached his amendment to the 1967 ESEA extension, and Oregon Democrat Edith Green added a stipulation that the guidelines include a legal justification. After Georgia Democratic senator Richard Russell amended the bill to prevent the withholding of federal school aid during an academic year, the administration secured the removal of the amendment with a promise to announce all noncompliance hearings before September 1 each year.[12]

The administration's enforcement of Title VI remained under fire from the other side as well. At Johnson's May 18, 1967, press conference, a reporter forced the president to deny that the administration was trading civil rights enforcement for votes on the ESEA extension. A U.S. Civil Rights Commission report in July 1967 concluded that "problems of intimidation and other denials of rights still are prevalent, and progress in obtaining compliance has been relatively slow." Commission staff director William Taylor wrote to the White House, "I believe the report may be of particular value in refuting the arguments of those in Congress who have said that HEW has been to[o] zealous in enforcing Title VI." Senators Morse and Jacob Javits, the ranking Republican on the Labor and Public Welfare Committee, filed a statement urging HEW to expedite school desegregation. Clarence Mitchell, Washington director of the NAACP, repudiated the Fountain amendments as the products of "an unholy alliance between advocates of racial segregation . . . and those who are unwilling to face . . . *de facto* segregation." In a March 1968 article in *The New Republic,* political scientist Gary Orfield claimed that school desegregation was "on the verge of final success," if only the administration would enforce it. Following Johnson's March 31 announcement that he would not seek reelection (due largely to the Vietnam War), Orfield wrote to Cater, "Given the real possibilities that Republican [Richard] Nixon might become President with Southern support or that [third-party candidate George] Wallace might have the balance of power in the Electoral College," Johnson should approach the "final settlement" on de jure school desegregation. "Far too much time and effort and political capital have been invested," Orfield concluded, "to risk reducing the desegregation effort to a curious historic footnote."[13]

In the face of such relentless criticism, the administration—and the guidelines—remained firm. Libassi decided on "refining present policies rather than introducing new approaches." He directed the Office of Civil Rights to "on a case by case basis, negotiate comprehensive desegregation plans, replacing freedom of choice where it has not proven effective; conduct these negotiations on a year-round basis and thus avoid the usual summer crisis; establish for each district a fixed target date by which time the elimination of the dual school system will be completed, preferably in two steps by September 1968 or by an earlier or later appropriate date; and continue focusing on districts with less than fifty percent Negro student population." Libassi concluded that "no major revision in the guidelines is necessary to carry out this program." While "I agree with Professor Orfield that . . . in many districts freedom of choice plans have not resulted in the year-by-year progress required toward the elimination of the dual school system," Libassi added, "the recently-issued school compliance policies require abandonment of freedom of choice where it has not resulted in . . . the adoption of an effective plan . . . to eliminate the dual school system by the opening of the 1969–70 school year."[14]

As the Johnson administration came to a close, its de jure school desegregation policies offered comfort for both camps. Despite the guidelines, as the 1968–69 school year began, 86 percent of African American pupils in the South still attended all-black schools, a mere 2 percent decrease from the previous year. Largely because of the guidelines, 650 school districts had converted from dual to unitary nonracial systems between September 1965 and September 1968. Most importantly, Lyndon Johnson had finally entered the fray. In his January 1968 civil rights message, Johnson noted that "the Secretary of HEW is now examining statistical reports from some 2,000 school districts throughout America to insure compliance with Title VI of the 1964 Civil Rights Act." The president added that "our national goals are clear—desegregated schools and quality education. They must not be compromised." A written presidential statement to Congress helped secure passage of the FY 1970 Labor-HEW appropriations without a House-passed amendment sponsored by Jamie Whitten of Mississippi, which would have prohibited the expenditure of HEW monies to "force attendance of a student at a particular school, or to force the busing of students, or the abolishment of any school."[15]

## De Facto Desegregation

"Desegregation means the assignment of students to public schools and within such schools without regard to their race, color, religion, or national origin," states the Civil Rights Act of 1964, "but 'desegregation' shall not mean the assignment of students to public schools in order to overcome racial imbalance." So after much internal debate, the administration opted not to include de facto segregation as a target of the Title VI guidelines. Despite this omission, Vice President Hubert Humphrey told Johnson in September 1965 that Northern school segregation "promises to be more emotion-laden as time passes." Humphrey warned that "the Federal government as a whole has not charted any clear course in this area." He was right on both counts.[16]

Amidst such uncertainty, Keppel in October 1965 investigated complaints that Chicago school superintendent Benjamin Willis was practicing racial discrimination in the distribution of Title I monies. "I want this slowed up," Keppel wrote to Willis. "I don't want any money handed out from the state until I'm satisfied." Keppel's firm stance provoked civil rights leader Martin Luther King Jr. to telegraph the president with a message of support. When Willis called a press conference to attack Keppel, however, Cater telephoned Johnson to assure him that Chicago's Democratic mayor Richard Daley "bears no responsibility for any discrimination that may exist" and that "HEW believes that the Chicago problem can be worked out quickly." But Daley could not wait. He demanded a meeting with Johnson in New York City, where the president was about to meet with Pope Paul VI at the United Nations. Johnson would later recall, "Do you know he kept me waiting ten minutes for the Pope?"[17]

"Fix it!" the president bellowed to acting HEW secretary Wilbur Cohen upon Johnson's return to Washington. And so Cohen did. After a day of negotiations with the secretary, the Chicago School Board promised to solve the funding inequities, Cohen restored the Title I monies, and the White House did not acknowledge King's telegram. But when Attorney General Nicholas Katzenbach found that Chicago's compliance plan, submitted two months later, "contains no meaningful program proposals," Keppel claimed that partisan politics had motivated the settlement and cost him his job. As "the chief SOB with the Northern Democrats in one city," Keppel would remember, "I was hopeless." But Keppel's assistant commissioner for equal opportunity David Seeley blamed "procedural and substantive weakness" for the faulty deal. "Undersecretary Cohen got about the same kind of promises of action from the city of Chicago," Seeley would recall, "that the Office of Education had accepted from a large portion of the Southern school districts as a basis for lifting the deferral of funds." Indeed, a year later Chicago submitted a second plan, which set racial quotas in school enrollments, mandated busing of black children to white schools, and established exchanges of black and white teachers.[18]

The political and procedural fallout from the Chicago case provoked reassessments within the White House. The lesson learned by Cater was that "political dynamite lies on both sides of the path" of de facto school segregation—from civil rights advocates on the one hand, and from local and state officials on the other. He therefore recommended the transfer of responsibility for enforcement of school desegregation from the OE and the Justice Department to "an independent quasi-judicial tribunal . . . apart from the Executive Departments" that could "withstand the political assaults from both sides." The lesson Johnson learned was that the nation had not learned enough: "Although we have made substantial progress in ending formal segregation of schools, racial isolation in the schools persists," wrote the president. "The problems are more subtle and complex than those presented by segregation imposed by law." Johnson therefore asked the U.S. Civil Rights Commission to study de facto school segregation. "The remedies may be difficult," Johnson conceded, "but as a first and vital step, the Nation needs to know the facts."[19]

As the administration awaited the report, its internal effort against de facto segregation remained virtually nonexistent. Howe complained in June 1966 that "quicksands of legal interpretation" were thwarting such endeavors. Gardner lamented in August that "HEW's efforts to do something about Northern urban segregation ... have scored zero ... [and] this reflects a failure of HEW staff to tackle the problem vigorously." The administration adopted no position on a bill, sponsored by Massachusetts Democratic senator Edward Kennedy, which would have provided special federal aid to help school districts confront de facto segregation, or one sponsored by New York Democratic representative Adam Clayton Powell, which would have withheld federal aid from school districts that practiced de facto segregation.[20]

When accused of actually doing something to confront de facto segregation, Howe was quick to deny it. In August 1966 Democratic representative William Cramer of Florida alleged that the OE was granting more than $730,000 "to implement experiments attacking *de facto* segregation or racial imbalance." In September, Republican representative William Brock of Tennessee charged that the administration was drafting a "multi-billion-dollar national school busing scheme." Howe rejected Cramer's claim and attributed Brock's allegation to a "draft document that we had around the office [that] was an effort to explore the possibility of making federal funds available to local school districts that wanted help in dealing with problems of school desegregation." The document, called the "Equal Opportunity Act of 1967," proposed such integrationist schemes as "magnet schools, clustering and pairing, busing, and mergers of urban and suburban school districts."[21]

Not only was his office not advocating racial balance and integration of Northern schools, the commissioner protested, it could not even define the terms. Howe's November 1966 interview with *American Education* included the following exchange:

Q. What is racial balance?
A. I don't know. I really don't know.
Q. Doesn't it seem that with all this talk about racial balance somebody ought to define it?
A. Don't blame me. I didn't originate the phrase.
Q. Another word that's being used a lot today is "integration." What is integration in a school?
A. I don't know in any quantitative sense. This is like the racial balance question.[22]

Uncertain of the goals of an assault on de facto segregation, the administration continued to resist employing methods to achieve them. When asked "Are we moving toward a time when youngsters are going to be transported from city to suburb and from suburb to city in order to achieve racial balance in schools?" Howe responded in November 1966 that "we are not moving when the federal government is going to get involved in pushing cities and suburbs to do this or requiring them to do it." The administration's "best possible defense," advocated in September by HEW deputy secretary Samuel Halperin against an antibusing addition to the ESEA extension, never arrived, and Johnson signed the law with the amendment in November. In February 1967 Libassi wrote that the Title VI guidelines did not apply to "the transfer of children in school systems *not* officially segregated." So when the February 1967 U.S. Civil Rights Commission report requested by the president defined "racial balance" as "fifty-percent minority" and integration as an avenue toward superior education for African American children, the president changed the subject. His civil rights message that month called not for mixing schools but for mixing neighborhoods through open housing legislation.[23]

Despite Howe's contention that "this whole business of excitement about transporting children [on buses] has gotten exaggerated" and Gardner's conviction that Title VI should apply to the North as well as the South, political realities continued to prevent a major federal campaign against de facto school segregation. "If 'guidelines' are a red flag to Southern legislators," wrote *U.S. News and World Report*, "busing is a fighting word to some Northerners." The *New York Times* and the *Washington Post* editorialized that the U.S. Civil Rights Commission's call for a "massive federal effort" in this area was politically unrealistic. In April 1967 the Education Task Force, for political reasons, warned against any "stress on minorities as a primary target" of the administration's education policies and "discussion of racial balance in precise terms." In the same month, citing the Fountain and Green amendments, Libassi lamented the "serious moves within Congress to cripple the school desegregation efforts of HEW both in the North and the South." The Justice Department would wait until after Johnson's March 31, 1968, decision not to seek reelection before initiating its first four de facto segregation suits.[24]

"It is time to stop repeating 'end *de facto* segregation!' as though this virtuous incantation were a magical spell," wrote Joseph Alsop in *The New Republic*. With black majorities in the public schools of Baltimore, Chicago, Cleveland, Detroit, Philadelphia, and St. Louis, and a 93 percent black student population in Washington, D.C., Alsop declared that "it is time to start dealing with the hard, cruel facts of the problem of the ghetto schools."[25]

A federal court seemed to agree. In June 1967, Judge J. Skelly Wright of the U.S. Court of Appeals ordered the implementation of busing, the abolition of "freedom of choice," and the end of academic tracking. While stopping short of outlawing de facto school segregation, the decision found it "of very shaky status, morally, socially, and constitutionally." Gardner warned Johnson that the order, "while not undoing previous court rulings, will stimulate litigation and local action."[26]

Yet another case for modification of the administration posture arose from the nation's cities. From 1964 to 1968, according to federal statistics, there were 225 "hostile outbursts" in predominantly black urban neighborhoods, killing

191, wounding 7,942, and resulting in 49,607 arrests. The President's Commission on Civil Disorders, chaired by Illinois Democratic governor Otto Kerner, largely blamed the rioting on the widening gulf between "two societies, one black, one white—separate and unequal." Prominent among its recommendations was a plea for enforcement of the Civil Rights Act of 1964 in the North as well as the South. "We support integration as the priority education strategy," the commissioners wrote. "It is essential to the future of American society."[27]

But obstacles to meaningful change hardened on Capitol Hill, where Republicans gained forty-seven House and three Senate seats in the 1966 midterm elections, and congressmen from Northern cities joined senators from Southern states in an unusual Democratic alliance against busing and in favor of uniform (read: lax) enforcement of the Civil Rights Act in all parts of the country. After reading the congressional mood, Libassi wrote in April 1967 that "We consider the prospect for avoiding a major civil rights setback most discouraging."[28]

Significant resistance to a more aggressive school desegregation policy came from Johnson himself. In only three years the president went from chief legislator to lame duck, and from a leader to a victim of public opinion. The number of Americans who viewed civil rights as the nation's most important issue slipped from 52 percent in March 1965 to 9 percent in May 1966. Only 47 percent approved Johnson's job performance in June 1966. On the eve of the November 1966 congressional elections, Johnson pronounced the Great Society "just about all wrapped up."[29]

Before the February 1967 announcement of its *Racial Isolation in the Schools* report, McPherson urged Johnson to meet with the U.S. Civil Rights Commission. "Among other things, [Chairman John] Hannah is President of Michigan State, and a close friend of [Michigan Republican governor and potential presidential candidate George] Romney," wrote McPherson. "I don't believe that he should be in a position to say that the Commission has never met with the President." When the Kerner Commission report in March 1968 failed to acknowledge his administration's civil rights successes, Johnson waited three weeks before tepidly endorsing it. Moynihan lamented in 1968 that Johnson's domestic agenda, including civil rights, was going the way of Kennedy's Alliance for Progress, "a vast and noble commitment pretty much in mothballs. He had a lot of other things like Vietnam . . . that obviously were eating on him more [from 1966 to 1968] than they had been in '64 or '65." Johnson himself omits mention of school desegregation in his memoir.[30]

## The Johnson Record

For Lyndon Johnson, school desegregation was less moral imperative than legal mandate and political challenge. The Supreme Court's June 1968 *Green v. County School Board of New Kent County* decision, declaring the inadequacy of voluntary "freedom of choice" plans in creating "nonracial" public school systems, signaled that the president would continue, however tentatively, to fight de jure school segregation. At a May 1967 meeting with his Education Task Force, Chairman William Friday would recall, "We talked about the report of the Task Force maybe for minutes and then he spent the next forty-five minutes talking about Vietnam." But unless and until the high court ruled on de facto segregation, Johnson refused to expend the enormous political capital required to wage war against it. Johnson "had no intention of pressing the issue [of school desegregation] beyond the bounds of political reason in the North," writes Robert Dallek, "where he feared provoking more of a backlash than was already evident." The last thing this president, already battling poverty and Vietnamese communists, wanted was another war—and another losing one.[31]

Most Americans wanted integration, but on their own terms—in their neighborhoods, without forced busing, and with "all deliberate speed." The assassinations of prominent integrationists Martin Luther Luther King Jr. in April 1968 and Robert Kennedy in June heightened similar sentiments within the black community. The Kerner Commission's prophecy of two Americas seemed to be coming true.

Historians have either extolled or assailed Johnson for elevating the expectations of the nation's politically and economically disenfranchised. The Civil Rights Act of 1964 certainly lifted the hopes of many Americans of all races. But like so much of the Great Society, this law in many ways was a triumph of Johnson's vigilance rather than his vision. So the image that the act invokes is not of a young Lyndon Johnson teaching Mexican American schoolchildren in Texas but of a vindictive Bull Conner unleashing dogs and fire hoses on black demonstrators in Alabama. The words that the act calls to mind are not those of Lyndon Johnson while signing the act at the White House in July 1964 but of Martin Luther King addressing the masses on the Washington Mall in August 1963. Indeed, the president most associated with the act is not even Lyndon Johnson— it is, by Johnson's own admission, his martyred predecessor, John Kennedy.[32]

If the Civil Rights Act of 1964 was not truly his own at the time of its passage, then one can understand why Johnson was reluctant to embrace the far more difficult task of its implementation. So the president who did little personally and publicly to fuel the expectations that accompanied his signature on the legislation did even less to sustain those hopes throughout his presidency. And judging by public opinion polls, election returns, and congressional roll calls, most Americans' expectations for enforcement of Title VI of the Civil Rights Act, formally in the South and informally in the North, were never all that high anyway.

## Richard Nixon

In many ways Richard Nixon chose a terrible time to be president. He followed an administration that comprehensively safeguarded civil rights and financed education. Through the Civil Rights Act of 1964, the Voting Rights Act of 1965, the ESEA of 1965, the Higher Education Act of 1965, and the Fair Housing Act of 1968, the country's leaders finally responded to the public's demand for equality of opportunity in school and society. Yet by 1968 the leaders were not meeting the extraordinary expectations raised by such legislation, and they were losing the public's trust. Nixon's challenge was therefore to realistically adjust his expectations without dangerously abdicating his leadership. If he succeeded, he could help accelerate the considerable progress that the country was making in race relations and educational achievement. If he failed, he might help alienate a generation of Americans from their leaders.

Some scholars claim that Nixon succeeded by leading a principled assault on de jure school desegregation. Others claim that he failed by orchestrating a politically expedient surrender to de facto school segregation. A close examination of the evidence, however, reveals that in the area of school desegregation, Nixon's record was a mixture of principle and politics, progress and paralysis, success and failure. In the end, he was neither simply the cowardly architect of a racially insensitive "Southern strategy" that condoned segregation nor the courageous conductor of a politically risky "not-so-Southern strategy" that condemned it. Because of his ambivalent past and his country's ambivalent present on civil rights, President Richard Nixon was both.

## The "Southern Strategy"

Writing in National Review in 1964, William Rusher argued that the "Republican Party is poised to shatter the Democrats' century-old grip on the 'Solid South.'" Of the six states that Republican Barry Goldwater carried in his landslide defeat by Lyndon Johnson that year, five were in the Deep South. Four years later, Nixon campaign strategist Kevin Phillips expanded upon the Rusher thesis. "[Southern] white Democrats will desert their party in droves," said Phillips, "the minute it becomes a black party." After Nixon divided the Southern electoral vote with independent George Wallace in 1968, Phillips predicted, "We'll get two-thirds to three-fourths of the Wallace vote in nineteen seventy-two." Nixon then swept the South in his landslide victory (largely because of the outbreak of peace in Vietnam) over George McGovern in 1972. There was no denying Nixon's "Southern Strategy" in 1968 and 1972—Phillips openly admitted it. "The Right just will not learn to keep its mouth shut," wrote Garry Wills in 1970, "to work on a strategy without confessing it."[33]

Nixon's public and private statements often reflected this strategy. In the 1968 campaign, candidate Nixon strongly opposed forced school busing to achieve racial balance. "I feel home environment has more to do with success in life than any amount of integrated education," Nixon would later explain. President Nixon occasionally uttered racial slurs, such as when he urged National Security Advisor Henry Kissinger to include "something . . . for the jigs" in the president's first major foreign policy address in February 1970. In 1976 former president Nixon counseled the Gerald Ford campaign, "The Negro vote's lost; don't let it lose you white votes."[34]

Nixon not only preached the Southern strategy, he practiced it. On January 19, 1969, HEW secretary Robert Finch announced that while the new administration would honor its predecessor's deadline for the defunding of five segregated Southern school districts, the districts could reclaim the funds if they desegregated within sixty days of the deadline. Finch's nod toward the South gained more skeptics than followers in the region, however. At a meeting with Nixon administration representatives, Republican Party Southern state chairmen suggested that Nixon "take a hard look at existing [school desegregation] guidelines; advise Republican leadership if funds are to be cut off in a district; [and] have HEW review the overall situation before any further action is taken." When told that the president would not carry any Southern state in the electoral college if he continued the Johnson policies, Nixon aide Bryce Harlow reassured them, "We were desperately sandbagged by the previous Administration. Finch is trying—which is more than the previous Administration did. . . . There will not be continuation of the policies of the Johnson Administration."[35]

Harlow's words were prophetic. In a March 14 meeting with Finch and Attorney General John Mitchell, Nixon noted that most of the letters received by his administration were "very critical" of the Johnson guidelines. A month later, two of Nixon's staunchest supporters, Republican senators John Tower of Texas and Howard Baker of Tennessee, told the president that the defunding of segregated Southern school districts had created a rift between the federal government and Southern schools. "Both Senators are up for re-election in 1972," Harlow had reminded Nixon before the meeting. "Both therefore actively share your interest in a strategy that will carry Southern states."[36]

In July this strategy helped produce a measured federal retreat on school desegregation. Mitchell and Finch called for "full compliance" with the Johnson administration's autumn 1969 deadline for full desegregation throughout the South, except in black-majority districts (given until 1970) or areas with inadequate facilities. They added, however, that "in some districts there may be sound reasons for some limited delay. . . . Examples of such problems would be serious shortages of necessary physical facilities, financial resources, or faculty." The Department of Justice would join HEW in enforcing this desegregation. Liberal Republican senator Jacob Javits of New York called the new policy "disastrous." Roy Wilkins, executive director of the NAACP, accused the administration of "breaking the law." Nixon's own appointees on the U.S. Commission on Civil Rights assailed this deferral of justice.[37]

The administration nevertheless moved to implement its new procedure. When the Fifth Circuit Court of Appeals granted a four-month delay to thirty-three Mississippi school districts facing an August 11 desegregation deadline,

White House aide Harry Dent noticed that for the first time, "the Department of Justice was seated at the table with the South rather than with the NAACP." Two months later, when the Supreme Court unanimously overturned the Fifth Circuit decision and ordered the immediate desegregation of the Mississippi schools, Dent consoled Nixon: "The reaction we are getting today regarding the Supreme Court decision yesterday is that this is working in our favor at the moment. . . . The Supreme Court is being blamed." Finch followed a similar line in preparing a response to Alabama Democratic governor George Wallace's January 19, 1970, appearance on CBS-TV's *Face the Nation*. To Wallace's contention that "we had freedom of choice up until Mr. Mitchell went into the Fifth Circuit Court of Appeals," Finch replied, "it was not Mr. Mitchell but the Supreme Court that . . . held freedom of choice plans unacceptable if they prove effective. Mr. Mitchell was merely enforcing that decision."[38]

Despite this judicial setback, Nixon pressed forward with his "Southern strategy." Two weeks before Georgia Democratic senator Richard Russell warned Nixon of "HEW people going around stirring up trouble," Nixon fired HEW assistant secretary Leon Panetta for his overly aggressive pursuit of school desegregation. On February 11 Nixon publicly reiterated his opposition to "compulsory busing of school children to achieve racial balance," cited the importance of "neighborhood schools" and "quality education," and offered his support for the concept, if not the substance, of Mississippi Democratic senator John Stennis's disingenuous amendment calling for "uniform application" of desegregation enforcement throughout the country. On February 16 Nixon bowed to segregationist South Carolina Republican senator Strom Thurmond in forming a Cabinet Committee on Education. The committee, nominally headed by Vice President Spiro Agnew, aimed to ease the burden of Southern desegregation through reassuring words and targeted monies.[39]

Nixon's major address on school desegregation on March 24 in many ways embodied the "Southern strategy." "Where school boards have demonstrated a good-faith effort to comply with court rulings," the president observed, "the courts have generally allowed substantial latitude as to method." He added, "When there is racial separation in housing, the constitutional requirement has been held satisfied even though some schools remained all black." He concluded that "transportation of pupils beyond normal geographic school zones for the purpose of achieving racial balance will not be required." Panetta and his former assistant, Paul Rilling, denounced the speech's "perpetuation" of segregation and "slick rationalization for retreat." "Anonymous government civil rights lawyers" concurred with this criticism in press reports, prompting Nixon to demand their names and resignations.[40]

In June HEW secretary Finch, whom Thurmond had earlier implored to "keep his mouth shut," became Special Counselor Finch. "Finch [is] a poet," domestic affairs advisor John Ehrlichman would write, citing the need for "prose guys" to "get things done." In August, Nixon's prose assured a New Orleans audience that Southerners were not "second-class citizens" and condemned "those from the North that point the finger at the South."[41]

In September, Southern concerns came north as Nixon and Mitchell conferred with Congressman Charles Jonas, armed with the antibusing petition of the Concerned Parents Association of Charlotte. Mitchell explained that in a case pending before the Supreme Court, the Nixon administration supported Charlotte "in principle, in that we are taking the position that the Fourteenth Amendment does not require racial integration as a matter of law." But seven months later, Charlotte and the administration lost. In a unanimous ruling in *Swann v. Charlotte-Mecklenburg School District,* the Supreme Court ordered the busing of students between white suburban and black inner-city schools to reverse the effects of pre-1954 de jure segregation within the district. (The average one-way trip lasted an hour and fifteen minutes and exceeded fifteen miles.) Asserting that the "busing problem has now turned against us and can do us considerable harm," Nixon explored ways to "get clearly on the record again by being against busing in spite of the court decision."[42]

But the judiciary was not finished. In January 1972 in Richmond, Virginia, and in June in Detroit, federal judges ordered the busing of schoolchildren across school district lines to overcome residential segregation patterns. Asserting that "I totally disagree with those decisions," Nixon insisted, "I am for action now; I prefer the legislative route to do it; but if we can't that way, I will go for a constitutional amendment [to outlaw busing]." The president then signed education legislation amended by Michigan Republican representative William Broomfield to prohibit future court-ordered busing until all appeals, or the time for all appeals, had elapsed and amended by Ohio Republican representative (and presidential candidate) John Ashbrook to outlaw federal spending for busing. Anticipating a legal challenge to the sweeping language of the former provision, Nixon decried the "manifest Congressional retreat from an urgent call for responsibility" and promised more specific antibusing legislation.[43]

Congress "retreated" further in October, when a Senate filibuster led by Democrats Edmund Muskie of Maine and Philip Hart of Michigan sank an administration bill that would have compelled the courts to implement specific desegregation plans, limit busing to the next closest school to a pupil's neighborhood, and reopen court orders that exceeded these restrictions. In March 1974 the House of Representatives, by a vote of 293–117, passed an antibusing addition to HR 69, the ESEA Amendments of 1974. The rider, sponsored by Michigan Republican Marvin Esch, "prohibited federal courts or agencies from ordering busing of students to any but the school closest or next closest to the student's home" and "provided that any school district under a federal court order or desegregation plan in effect on the date of HR 69 could ask that the case be reopened and made to comply with the provisions of Title II." The Senate passed HR 69 but rejected the Esch amendment, 46–47. The conference report on the bill adopted the Senate amendment prohibiting busing "beyond the school next closest" to a student's home "but allowing courts to mandate additional busing" if it were required to guarantee the student's civil rights. The conferees also replaced the House reopener provision with language permitting "parents or the school district to reopen a case only if the time or distance traveled was so great as to endanger the health of the student or impinge on the educational process." Whereas the House bill had *required* the termination of a busing order if a federal court determined that desegregation had been achieved, the conference report merely *permitted* such a termination.[44]

Before the HR 69 conference report could come to a vote, Nixon signed a bill prohibiting Federal Legal Service offices from using public or private funds to litigate school desegregation cases. Then, on July 25, 1974, the Supreme Court, in overturning the Detroit busing plan, "refused to recognize a power in the federal courts to order the amalgamation of urban and suburban school districts to obtain a desirable racial mixture in the schools, where *de jure* segregation existed only in the urban district." Encouraged by this rare judicial victory in *Milliken v. Bradley,* the House adopted the HR 69 conference report, 323–83, with Esch among the fifty-eight antibusing representatives who rejected the bill's moderate language. After the Senate adopted the conference report, 81–15, it reached President Nixon's desk on August 7. While "the bill's busing provisions fall short of your desire to retain the House provisions," HEW secretary Caspar Weinberger wrote to Nixon, the measure does "strengthen the existing law against busing and certains many of the provisions you originally sought." Noting the "obdurate attitude of the Senate and the size of the House vote accepting this compromise," Weinberger recommended that Nixon sign the legislation. But when Nixon resigned (due to the Watergate scandal) on August 9, the busing controversy fell to President Gerald Ford.[45]

## The Not-So-Southern Strategy

While many contemporary critics would have ended the story of Nixon and school desegregation here, the "Southern strategy" cannot fully explain the politics of busing. The president and the issue were far more complicated than that.

Richard Nixon traced his respect for civil rights to his Whittier College football coach Wallace "Chief" Newman, an American Indian. "It did not occur to me at the time," Nixon would recall, "but Chief taught us a lot about civil rights forty years before that movement became popular on college campuses." When Nixon attended Duke University Law School in the Jim Crow South, "I saw for the first time two nations, black and white, in twentieth-century America." When he ran for vice president in 1952, Nixon committed himself to one nation: he was against the poll tax, against segregation in the District of Columbia, and in favor of antilynching legislation. As vice president he endorsed the *Brown v.*

*Board of Education* decision of 1954, lobbied hard for the Civil Rights Acts of 1957 and 1960, and spearheaded the Eisenhower administration's effort to eliminate discrimination in the issuance of government contracts. He defended Eisenhower's dispatch of federal troops to enforce the desegregation of Central High School in Little Rock, Arkansas, in 1957 as the "moral" thing to do. Nixon refused to sign a restrictive covenant on his home, and the Quaker vice president sent his two daughters to the desegregated Sidwell Friends School.[46]

Martin Luther King Jr. saluted Vice President Nixon's "assiduous labor and dauntless courage" as a civil rights advocate. Martin Luther King Sr. endorsed Nixon for president in 1960 after the candidate, in Jonathan Aitken's words, "held out for the most liberal platform on civil rights ever to be accepted by the Republican Party." Four years after receiving one-third of blacks' votes in his narrow loss to John Kennedy, Nixon urged Southern Republicans not to "climb aboard the sinking ship of racial injustice." In 1968 Nixon chose Maryland governor Spiro Agnew as his running mate, in part because he "had very good credentials as a moderate Republican [who] had defeated a racist Democrat." As a presidential aspirant in 1968, Nixon championed "black capitalism," and as president he overcame the opposition of organized labor and a Senate majority to introduce the Philadelphia Plan, an affirmative action system for training and hiring black construction workers. Nixon's urban affairs advisor Daniel Patrick Moynihan recalled that "there weren't any more race riots under Nixon because of the hope generated in the black community by his welfare reform, revenue sharing, and job training proposals." White House aide Robert Brown, an African American, remembered Nixon's record number of black appointees and "eightfold increase in the budget for civil rights enforcement." Kenneth Cole, assistant to Ehrlichman and liaison to Nixon's Domestic Council, observed that liberal ideas often attracted Nixon. Martin Anderson, deputy to White House counsel Arthur Burns, added that Nixon's ideology was highly vulnerable to political influences from the Left as well as the Right. Finch recalled that the "Southern strategy" did not necessarily foreclose attracting liberals and minorities to the Republican Party.[47]

At a time when "liberal Republican" was not an oxymoron, there indeed was much in the Nixon policies that the Left could embrace. Nixon's Task Force on Education, which issued its report on January 3, 1969, correctly predicted that the new administration would face "continuous pressure" to "adopt a lower standard of policy generally with regard to desegregation than that enunciated by the Supreme Court." But it urged the Nixon White House to "do all in its power to assure that the Constitutional rights of children as defined by the courts are fully protected." The task force concluded that the administration should augment the "woefully inadequate" funding required for enforcing school desegregation. The administration would largely accept the task force's counsel. A July 1969 sit-in at Mitchell's office by thirty African Americans from four Southern states ended when Mitchell encouraged them to "watch what we do instead of listening to what we say" on school desegregation. At the same time, warnings to Nixon from Republican governor Winthrop Rockefeller of Arkansas and Republican senators Hugh Scott of Pennsylvania and Marlow Cook of Kentucky helped lead to the July 3 Mitchell-Finch statement expressing general adherence to the Johnson administration guidelines.[48]

Nixon's "not-so-Southern strategy" also emboldened Finch to argue to Nixon privately in September that the administration was actually "for busing" in many instances, then to oppose publicly in October a House-passed antibusing amendment sponsored by Democrat Jamie Whitten of Mississippi. Finch contended that the measure, which would have prohibited HEW from spending federal money to force busing, was unconstitutional because "where racial isolation or segregation exists as a result of discrimination, the courts have required affirmative action based on constitutional principles to correct the situation." Finch's explanation hardly satisfied Thurmond, who admonished the secretary that "Things like this do not go well in the South."[49]

Confusing? Well, yes—deliberately so. At a meeting on January 8, 1970, Nixon told Finch that the administration strategy on school desegregation was to "keep it confused." Nixon's straddle of the Stennis amendment prompted the following exchange between the president and the attorney general at a February 18 Cabinet meeting:

> Nixon: Mr. Attorney General, are you here?
> Mitchell: I think so.
> Nixon: I thought you were out with Finch working on the Stennis
> Amendment. Which side are you on?
> Mitchell: In the right place: right in the middle.[50]

"The middle" meant lukewarm rejection of the Stennis amendment coupled with lukewarm acceptance of a substitute sponsored by Hugh Scott. In a letter to Scott, the administration wrote: "It is unfortunate that confusion has arisen over the Administration position in this matter. . . . Several days ago, the President indicated support of the concept of Senator Stennis' amendment to the extent that it could encourage equal application of the law throughout the country. The Administration has proposed, alternatively, the revised language which you have submitted for the reason that it would not prejudge *de facto* segregation [as the Stennis amendment would] but would validate it in the south as elsewhere as long as the courts have not held such segregation unconstitutional."[51]

The administration's ambivalence, while encouraging the defection of enough Republicans to pass the Stennis amendment in the Senate in February, ensured that it would go no further. The "confusion" that the White House had disingenuously lamented to Scott was in fact quite intentional. "It's true that our current posture has an overlay of fuzz," Nixon aide Bryce Harlow wrote to the president on February 23. "The Administration posture is a calculated waffle."[52]

But this ambiguity risked fatally alienating the South, warned White House aide Patrick Buchanan. "My great concern," wrote Buchanan, "is that the people of the South will start to say that President Nixon is a fair weather friend; he clearly agrees with us, and yet he will do nothing to help us." Buchanan implored Nixon to emphatically and publicly state the "current case against continuing compulsory integration anywhere." Yet HEW assistant secretary James Farmer, an African American, conveyed to the president "the prevalent feeling among Negroes that [the] Administration is embarked upon a Southern Strategy designed to slow down school desegregation to the detriment of Negro children." He urged Nixon to "make a public statement putting [the] Administration unequivocally on record in support of court-ordered desegregation."[53]

For all the attention paid to Nixon's acceptance of Southern "good faith" and aversion to "unreasonable" busing, his March 24 school desegregation address sounded closer to Farmer than to Buchanan. "Some have interpreted various administration statements and actions as a backing away from the principle of *Brown*," said the president. "We are not backing away. The constitutional mandate will be enforced." Nixon continued, "Deliberate racial segregation of pupils by official action is unlawful wherever it exists. In the words of the Supreme Court, it must be eliminated 'root and branch'—and it must be eliminated at once."[54]

African American Republican senator Edward Brooke of Massachusetts praised the speech's "unequivocal commitment" to school desegregation and Nixon's allocation of $1.5 billion to help enforce it. Yale law professor Alexander Bickel wrote approvingly in *The New Republic* that "the President's statement on school desegregation cannot have gladdened Senators Stennis and Thurmond." Johns Hopkins University professor James Coleman, a leading authority on school desegregation with whom Nixon consulted before the speech, applauded the enforcement monies as "an incentive to desegregate rather than an incentive not to."[55]

While Nixon was announcing his policy on school desegregation, his aides were formulating his policy on school resegregation. In the fall of 1969, Internal Revenue Service (IRS) commissioner Randolph Thrower had quietly begun to avoid ruling on applications by private schools for tax-exempt status. By 1970, several Southern private schools had filed suit against the IRS, demanding tax exemption. Nixon's assistant Peter Flanigan then organized a working group that included Thrower, Dent, and Finch, among others. The group presented the president with three options: (1) privately grant tax exemption to Southern private schools that discriminated on the basis of race, evade press questions on the subject, and await a Supreme Court decision on the matter; (2) publicly grant tax exemptions to schools that clearly did not discriminate, tax schools that clearly discriminated, and leave unclear cases to the courts; and (3) publicly grant tax exemption to schools that professed and adopted nondiscriminatory policies, tax schools that did not, and dispatch federal officials to enforce the policy.[56]

The "Southern strategy" argued for option 1 or 2, as did Buchanan. "What possible good can come out of denying the tax exemption? . . . There is no reason for the President to take this action—it would be a political error for which we would reap absolutely nothing in return." The "not-so-Southern strategy" chose option 3, as did Harlow. "I recognize the temporary political expediency to be served by Option 2. But I think this is an ephemeral advantage. It will not persuade the South, who will know better, and it surely will further abrade the President's relations with the blacks and whites who fondly regard civil rights. . . . The failure to stand up to this issue will be a total loss on all sides."[57]

Nixon's selection of option 3 on July 10 reversed his previous private opinion, conflicted with his Justice Department's position in federal court two months earlier, moved him to the left of his predecessor, and enraged his erstwhile Southern allies. Calling the decision "arbitrary, vindictive, and anti-South," Thurmond predicted Nixon's electoral defeat in 1972 unless he abruptly reversed course (he would not).[58]

On January 14, 1971, Finch's successor as HEW secretary, the equally liberal Elliot Richardson, declared victory for the Nixon administration's school desegregation efforts. Eighty percent of black children in eleven Southern states attended public schools with whites. More black children attended predominantly white public schools in the South than in any other region of the country.[59]

## The Nixon Record

Amid all the political machinations, one can find a coherence to Nixon's school desegregation policies: in favor of desegregation (*Brown*) but against busing (*Swann*). Yet most of the time, the latter position muffled the former—just as the president intended. An August 4, 1970, memorandum from aide H. R. Haldeman to Nixon revealed this imbalance. On desegregation: "You wanted to emphasize [that] . . . all people concerned are to do only what the law requires, and they are to do it quietly without bragging about it." On busing: "Hit hard on the Administration position against busing at every opportunity." Ehrlichman would remember that "His [Nixon's] political compass told him to stay away from the whole subject of race. And if he could not stay out of it, the best political position was on the side of the white parents whose children were about to get on those hated buses." So despite all his heartfelt resentment of the "hypocrisy" of Northern liberals in condemning racial segregation in the South but tolerating it in their backyard, Nixon firmly safeguarded de facto segregation. When Senator Abraham Ribicoff, a liberal Connecticut Democrat, called Stennis's bluff and supported his "uniform application" amendment, Nixon warned his cabinet that "He [Ribicoff] is trying to force this Administration to visit the troubles of the South on the North. . . . The cynical Northern liberals who don't have any problem with the civil rights issue in the coming elections will try to needle this Administration to enflame the situation."[60]

Nixon's efforts to delay implementation of the *Brown* decision were unprincipled, but they were also unpopular in most of the nation. Seventy-four percent of Americans favored school integration in 1970. Nixon's attempts to undermine implementation of the *Swann* decision were popular among the public (only 2 percent of Americans favored forced busing to achieve racial balance in 1969), but they were also principled (Nixon had *always* opposed forced busing to achieve racial balance) and unpopular in Congress. "Never in fifteen years of testifying up on the Hill," said Richardson, had he encountered the degree of resistance that Nixon's antibusing legislation engendered. Nixon's instincts on tax-exempt Southern "academies" were political, but his actions were based on politics *and* principle. In choosing option 3, Nixon not only accepted Harlow's counsel that the "straddle" offered by option 2 would be politically expedient in the short term, but he also agreed that in the long run, "it is certain to play pluperfect hell throughout the South," while following "no principle at all."[61]

To condemn the Richard Nixon who vigorously opposed de jure school segregation in the 1950s for timidly perpetuating de facto school segregation in the 1970s is to overlook two important realities of those two decades: the country had changed, and Richard Nixon had changed. As blacks arrived in Northern cities and whites departed for Northern and Southern suburbs, New York went from 10 to 21 percent black, Chicago from 14 to 33 percent black, and Washington, D.C., from 35 to 71 percent black. In 1972 only 23 percent of African American schoolchildren attended school with whites. So when Vice President Agnew opined that "massive rioting" might result from a federal assault on such de facto segregation, Nixon concurred, citing the "many schools in which full-time policemen are stationed in the halls and classrooms."[62]

To his critics, "law and order," like "neighborhood schools" and "quality education," were racial code words. But to Richard Nixon and to most Americans of whatever color, they were legitimate priorities. And busing was not. "The ideal is a situation in which race is irrelevant to [school] assignment," wrote African American journalist William Raspberry. "Preoccupation with mathematical precision, unfortunately, is not the way to achieve that ideal." Even liberal Democratic presidential candidate Hubert Humphrey had come to that conclusion by 1972. So unless and until the courts forced him to act—in enforcing the *Brown* decision after October 1969 and in seeking a moratorium on busing after the *Swann* decision of March 1971—Nixon was largely content to uphold the status quo.[63]

"Most of the present population," Vice President Richard Nixon had predicted in 1956, "[will] live to see racial integration accomplished in the nation's public and private schools." Then Nixon witnessed the assassinations of John and Robert Kennedy, Malcolm X, and Martin Luther King; observed three waves of race riots in Northern cities; and read gloomy analyses by Johnson administration Assistant Secretary of Labor Moynihan of the deterioration of the black family, Coleman of the dubious value of school desegregation, the Kerner Commission of the country's widening racial gulf despite de jure desegregation, and Bickel of the limitations of federal desegregation efforts. His defense of civil rights hardly helped in his defeat by Kennedy in 1960, and his ambivalence toward civil rights did not hurt in his victory over Humphrey and Wallace in 1968. So by 1970, President Richard Nixon decided that "integration is not the wave of the future," after all.[64]

"There may be some doubt as to the validity of the *Brown* philosophy that integrating education will pull up the blacks and not pull down the whites," Nixon wrote in January 1972, ". . . but there is no doubt whatever . . . that education requiring excessive transportation for students is definitely inferior." Two decades in the life of the United States and the career of Richard Nixon had culminated in this marriage of principle and politics.[65]

## Gerald Ford

In 1957, as Little Rock, Arkansas, began its court-ordered school desegregation, a Boston clergyman telephoned a colleague, a Little Rock priest, to ensure that his church was doing its part. In 1974, as Boston commenced its court-ordered school desegregation, the Little Rock priest called his old friend in Boston, who refused to take the call.[66]

Like the Boston priest, Rep. Gerald Ford had supported the 1954 *Brown v. Board of Education* decision that led to the Little Rock desegregation, but he had opposed the 1971 *Swann v. Charlotte-Mecklenburg School District* verdict that cleared the way for the Boston desegregation. And when President Gerald Ford responded to violent resistance in Boston and elsewhere by speaking equivocally and acting reluctantly, advocates of busing to coerce desegregation accused him of refusing to answer the call of leadership that beckons a powerful individual to steer society on a proper, if unpopular, course.

As a politician, Ford knew that busing was not popular. As a conservative Republican, however, he believed that a substantial federal alternative to busing would not be proper. So he haltingly led the country on a search for a more palatable remedy for school segregation. In the years of his administration, however, neither he nor the country ever really found one.

### Speaking for "Quality Education"

Ford's record, like Nixon's, had been consistently in favor of the goal of school desegregation but opposed to forced busing as a means of achieving it. In 1956 Michigan representative Ford voted for an amendment to a school construction aid bill "prohibiting allotment of funds to states failing to comply" with the Brown decision. In 1970 Ford voted for a motion to retain provisions of an education appropriations bill "prohibiting use of funds to force busing or closing of schools, and providing for freedom of choice plans." A year later Ford agreed to an amendment to the Higher Education Act of 1971 that postponed "any federal court order requiring busing for racial, sexual, religious, or socioeconomic balance until all appeals . . . had been exhausted." In 1972 he opposed as unnecessary an amendment to an antibusing bill "providing that nothing in the act was intended to be inconsistent with or violate any provision of the Constitution."[67]

The new president received counsel similar to that of his predecessor: HR 69's busing provisions, if not ideal, were acceptable. "While falling short of the Administration's wishes," White House aide Roger Semerad wrote, "the bill includes several favorable new measures to limit forced busing and holding that remedy as a last resort." The Office of Management and Budget and HEW recommended that Ford sign the bill, while the Department of Justice offered no objection.[68]

Professing "special pleasure" in "the first major legislation to become law during my administration," Ford signed HR 69 on August 21. In his first pronouncement on the issue since becoming president, Ford asserted that "I am opposed to the forced busing of school children because it does not lead to better education and it infringes upon traditional freedoms in America." While lamenting that "H.R. 69 lacks an effective provision for automatically reevaluating existing court orders," the president nonetheless praised the bill's "ordered and reasoned approach to dealing with the remaining problems of segregation in our schools."[69]

The president's "special pleasure" would be short-lived. Despite their best efforts, the legislature and the executive branch could not prevent the judiciary from exacerbating the busing controversy. In October 1974, Judge Arthur Garrity of the First Circuit Court ordered Boston to develop a busing plan to "provide for the greatest possible degree of actual desegregation of all grades in all schools in all parts of the city."[70]

"I respectfully disagree with the judge's order," said Ford, "but having said that, I think it is of maximum importance that the citizens of Boston respect the law." Such ambivalence did much to create confusion and little to quell the violence that greeted Garrity's order. Two days after twenty-four whites and fourteen blacks were injured in a series of racial incidents, the president rejected Boston mayor Kevin White's plea for federal marshals, maintaining that "the marshals are under the jurisdiction of the court." As the violence escalated, Ford turned down Massachusetts governor Francis Sargent's appeal for federal troops, viewing such a deployment as a "last resort" that had not yet been reached. White, Sargent, and the state's Democratic senator Edward Kennedy decried the president's inaction, while Republican senator Edward Brooke, an African American, received from the chief executive a tape-recorded statement, for broadcast in the Boston area, that condemned the violence.[71]

In December, the U.S. Court of Appeals for the Sixth Circuit reaffirmed its decision that the Louisville (more than 50 percent black) and Jefferson County, Kentucky (more than 95 percent white) school districts merge to facilitate the busing of 30,568 students. The ruling was a response to the Supreme Court's request for a review of the Sixth Circuit decision in the wake of the *Milliken v. Bradley* verdict. Sporadic violence and peaceful demonstrations against the decision would mark the opening of school the following September and would cause Ford to cancel an October campaign visit.[72]

"Can you clarify your position on busing?" a reporter urged the president in Newport, Rhode Island, on August 30, 1975. After citing the hands-on involvement of the Justice Department and HEW in Boston to ensure that "any court order is enforced," Ford nonetheless added, "I just don't think court order, forced busing, is the way to achieve quality education."[73]

"I think there is a better way to do it," Ford continued, obliquely referring to the "five or six rules" of "a law that was passed . . . maybe two or three years ago." Barely a month into his second year as president, Ford had apparently already forgotten his first major Oval Office signing ceremony, at which he approved HR 69 and its diluted Esch amendment. The amendment nonetheless provided that federal courts and agencies exhaust the following remedies before resorting to forced busing:

1. Assign students closest to their homes, taking into account school capacities and natural physical barriers.
2. Assign students to schools closest to their homes, taking into account only school capacities.
3. Permit students to transfer from a school in which their race, color, or creed was a majority to one where it was a minority.
4. Create or revise attendance zones or grade structures without requiring busing beyond that described elsewhere in the bill.
5. Construct new schools or close inferior ones.
6. Construct or create magnet (high-quality) schools.
7. Implement any other plan that was educationally sound and administratively feasible.[74]

Ford's supporters, such as Representative Esch, applauded the president's suggestions of meaningful alternatives to busing. His critics, such as General Counsel Nathaniel Jones of the NAACP, contended that the president's remarks invited further violent resistance to federal court orders. A Justice Department study provided ammunition for both sides: the Esch amendment figured in only two of sixteen court-ordered busing plans since the passage of HR 69, but Boston and Louisville were those instances.[75]

Ford continued to say little about desegregation and much about the Esch amendment and the pursuit of "quality education." "We can increase pupil-teacher ratios; we can improve facilities, have more and better equipment, rely more heavily on the neighborhood school concept," the president told the National Federation of Republican Women on September 13. "There is a better way to achieve quality education in America than by forced busing."[76]

"We have got to get judges to use the alternatives listed in the Esch Amendment," Ford assured Kentucky governor Julian Carroll on October 7. "I don't agree that it [busing] is the way for quality education." On October 30 Ford told a group of reporters in Los Angeles that "I think we ought to spend whatever money is necessary for what we call magnet schools, to upgrade teachers, to provide better facilities, to give greater freedom of choice." He proudly reminded them, "I was one of the original members of the House or the Senate that said that court-ordered forced busing to achieve racial balance was not the way to accomplish quality education."[77]

## Speaking for "Quality Education and Desegregation"

Even as the president publicly defended the Esch amendment and insisted upon "quality education," key members of his administration began to privately question these emphases. At a September 17, 1975, cabinet meeting, Attorney General Edward Levi argued that the Esch alternatives to busing were unrealistic and expensive. Secretary of Transportation William Coleman, the only African American in the cabinet, assailed Ford's implication that busing had been less than a last resort: "History will show . . . that the Federal judges acted with great restraint, judgement, and wisdom in assisting the court-ordered busing."[78]

A month later, Richard Parsons of the president's Domestic Council addressed "the conceptual and political inadequacies" of Ford's positions:

> As a conceptual matter, if one opposes busing, for whatever reason, one must either indicate the alternative means by which the constitutional objective (indeed requirement) of desegregation of public school systems can be achieved or simultaneously indicate his opposition to the very objective which busing seeks to facilitate. The alternatives which we have focused on—i.e. improving teacher-pupil ratios, physical plants and curriculum—address the broader question of quality education, not the question of school desegregation. Having failed to indicate the alternative methods by which we believe school desegregation may be achieved, the question arises: Do we, in fact, oppose desegregation? Many in the civil rights community believe, on the merits, that busing is an important and useful tool. More importantly, there are many more who, while questioning the utility of busing, believe that it is incumbent upon the president to provide positive leadership in these difficult times. That is to say, since busing is the law of the land, like it or not, he ought to be actively encouraging people to comply with the law and not fueling frustrations with the law by criticizing it.[79]

Noting that "a review of the cases from *Swann* on up to Boston and Louisville clearly shows that the courts have always turned to busing as a last resort," Parsons concluded that "it is not enough [for the president] to point to the Esch Amendments of 1974." Instead, he urged that Ford consider a variety of alternatives to busing, including a presidential commission or conference on school desegregation, a constitutional amendment to establish guidelines by which courts may order busing, litigation by the Justice Department to test current judicial procedures, and "lowering our profile (and rhetoric) and simply roughing it out." The president then began to explore such alternatives, asking Attorney General Levi to consider litigation in the Louisville busing case and requesting that the Justice Department and HEW seek desegregation remedies other than busing.[80]

As the White House studied the busing issue, the Ninety-fourth Congress moved forward, introducing no fewer than six types of constitutional amendments to prohibit forced busing. Although Ford was publicly neutral on such proposals, he privately believed that such an amendment would unreasonably tamper with the Constitution, take too long to enact, and jeopardize alternate desegregation strategies.[81]

Four months of study by the Justice Department and HEW produced the following alternatives to busing for consideration by the president:

A. There should be greater involvement in supporting and drawing advice from the professional educators who have been most successful in implementing voluntary desegregation and improving the quality of education. . . .

B. Further, you could direct the Office of Education to utilize supplemental funds to conduct a series of seminars for public school administrators which would enable those administrators who have dealt successfully with desegregation to share their views with their colleagues. . . .

C. Existing Federal programs which seek to assist localities to preserve desirable racial/ethnic neighborhoods (e.g. HUD's Neighborhood Prevention Program) should be redirected to have an impact on neighborhoods where further "white flight" would greatly increase the likelihood that local schools would become racially identifiable. . . .

D. You could direct a tripartite study by the Office of Education, the National Institute of Education, and the Civil Rights Division of the Department of Justice to report to you on the accuracy of . . . studies [on busing].

E. You could direct the Department of Justice to propose legislation which would effectively accomplish what the Esch Amendments were meant to accomplish but failed to do.[82]

"Good beginning," Ford responded on February 17, 1976. "I suggest we pursue A, B, D, and E."[83]

Ford's public utterances reflected his administration's private analyses. On February 20, while continuing to attack those "judges [who] don't seem to understand that it is counterproductive to go as far as they have gone," Ford nonetheless applauded the "responsible, moderate" course of a federal judge in Detroit, who seeks to achieve "quality education *and desegregation*." The next day, while again invoking the Esch amendment, Ford nevertheless acknowledged that "local district courts [may order] a remedy, to *end segregation* on the one hand, and provide quality education in disadvantaged areas on the other."[84]

On April 27, Solicitor General Robert Bork informed the Supreme Court of the administration's intention to challenge future busing. He promised to continue his search for busing cases suitable for litigation and for busing alternatives suitable for legislation. After three meetings with Levi, Ford announced on May 29 that the attorney general had decided not to file a brief in the Boston school desegregation case. Levi concurred with the administration's critics in the civil rights community that to intervene in the Boston case would be to reward those who resisted court orders.[85]

## Acting to Remedy School Segregation

Although Ford was moving toward a more coherent statement of his position on busing, he had never actually made that statement. "The President's position has evolved piecemeal, through leaks and questions," acknowledged White House aides Art Quern and Allen Moore. "The failure to make a comprehensive statement feeds speculation on the President's motives and precise position."[86]

In the midst of the presidential primary season, the press had seized upon such speculation. "Mr. President, there is an element of skepticism about your initiative on the busing issue," a Kentucky reporter had noted on the eve of that state's May 1976 primary. "Why are you doing this now?"[87]

On June 2, 1976, Levi, HEW secretary David Mathews, and members of their staffs presented the president with a concrete set of proposals to implement the general alternatives to busing that he had previously approved. These remedies included a Community Mediation Service, a presidential representative, and a National Community and Education Commission, created by executive order, appointed by the president, and intended to prepare for desegregation at the local level.[88]

Just as the president seemed to be hitting his stride on the busing issue, a new complication arose. In an appearance on CBS-TV's *Face the Nation* on June 5, Ford seemed to defend racial discrimination in nonpublic schools. When asked if he "would . . . approve of a private school turning someone away on the basis of color," Ford replied, "Individuals have rights. I would hope they would not, but individuals have a right, where they are willing to make the choice themselves, and there are no taxpayer funds involved." As Richard Parsons wrote five days later, Ford's position not only belied his defense of school desegregation but contradicted his own Justice Department and would be repudiated by the Supreme Court.[89]

On June 24, 1976, after months of study by the Justice Department and meetings between concerned groups and the president, Ford appeared on television to unveil the School Desegregation Standards and Assistance Act. "It is my responsibility, and the responsibility of the Congress," said Ford, "to seek a solution to this problem—a solution true to our common beliefs in civil rights for all Americans, individual freedom for every American, and the best possible public education for our children." He added that "We will act swiftly and effectively against anyone who engages in violence." The legislation required that courts "determine the extent to which acts of unlawful discrimination have caused a greater degree of racial concentration in schools or school systems than would have existed otherwise, and to confine the relief provided to correcting the racial imbalance caused by these unlawful acts." The bill generally would have limited court-ordered busing to no more than five years and would have established a bipartisan National Community and Education Committee to help communities prepare for desegregation and preclude violence.[90]

Four months later, after declining to enter the Louisville case, the Ford administration for the first time challenged a busing decision. In a brief filed with the Supreme Court, Solicitor General Bork argued that a federal court "went too far" in ordering the consolidation of the city and ten suburban Wilmington, Delaware, school districts.[91]

A week later, Ford narrowly lost his election bid to former Georgia governor Jimmy Carter. Rising unemployment, the impact of Ford's pardon of Nixon, and the scars from Ford's bitter primary campaign against former California governor Ronald Reagan helped defeat the incumbent. But while a new administration augured change in many areas, school desegregation did not appear to be one of them. One busing opponent was about to replace another.

## The Ford Record

Of all of the issues that Gerald Ford inherited from Richard Nixon, busing in many ways appeared to be one of the easiest. Public opinion was strongly on the side of the new president. Congress had just overwhelmingly passed antibusing legislation, and all Ford had to do was sign it. He not only had compiled a consistent, substantive record while in the House of Representatives, but he knew whereof he spoke—his own daughter had been bused in the pursuit of school desegregation.[92]

And by the end of his abbreviated presidency, Ford had done many things right in addressing the issue. He had chosen legal counsel over political expediency in refusing to intervene in the contentious Boston and Louisville court cases. He had listened to the disparate voices of educators, school board representatives, community leaders, civil rights spokespersons, politicians, and members of his own administration. He had condemned antibusing violence, promoted school desegregation as well as quality education, and promised to uphold the Constitution in a nationally televised address. He had not simply denounced busing; he had introduced legislation that offered alternatives to it.

Yet between his signing of the Education Amendments of 1974 and his proposal of the School Desegregation Standards and Assistance Act of 1976, Ford committed several errors that exacerbated a volatile issue. First, his ambiguous responses to the Boston, Louisville, and other instances of court-ordered busing inadvertently encouraged violent resistance to federal court orders. "The President has promised to uphold court orders, while insisting that the courts have gone too far," editorialized the *Christian Century.* "He has told those who have fought desegregation bitterly that his legislation will not affect court orders and litigation in progress."[93]

Second, Ford repeatedly offered the Esch amendment as a realistic program of alternatives to busing, even after his administration had discredited it. Of all of Ford's statements on busing, perhaps his least ingenuous was his promise to "spend whatever money is necessary" to implement the Esch alternatives—a pledge betrayed by his veto of the "inflationary" Education Appropriations Act of 1976, which included an antibusing amendment sponsored by West Virginia Democratic senator Robert Byrd but provided "$150 million more than the President's budget request for elementary and secondary education" for FY 1976 and FY 1977. (Congress would override the veto, and Ford would increase education spending in his next budget.)[94]

Third, Ford overestimated the political impact of the busing issue. His initial emphasis on "quality education," his awkward defense of the "constitutional rights" of children to refuse to be bused, and his election-year introduction of an antibusing bill with virtually no chance of passage were largely counterproductive overtures to conservatives of both parties. In a May 26, 1976, news conference in Columbus, Ohio, Ford found himself having to respond to a reporter's implication that "quality education" were code words for "segregation." The next month Art Quern and Richard Parsons of the president's Domestic Council worried that the "symbolic value" of the School Desegregation Standards and Assistance Act "may stiffen the resolve of those who would resist desegregation."[95]

In his June 5 *Face the Nation* appearance, Ford said that "the Justice Department . . . is in the process of preparing legislation . . . which would seek to limit the courts . . . to . . . the areas where the local school board has violated the constitutional rights of individuals—in this case, students." He then disavowed such "rights": "Busing itself is not a constitutional right, nor is it a lack of a constitutional right. It is only a remedy."[96]

On August 25, White House aide James Cannon wrote to the president, "There seems to be little enthusiasm on the part of Ford supporters to bring this [busing] issue to a head now . . . because at this point we have as an issue the fact that the Democratic Congress has not acted, and we may be better off that way." On September 13 Cannon concluded that "the last opportunity for Congressional action on the busing legislation you have submitted is passed."[97]

Not only did Ronald Reagan's and Jimmy Carter's similar views rob the Ford campaign of a defining issue, but a June 1976 survey found busing a dismal nineteenth on a list of issues most important to voters. Busing had not even significantly diminished Ford's standing among liberals—in 1976, as in 1972, the number of voters who viewed the Republican Party as unresponsive to minorities outnumbered those who did not by only four to three.[98]

Fourth, and most important, Ford never authorized a study of whether busing actually worked. As early as October 7, 1975, Governor Carroll of Kentucky urged Ford to conduct such research. Attorney General Levi, in drafting his legislation, conceded that "an admission that we know too little about the effects of court-ordered busing to frame responsible government policy could be seen to be in tension with the proposal . . . that we now develop additional legislation on busing."[99]

On June 11, 1976, contending that "in most cases in the South busing has worked," Ford aide Judith Richards Hope wrote, "Bill Coleman has suggested, and I concur, that before precipitously submitting legislation on this issue, the Secretary of Health, Education, and Welfare should conduct a study on the actual facts in connection with . . . busing." Three days later, Ford was speechless when challenged by the NAACP's Clarence Mitchell to name a specific instance of court-ordered busing "going too far." On June 15, educator Diane Ravitch urged the president to commission a "Coleman II" report, to follow up sociologist James Coleman's 1966 *Equality of Educational Opportunity* findings that "blacks in all-black schools actually scored higher on many tests" than blacks in integrated schools that were at least half black. Ravitch suggested that a second study "should examine two questions: first, what has been the educational impact of busing . . . ; and second, what educational methods or programs are known to produce better education results for . . . minority children and poor children."[100]

The U.S. Civil Rights Commission concluded in August 1976 that busing had succeeded. The report noted that "eighty-two percent of the nation's school districts had desegregated without serious disruption, and only ten percent report any decline in the levels of education." Without counterevidence from the Ford administration, critics such as commission researcher Duane Lindstrom, who resigned to protest the report's findings, could only say, "I don't think the report proves desegregation does not work. It just doesn't prove anything."[101]

In October 1976, on the eve of the election, HEW finally agreed to conduct its annual survey of the racial characteristics of the nation's school systems. While the administration had claimed that "some smaller school systems will have difficulties complying with the census," its detractors attributed the two-year delay to the fear of exposing persistent school segregation.[102]

"Perhaps from the very beginning the achievement of a unitary society was beyond the capacity of judges," wrote Harvie Wilkinson in his gloomy assessment of school desegregation from 1954 to 1978. Such a challenge certainly seemed beyond the grasp of this president—despite what Ford considered his "commendable record, publicly and privately, on racial matters." Ford confidant and chief of staff Robert Hartmann conveyed the president's accurate belief that "many blacks agreed with him" on busing. One who did not, William Coleman, nonetheless lauded his former boss's devotion to civil rights.[103]

Though Ford's own education in neighborhood schools had been fruitful, he acknowledged that many children, especially minorities, did not share in this experience. For them, he believed that busing would only make a bad situation worse.[104]

During the Ford administration, most Americans of all races sought quality education and desegregated schools. But in the pursuit of both of these goals, they and their president too often achieved neither.

## Jimmy Carter

Today, scholars, politicians, and the public find themselves in unusual agreement about busing to coerce school desegregation: by and large, it has not worked. Such is the lesson of time passed and battles won and lost.

But thirty-five years ago, the lesson was still being learned, and the issue had more than one side. As a presidential candidate in 1976, former Georgia governor Jimmy Carter took his stand, expressing his support for the Atlanta Plan of racial desegregation of that city's elementary and secondary public schools. Though prohibiting mandatory busing, the plan permitted voluntary busing to promote racial integration and to further racial cooperation. "I'm strongly opposed to forced busing," said candidate Carter. "The only kids that ever get bused are poor children."[105]

Carter's campaign stance was popular among the public, which overwhelmingly opposed busing to coerce school desegregation. His position also would be welcome in Congress, which continued to attach antibusing amendments to annual appropriations for HEW and, later, the Department of Education. However, Carter's desegregation stand was disappointing to those liberals and civil rights groups who supported him as the "lesser of evils" in 1976.

The position of candidate Carter was also unsettling, as things turned out, to President Carter. Clinging to the campaign escape clause that he would uphold the law even if it differed from what he believed, the president opposed additional congressional restrictions on busing and deployed the Justice Department on the side of mandatory school desegregation.

Which was the real Jimmy Carter—the antibusing candidate or the probusing president? Carter's true philosophy in some ways combined both positions. But only after leaving "Atlanta" on the campaign trail did the president finally find a home.

## Carter, Congress, and Busing

THE BYRD AMENDMENT    The Atlanta Plan had prohibited forced busing but permitted voluntary busing at public expense if it "contributed to increased integration" and invited "local participation by all racial groups in the formulation of a desegregation plan." The question thus arose as to whether President Carter, like Nixon and Ford, would seek and support legislation that strengthened his antibusing stance.[106]

The answer arrived in the second month of the Carter presidency. Attorney General Griffin Bell, a boyhood friend of the president and whose own antipathy to forced busing had provoked the opposition of civil rights groups to his nomination, nonetheless urged Carter to "leave the law just where it is." The *Milliken* decision, Bell argued, essentially reflected Carter's contention that busing should be a "remedy of last resort." So there was no need for Carter to enter the perilous legislative arena that his predecessors had visited with mixed results.[107]

The new president's aversion to proposing antibusing legislation nevertheless could not insulate him from the issue. He would have to take a stand on antibusing legislation proposed by someone else, most notably Senate majority leader Robert Byrd of West Virginia. In May, HEW secretary Joseph Califano drafted a letter to Washington Democrat Warren Magnuson, chairman of the Senate Subcommittee on Labor and HEW Appropriations of the Committee on Appropriations, urging him to delete the Byrd amendment from his department's annual expenditures. Califano explained that in accordance with the *Swann* decision, "it may be necessary to require transportation of students beyond the school closest to their homes [when] . . . no other remedy will serve to undo the official acts that created the dual [school] system." He therefore concluded that the Byrd amendment poses "serious constitutional questions."[108]

Or so it seemed. Before sending the letter to Magnuson, Califano solicited a legal opinion from the Justice Department. No, Assistant Attorney General Drew Days corrected Califano, the Byrd amendment "is not unconstitutional on its face." Days nonetheless argued that "even a narrow reading" of the amendment could "preclude all HEW action to desegregate schools" and violate the due process clause of the Fifth Amendment. He therefore upheld Califano's opposition to the Byrd amendment and contended that should the measure pass, the secretary must interpret it so as to facilitate, rather than obstruct, school desegregation. The Ford administration identified the "school nearest the pupil's home" before court-ordered desegregation; the Carter administration would identify it after the court order. "Thus, if the nearest school serving your grade is four schools away under that [desegregation] plan, this becomes the nearest school for purposes of compliance with the law," explained Kurt Schmoke of the domestic policy staff. "Justice argues this interpretation is justified by the doubtful constitutionality of the amendment as previously construed."[109]

On June 6 Bell announced a further modification of the Ford policy. Instead of prohibiting "pairing" and "clustering" of schools (by which two or more schools are merged to coerce desegregation), the Byrd amendment actually permitted these practices, according to the attorney general.[110]

THE EAGLETON-BIDEN AMENDMENT   In the same week, the Third Circuit Court of Appeals upheld the District Court busing order of up to 62 percent of Delaware's schoolchildren. So on June 14 that state's congressional delegation (Democratic senator Joseph Biden, Republican senator William Roth, and Republican representative Thomas Evans) solicited Carter's support of Biden's and Missouri Democratic senator Thomas Eagleton's version of the Byrd amendment, which would prevent busing beyond a pupil's nearest school except for purposes of special education. In his talking points for the meeting, Schmoke wrote, "The President is probably best served by going no further than his campaign statements, i.e. supporting the basic Supreme Court decision, preferring the Atlanta Plan, but *executing* the law as formulated by the federal courts." Carter's top domestic policy advisor, Stuart Eizenstat, concurred, urging the president to explain his advocacy of the Atlanta Plan and be "sensitive to human and emotional concerns" but to "emphasize [his] obligation to enforce civil rights laws, including the Constitutional mandate to bring about desegregated school systems where there has been discrimination."[111]

The president chose to ignore the advice. Because "Congress has the authority to decide how a federal agency acts in these matters," Carter told the legislators, the Byrd amendment had been the "proper approach." When informed that such an endorsement contradicted his administration's public policy, the president retreated, promising that he would seek and accept a private decision on the Eagleton-Biden rider by the attorney general, who "ran the Mississippi school system for years as a federal judge."[112]

Two days later the House of Representatives passed its version of the Byrd amendment, sponsored by Ohio Democrat Ronald Mottl, who called the administration's public statements "legalistic somersaults" designed to "circumvent the will of Congress." Opponents of the Mottl amendment charged that rather than preventing court-ordered busing, it would simply preclude HEW from paying for the buses. "It ain't going to stop one bus," argued Wisconsin Democrat David Obey, while black Democrat Parren Mitchell of Maryland branded the proponents of the measure as racist. On June 28, the Senate followed the House in adopting the Eagleton-Biden amendment.[113]

On July 8 the members of the U.S. Civil Rights Commission met with Carter to register their displeasure with the Mottl and Eagleton-Biden amendments. "Both student reassignment and student transportation are judicially approved remedies for school segregation," the commissioners argued. "Although the federal courts have attempted to minimize the use of these remedial techniques,

[they] have found that constitutionally adequate school desegregation cannot be accomplished in many communities without resort to student reassignment and transportation to a school other than the school nearest the student's home." So they urged the president to veto the Labor-HEW appropriations bill if it emerged from the conference committee with an antibusing addition.[114]

Five days later, Bell offered Carter his private assessment of the Eagleton-Biden amendment. While the legislation was constitutional, the attorney general decided, recent court decisions rendered it unnecessary. "The Supreme Court decision in the Dayton, Ohio case . . . gives him [Biden] almost everything that the bill would bring about," Bell contended, citing the unanimous verdict by the high court that desegregation remedies may only be as widespread as the violations they intend to address. Bell worried that passage of the Eagleton-Biden amendment, by relegating federal enforcement of school desegregation entirely to the Justice Department, would burden his agency with excessive litigation.[115]

On July 19, in a memorandum to the president, Eizenstat echoed Bell's opinion. On July 21 Clarence Mitchell, Washington bureau representative of the NAACP, spoke for the "142 organizations that comprise the Leadership Conference on Civil Rights" in opposing the Eagleton-Biden amendment. When the U.S. Civil Rights Commission reiterated its position in a September 15 letter to Carter, Eizenstat replied, "We are aware of the problems raised by the Eagleton-Biden Amendment, and we recognize the need to develop an adequate response to it."[116]

The president's response came two months later. Despite considerable misgivings about the "vexing constitutional questions" and "additional expense and delay" posed by the Eagleton-Biden amendment, Carter signed the Labor-HEW Appropriations bill on December 9, 1977.[117]

But Carter's pen was mightier than his words. The Leadership Conference on Civil Rights challenged the law's constitutionality in a brief filed with the Federal District Court in Washington, D.C. NAACP officials, in a White House meeting, asked the president to veto future appropriation bills containing antibusing riders, and if Congress overrides his vetoes, he should take the legislators to court. David Tatel, director of HEW's Office of Civil Rights, told the *New York Times* that "We can't get an effective remedy [for school segregation] without using some transportation. The districts are so big and the black areas so large that without busing, all we can do is desegregate the edges." Califano asked the Senate Subcommittee on Labor and HEW Appropriations to omit the Eagleton-Biden amendment from its FY 1979 bill. Tatel and Califano then urged Bell to side with the Leadership Conference on Civil Rights in its lawsuit against Eagleton-Biden.[118]

Yet the administration—consistent with Carter's campaign rhetoric, the views of his Justice Department, and his words to Biden, Roth, and Evans—defended the amendment in court as constitutional, despite opposing it on

Capitol Hill as unnecessary. In July 1978, in *Brown v. Califano,* Judge John Sirica of the U.S. District Court of the District of Columbia rejected the suit brought in the name of several public school students. The court held that the Eagleton-Biden amendment did not "violate equal protection guarantees as impermissibly inhibiting desegregation of schools because of the availability of litigation in federal courts as an alternative device to effectuate federal guarantees." After two more years of fighting Eagleton-Biden, Carter nonetheless signed the education appropriations bills for FY 1979 and FY 1980, and in January 1980, in *Adams v. Harris,* the administration successfully defended Eagleton-Biden in the U.S. Court of Appeals.[119]

THE HELMS-COLLINS AMENDMENT    While a congressional majority (with the Carter administration's unhappy acquiescence) was preventing HEW from paying for court-ordered buses, a congressional minority had been attempting to stop the court orders themselves. Over the fierce objections of civil rights organizations and the Carter administration, the Senate Judiciary Committee in September 1977 reported a bill outlawing federal busing orders without evidence of intentional discrimination. The following year, an effort to add the bill to legislation extending the ESEA of 1965 failed in the Senate, 47–49. The next year Representative Mottl challenged the courts with his proposal of a constitutional amendment to ban all busing to coerce school desegregation. The Carter administration's "unequivocal opposition" to the amendment helped seal its defeat in the House, 209–216, on July 24, 1979.[120]

Unable to preempt the judiciary, congressional busing opponents tried the next best thing: stopping the Justice Department from defending busing in court. In November 1980, both houses of Congress passed bills that included such a prohibition. White House counsel Lloyd Cutler urged the president to sign the legislation anyway because the Congress was nearing adjournment, and the next session (with a Republican president and a Republican Senate) would likely "add even more regressive items." But Frank White of the Domestic Policy Council countered that civil rights groups would not accept Cutler's argument. "They would rather fight in January than accept the loss now. Lloyd may be right, but they will never accept throwing in the towel now." Charging that "these [antibusing] riders are just the tip of an iceberg," White House aide Louis Martin, an African American, advocated a presidential veto. "We cannot permit racists and reactionaries to turn the lights out in America."[121]

With the additional support of the Justice Department and Vice President Walter Mondale, Carter on December 13 vetoed a measure providing appropriations for the Departments of State, Justice, and Commerce and containing the antibusing provision sponsored by Republican senators Jesse Helms of North Carolina and James Collins of Texas. The president argued that the Helms-Collins amendment, by restricting the Justice Department, "would effectively allow the Congress to tell a President that there are certain constitutionally mandated remedies for the invasion of constitutional rights that he cannot ask the courts to apply." The Senate then removed the Helms-Collins amendment, and in one of his last acts as president, Carter signed the appropriations bill.[122]

## The Carter Record

The search for an explanation of why the presidential candidate who condemned busing to coerce racial desegregation became the president who preserved it begins with Jimmy Carter's political career. As Carter's biographers attest, Carter had always acted cautiously toward civil rights. Carter's caution, according to Betty Glad, prevented him from confronting the issue of school desegregation as governor. "Somehow, Jimmy Carter kept out of most of [the] turmoil [of the civil rights movement]." John Dumbrell adds that Carter became governor by courting white segregationists and conceding black voters to his Democratic primary opponent. "It would be wrong to imagine that either Jimmy or [wife] Rosalynn were in the vanguard of Southern civil rights," Dumbrell concludes, "and indeed, neither of them fell to the temptation of describing themselves in those terms."[123]

But Carter's caution in his prepresidential years had not erased his conviction on civil rights issues. Glad notes that Carter refused to join the Georgia States' Rights Council in the 1950s, opposed the exclusion of blacks from the Plains Baptist Church, helped persuade the merchants of Plains to lift their boycott of a white farmer sympathetic to blacks, and publicly defended his personal attorney's advocacy of civil rights. Dumbrell observes that Carter's first speech in the Georgia Senate was a defense of black voting rights, his inaugural address as governor contained a vigorous denunciation of racism, and his first campaign for president earned him 94 percent of the African American vote.[124]

Carter could even convince himself that his stance toward the Atlanta Plan continued this early pattern of cautious conviction on the side of civil rights. While caution dictated Carter's defense of the plan's ban on mandatory busing, conviction fueled his attraction to the plan's allowance for voluntary busing and backing by local civil rights groups, which seemed to placate busing proponents as well as opponents.[125]

Carter's presidency continued this blend of caution and conviction. In February 1977 Schmoke outlined three options for Carter to "explain his Administration's approach to busing":

Option 1: Decline to comment at all on the issue on the grounds that his views may be perceived as an attempt to influence judicial consideration of busing cases pending before the courts. The disadvantage to the option is that he may appear to others to be withdrawing from his campaign position and his commitment to enforcing civil rights law.

Option 2: Reaffirm stance taken in the campaign. The problem here is that the Atlanta plan he prefers is under review; therefore, merely repeating the campaign position would raise the specter of Executive interference with the judiciary.

Option 3: Respond by noting:
a) that as President he will uphold the law as stated by the Supreme Court;
b) that this administration is committed to enforcing laws designed to end discrimination;
c) that federal intervention into school desegregation cases will be decided not by the White House but by appropriate officials of the Justice Department. This option seems to overcome the disadvantages of #1 and #2. By saying that he will uphold the law as stated by the Supreme Court, the president avoids having to comment on the disparate busing orders prescribed by lower federal courts.[126]

The minutes of a March cabinet meeting note that "Mr. Califano said that the President may be asked about the Byrd Amendment on school desegregation at his press conference this afternoon, and suggested that he make no comment." In June HEW general counsel Peter Libassi recommended that while Carter should oppose the Eagleton-Biden amendment, he should not make the "futile" attempt to overturn it. In February 1979 Eizenstat and Martin suggested that the president commemorate the twenty-fifth anniversary of the May 17, 1954, *Brown v. Board of Education* decision with a "symbolically important" White House reception for participants in the case and civil rights leaders.[127]

In accepting the counsel of Schmoke, Califano, Libassi, Eizenstat, and Martin, Carter again proceeded with caution. "Aside from his notes and conversations urging me to hire more minorities and women," Califano, who worked for Presidents Johnson and Carter, would recall, "I never heard Carter speak privately with . . . the passion of Lyndon Johnson about civil rights or race in America. . . . I sensed his desire was to appease constituencies as much as to satisfy a fundamental commitment to civil rights." Elizabeth Abramowitz, education specialist on Carter's domestic policy staff, would remember that the idea for the *Brown* reception came not from the president or his closest aides but rather in "the fall of '78 someone said to me that the twenty-fifth anniversary of *Brown* is next May. Aside from the fact that I felt immediately old, I thought we need to do something." Bell would observe that Carter was largely "satisfied to leave" school desegregation "to the courts." Abramowitz concluded that regarding school desegregation, the Carter administration was "trying to do two things. The primary decision is to keep the issue in the agency and not in the White House. . . . You don't bring controversy in. You keep it out there. So you leave yourself a little wiggle room."[128]

Carter's careful "wiggling" nonetheless again allowed for principled opposition to racial segregation and antibusing legislation. On the twenty-fifth anniversary of *Brown v. Board of Education,* in what Abramowitz would call "one of his best speeches," Carter recalled the "cattle prods and high-pressure hoses" that had perpetuated "the national shame of racial oppression." The administration opposed the Byrd, Eagleton-Biden, and Helms-Collins amendments because "often, some busing may be necessary to carry out a desegregation plan." Bell would recall that Carter appointed "a lot of people who were in favor of forced busing," including Assistant Attorney General for Civil Rights Drew Days and Solicitor General Wade McCree. Carter administration Secretary of Education Shirley Hufstedler argued that Carter's view of the "critical federal role in dismantling apartheid in public schools didn't change at all."[129]

If Carter's prepresidential and presidential school desegregation positions combined caution with conviction, however, his reelection effort chose caution over conviction. To President Carter, busing to force racial balance was a "last resort." To candidate Carter, it seemed no resort at all. As a result, confusion marred Carter's 1980 campaign, as in the following September exchange between the candidate and a reporter:

> Q. You said recently in Texas you didn't think that busing for school desegregation was a very good idea.
> A. That's right.
> Q. But under your Administration the Justice Department has defended judicial authority to order busing in a number of cities around the country. Does your public statement suggest that you are withdrawing from the position of leadership in that area and that the Justice Department policy consequently will change?
> A. No. I have never known a massive busing system that was mandated in this country to work with effectiveness.[130]

Once Carter's campaign (and, effectively, his political career) was over, however, conviction could finally overcome caution. Carter vetoed the Helms-Collins amendment, heeding the advice of aides Frank White and Donald Donavan that "such a move would have symbolic importance by demonstrating that he and the Democratic Party do not interpret the recent election results as an excuse to turn their backs on long-standing commitments."[131]

President Carter fulfilled many of his long-standing commitments on school desegregation. He advocated affirmative action in higher education and practiced it in his administration. He vigorously enforced federal policies removing tax exemptions from racially exclusive nonpublic schools and imposing federal regulations that mandated bilingual education. He helped desegregate hundreds of public elementary and secondary schools. But while carrying the big stick of school desegregation, President Jimmy Carter spoke softly. Echoing the ambivalence of federal school desegregation politics and policy from 1965 to 1981, his words were loud enough for antibusing congresspersons to criticize him for too little consistency and for probusing civil rights leaders to attack him for too little courage—but not loud enough for most of the American people to hear.

CHAPTER 3

# Nonpublic School Aid
# 1965–81

## Lyndon Johnson

"The kids is where the money ain't" is the way Lyndon Johnson characterized the U.S. education system when he took office. The nation's Catholic bishops concurred. From 1940 to 1960, Catholic elementary and secondary school enrollments increased at a rate three times that of public schools. By the 1960s, nine of every ten nonpublic school children, and one of every nine schoolchildren, attended Catholic elementary and secondary schools. Forty-nine percent of Americans in 1963 favored federal aid to help keep those schools open. Lyndon Johnson was one of them.[1]

But Titles I, II, and III of the Elementary and Secondary Education Act (ESEA) of 1965, like Title VI of the Civil Rights Act of 1964, were only as good as their implementation. The euphoria in the nonpublic school community over the ESEA's church-state compromises, like the response to Title VI, soon dissolved into acrimonious disputes over its execution. Priorities and politics again left the president largely on the sidelines.

### The Elementary and Secondary Education Act Amendments of 1967

The early returns on the ESEA's impact on nonpublic schools were not promising. A National Catholic Welfare Conference (NCWC) Task Force in November 1965 argued that Title II of the act needed to "be broadened in every possible way." In February 1966 James Cardinal McIntyre of Los Angeles claimed that the ESEA "lacked any provision to enforce inclusion of parochial school students in its benefits." The NCWC's Monsignor James Donohue told the House Education Subcommittee in March that some state constitutions were blocking participation of nonpublic school students in ESEA programs. The first report of the National Advisory Council on Disadvantaged Children, summarizing the ESEA's first year, appeared to confirm these charges by concluding that nonpublic school children were "participating in only 180 of 256 areas where they were eligible."[2]

Church-state separationists continued to view the ESEA differently. George LaNoue of Columbia University told the House Subcommittee on Education in March that because "the Office of Education [OE] encourages the lending of library materials to nonpublic schools," the ESEA was not "consistent with the child benefit theory" upon which it was enacted. In his testimony before the Senate Education Subcommittee on the ESEA extension in April, Leo Pfeffer, special counsel of the American Jewish Congress, charged that the ESEA was attempting to "finance a private and parochial school system paralleling the American public school system." According to Pfeffer, "there is a widespread impression among public school administrators . . . that a local public school board will not be able to get funds under [the ESEA] unless it agrees to set aside a portion . . . for the parochial school system within its district." In June, Protestants and Other Americans United for Separation of Church and State filed suit in U.S. District Court in Ohio alleging that the ESEA was violating the First Amendment by directly distributing Title II monies to Dayton's parochial schools.[3]

With both sides unhappy, the administration feared the unraveling of its delicate handiwork. HEW deputy secretary Samuel Halperin blamed the separationists for threatening the "religious coalition which helped bring PL 89–10 [the ESEA] into being" with their charges of "imprecise administration of the program particularly in Title II, which 'enriches' private institutions more than it aids private students." Education commissioner Harold Howe was more concerned about administration concessions to nonpublic school interests: "As time goes along, we are building larger and federal commitments into a structure which results from political compromise and which may or may not stand the test of constitutionality." The commissioner concluded that "I see the dangers of our making errors of principle simply because the arrangements we suggest are acceptable in a community."[4]

If confrontation over church-state issues reappeared in the ESEA's first full year, compromise returned in its second. "If you don't like the ESEA," the administration seemed to be telling both sides in 1967, "consider the alternative." The alternative was the proposal, sponsored by Republican representative Albert Quie of Minnesota and supported by most Republican and Southern Democratic representatives, to transform the ESEA into "block grants" to be distributed by state boards of education. The adversaries in the church-state wars considered it, and they liked it even less than the original.

Although Quie included in his bill a prohibition on the mixing of state and federal education funds and a requirement that 50 percent of the monies reach impoverished school districts, the NCWC opposed the measure for two major reasons: (1) "We're a little gun shy of chief state school officers because of their historical opposition to aid to private schools," and (2) "It's a bad education measure since it takes the thrust away from being a poverty program." The National Catholic Education Association (NCEA), representing Catholic school teachers and administrators, worried that the Quie proposal would leave nonpublic schools vulnerable to "the interpretations of some state attorneys general" of "state constitutional barriers which prohibit assistance to church-related schools" in thirty-four states. The National Education Association (NEA) called the Quie proposal premature: "you have to have experience with new programs before you take on a substitute." New York state commissioner of education James Allen warned that the "momentum achieved under this Act [ESEA] . . . must not be lost." Pittsburgh superintendent Sidney Marland said that "block grants should supplement, not supplant, the ESEA." The lay Catholic organization Citizens for Educational Freedom and the American Federation of Teachers (AFT) also opposed the Quie substitute.[5]

The administration was therefore able to reassemble the fragile coalition that had helped enact the ESEA in 1965. After Johnson publicly castigated the Republicans for "fanning the church–public school controversy," his staff worked closely with both constituencies. In April, Charles Roche wrote to William Consedine of the United States Catholic Conference (USCC) identifying the logical targets of their joint lobbying efforts as Catholic members of Congress, freshmen congresspersons from districts with large private school populations, and congresspersons from heavily Catholic districts. In May, Roche noted approvingly that "The Catholics have been very industrious in recruiting support" for the administration version of the ESEA. "I don't know whether you watched the Walter Cronkite [television news] show last night," aide Robert Kintner wrote to the president in May. "But they had an excellent feature on the Republican plans to change the education bill [and] . . . the issue seemed to settle on whether the parochial schools would be affected. The Democrats said 'Yes' and the Republicans said 'No.' "[6]

Three days later, a House majority said "no" to the Quie substitute, and, as in 1965, the administration again received acclaim for constructing the church-state consensus that preserved the ESEA. A review of both votes, however, shows that the acceptance of a major federal role in elementary and secondary education was more important than the protection of token concessions to nonpublic schools. The defeat of the Quie substitute and the extensions of the ESEA were therefore Pyrrhic victories for the nonpublic school forces. An OE study released in January 1968 concluded that nonpublic school children were not receiving their fair share of ESEA funds because of three factors. First was the attitude of public school authorities toward the inclusion of nonpublic school pupils. Second were the interpretations of state constitutions by judges and attorneys general. Third was the amount of energy expended by nonpublic school officials to ensure fair treatment for their students.[7]

These obstacles continued to discourage nonpublic school aid after the report. First, the NEA, representing most public school administrators and teachers, announced its opposition to additional categorical aid within the ESEA. "We still have to convince the Congress and the public that granting funds for specific purposes which Congress selects, which are reviewed in the federal government, is not the best way to guard against federal control in education," William Carr, having completed his fifteen-year tenure as executive secretary, told the Representative Assembly as it returned to its pre-ESEA advocacy of general federal aid for public school construction and faculty salaries. Second, the Supreme Court, in *Flast v. Cohen* in June 1968, supported the right of taxpayers to sue and test the constitutionality of the ESEA's provisions for textbooks, "supplemental services and centers," and "shared time" programs for nonpublic as well as public school children. John Lumley, the NEA's executive secretary for legislative and federal relations, pronounced his organization "gratified that the Supreme Court has endorsed a long-standing NEA position that the use of public funds in the private sector be subject to constitutional tests." Third, Catholic lobbyists struggled to maintain their enthusiasm in the face of such resistance. Johnson administration congressional liaison Harold "Barefoot" Sanders concluded that on Capitol Hill, the "church groups were . . . rather ineffective." In the fourth consecutive year of declining enrollments and the third successive year of underutilization of federal funds by Catholic schools, Joseph Cardinal Ritter of St. Louis lamented, "If we were confronted with the question of whether we should start parochial schools today, I am sure they wouldn't be started." Finding that ESEA monies were largely bypassing one thousand California nonpublic schools, *American Education* writers Frank Largent and William May quoted Thomas Dekker: "Swim'st thou in wealth, yet sinkest in thine own tears! O punishment!"[8]

Not all of the news was bad for nonpublic school interests, however. USCC director of education Monsignor James Donohue told the Senate Education Subcommittee in August 1967 that the ESEA had already served more than 1.2 million nonpublic school students. Howe, addressing the 1968 convention of the NCEA, applauded Catholic schools' commitment to the urban poor. The Supreme Court, in *Board of Education v. Allen* in June 1968, upheld a New York law providing secular textbooks to nonpublic school children. The NEA's Lumley praised the decision: "We agree with the United States Supreme Court that the textbook loaning program—the basis for NEA support of Title II of the Elementary and Secondary Education Act—. . . does not constitute state support of religion."[9]

## The Johnson Record

Just as the Southern white president had become an unlikely crusader for civil rights, so the Protestant liberal president had become a surprising champion of nonpublic schools. But as in the school desegregation arena, Johnson seemed largely intent on preserving rather than enlarging the scope of nonpublic school assistance. Yet according to the nonpublic school interests, by the end of his presidency he had not met even this minimal standard.

Despite the enactment of the ESEA, 1,023 Catholic schools closed during the Johnson presidency, reducing enrollment by 14 percent. In its November 1968

meeting, the USCC's Division of Elementary and Secondary Education condemned the "persisting inequities for children attending nonprofit private
schools." It advocated adding a withholding authority and bypass provision in
Title I and specific provisions in Title III for "proportionate participation of
children attending nonprofit private schools; for stressing of supplementary
centers; for independent control of these centers where necessary; and for con-
tinuance of one hundred percent federal funding."[10]

The nonpublic school interests could also blame themselves for the lack of
progress on nonpublic school aid—and they did. A 1966 Carnegie Foundation
study, *The Education of Catholic Americans,* conducted by a team of researchers
including Catholic sociologist Rev. Andrew Greeley, offered a lukewarm defense
of Catholic schools as "neither as bad as their most severe critics would portray
them nor as good as they might be." Three years later, the USCC Committee on
Education, charged with defending those schools before Congress, admitted
that "inconsistency" had marred its lobbying efforts in the 1960s. Not only had
its constituents not received the full benefits of federal legislation, but the USCC
had not clearly communicated what those benefits should be: "There had never
been a positive statement on federal aid by the Conference of Bishops."[11]

Having failed to achieve its short-term objective of fair access to ESEA funds,
the USCC pondered "long-range goals" of $100 federal tuition grants for stu-
dents, teachers, and instructional materials in nonpublic schools. Rather than
settling for less, the nonpublic school interests would be seeking more from the
federal government. They would have a lot of company.[12]

Lyndon Johnson's educational legacy in the areas of public school aid, school
desegregation, and nonpublic school aid, therefore, was one of legislative success
and administrative uncertainty. Federal aid to public and nonpublic schools was
here to stay, and de jure school segregation was on the way out. But if Johnson's
rapid enactment of his education policies invited praise from many and resignation from a few, his moderate implementation ignited new conflicts for a new era.

## Richard Nixon

Richard Nixon told a story about a candidate who sought his advice on whether
to raise money before seeking office or to seek office before raising money.
Nixon advised the candidate to "run first, but with a solid plan, and the money
would then come." In his first, unsuccessful bid for the White House, Nixon had
opposed loans to nonpublic schools. In his second, successful presidential campaign in 1968, he called upon states "to present plans for federal assistance to be
distributed by the states to nonpublic school children and includ[e] nonpublic
school representatives in the planning process." Just like the supplicant in his
story, Nixon appeared to have a "solid plan" for nonpublic school assistance.[13]

As Nixon's proposal evolved, it came to focus primarily on tax credits to help
parents of nonpublic primary and secondary school pupils pay their children's

tuition. But Congress was largely disinterested, the nonpublic school interests were badly divided, and the president was too often distracted. So the "solid plan" of nonpublic school aid would help elect and reelect Richard Nixon, but the "money" for tuition tax credits would not follow.

## The "Crisis"

One of the most popular rationales for a departure from the tradition of state and local regulation of education in the United States is the perception of a "crisis." The "crisis" of the Great Depression of the 1930s provoked numerous congressional attempts to build public school classrooms and pay public school teachers. The "crisis" of the Soviet launch of Sputnik I in 1957 helped enact the National Defense Education Act of 1958. The "crisis" of the baby boom of 1947–62 led to the Higher Education Facilities Act of 1963. The "crisis" of poverty helped secure passage of the ESEA of 1965.

And by the end of the 1960s, proponents of federal aid to nonpublic schools were invoking their own "crisis"—the rapid decline of Catholic elementary and secondary school enrollments. To its purveyors, this crisis was not exclusively Catholic. Noting that the cost of educating a public school pupil was double that of educating a child in a Catholic school, *Time* pronounced Catholic education "a bargain for society." Although less than 25 percent of the U.S. population in 1970 was Catholic, 37 percent of Americans supported public funding for nonpublic elementary and secondary schools.[14]

To proponents of nonpublic school aid, the time seemed right. "Many things have combined to create a situation more favorable to providing tax funds for the education of children in nonpublic school," wrote Rev. Virgil Blum in 1969, his sixteenth year of writing and lecturing on the issue. He listed "the Christian benevolence of Pope John XXIII, the ecumenical impact of the second Vatican Council, the public relations efforts of Citizens for Educational Freedom [the leading citizens' lobby for such assistance], growing concern for the religious liberty of school children and their parents, wider acceptance of the pluralistic nature of American society, the precedents of federal and state aid for Christian and Jewish college education, the enactment of the Elementary and Secondary Education Act of 1965, [and] the growing state monopoly in education." As the Nixon era dawned, twenty-five states provided some form of aid to public schools. Twenty-three offered bus transportation, eight provided secular textbooks, three supplemented the salaries of teachers of secular subjects, and one issued tuition tax credits.[15]

## The Response

President Nixon privately and publicly demonstrated a genuine commitment to nonpublic school assistance. At a White House staff meeting in January 1970, Nixon repeatedly stressed that he "supports private schools." A month later, he

remarked that even though he "always went to public school," he did not consider himself "a public school man." Finn lent urgency to Nixon's interest, concluding that a total collapse of nonpublic schools would require public
education to hire 250,000 more teachers, build 222,000 more classrooms, and
spend $5 billion more. Responding to what its president called an "unprece-
dented" invitation to discuss the "crisis" in Catholic schools, the leadership of
the NCEA met with Nixon at the White House in February 1970. Nixon conveyed his "deep concern" that his Right-to-Read program reach private as well
as public schools. Recognizing the "strong commitment" of Catholic schools to
the inner city, the president implored the educators, "You cannot retreat, you
must not retreat; we must find ways to get public opinion behind you." Following the meeting, Nixon ordered Colson to "get the Commission on Nonpublic
Education announced immediately."[16]

In his "Special Message to the Congress on Education Reform" on March 3,
Nixon formally announced the creation of the Commission on School Finance
to "help states and communities to analyze the fiscal plight of their public and
nonpublic schools." On the same day he wrote to USCC general secretary
Bishop Joseph Bernardin of Cincinnati, "In the section [of the speech] dealing
with the Commission on School Finance, I have specifically directed that special
attention be given to the grave problems confronted today by the non-public
schools of this country." Two weeks later Nixon admonished the commission's
chairman, Neil McElroy, "You've got to do this Catholic school job. I want it
done well. If you don't do it, I will have to set up a separate commission." Within
a month, Nixon had done just that, establishing a Panel on Nonpublic Education, chaired by Clarence Walton, president of Catholic University.[17]

While the commissions deliberated, the Office of Economic Opportunity
(OEO) acted, unveiling a plan to test tuition vouchers for parents of children in
nonpublic schools in selected communities. At a November 1970 meeting at the
OE, representatives of the USCC expressed "friendly interest" in the study, while
leaders of the AFT and NEA registered their strong opposition to the proposal's
purported affront to public education. By the end of the year, Nixon had
approved the experiment, to be conducted by Christopher Jencks of the Center
for the Study of Public Policy.[18]

Just as the campaign for nonpublic school aid was gathering momentum, it
suffered a serious setback. On June 28, 1971, in the *Lemon v. Kurtzman* and *Early v.
Dicenso* decisions, the Supreme Court ruled that Pennsylvania and Rhode Island
laws permitting public aid for nonpublic schoolteachers' salaries were unconstitutional. In a unanimous opinion in the *Lemon* case (only Justice Byron White dis-
sented in *Dicenso*), Chief Justice Warren Burger rejected the separation of
"secular" and "sectarian" aspects of parochial school education so that teachers of
the former could constitutionally receive funds. The Court thus added a third cri-
terion to the 1963 *Schempp* formula for interpreting the First Amendment: not

only whether legislation "is a mask to advance religion" or if its primary effect is to help or harm religion, but whether it constitutes an "excessive entanglement" with religion. On the same day, in the *Tilton v. Richardson* case, the Court, by a 5–4 margin, upheld the Higher Education Facilities Act of 1963, which authorized federal monies for construction at religious as well as secular colleges. In its majority opinion, the Court argued that "since religious indoctrination is not a substantial activity or purpose of these church-related colleges and universities, there is less likelihood than in primary and secondary education that religion will permeate ... secular education."[19]

As had happened so often before, the Supreme Court forced the nonpublic school interests to reassess their positions. "The Court, while refusing to go so far as to say that all direct aid to sectarian educational institutions is forbidden," wrote USCC general counsel William Consedine in July 1971, "has raised serious doubts as to whether it is prepared to sustain any substantial amount of direct assistance." USCC legislative liaison James Robinson added that the Court's actions had rendered general federal aid to nonpublic schools "politically impractical." The President's Panel on Nonpublic Education concluded that "the Court's decisions appear to rule out the concept that secular and religious teaching in church-related schools can be distinguished and separated for purposes of providing support. Also ruled out would be any form of aid to church-related schools that would require a continuing process of distinguishing between secular and religious functions." Although the Supreme Court had precluded direct federal aid to nonpublic schools, these analyses agreed, it had not prohibited all forms of assistance. "The school aid decisions are disappointing and disturbing," wrote Consedine, "but they should not be the occasion for despair. The history of constitutional law in the last twenty-five years is full of twists and turns." The newest twist, the USCC and the president's panel concurred, should be tuition tax credits, a form of indirect federal aid that could pass the three-pronged *Lemon* test. Such a provision for nonpublic school expenses on a parent's federal income tax return, proponents believed, would favor lower-income taxpayers; enlist the support of various Protestant, Jewish, and independent schools; invite bipartisan backing in Congress; and win the endorsement of the president.[20]

Robinson and Auxiliary Bishop Thomas Kelly of Washington, D.C., launched the tuition tax credit effort at an August meeting with House minority leader Gerald Ford, Republican of Michigan, who "enthusiastically" promised to cosponsor such a bill and act as a liaison between the House Ways and Means Committee and the White House. Later in the same month, Nixon told the Knights of Columbus Supreme Council that Catholic education transmits "the moral, spiritual, and religious values so necessary to a great people in great times." Lamenting that parochial schools are "closing at a rate of one a day," Nixon voiced his determination "to stop that trend and turn it around. . . . You may count on my help." The day after the speech and two months after the Supreme Court decisions outlawing Pennsylvania and Rhode Island nonpublic school salary supplementary laws, Nixon conferred with New York officials about a similar law just passed by that state's legislature.[21]

The nonpublic school interests moved to transform Nixon's rhetoric into reality. At an October meeting with the USCC's Bishop Bernardin, White House aide Peter Flanigan rejected as politically "impossible" the bishop's call for a tuition tax credit amendment to the administration's tax bill in the Senate Finance Committee. But he agreed to pursue tuition tax credits as a separate piece of legislation for enactment before Congress adjourned. At a November conference of parochial and public school administrators to "explore ways of further implementing the President's pledge to assist nonpublic schools," Commissioner Marland appointed a coordinator to help nonpublic school students "obtain all federal aid services for which they are eligible." But the year ended with Chairman Wilbur Mills, Democrat of Arkansas, refusing to allow the House Ways and Means Committee to report a tuition tax credit bill.[22]

The new year began in familiar fashion. Nixon again professed his devotion to the nonpublic school cause. In March 1972 he approved the final reports of the Commission on School Finance and the President's Panel on Nonpublic Education. Among the former group's recommendations were "the provision of child benefit services and considerations of additional forms of assistance to nonpublic schools." The major recommendation of the latter group was "a federal income tax credit for tuition, limited to a fixed percentage of tuition paid for nonpublic schools only, with both a maximum credit for children and a phase-out of higher income taxpayers." In April, Nixon told the NCEA Convention that "I am committed to these propositions: [that] America needs her nonpublic schools; that these nonpublic schools need help; that therefore we must and will find ways to provide that help."[23]

But there were signs that this time, Nixon would deliver. First, the nonpublic school interests had broadened their base, with the establishment of the Citizens' Relief for Education by Income Tax (CREDIT), to be chaired by Rabbi Morris Sherer of Agudath Israel, with Vice Chairmen Dr. Al Senske of the Lutheran Church–Missouri Synod, Cary Potter of the National Association of Independent Schools, and Rev. C. Albert Koob of the NCEA. Second, it was a presidential election year, Catholics were largely one-issue voters, and parochial school aid was that issue. Third, and not coincidentally, Mills not only pledged to report a tuition tax credit bill—he was cosponsoring it, and Nixon was supporting it.[24]

Hearings on the Mills bill, HS 16141, began before the House Ways and Means Committee in August 1972. Health, Education, and Welfare (HEW) secretary Richardson, Treasury secretary Shultz, and Budget Director Weinberger strongly endorsed the legislation, and Mills announced that he hoped that the bill would reach the House floor before the end of the session. The AFT and the NEA led the opposition to the measure. AFT director of nonpublic school teachers John Murray considered tuition tax credits "unconstitutional," while NEA president Catherine Barrett worried that "all taxpayers with no school-age children, or those who send their children to public schools, will be taxed to make up the difference of the loss to the Treasury." The committee reported HS 16141 on October 2 by an 18–6 vote. But the press of other legislation and the final month of election-year campaigning assured that tuition tax credits went no further in 1972.[25]

Following Nixon's landslide victory over Democratic senator George McGovern of South Dakota in the November election, the president recommitted himself to nonpublic school assistance. In December, Nixon told Schultz that "the two specific [tax] programs" that he advocated were "tax credits for nonpublic school tuition, and property tax relief for the aged." Nixon's FY 1974 budget allocated $600 million for tuition tax credits. In April 1974 Schultz presented Congress with the administration's proposal for a tax credit up to half of tuition costs but not exceeding $200 to all parents of nonpublic school children earning less than $18,000. Parents earning between $18,000 and $30,000 could receive a reduced tax credit, and those with income above $30,000 would receive no credit at all.[26]

The attention of the education interests, however, had returned to the ESEA, due to expire on June 30, 1973. All sides advocated its renewal, but for different reasons. The USCC seized the chance to expand coverage of nonpublic school children under the legislation. It therefore supported a so-called bypass provision that permitted the education commissioner to directly provide ESEA services to nonpublic school pupils when state and local public education agencies failed to do so. The AFT and NEA saw the opportunity to reemphasize public education. "By constantly calling attention to the failures of public education, to the need for a voucher program, and aid to private and parochial schools," the AFT's Megel complained in February 1973, Nixon "has diverted attention from the good that ESEA has been doing." The AFT and NEA opposed the bypass as yet another invitation for funds to be transferred from public to nonpublic education. The Nixon administration still hoped to reform the ESEA and opposed the bypass as, in Weinberger's term, "unadministrable."[27]

The nation's attention, however, had largely turned to the constitutional crisis enveloping the White House. "The Watergate scandal and its high-level interest has slowed all activities in Washington," Megel observed. On August 9, 1974, it ended the Nixon presidency.[28]

## The Nixon Record

"The climate is right for proposals such as tax credits and vouchers," wrote Donald Frey of Wake Forest University in March 1973, "because the public schools are bearing the brunt of an unprecedented polemic against public education." Yet tax credits and vouchers did not become law, as conflict precluded consensus.[29]

The first major conflict that undermined the nonpublic school cause was within Nixon himself. The political attraction of aid to nonpublic schools was undeniable. In 1960, opposing nonpublic school assistance and running against Catholic John Kennedy (who also opposed it), Nixon received 22 percent of Catholics' votes. In 1968, supporting nonpublic school assistance and running against Protestant Hubert Humphrey (who opposed it), Nixon received 33 percent of Catholics' votes. Republican political strategist Kevin Phillips largely attributed Nixon's victory to Catholic support. In each of the four large states (Pennsylvania, New York, Ohio, and Michigan) that enacted nonpublic school aid after the election, Republican administrations led the way. In July 1969 Finn acknowledged that "parochial schools . . . have a certain appeal because they affect the lower-middle and working classes [who] are neglected by many federal programs." When September polls showed that Nixon would carry more than 60 percent of the Catholic vote in 1972, his Democratic opponent, Protestant George McGovern, endorsed nonpublic school tuition tax credits. McGovern's "Catholic strategy" was too little too late: California, New York, Ohio, Pennsylvania, Illinois, New Jersey, and Michigan, which would have absorbed 70 percent of the burden of the closing of Catholic schools, provided Nixon with 202 of his 520 electoral votes in 1972.[30]

But next to getting elected, Nixon's primary domestic concern, as has been documented, was the economy. It became increasingly difficult, with each successive veto of an education appropriations bill and proposal for state-federal revenue sharing, for Nixon to justify an expensive Washington program such as tuition tax credits—a fact acknowledged within his administration. During his confirmation hearings in November 1970, Marland expressed "serious misgivings" about the "effectiveness" of vouchers. Buchanan warned Nixon in October 1971 that the impending report of the Commission on School Finance would call for "another multibillion-dollar crisis-type recommendation for the federal government to carry out, which would put the President on the hot seat this spring [when] the Democrats would echo the commission's recommendations." But while the report advocated such a plan, it rejected tuition tax credits in part because they would be even more costly. "We are somewhat disappointed by the generally negative attitude toward tax credits taken by Commissioner of Education Sidney Marland and HEW Secretary Elliot Richardson," the USCC's Robinson wrote in May 1972.[31]

In choosing rhetoric over revenue, Nixon falsely encouraged Catholics, conservatives, and, most of all, conservative Catholics. "Skeptics will say that words are cheap and that after all, we are now in the fourth year of the Nixon Administration," *National Review* editorialized after Nixon's speech to the NCEA in April 1972. "Parochial schools . . . are closing at a rate of approximately one per day." The conservative journal asked when nonpublic school aid would finally come in the Nixon administration. "About the same time he balances the budget."[32]

A second major conflict that derailed nonpublic school assistance was on Capitol Hill, where public and nonpublic school interests vied for votes. The former emerged the clear winner. Kenneth Young, lobbyist for the AFT's parent AFL-CIO, begrudgingly praised the rival NEA as "the most effective of all the education groups in terms of lobbying." Nixon budget director and HEW secretary Caspar Weinberger would remember the NEA as "perhaps equal to the National Rifle Association" in its lobbying prowess. The NEA agreed, claiming credit for 30 percent of the 435 representatives and 40 percent of the 33 Senators elected in 1972. Due in large part to the effectiveness of the AFT and the NEA, the Democratic Party controlled both houses of Congress throughout the Nixon years and beyond. "A [tuition] tax credit proposal has no political viability at present or in the foreseeable future as long as the Democrats control Congress," Dick Riddell, confidant of Rep. Wilbur Mills, told the USCC.[33]

And due in large part to the ineffectiveness of the USCC, the advocates of nonpublic school assistance could not exploit the advantages of a friend in the White House. In February 1970 the bishops were miffed that Nixon had met with the NCEA instead of the USCC to discuss the Catholic school situation. In May 1972 Nixon told John Cardinal Krol of Philadelphia that in spite of a USCC letter-writing campaign, his mail was running three to one against tuition tax credits. Despite the presence of 12 Catholic senators and 101 Catholic representatives from 1971 to 1973, 90 percent of Catholics were unable to name a single decision by the USCC, their leading advocates in the halls of Congress.[34]

The bishops' task became even more onerous with the exacerbation of a third conflict—the age-old tension between church and state. The First Amendment's "establishment clause" influenced thought within the administration and action outside it. The first Task Force on Education warned in January 1969 that "state constitutional restrictions" portended a "major struggle" for federal aid to nonpublic schools. Marland predicted in December 1971 that the *Lemon*, *Dicenso*, and *Tilton* decisions would forestall any nonpublic school assistance beyond the "marginal" relief provided by the ESEA. "Dubious constitutionality" was among the reservations of the McElroy Commission toward tuition tax credits in March 1972.[35]

Outside the administration, the Rochester, New York, Board of Education voted 6–1 in February 1973 to reject, largely on constitutional grounds, a $5 million OEO voucher demonstration project for a city in which one-third of its children attended Catholic schools. The next month the NEA enlisted the American Civil Liberties Union, the American Jewish Congress, the Baptist Joint Committee, and the National Coalition for Public Education and Religious Liberty in a national alliance against "government aid to religiously-affiliated schools." In 1974, the Supreme Court ruled that a California law granting parents a $125 tax credit for each child enrolled in nonpublic schools was an "excessive entanglement" of church and state. "It is generally conceded by proponents and opponents of public aid to nonpublic schools," concluded NEA director of government relations Stanley MacFarland in the waning days of the Nixon era, "that the issue will ultimately have to be resolved not by Congress, but by the courts."[36]

The final conflict that undercut the movement for nonpublic school assistance was a rift within the Catholic community in the United States. "A majority of American Catholics feel free to ignore the Holy Father's condemnation of contraceptives," a *Newsweek* survey found in 1971, "and on other public issues such as abortion and aid to parochial schools, conflict has replaced consensus in Catholic circles." This division threatened the strongest rationale for federal aid for nonpublic schools: the "crisis" in Catholic schools.[37]

According to the prominent Catholic interest groups that pressed for nonpublic school aid, parochial schools were closing because of too few clergy and too little money. Terence Cardinal Cooke, archbishop of New York, testified for the USCC on the Mills tuition tax credit bill (HR 16141) in September 1972. "The area of finances is the focal point of the various elements of the Catholic school crisis. . . . Traditionally, Catholic elementary schools have charged very low tuitions, preferring to balance their budget[s] with parish funds. However, this is changing drastically. For example, in 1970–71, about seventy-one percent of the elementary schools charged tuitions of less than $100, but during 1971–72 about fifty-six percent were charging between $100 and $300. This trend will continue to accelerate."[38]

But other Catholics disagreed about the causes of the "crisis." Conservative Catholics attributed the loss of parochial school students to the liberal post–Vatican II bent of the schools' faculties, while liberal Catholics found the schools too conservative. Some Catholics blamed mismanagement by school administrators who either were distracted by other political causes such as abortion or unprepared for the Catholic rush to the suburbs. Another faction bemoaned a "crisis of belief" in parochial schools—Catholic educators were no longer sufficiently devoted to their enterprise.[39]

Still other Catholics denied that there was a crisis at all. They attributed the decline in Catholic school enrollments to more widespread use of birth control by Catholic parents and greater social acceptance of Catholic children in public schools. A report by the New York City Department of City Planning noted that enrollment at non-Catholic private schools was increasing in New York City and throughout the country. The New York State Commission on the Quality, Cost, and Financing of Elementary and Secondary Education, chaired by Manly Fleischman, found that twenty-five of the state's seventy-six Catholic elementary schools that closed between 1967 and 1969 charged no tuition. Rev. Andrew Greeley and Peter Rossi, who conducted the 1966 Carnegie Foundation study, observed that only 22 percent of parents of public secondary school pupils and 18 percent of parents of public elementary and secondary school pupils cited "cost" as the primary reason their children did not attend Catholic schools. A study by Rev. Ernest Bartell for the President's Commission on School Finance concluded that tuition increases accounted for only 20 percent of the enrollment decline in Catholic schools since the peak years. The findings of George Madaus of Boston College and Donald Erickson of the University of Chicago, submitted to the commission but not included in its final report, showed no evidence that parents were withdrawing their children from Catholic schools because of rising costs. When informed of the Madaus-Erickson study, Nixon argued that more money nonetheless would improve the Catholic schools and increase their enrollments—precisely the "cost-quality" rationale for greater *public* school expenditures that Nixon had questioned.[40]

Even if Catholic schools were not in crisis, the USCC and its allies contended, they would deserve federal aid. They provided secular as well as religious education, educated non-Catholic as well as Catholic poor and minorities, stabilized and desegregated urban neighborhoods, saved taxpayers money by diverting students from public schools, promoted healthy competition for public schools, and offered parents choices between nonpublic and public education for their children.[41]

But critics countered that Catholics themselves did not appreciate these benefits. Catholics contributed only 2 percent of their incomes to parish churches (which covered more than half the cost of parochial schools), with poor Catholics donating the same proportion as rich Catholics. The National Association of Catholic Laity's First Annual Report on Catholic Schools in 1972 advocated a redistribution of these resources because "ninety-six percent of the [Church's] educational funds go to the 4.4 million children in parochial schools and only four percent to the religious instruction of an estimated 7.6 million Catholic young people attending public schools." According to information gathered by the White House, Nixon told Cardinal Krol in May 1972, "Catholic people do not really care that much about Catholic schools. . . . When Catholics move to the suburbs, they are satisfied to send their children to good public schools."[42]

Richard Nixon did care about Catholic schools, but he could not overcome the economic, constitutional, and political conflicts generated by his concern. He could not persuade donors of the need for federal aid for nonpublic schools if recipients could not even persuade themselves.

In the end, then, Nixon's unfinished presidency offered an appropriate metaphor for his performance in the areas of public school aid, school desegregation, and nonpublic school aid. While he successfully completed the institutionalization of federal aid to, and de jure desegregation of, public and nonpublic schools, he barely began to reform public schools, fight de facto school segregation, and seek substantial assistance to nonpublic schools. He promised a new beginning; he delivered a false start.

## Gerald Ford

In August 1971, when the USCC wanted a sponsor for its nonpublic school tuition tax credit bill, it turned to House minority leader Gerald Ford, who accepted the offer. The legislation never came to a vote, but Ford's acquiescence identified him as a firm supporter of federal aid to nonpublic schools. So three years later, when Ford became president, advocates of such aid hoped that their time had finally arrived.

They should have known better. In what was becoming a familiar pattern, the courts, the public education interests, and Congress would stand in their way. And by the end of his tenure, their ally in the White House was barely standing at all.

### Vouchers

Among the elementary and secondary education programs that Ford inherited from Nixon were the OEO (later National Institute of Education [NIE]) voucher experiments. HEW executive secretary David Lissy reported "considerable pressure" from representatives of East Hartford, Connecticut, for White House funding of its voucher project. Roger Semerad of the White House staff acknowledged "continued pressure" from New Hampshire State Board of Education chairman William Bittenbender to increase the federal budget for that state's voucher experiment. "The Administration's commitment to the project in New Hampshire," Semerad added, "is well-known."[43]

That commitment was also in jeopardy. The AFT and the NEA continued to oppose vouchers as threats to public education. Congress continued to reduce the budget of the NIE, which housed the voucher projects. And the courts continued to narrowly interpret the First Amendment prohibition on the federal "establishment of religion." On May 19, 1975, in *Meek v. Pittenger,* the Supreme Court overturned a Pennsylvania law permitting publicly funded auxiliary services (for disabled, disadvantaged, or exceptionally talented students) administered with publicly owned instructional equipment and materials by public school personnel at nonpublic schools.[44]

The nonpublic school interests expressed dismay over the decision. "The implications of the Supreme Court's decision are incredibly absurd and terrifying," wrote John Cardinal Krol of Philadelphia in May 1975. "If pluralism in education is a danger to be avoided, is not the same applicable to pluralism in political parties, pluralism in religious beliefs, pluralism in the press? . . . If we are liable for things someone thinks we might do in the future, is any one safe?" The USCC Committee on Education concluded in August that "the United

States Supreme Court has nullified in large measure laws which reflect a policy of granting [nonpublic school] aid."[45]

The Ford administration reached a similar conclusion. Education commissioner Terrel Bell wrote in July 1975 that "it is my understanding that the constitutionality of the solutions [to declining nonpublic school enrollments], if anything, has been more restricted by *Meek v. Pittenger.*" Two weeks later, White House aide Arthur Quern advised the president that "almost any new form of aid which might be considered [tax credits, tuition reimbursement, vouchers] would only survive a constitutional challenge if they were available to both public and private school students. Making them available to both is fiscally impossible." Quern thus recommended that "the President not give any expanded aid to nonpublic education since almost any course would be unconstitutional or too expensive."[46]

## Tuition Tax Credits

Two months after taking office, Ford announced, "I'm thinking a [tuition] tax credit proposal is a good proposal. . . . There is no reason why there should be a monopoly on education just on the public side. . . . And I would hope that we could find some constitutional way in which to help private schools." His administration then began its search, only to have Bell and Quern find tuition tax credits, like vouchers, to be unconstitutional. Another year of inaction on tuition tax credits indicated that the president did, too.[47]

Election-year politics reawakened Ford to the issue of tuition tax credits. Public opinion polls showed most Americans in favor of federal aid to nonpublic schools and most Catholic Republicans in favor of Ford's major presidential primary opponent, former California governor Ronald Reagan. "The nonpublic schools are dying fast, but there is still a very strong sentiment among Catholics and other religious factions that children have a right and a privilege to a religious education which should in some degree be federally subsidized," White House aide Henry Cashen wrote in July 1976. "Support of nonpublic schools is vital to the hierarchy of the Church."[48]

Many Catholics were uneasy with the nonpublic school aid stance of the Democratic Party presidential candidate, former Georgia governor Jimmy Carter. In June 1976 Carter pronounced himself firmly committed to an "absolute separation of church and state" and opposed to "public support for parochial schools." In July, Carter omitted nonpublic schools from his convention acceptance speech. In August he expressed support for secular funding of secular subjects in parochial schools only "if the laws and the interpretation of the Constitution would permit." According to Cashen, "Catholics interpret such statements as reactive and defensive, rather than offering clear unequivocal leadership to redress wrongs in constitutionally acceptable ways." The USCC urged Carter to "move from general statements of tax aid to a specific program of tax credit legislation for all public and nonpublic school parents." Some Catholics were also uncomfortable with Carter's "born-again" evangelical Protestantism. "Catholics are very privately religious people," Cashen wrote. "They don't like religion flaunted openly, which Carter has done and continues to do."[49]

Ford, on the other hand, was politically and personally attractive to many Catholics. The nonpublic school aid lobby Citizens for Education Freedom praised the president for "consistently and frequently" supporting "equal treatment of all parents and children in education benefits." The *Church/State News Service* asserted that "there has never been a more clear-cut choice between the two parties on the major church-state issues than in this election." Cashen wrote that "President Ford has established himself as an honest, hard working family man who is very religious but in a quiet, personal way. These qualities are the foundation of the Catholic community."[50]

"With so many feeling so deeply about the question of aid to nonpublic schools," Cashen added, "it seems inevitable that this . . . will become a major issue in the current political campaign." So he urged Ford to "go beyond" Carter's "nominal" support for the "plight of nonpublic schools." But nonpublic school assistance did not become a major issue in the campaign, and Ford continued his retreat on tuition tax credits. The Republican Party platform favored only "consideration" of tuition tax credits, while Ford echoed Carter in saying, "I hope we can find . . . a constitutional way . . . to help nonpublic schools so that they can compete adequately with the public school system."[51]

## The Elementary and Secondary Education Act

The courts, Congress, the public education interests, and their presidential candidate largely permitted Gerald Ford to avoid censure from the nonpublic school community for the failure to expand vouchers and enact tuition tax credits. But when the nonpublic school interests failed to achieve a greater role for their schools in the ESEA, the president could not escape the blame.

Ford's opposition to expanding ESEA benefits for nonpublic schools was primarily an economic decision. "Inflation" was the reason cited for his veto of congressional education appropriations in 1975. Inflation was also the cause of the USCC's opposition to the veto. Contending that in the previous seven years education costs had risen 211 percent while the consumer price index had increased only 57 percent, the USCC accused Ford of accelerating the "gradual erosion of the [ESEA's] program benefits to the Nation's educationally disadvantaged children." Sounding very much like their counterparts in the public school community, the bishops asserted that "there must be a reordering of the Nation's spending priorities, with education spending as a higher priority." Over the USCC's objections, Ford would veto two education appropriations.[52]

Ford also based his resistance to expansion of the ESEA on constitutional grounds. In the wake of the *Meek v. Pittenger* decision, Quern advised that "the

President not give any indication of expanded aid to nonpublic education since almost any course would be unconstitutional." Yet the 1972 "Report of the President's Commission on Nonpublic Education," which Ford implicitly embraced, had called upon the federal government to "tighten participation requirements in existing programs, e.g. Title I, so as to ensure the genuine and equitable participation of nonpublic school students." So in a June 1975 White House meeting, USCC representatives reminded Ford that "nothing in the [*Meek v. Pittenger*] decision deals with existing state or federal aid programs, including in particular the ESEA." The following February, however, the OE announced a narrower interpretation of ESEA regulations to conform to the *Meek* decision. Only after the USCC protested that such a change "would have given the opponents of aid to public schools their victory without having to go to court" did Commissioner Bell reverse the decision and restore the original guidelines.[53]

The Ford administration thus ended with the same limited provisions for nonpublic school aid in the ESEA as when it began. A 1976 administration issue paper identified as a "major problem in education" the fact that "nonpublic schools, which make a valuable contribution to the Nation's total education effort, face serious financial difficulties." As for "what President Ford proposes to do about their problems," however, the paper merely cited existing components of the ESEA: "The Ford Administration is providing aid to students at non-public schools for such services as compensatory education in reading and math, child nutrition programs, and training of children with learning disabilities."[54]

## The Ford Record

Gerald Ford was not only in office when the nation commemorated its bicentennial; he was also president when the ESEA of 1965 passed its tenth year. Msgr. Olin Murdick of the USCC appealed for a rekindling of the "significant dialog" between public and nonpublic school interests that had led to the ESEA. But there was little immediate prospect for such outreach, even with a president temperamentally disposed to dialogue. Not only would Ford not bring the AFT, NEA, and USCC together, but Weinberger would advise the president against convoking a 1977 White House Conference on Education "as recommended by the Education Acts of 1974," lest it become a forum for new budget demands by the public school groups.[55]

Before Catholics talked with others, however, perhaps they should have talked among themselves. A USCC analysis of opposition to nonpublic school aid predictably identified "persons who for reasons of deep religious feeling and belief (prejudice) fear Catholic power" as well as "secular humanists who oppose the extension of religion into public life" and "the public school establishment which, for reasons of economic advantage (consciously pursued by the AFT and the NEA) and/or professional or proprietary pride, opposes any public policy which would give new advantages to nonpublic schools and thus jeopardize the public school monopoly." Yet it added a fourth obstacle: "opposition to Catholic schools variously motivated, manifested within the Catholic community itself."[56]

As significant divisions among Catholics lingered, so too did doubts within their leadership as to how to overcome these differences. Murdick lamented in August 1975 that "We have yet to develop or permit to develop in the Catholic community a capability for political action." Rev. William McManus, chairman of the USCC Committee on Education, wondered a year later if the bishops had a "strategy for federal aid," noting that the subcommittee charged with devising one had yet to meet.[57]

Despite any apprehension about Jimmy Carter's unambiguous religiosity or ambiguous stands on abortion and nonpublic school aid, Catholics would award him a majority of their votes in the 1976 election. After eight years of effort by Nixon, Ford, the USCC, and others had failed to solve or even certify the "crisis" in their schools, perhaps Catholics were no longer sure who their friends were.[58]

In the final analysis, it seems almost unfair to evaluate Gerald Ford's presidency. Yet despite the disadvantages of his predecessor's inheritance—a bad economy, a disillusioned public, an increasingly adversarial Congress—Ford possessed one overriding strength. He was not Richard Nixon. In the areas of public school aid, school desegregation, and nonpublic school aid, however, Ford was less serious than Nixon about reform, more serious about retrenchment, and, in the end, just as unsuccessful.

## Jimmy Carter

A cosponsor called it "among the most important debates in education history." A leading critic asserted that it "could lead American society [to] use its own hands to destroy itself." On August 15, 1978, by a vote of 57–41, the U.S. Senate would delete the provision for federal tuition tax credits for parents of nonpublic school children from a bill cosponsored by Democrat Daniel Patrick Moynihan of New York and Republican Robert Packwood of Oregon.[59]

The failure of tuition credits would be a setback for the Roman Catholic bishops of the United States, whose parochial schools were closing at an alarming rate. It would be another triumph for church-state separationists, in the wake of several favorable court decisions. And it would be at once a defeat for candidate Jimmy Carter, who had appeared open to tuition credits, and a victory for President Jimmy Carter, who would never seriously consider them.[60]

### The Moynihan-Packwood Bill

Because the right to a religious education for low-income and middle-income American children "lies at the core of America's diversity and strength," presidential candidate Jimmy Carter, after considerable vacillation, pronounced

himself in October 1976 "firmly committed to conducting a systematic and continuing search for constitutionally acceptable methods of providing aid to parents whose children attend nonsegregated private schools." At the time, 85
percent of nonpublic elementary and secondary schools were religiously affiliated, and 75 percent of these religious schools were Catholic. Many Catholics
applauded the promise by the former Georgia governor, whom they would
reward with 57 percent of their votes in the 1976 presidential election.[61]

Within eight months, however, the Supreme Court had dampened such
enthusiasm. In June 1977, in its sixth nonpublic school aid decision in seven
years, the Court ruled in *Wolman v. Walter* that Ohio could provide parochial
schools with speech, hearing, and psychological tests; remedial training and
counseling outside the school; and standardized examinations. But the state
could not loan instructional materials or finance field trips. While the former
types of assistance "will not create an impermissible risk of the fostering of ideological views," wrote Justice Harry Blackmun for the majority, the latter forms
of aid blurred the distinctions between "secular" and "sectarian" education.[62]

The latest setback from the high court was not enough to deter nonpublic
school aid's congressional advocates, however. Senators Moynihan and Packwood devised a bill that provided a tuition tax credit of up to $500 for parents
in nonpublic schools and colleges. Congressional opponents cited the measure's
$4.7 billion price tag in an era of inflation; claimed that two-thirds of the credit
would reach the wealthiest 15 percent of parents; predicted that nonpublic
schools would nullify the credit by raising tuition; and, in the wake of the *Wolman* decision, challenged its constitutionality. The Carter administration
agreed that it was "very expensive" and "probably unconstitutional." Even the
country's Catholic bishops (the USCC) withheld their endorsement of the kind
of bill that they had not supported since the *Nyquist* decision in 1973. The bishops'
general counsel, George Reed, privately considered the Moynihan-Packwood bill
"patently unconstitutional."[63]

But these principled objections could not conceal the bill's political promise.
When Moynihan and Packwood introduced their legislation in the Senate on
September 26, 1977, they enlisted forty-six cosponsors, including thirteen of the
eighteen members of the Senate Finance Committee, where the bill would originate. *Newsweek* concluded that the bill's passage seemed "irresistible." The
*Washington Post* declared it virtually "unstoppable." And for many Catholics, the
bill's prospects seemed too good to be true. On October 19, the first anniversary
of Carter's pledge to their organization, the chief administrators of the NCEA
passed a resolution at their annual meeting urging the president to enact nonpublic school tuition tax credits. In November the USCC's administrative board
directed the bishops to resurrect their campaign for tuition credits.[64]

But the Carter administration held firm. HEW secretary Joseph Califano, the
administration's most prominent Catholic, testified against the Moynihan-

Packwood bill before the Senate Finance Committee in January 1978. While recognizing the financial burdens faced by parochial school parents, Califano nonetheless argued that "other needs are much more desperate." While acknowledging Carter's campaign promise, Califano questioned whether nonpublic school tuition tax credits would be constitutional. Moynihan found Califano's testimony "puzzling" in light of Carter's pledge. "As the President is a man of his word," the senator wrote to Archbishop John Quinn of San Francisco, "I can only suppose that his bureaucracy is out of touch with his views on this issue."[65]

But the bureaucracy pressed on. A month later Califano announced the administration's alternative to the college portion of the Moynihan-Packwood bill—expansion of existing student grant, loan, and work-study programs. He offered no substitute for the primary and secondary school part of the legislation, which, by helping to fund nonpublic schools, "could mark a total erosion of public education" and "could create problems in terms of perpetuating or beginning academies to avoid racial integration." Noting that "I am one who sends my children to private school," the secretary added, "I think I should pay the tuition." Califano denied that Carter was breaking his promise to constitutionally aid nonpublic schools, citing administration proposals for increased funding of the nonpublic school provisions of the ESEA on the one hand and the "questionable constitutionality" of tuition credits on the other. He assured the committee that he would request from the Justice Department a legal opinion on the Moynihan-Packwood measure. "I draw a very sharp distinction between the candor with which President Carter dealt with this question [in October 1976]," Califano concluded, "and the absolute false integrity, false hope with which President Nixon . . . promised the Catholic schools . . . aid he knew he could not provide in a constitutional manner."[66]

But many Catholics begged to differ. On February 8 the chief administrators of the NCEA responded to the secretary's remarks by dispatching a telegram to the president accusing Carter of "contradict[ing] your explicit campaign pledge communicated to us at our October 1976 meeting." On February 14 Califano summarized Carter's political dilemma: while the NEA "would be annoyed" if Carter supported tuition credits, expansion of the ESEA without the Moynihan-Packwood bill "may not be enough to satisfy private school interests."[67]

Carter's alternative to college credits and his opposition to elementary and secondary school credits could not prevent the Senate Finance Committee from reporting by a 14–1 margin on February 23 a consolidation of Delaware Republican William Roth's $250 college tuition plan and the Moynihan-Packwood $500 primary-secondary school proposal. The "modest efforts" of Carter's ESEA expansion, Budget Director James McIntyre and domestic policy advisor Stuart Eizenstat informed the president the next day, had not stalled the "momentum building behind the Moynihan-Packwood tuition credit."[68]

Carter nonetheless defended his ESEA expansion and tuition tax credit omission in his education message to Congress on February 28. While "I am committed to doing all that the Constitution allows to ensure students in private schools benefit from Federal programs," Carter asserted, "I cannot support a tax credit for private elementary and secondary school tuition." The president explained: "First, there is grave doubt that such a tax credit program can meet Constitutional requirements concerning separation of church and state. Second, the federal government provides funding primarily to help meet the needs of public school children . . . who have some . . . form of special need." He concluded that "we do not provide general support for public schools, and it would be unfair to extend such support, through a general tax credit, to private schools."[69]

The Carter message, while not unexpected, was nonetheless discouraging to many Catholics. "We urgently need more Democrats who are willing to withstand the pressure which we know will be forthcoming from the Administration," James Robinson, the USCC's chief government liaison, concluded in the aftermath of the statement. The bishops therefore postponed any personal lobbying of the president until a majority in the Ways and Means Committee was secure for the House version of the Moynihan-Packwood bill. Moynihan shared the bishops' disillusionment. HEW assistant secretary Hale Champion admitted to the senator that despite Carter's public protests to the contrary, "no significant assistance will accrue to private school students or their parents as a result of the President's proposed changes in existing education legislation." Califano conveyed to Moynihan the administration's judgment that tuition credits were not "necessary as a matter of politics," so the secretary was "under direct instructions from the President to try to kill our bill in the House of Representatives."[70]

While Moynihan feared the worst for tuition credits, the White House feared the best. Republican representatives Albert Quie of Minnesota, William Frenzel of Michigan, and Lawrence Coughlin of Pennsylvania requested that their version of the Moynihan-Packwood bill be attached to the administration's college aid measure. Eizenstat then summoned congressional Democrats to the White House to devise a strategy to foil the plan. Majority whip John Brademas of Indiana, Education Subcommittee chairman William Ford of Michigan, and the administration's House liaison William Cable produced a scheme that Eizenstat called "political hardball" and Quie and Frenzel termed "parliamentary chicanery." Ford would introduce the Carter bill the following day under a suspension of the House rules, thus requiring a two-thirds vote for passage but prohibiting any amendment. Ford executed the plan on March 20, but the 218–156 vote for the administration's measure fell short of the necessary two-thirds majority.[71]

At the same time, the Justice Department concluded that while nonpublic college tuition tax credits would be constitutional, their elementary and secondary school counterparts would not. Citing the *Nyquist* precedent, Assistant Attorney General John Harmon argued that Moynihan-Packwood "would appear to violate the first amendment guarantee against establishment of religion."[72]

"I respectfully submit that the Attorney General is wrong," said Moynihan. The bishops concurred, redirecting their national letter-writing campaign to persuade representatives to add elementary and secondary school tuition credits to the college-only bill that emerged from the House Ways and Means Committee. But during Carter's April 11 news conference, he pledged to veto any such "costly and unconstitutional" measure. A month later, Elizabeth Abramowitz, education specialist on the administration's domestic policy staff, denied that Carter had abandoned his campaign promise. "We are fulfilling President Carter's pledge to aid private schools," she wrote to Rev. John Meyers, president of the NCEA, "by creating an Office of Nonpublic Schools within the Office of Education, by requiring states to guarantee equitable participation in various Federal programs, and by including nonpublic school representatives on all advisory committees in the Education Division of the Department of Health, Education, and Welfare." She estimated that the Carter administration would add $100 million in federal assistance for nonpublic elementary and secondary school students for FY 1980.[73]

But neither the president's stick nor his advisor's carrot deterred the proponents of tuition tax credits. After a Harris Poll showed two-thirds of Americans in favor of nonpublic elementary and secondary school tuition tax credits, the issue came to a vote on the House floor. On June 1, a 209–194 vote restored elementary and secondary schools to the college tuition tax credit bill reported by the Ways and Means Committee. Proclaiming "freedom of choice" in education, 107 Democrats joined 102 Republicans in the majority. The House then passed, 237–158, a bill providing tuition tax credits at all levels of education. The $1.206 billion House measure, sponsored by Democrat Charles Vanik of Ohio, included a $50 elementary and secondary school tuition credit for 1978, up to $100 for 1979 and 1980. The credit would extend solely to nonpublic schools, and about 50 percent of the recipients would be families with incomes over $20,000. The $5.29 billion Moynihan-Packwood bill included a $500 elementary and secondary school tuition credit beginning in 1980. It would extend to nonpublic as well as public schools that charged tuition, and about 40 percent of the beneficiaries would be families with incomes over $20,000.[74]

Five days after the House vote, Moynihan shared with Archbishop Quinn "the very considerable success" enjoyed by the tuition credit forces. He assessed the chances of such legislation in the Senate as "excellent," despite the president's resistance. He noted, however, that "I will have an opportunity to review it with him in the near future." The "near future" arrived that afternoon, when Moynihan met with Carter at the White House. In the ten-minute meeting, the president wasted no time reiterating his strong stance against tuition credits:

1. Tax credits provide benefits to those who need them the least;
2. Tax credits further fragment federal education policy, making the Treasury Department-IRS the largest contributor to federal aid to education;
3. Tax credits are expensive;
4. Tax credits add administrative burdens and increase paperwork for institutions, the IRS, and the taxpayer;
5. Tax credits signal and encourage white flight from public schools along with middle-income flight;
6. At the elementary and secondary level, tax credits to church-related schools are probably unconstitutional; and
7. At the higher education level tax credits would have little effect on choice because a $250 or $500 tax credit would provide minimal help for families facing college costs of several thousand dollars.[75]

Unable to change the president's mind, the tuition credit forces intensified their pressure on Congress. Washington, D.C., Auxiliary Bishop Thomas Kelly, chairman of the USCC's Education Department, authorized a "last personal effort" on June 19 to influence the Senate floor vote on the Moynihan-Packwood bill, which forty-one Senators clearly favored and twenty clearly opposed, with thirty-nine still undecided. Proponents as well as opponents expected the measure to pass. "We still expect to win," wrote the USCC's James Robinson on July 24. "With fifty cosponsors on record," wrote Paula DiPerna in *The Nation*, "it is likely that the Moynihan-Packwood bill will pass the Senate."[76]

By August 2, however, the pendulum had swung against the legislation. John Cardinal Krol of Philadelphia emerged from a meeting with Republican senator Richard Schweiker of Pennsylvania with a count of forty-six supporters, forty-eight opponents, and six undecided. Moynihan responded by circulating copies of the 1972 and 1976 Democratic Party platforms to all congressional Democrats, including 1972 presidential candidates Senator Hubert Humphrey of Minnesota and Senator George McGovern of South Dakota, to remind them of their party's past support for nonpublic school tuition tax credits. On August 3, the Senate Finance Committee halved the cost of the Moynihan-Packwood credit. Four days later, Carter met with Senator Kaneaster Hodges of Arkansas to plot the administration's strategy. On August 15 the Senate voted 65–26 in favor of college tuition credits but 57–41 against elementary and secondary school credits. Twenty-eight Senators supported the former but opposed the latter. Two days after the votes, Carter spoke more vigorously than ever against tuition credits: "I do not favor the tuition tax credit approach to college students, and I even more strongly oppose on constitutional grounds government financing of the elementary and secondary schools which are privately operated."[77]

Carter reiterated his "strong opposition to any tuition tax credits" at his September 26 breakfast meeting with the congressional leadership. On September 28, after the House conferees voted 4–3 to drop elementary and secondary school credits from the House bill (with Catholic Democrats Vanik, Daniel Rostenkowski of Illinois, and James Burke of Massachusetts in the minority), the House-Senate Conference Committee reported a college tuition tax credit bill. Califano would recall Carter's relief that "he would not have to veto a bill with widespread Catholic support."[78]

The bishops were furious. Calling the conference report "a case of discrimination against the five million children whose parents have, at considerable sacrifice, exercised their constitutional right to choose a nonpublic school education," Bishop Kelly urged all members of Congress to recommit the bill. The House obliged on October 12, voting 207–185 to attach elementary and secondary school credits to the conference report. The next day, the conference committee compromised by restoring secondary school, but not elementary school, credits. But Congress would adjourn before the measure could reach the floor of either house.[79]

In November, President Carter declared victory, signing the package of college grants and loans (but not tuition tax credits) known as the Middle Income Student Assistance Act. But after the congressional elections that month, the bishops could claim some measure of success as well. They estimated a gain of up to twenty tuition credit advocates in the House and perhaps as many as five in the Senate, based on the campaign positions of the new members.[80]

The bishops' Executive Committee, in an attempt to "scare" and "neutralize" their chief adversary, met with the president at the White House on November 11. Contrary to Carter's claims, they argued, the Moynihan-Packwood bill would be less expensive and more efficient than the Middle Income Assistance Act; there was no danger of federal nonpublic school aid surpassing public school assistance; nonpublic school competition would help, not hinder, the public schools; the credits would help the poor more than the rich; and such legislation would be constitutional because it aids parents, not schools. Noting that "the Catholic Community has had a long history of support for the Democratic Party," the bishops warned that the "rising anger" among Catholics "will have an effect on future election results just as it affected the recent election."[81]

Four months later the bishops approved a two- to four-year campaign for tuition tax credits, and Moynihan and Packwood reintroduced their legislation. But on May 25, 1979, in *Beggans v. Public Funds for Public Schools,* the Third Circuit Court found a New Jersey nonpublic school tuition tax credit plan unconstitutional. "Even if parents of dependents in nonpublic schools do have greater expenses than those supporting dependents in public schools," the court decided, the state "may not equalize the burden by granting a benefit to taxpayers with dependents in private or parochial schools." The Supreme Court, despite the clamor by tuition credit partisans, let the decision stand. *Beggans* thus threatened to repeat what *Nyquist* had accomplished six years earlier: derail the national tuition credit effort. USCC general counsel Reed interpreted the

Supreme Court's inaction as a "signal to Congress reaffirming the entanglement concept developed in *Nyquist*." Reed advised the bishops that tuition credits "should not be vigorously pressed at this time."[82]

In June, Bishop Daniel Pilarczyck presented the USCC Education Committee with three options: "withdraw the effort entirely and stop; slow down, scale-down, or refocus the effort"; or "continue with plan as approved . . . full speed ahead." Reasoning that a federal tuition credits case would not reach the Supreme Court for two or three years anyway (at which time the composition of the Court may well have changed), the committee unanimously chose to continue the effort—a decision ratified by the Administrative Board in September. But the campaign never reached Congress, which had turned its attention to Carter's proposal of a cabinet-level Department of Education, opposed by the bishops as an invitation to federal control of nonpublic as well as public education and as a campaign promise kept by Carter to the bishops' nemesis, the NEA. After the House approved the creation of the Department of Education by only four votes on July 11, Budget Director James McIntyre consoled the bishops with the promise of a high profile for the newly created Office of Nonpublic Education within the new agency. While the bishops "appreciate this action," wrote the USCC's Robinson, they "do not see it as adequately addressing the broad-range problems which we have with the proposal to create a new Department."[83]

On August 28, Carter again reached out to Catholic interests, appointing Auxiliary Bishop Edward Hughes of Philadelphia to the Advisory Panel on Financing Elementary and Secondary Education authorized by the extension of the ESEA in 1978. Within six months, however, Hughes had determined that the fifteen-member panel was "weighted clearly in favor of public schools" and against nonpublic school tuition tax credits.[84]

In April 1980 the administration and Catholic interests were actually on the same side in court. In *PEARL v. Harris,* a District Court in New York unanimously upheld ESEA Title I services provided to nonpublic school students on nonpublic school grounds during school hours. Yet in her election-eve review of the administration's policies toward nonpublic schools, Debbie Hyatt, assistant director of the domestic policy staff, admitted that "I am still not very happy with this piece, but I think we've about exhausted the scanty information available on the subject." Many Catholics apparently agreed. In November 1980, 51 percent of Catholics' votes went to Republican Ronald Reagan, 46 percent to Carter, and 9 percent to Independent John Anderson. Reagan's Catholic vote came despite a majority of Catholic voters choosing Democratic congressional candidates.[85]

While Catholics voted for Reagan, Carter, and Anderson (or not at all) for a variety of reasons, the USCC and other Catholic groups believed that Reagan's election augured well for tuition credits. In all-too-familiar words, Rev. Thomas Gallagher of the USCC cited the Republican Party's "strong and specific commitment" to nonpublic school assistance, a "solid base of support" in the House, and "a good chance of obtaining support in the Senate" for tuition credits. But, as if to distinguish Reagan in 1980 from Carter in 1976, Rev. Virgil Blum, president of the Catholic League for Religious and Civil Rights, observed that "President-elect Reagan *repeatedly stressed* his *strong* support for tuition tax credits, calling them the best way to aid parents whose children attend nonpublic schools." He concluded, "Now it is up to Catholic parents to organize with other parents of private school children so they can effectively influence Mr. Reagan to keep his promise to them." For a variety of reasons, the new president, like his predecessor, would not.[86]

## The Carter Record

The Moynihan-Packwood tuition tax credit bill failed for two major reasons. First, the Carter administration consistently opposed it. While the White House perpetuated the president's campaign pledge to seek "constitutionally acceptable" means of funding nonpublic schools, its performance belied the promise. Yet both rhetoric and reality remained constant. As late as April 1980 a Department of Education summary of the Carter policies toward nonpublic schools asserted that "the Administration believes that we must take all constitutionally appropriate steps to ensure that nonpublic school children receive an equitable share of funds provided under federal elementary and secondary education programs." Yet Califano announced the administration's resistance to tuition credits even before the Justice Department found them unconstitutional; Carter privately equivocated to Moynihan that tuition credits were *probably* unconstitutional even after the Justice Department's ruling.[87]

Carter opposed tuition credits regardless of their constitutionality. At his April 11, 1978, news conference, after calling such credits "very detrimental to the future of education in our country," the president concluded that "I think the whole concept is fallacious, and I don't like it." On August 17 the president, who refused to veto appropriations increasing education spending 73 percent during his term, expressed "no reticence" about vetoing a tuition tax credit bill. On September 25, when Texas Democratic senator Lloyd Bentsen suggested that the House-Senate conference report provide for a "declaratory judgment" by the federal courts on the bill's constitutionality, Carter concurred with Eizenstat that "we do not want to imply that a court decision upholding the constitutionality of such credits would have our support on policy grounds." Three days later, Moynihan elicited the administration's position on a prospective minimal tuition tax credit of "perhaps $10 per student per year" simply to provoke the court test Carter had appeared to invite during the campaign. "I told the Senator," Eizenstat wrote to Carter, "that the Administration opposes elementary and secondary tuition tax credits of any amount." The president replied that the issue of a judicial challenge was "moot"—as it had been since his inauguration.[88]

The political lesson conveyed by the Carter administration seemed to be that if a president is to break a campaign promise, he should break it early yet restate it often. "I have not changed my position at all," Carter asserted at his August 17, 1978, news conference, two days after the defeat of the Moynihan-Packwood bill and before pledging to continue his search for "constitutionally acceptable" ways to aid nonpublic schools.[89]

Without a prominent advocate for nonpublic schools within the administration and with the firm allegiance of public school and civil rights interests, Carter was able to lead a united effort against tuition credits. In February 1978 the NEA, the United Auto Workers, and the National Parent-Teachers Association formed A Coalition to Save Public Education by defeating tuition credits. The National Association for the Advancement of Colored People (NAACP) and the Urban League soon joined this campaign in the name of public school desegregation. To preserve this fragile alliance, the administration tabled its major educational priority, a Cabinet-level department, an issue that would have divided the coalition.[90]

Friends and foes alike saluted the administration's persistence. Elizabeth Abramowitz of the domestic policy staff would remember that "we won on tuition tax credits" after spending "half of every day, which is a lot of time on any one thing," in September and October of 1978. AFT president Albert Shanker concluded that tuition credits had failed "only because of President Carter's active opposition." Moynihan wrote that "the largest remaining challenge is to persuade the President." Packwood called Carter the "overwhelming and decisive factor" in the defeat of his bill.[91]

A second reason for the defeat of Moynihan-Packwood was that the unity and perseverance of the opposition starkly contrasted with the division and uncertainty that plagued the tuition credit forces. While the Carter administration's presumption of the Moynihan-Packwood bill's unconstitutionality preceded the opinion of its legal counsel, the Catholic bishops' presumption of the bill's constitutionality defied the opinion of its legal counsel. After a *Washington Post* editorial against Moynihan-Packwood conceded that "what the Supreme Court might finally say about a tax credit for tuition is impossible to guess with any certainty," Moynihan wrote in March 1978, as if in wonderment, "Our bill may in fact be constitutional!"[92]

The strategy of attaching elementary and secondary school credits to the more popular college credits could not prevent twenty-eight senators from voting for the latter but against the former in August 1978. So when the conference committee reported a college-only bill in October, the bishops found themselves awkwardly allied with the president against the measure. Such legal and political rifts over tuition credits not only contributed to the death of Moynihan-Packwood but helped forestall its resurrection. Noting the split in the nonpublic school aid community between advocates of tuition credits and supporters of educational vouchers, Bishop Hughes wrote in March 1980 that "the easiest way to defeat any substantive aid [to nonpublic schools] is to keep our supporters divided, and our opponents are quite familiar with this tactic."[93]

Even if the tuition credit forces had united, they may have fallen short, because at times their hearts did not seem to be in the fight. After three conversations with Louisiana Democratic senator Russell Long, chairman of the Senate Finance Committee, Archbishop Philip Hannan of New Orleans reported on September 28 that Long was "under pressure from Senators to fight for the Senate position [college credits only] in the conference on tax credits." So although Long assured Hannan that he would vote for elementary and secondary school credits, he added that he would not "fight" for them.[94]

The bishops revealed a distaste for politics in general and for Republican politics in particular. In March 1978, Moynihan observed "how audible the silence of the [Catholic] hierarchy has been at the White House," and he deplored the "image of defeatism" surrounding the campaign for his legislation. Two months later, the senator lamented that "the President has not met with any leaders of the Church" on tuition credits. Yet the USCC kept postponing such a meeting to "avoid the appearance of conflict" with the president. When the meeting finally occurred in November 1978, it came *after* the defeat of Moynihan-Packwood.[95]

Because there were far more Catholic Democrats than Catholic Republicans, and since the bishops tended to be liberal on most social issues, the USCC appeared uncomfortable siding with so many conservative members of the Republican Party. In April 1978, Chester Finn of Moynihan's staff chided the USCC's Robinson for aligning himself with "right-wing Protestant Republicans" in the tuition credit effort. Robinson replied that "it was none of his [Finn's] nor the Senator's business as to which Protestant I decided to work with." In January 1979 the USCC's Russell Shaw warned the bishops not to "allow themselves to be co-opted by the Republicans." In her 1979 book *Catholics and American Politics*, Mary Hanna concluded that the USCC had remarkably little influence on Catholic congresspersons. Wisconsin Democratic representative Rev. Robert Cornell, one of two Catholic priests in the Ninety-fourth and Ninety-fifth Congresses (Massachusetts Democratic representative Rev. Robert Drinan was the other), would recall no contact with the USCC during his two terms.[96]

In a letter to the bishops, Moynihan ascribed the defeat of tuition credits in large part to anti-Catholicism, which he called "one form of bigotry which liberalism curiously seems to tolerate." Yet twenty-three Catholic representatives and five Catholic senators voted against tuition credits. When Moynihan contended on the Senate floor that without tuition credits many nonpublic schools "could very easily go out of operation entirely," Catholic Democrat Edmund Muskie of Maine, whose children had attended parochial schools, replied, "I doubt that it is that simple." Another Catholic member of the Ninety-fifth Con-

gress recalled that he supported tuition credits "on a tax basis, not religious. . . .
Maybe all that means is that I'm not a good Catholic."[97]

Not all Catholics were loyal to their schools. According to a November 1981
*U.S. Catholic* survey, only half of the country's Catholics disagreed with the
statement, "A good CCD [religious education] program with a public school
education produces just as many good Catholics as the Catholic schools produce." And over half disagreed with the assertion that "Catholic parents have a
religious obligation to send their kids to Catholic schools, even at a substantial
financial sacrifice."[98]

Evangelical Protestants, whose schools had tripled in number in the 1970s,
were as vulnerable to religious innuendo as Catholics. "I'm a Thirty-Third
Degree Mason," one senator told Packwood, "and I'm opposed to giving aid to
Catholic schools." But another said, "I'm opposed to giving aid to those damn
holy rollers," whom Packwood identified as "fundamentalist Protestant
schools." As John Swomley wrote in *Christian Century* in May 1978, Moynihan
seemed to want things both ways: arguing for his bill as a benefit to Lutherans,
Seventh-day Adventists, and Southern Baptists as well as Catholics, then casti-
gating opponents of the legislation as "anti-Catholic."[99]

In the end, support for elementary and secondary nonpublic school tuition
tax credits proved to be broad but not deep. The impact of religious prejudice
on the issue was deep but not broad. Most importantly, the president who
promised to find new constitutional ways to aid nonpublic school children
never really looked.

As in other areas of Jimmy Carter's presidency, his public school aid, school
desegregation, and nonpublic school aid policies offered conflicting signals. He
kept his promises to restore a federal Department of Education and increase
public school aid, broke his promise to seek greater nonpublic school aid, and
opposed and supported mandatory busing at the same time. If Carter knew
where he wanted to take the country in the era of education, he was not very
good at letting the country in on his plans.

# CHAPTER 4

# Public School Aid
## 1981–2001

## Ronald Reagan

> Public education is vital to the security and prosperity of our nation. . . . If we are to remain competitive as well as secure, we had better have educated, technically competent citizens in the coming years.
> —Ronald Reagan (1984)

History will remember Ronald Reagan as a pivotal figure.[1] In foreign and domestic policy, he dared to say what many Americans had long been thinking: that the Soviet Union was an "evil empire," and the federal welfare state had bred a dangerous dependency. In elementary and secondary education policy, he tapped the frustrations of many Americans that children seemed to be learning less even as their parents were paying more.

But history follows no script. So the former actor's deeds could be as unpredictable as his words were consistent. The president who liberally escalated defense expenditures radically reduced nuclear weapons. The president who helped cut taxes helped increase deficits. And the president who insisted that education was a state and local issue helped ensure that it would remain a national one.

"Whether he intended it or not," National Education Association (NEA) president Mary Hatwood Futrell (1983–89) would remember, "President Reagan elevated education. We had never had that kind of visibility." Ronald Reagan had not intended it. As a presidential candidate in 1980, he promised to abolish the Department of Education and to reduce federal spending on elementary and secondary public schools, but otherwise he had little to say about education. As president, he would institutionalize the Department of Education, increase federal spending on elementary and secondary public schools, and otherwise have a lot to say about education. The transformation of Ronald Reagan's elementary and secondary education policies owes much to the president's political acumen, ideological fervor, and oratorical brilliance. The transformation of the country's elementary and secondary education dialogue owes much to Ronald Reagan.[2]

## Reagan and Education

After attending four schools in four years as his father, a traveling salesman, traversed the country, Ronald Reagan settled in Dixon, Illinois, for four years of high school. When he enrolled at nearby Eureka College, a Christian Church liberal arts school, Reagan became one of only 8 percent of his high school graduating class to pursue higher education. As Hollywood actor turned California governor from 1967 to 1975, Reagan increased education spending to serve larger school populations (as mandated by state law) by transferring much of the financing from property taxes to income taxes.[3]

## The Education Department

At his first press conference on January 29, 1981, President Reagan asserted that he had "not retreated from" his campaign pledges to abolish the infant Departments of Education and Energy: "I have asked . . . Secretary [Terrel] Bell of Education and Secretary Jim Edwards of Energy to reorganize to produce the most effective streamlining . . . of their departments that they can." He added that Bell's principal mission was to "look at the appropriate role of the federal government in education—if there is one."[4]

The administration then followed two tracks: publicly advocating the abolition of the Department of Education while privately seeking to define the proper federal role in education. After Budget Director David Stockman announced that legislation to dismantle the department would reach Congress by October, Director of Cabinet Administration Craig Fuller lamented that "it is most difficult to determine whether or not there should be a Department of Education as an administrative agency until there is a consensus of what the role of the federal government should be." As Reagan's September 24 budget speech reiterated his determination to end the department's "intrusion . . . into an education system that had traditionally drawn its strength from diversity, adaptability, and local control," Bell battled "movement conservatives" within the administration who "wanted to cut every dime of federal expenditures for education."[5]

The administration considered three alternatives to the department. For those whom Bell called "movement conservatives," the first approach, restoring the Department of Health, Education, and Welfare (HEW), offered the advantages of reducing the visibility of education and the influence of education interests at the federal level. The disadvantages were potential increases in bureaucracy and regulation coupled with decreases in the efficiency and competence of administration and administrators. A second option, distribution of the department's functions throughout several federal agencies, was attractive to "movement conservatives" because it diminished the federal presence in education but was unattractive because it enlarged other federal agencies. The third proposal, replacing the department with a subcabinet foundation engaged in assisting rather than controlling education, embodied the pragmatic virtue but the ideological vice of eliminating the department while maintaining a substantial federal educational role.[6]

Division over these three options within the White House ensured that no legislation abolishing the department would reach Congress in 1981. White House aide Robert Carleson argued for returning the department to HEW, White House counselor Edwin Meese and domestic policy advisor Martin Anderson favored dispersing the department's functions, and Bell preferred a foundation that would "give financial support and do studies" but not "regulate and run things."[7]

In his 1982 budget Reagan sided with his Education secretary. The proposed Foundation for Educational Assistance would transfer twenty-three programs to other departments while eliminating twenty-three programs and eleven boards or commissions. The foundation would retain all of the major responsibilities of the department except civil rights, which would move to the Justice Department.[8]

Having agreed upon an alternative to the Department of Education, the administration undertook to sell the Foundation for Educational Assistance on Capitol Hill. Bell urged Republican senators William Roth of Delaware, chairman of the Government Operations Committee, and Howard Baker of Tennessee, majority leader, to cosponsor the legislation. But Roth, a self-proclaimed "fiscal conservative," told Bell that he nonetheless believed "there was an important federal role in education" that justified its cabinet-level status. Baker's fervent defense of the department's "effective leadership for education on the federal level" in a meeting with Reagan prompted the president to tell the secretary that he had "never seen Baker so stubborn on any issue." After visiting "virtually every member of the U.S. Senate on both sides of the aisle," Bell counted nineteen in favor and eighty-one opposed to the foundation concept. Carleson concluded that "our proposal for a foundation does not appear to have any realistic prospect of political success." So in 1982 the administration abandoned its legislative effort to abolish the department, in 1984 the Republican Party platform was silent on the issue, and Reagan broke one of his most memorable campaign promises.[9]

## *The Education Budget*

In the 1980 presidential campaign, candidate Ronald Reagan had argued not only that federal spending on elementary and secondary education had failed to make the nation's public schools better but had even made them worse. So he vowed to return control of public education, and the funds to finance it, to states and local communities.[10]

In his first term, President Ronald Reagan proposed a dual strategy to achieve these objectives. First, he sought to reduce federal education expenditures. His FY 1982 budget reduced the rate of increase by $4.4 billion, while his FY 1983 budget proposed a $2.1 billion reduction. Reagan's assault on the federal education budget prompted the *National Journal*'s Rachelle Stanfield to accuse him of killing the Department of Education by starvation and Massachusetts Democratic senator Edward Kennedy to assail his "scorched-earth policy" against the nation's public schools. Education commissioners Francis Keppel of the Kennedy administration, Harold Howe of the Johnson administration, and Sidney Marland of the Nixon administration rejected Reagan's "constant refrain that Federal programs haven't worked and that money spent on them is wasted."[11]

The most politically vulnerable budget proposals advanced by the administration were its reductions in the school lunch program. On March 27, 1981, conservative Republican Jesse Helms of North Carolina, chairman of the Senate Agriculture Committee, led a successful effort to restore $200 million to the program. On September 25 Reagan retreated from an Agriculture Department plan to help meet stricter budget guidelines through weakened nutrition requirements that would have, among other things, counted ketchup and pickle relish as vegetables.[12]

Reagan's fiscal strategy achieved mixed results. While each of his first three education budgets was leaner than the previous year's, they were also smaller than those subsequently enacted by Congress. While federal education spending would decrease as a percentage of overall education expenditures from 8.7 percent in Jimmy Carter's last year to 6.2 percent in Reagan's final year, total education spending at all levels would increase from $218 to $308 billion. Whereas federal outlays for education declined as a percentage of gross national product from 0.6 percent to 0.4 percent over Reagan's eight years, they grew in absolute numbers from $13.9 billion to $21.7 billion. And Reagan's three years of proposed reductions preceded five years of proposed additions. *A Nation at Risk,* the celebrated 1983 report by the National Commission on Excellence in Education (NCEE), helped assure an election-year FY 1985 budget from which there would be no turning back. "He gave his usual exhortation to cut back—the more the better," Bell would write of "formidable opponent" Stockman in preparing that budget. "But then he added . . . 'except for the sensitive area of education.'"[13]

The other major component of Reagan's budget plan was to streamline the federal role through education block grants. On April 29, 1981, Bell unveiled the administration's proposal to combine forty-four federal school aid programs into two block grants to the states. This "dramatic step toward restoring education to the people," the secretary explained, would virtually eliminate Title I of the Elementary and Secondary Education Act (ESEA), the Education for All Handicapped Children Act, and other legislation. Instead, states and localities would be free to target federal monies virtually as they wished.[14]

The ensuing legislative campaign for block grants largely became a philosophical and legislative confrontation between Reagan and Democrat Carl Perkins of Kentucky, chairman of the House Education and Labor Committee and "father" of Title I. According to committee counsel Jack Jennings, Perkins would hold "hundreds of hearings involving close to a thousand witnesses, [offer] amendments on the House floor, and [employ] every possible maneuver . . . to blunt the effects of the President's proposals." Since the highly regarded National Assessment of Educational Progress (NAEP) had never evaluated Title I, each side relied on more controversial sources to support its position. Perkins could cite a 1977 report by the Carter administration's National Institute of Education (NIE), which concluded that in a seven-month period, first-graders served by Title I achieved average gains of thirteen months in reading and fourteen months in mathematics, third-graders served by Title I gained seven months in reading and fourteen months in math, and disadvantaged students not served by Title I averaged seven-month gains over a ten-month school year. But Reagan could choose a 1981 study by William Cooley, former president of the American Educational Research Association, contending that Title I was not meeting expectations. Of the NIE report Cooley concluded, "Unfortunately, the evaluation did not help. Instead of looking for ways to improve the education of children who are somehow disadvantaged, they tended to look for evidence to justify the continuation (or discontinuation!) of a federal funding program."[15]

The passage of the Education and Consolidation Act of 1981, which created two block grants, was a victory for both sides. Perkins helped keep Title I largely intact as Chapter One of the new law. Reagan won consolidation of twenty-eight other categorical school aid programs into Chapter Two. Yet despite the controversy over the effectiveness of Title I, the measure contained no provision for its evaluation.[16]

## The Education Reforms

Terrel Bell arrived in Washington from his professorship at the University of Utah with only enough furniture as he would need for the year he expected his job to last. But by the time he resigned four years later, *U.S. News and World Report* had rated him the fifth most effective cabinet member (trailing only the secretaries of the Treasury, Transportation, Defense, and State Departments), and his formerly disposable department had became indispensable. The major reason was *A Nation at Risk.*[17]

On July 6, 1981, Bell wrote to Craig Fuller lamenting the "nationwide problem of declining college entrance scores and the overall lack of commitment to high standards of achievement in education." Bell therefore proposed to establish the NCEE to "call attention to an alarmingly persistent decline in the quality of education and to try to rally the entire academic community of the nation to reverse this trend." But Bell assured Fuller that the commission "will not in any way focus on or ask for 1) any increased federal expenditure or 2) an increased federal role in education." In fact, said the secretary, "The success of this endeavor will not require the continued existence of the Department of Education, and the plans for dismantling the Department will go forward."[18]

On August 26, 1981, Bell announced the formation of the eighteen-member commission, representing government, business, and education and chaired by University of Utah president David Gardner. The secretary instructed the commissioners to "do whatever is needed to define the problems and barriers to attaining greater levels of excellence in American education" and to "report and offer practical recommendations for action to be taken by educators and others having a vital interest in American education and a capacity to influence it for the better."[19]

A year later a Department of Education background paper noted that past federal education efforts had focused on "Equal Employment Opportunity goals to compensate for past societal deficiencies and inequities in the nation's schools and colleges." It called upon the administration to "establish excellence as a national goal to a level coequal with the equal opportunity goal" and to "fully capitalize on what has been and what can be learned about more effective schooling, and non-intrusive and cost-effective uses of Federal resources to help states and localities improve."[20]

A November 1982 Department of Education issue paper asked, "How can the nation's math and science teaching be improved to assure adequate skills to meet economic and national defense needs?" It offered five potential answers as "perfectly consistent with overall Administration policy": Presidential Science and Math Teaching Awards for elementary and secondary school faculty, a Presidential Science Teaching Scholar training program for elementary and secondary school faculty, Presidential Young Investigator Awards for young college faculty, a NIE-developed math-science model program for elementary and secondary schools, and a double tax deduction for companies that contribute computers to secondary and postsecondary schools.[21]

In January 1983 Bell proposed that outstanding public school teachers—"master teachers"—receive higher salaries than other faculty. He argued that such "merit pay could serve to help in recruiting talented new teachers who would otherwise seek other kinds of jobs" and that it "will encourage all teachers to work harder and teach better." The secretary asserted that "not only will those who get the money benefit, but all the students will benefit when teachers do a better job."[22]

A March review of the Department of Education's 1983–84 budget proposals by Planning, Budget and Evaluation undersecretary Gary Bauer noted that the administrative proposal on bilingual education would "authorize a broader range of instructional approaches rather than mandating one teaching method for all localities." An April memorandum from Ann Weinheimer of the department's Quality and Equality of Education Division recommended that the administration support research, pilot tests, model programs, a national commission, and college student aid to encourage effective elementary and secondary school teaching.[23]

The climax of these prescriptions for education reform came on April 26, 1983, when Gardner and Vice Chair Yvonne Carson, immediate past president of the San Diego City School Board, released the report of the NCEE. Claiming that a "rising tide of mediocrity" in American education imperiled the nation, the report recited a litany of discouraging statistics:

> Internationally, American student achievement was never first or second: compared with other industrialized nations, American students were last seven times.
>
> The College Board's Scholastic Aptitude Tests demonstrate a virtually unbroken decline from 1963 to 1980.
>
> One-fifth of all public four-year colleges must accept every high school graduate within the state....
>
> Twenty-five percent of the credits earned by general track high school students are in physical and health education, work experience outside the school, remedial English and math, and courses such as training for adulthood and marriage.
>
> Nearly forty percent of seventeen-year-olds cannot draw inferences from reading; four-fifths cannot write a persuasive essay; two-thirds cannot solve math problems.
>
> Thirteen percent of all seventeen-year-olds are functionally illiterate.
>
> Teachers are drawn disproportionately from the bottom quarter of graduating high school and college students, and the teacher education curriculum is heavily weighted with "educational methods" study instead of academic subjects.

The Commission recommended

> Strengthening state and local high school graduation requirements for all students by requiring at a minimum five new basics. All high school graduates should complete: four years of English, three years of math, three years of science, three years of social studies, and one-half year of computer science.
>
> Raising admission standards for four-year colleges and universities; restoring the value of grades as indicators of academic achievement and the use of standardized tests at transition points, such as from high school to college and college to work; revised standards for textbooks, including challenging texts for gifted and talented and learning disabled.
>
> Strengthening the teaching profession by revising teacher personnel policies to allow for the rewarding of excellent teachers, the encouragement of average ones, and the improvement or dismissal of poor teachers; lengthening the work year for teachers to eleven months, and establishing positions that distinguish among beginning, experienced, and master teachers; making teacher salaries

competitive, market-sensitive, and performance-based; requiring teacher candidates to demonstrate aptitude, meet high educational standards, and prove competence in academic disciplines; remedying teacher shortages by drawing graduate students, recent math and science graduates, and other nonschool personnel into the classrooms; assigning far more homework to high school students; [and] establishing discipline codes.

While acknowledging that "state and local officials have the primary responsibility for financing and governing the schools," it urged the federal government to "help meet the needs of key groups of students, enforce civil and constitutional rights, sponsor research, collect and disseminate data and statistics, provide student financial aid, and exercise leadership in carrying out the reforms outlined in the report."[24]

The virtually universal acclaim that greeted the report surprised even Bell. NEA president Willard McGuire pronounced himself "excited about the ideas and recommendations of the National Commission on Excellence in Education." American Federation of Teachers (AFT) president Albert Shanker emerged from a meeting with Reagan in "ninety-eight percent" agreement with the president on the need for more rigorous courses, testing of teachers, and "different methods of compensation" for faculty. A bipartisan House task force chaired by Illinois Democrat Paul Simon, with Futrell and Shanker among its members, unanimously advocated local experimentation with merit pay. Four of five school superintendents and six of seven public school teachers backed merit pay. The public embraced the commission's call for a basic public school curriculum, more homework, and a national student examination, as education reemerged as the country's "most important" issue. Bell hailed the "unprecedented opportunity to attain some far-reaching reforms in American education" afforded by the report, adding, "Let's not allow this great potential to go by." And Reagan, after initially mischaracterizing the report as a justification for tuition tax credits, prayer in schools, and abolition of the Department of Education, would attend two of the twelve regional, and the only national, NCEE forums and would deliver fifty-one speeches on education in the eighteen months following *A Nation at Risk*.[25]

In June in Tennessee, Reagan saluted Republican governor Lamar Alexander's Master Teacher program, asserting that "if we want to achieve excellence, we must reward it." In Kentucky and Kansas, Reagan urged a return to the "basics" of education, noting that employers seek "more people with a solid background in reading, writing, calculating, and thinking—people practiced in the art of modern learning." In California, Reagan advocated a "grassroots campaign for educational renewal" to "restore parents and local government to their rightful role in the educational process." The *Washington Post* lauded "President Reagan's campaign for better schools" as a "genuine service."[26]

In January 1984 Reagan announced that the administration would promote school discipline by filing court briefs on behalf of aggrieved teachers and administrators as well as studying methods to combat school violence. In a March 1984 article in the AFT's *American Teacher* magazine, Bell proposed three priorities—"commitment to literacy," "mastery of basic mathematics," and "citizenship education"—for American education. He added four performance goals to measure the progress of these priorities by 1989: all high school graduates would have studied four years of English and three years of math, science, and social studies; SAT/ACT scores in every state would exceed the 1965 totals; dropout rates in every state would be below 10 percent; and entry-level teaching salaries would compete with entry-level business and engineering salaries in every state.[27]

In August 1984 Reagan announced that the first citizen-passenger on the space shuttle would be a teacher. In May 1986 Bell's successor, William Bennett, released *What Works,* an Education Department report that offered forty-one suggestions for teachers and parents to improve students' learning. The president appointed a task force to study merit pay, backed a math-science teacher training bill in Congress, and proposed a broadening of bilingual education guidelines to permit English as the primary language of instruction.[28]

## *The Reagan Record*

Early in his presidency, Ronald Reagan expressed his opposition to the United Nations' Law of the Sea treaty. Secretary of State Alexander Haig attempted to change his mind by noting that every recent president and virtually every leader of both parties supported the treaty. "Well yes, but that's what the last election was about," Reagan replied. "About the Law of the Sea treaty?" asked an incredulous Haig. "No," Reagan responded, "it was about not doing things just because that's the way they've been done before."[29]

In elementary and secondary education, Ronald Reagan, throughout his presidency and particularly before *A Nation at Risk,* in many ways simply did things "the way they've been done before." Like Johnson, Nixon, Ford, and Carter, Reagan too often reduced the education debate to dollars and cents. "The total budget for education in the United States is far greater than the defense budget," Reagan claimed in May 1983. Yet in June, Reagan conceded that total education spending was only $1 billion more than defense spending. In May, he observed that "most politicians had felt that 'more money' was the solution to the nation's education problems; well, they tried that approach and failed." But in July he demonstrated his "concern for education" by noting that as governor of California he had "increased aid to the primary and secondary school system 105 percent while enrollment increased five percent."[30]

Like Nixon and Ford, Reagan thus chose to fight the education interests—especially the NEA—on their terms. AFT legislative director Greg Humphrey wrote in February 1981 that "few would find it responsible to cut over $1.5 billion," as Reagan's block grant proposal would. In July 1982 McGuire told the NEA Convention, "We are in a war" to defend against "the unprecedented attack on public education" by Reagan spending cuts. In May 1983 NEA government relations director Linda Tarr-Whelan called for a doubling of federal monies to meet the needs identified by *A Nation at Risk,* and Humphrey hoped that the report would "stimulate Congress to give education its fair share." Shanker wrote that because teachers were not "encyclopedia salesmen," merit pay was a "bad idea." McGuire agreed: "All teachers are woefully underpaid, so you can't even talk about adding salary incentives until you have adequate pay for everyone."[31]

The antipathy was mutual. In March 1981 special assistant to the president Gregory Newell told NEA executive director Terry Herndon that Reagan was too busy to meet with him. In May 1983 Bell excluded the NEA Convention from a list of potential presidential speaking engagements because of a "potentially hostile audience." Later the same month, after an exchange of letters between Reagan and McGuire, White House press secretary Larry Speakes announced that the two presidents would meet. But on July 18 McGuire received word that Reagan would not meet him alone, so the next day McGuire boycotted a meeting of Reagan, Shanker, and other educators. In June 1983 Reagan told the National Congress of Parents and Teachers that "until it [the NEA] relaxes its opposition to badly needed reforms the country wants . . . the improvements we so desperately need could be delayed." In August, Craig Fuller wrote that "the NEA's push for more Federal funds is understandable because its local affiliates find it increasingly difficult to prove genuine need to their communities and state legislatures."[32]

Former Nixon and future Reagan aide Chester Finn concluded that by 1983, administration attitudes and practices had "unified the education community more solidly than anything since Nixon's vetoes of Congressional school-aid appropriations." Former AFT official Myron Lieberman wrote in 1986 that "it would be unrealistic to propose reforms of the auto industry that did not take into account the interests of the UAW [United Auto Workers, the largest union in the industry]. It is even more unrealistic to propose education reforms that ignore the NEA and the AFT." Bell added in 1988 that "I do disagree with Secretary Bennett when he blames the NEA and AFT for the shortcomings of school reform. The accomplishments . . . would not have been possible, had not hundreds of thousands of teachers who belong to the AFT or the NEA pitched in to help."[33]

As with Johnson, Nixon, Ford, and Carter, politics often governed policy during the Reagan administration. "Until his pollsters and political advisors informed him that, guess what, Mr. President, the American people care about the kind of schools their kids attend," wrote the *Washington Post*'s David Broder, "Reagan's contribution to the education debate had been nil." Finn was equally skeptical of his fellow Republican: "After two years of total silence on the subject of public education, he [Reagan] cannot help but look a bit like an opportunistic reader of public opinion polls." Denis Doyle, director of education policy studies at the conservative American Enterprise Institute, wrote, "The most anti-education President in our history has succeeded in making education an issue." And veteran education writer Fred Hechinger of the *New York Times* wondered a year after Reagan's reelection, "Has the school reform engine run out of steam?"[34]

There was indeed much evidence to fuel such cynicism. When Bell conceived the commission that Reagan would embrace two years later, Fuller urged him to call it the "Secretary's [rather than 'National'] Commission on Excellence in Education" to create distance from the president. In September 1982, Fuller encouraged Reagan to meet with the commissioners to help defuse the perception that the president is "anti-education" and to demonstrate "that this Administration is in fact responsive to education issues considered vital to the American people." Before Reagan met with Jaime Escalante, the first Math and Science Award winner, in a White House ceremony, assistant to the president for policy development Edwin Harper wrote, "An important reason for early Presidential announcement of the awards is [that] the Democrats' response to the State of the Union message attempts to take credit for positive policies in the high technology area." In November 1982 the Department of Education warned that the cost of a grant program for training math and science teachers "will undoubtedly grow in the future," while pollster Richard Wirthlin noted that "a slight majority" of the public would support such a plan. In 1984 Reagan sided with Wirthlin and heartened Bell, who praised the president's uncharacteristic willingness "to provide federal funds, even in an era of huge deficits, to meet an emerging crisis in education."[35]

In June 1983 Weinheimer wrote that "merit pay is not a new idea," noted that "schools have had difficulties developing appropriate standards," and called for "financial assistance to school districts for planning and implementation of a merit pay system." But the Office of Policy Development reported that "basics, merit pay, and competency rate high" in public opinion surveys and that 46 percent of the public approved of the president's education policies with only 29 percent opposed, numbers "reversed from a few weeks ago." So Reagan continued to press for merit pay—without federal funding.[36]

Polls also showed 80 percent support for a school prayer constitutional amendment in 1984 and identified discipline as the major educational concern for sixteen of the seventeen years before 1986, helping to spur administration initiatives in those areas. In 1985 Bennett cited "the Gallup Poll" in explaining the administration's devotion to "two fundamental goals for our schools: that they teach our children how to read, write, speak, and count, and then teach them English, history, science, and math; and that the schools help our children develop reliable standards of right and wrong." He admitted in 1988 that "there has been a shift. Republicans and conservatives have come to realize that the Federal role in education is here to stay. . . . They also realize that it is silly to concede the issue to the Democrats."[37]

As was the case during the Johnson, Nixon, Ford, and Carter administrations, Congress would largely dominate elementary and secondary education policy in the Reagan era. In May 1983 Anne Graham, assistant secretary of Education for legislation and public affairs, accurately warned of *A Nation at Risk* "being used in Congressional debate . . . as a call for further federal funds." With the complete Senate Labor and Human Resources Committee and all but one of the members of the House Education and Labor Committee returning after Reagan's landslide reelection, Alfred Sumberg of the losing Walter Mondale presidential campaign observed in January 1985 that "Congress has its own education agenda." Bell noted that he was able to "keep [conservative] ideologues at bay" within his department in 1983, "once the Office of Management and Budget [OMB] yielded to the unrelenting pressure from Capitol Hill to respect the laws and the mandates that accompanied appropriations." Mike Casserly, legislative associate for the Council of Great City Schools, observed in 1985 that the administration had "submitted a series of [education] proposals that are very unpopular on Capitol Hill, [and] Congress has repeatedly [refused] to go along with these."[38]

Not only did Congress annually appropriate more education funds than Reagan requested, but it preserved most of the "sacred cows" that the administration attempted to wound, if not kill. In 1983, after he joined a majority of his House colleagues in reversing administration budget reductions in education for the disadvantaged, education for the handicapped, and vocational education programs, New York Republican Barber Conable quipped that he had just voted for "motherhood." In 1984 Reagan reluctantly signed the Bilingual Education Act, which amended the ESEA to require that 75 percent of annual local school district appropriations support bilingual education programs stressing native-language instruction; two years later he signed HJ Res 738, which extended the appropriations. In 1988, despite new evidence that the benefits that children served by Chapter One gained in the early grades disappeared by the middle grades, Congress and Reagan added $500 million to Chapter One and $2 billion, including a math-science instruction training grant, to overall education spending in the Hawkins-Stafford amendments of 1988. So by the end of the Reagan presidency the federal role in elementary and secondary education looked, as House Education and Labor Committee counsel Jennings saw it in the middle of the era, "very much like it did under Presidents Johnson, Nixon, Ford, and Carter."[39]

Like his three immediate predecessors, the "Great Communicator" never communicated a coherent philosophy to guide his elementary and secondary education policies. "Because of the high visibility of the education issue nationally and the obvious decision by the Democrats to make this a campaign issue," wrote

White House staffer Robert Sweet in May 1983, "it is important that the Administration coordinate its efforts and develop an overall strategy toward which each office works." In June, aide James Coyne observed that the question "What is the appropriate role of the federal government in education?" had "consistently followed the President in his trips to highlight the issue of excellence in education." But Sweet's suggestion that Reagan deliver a nationally televised speech on education fell on deaf ears. "The Administration deserves credit for trying to lift the level of public debate and concern," said "Education Governor" Bill Clinton, an Arkansas Democrat, in December 1988, "but there hasn't been any real leadership." Bell admitted that "the Administration's policy regarding education never was clarified through the development of a written policy."[40]

Yet the Reagan era was not simply more of the same in primary and secondary education policy. "Five years ago education seemed to be the liberals' issue," said Bennett in 1985. "Debate was focused on spending. . . . This has now changed. President Reagan has transformed the nation's education agenda. He has seized the issue and focused the debate on . . . standards, excellence, discipline, values, parental involvement, and choice." If price tags too often preceded prescriptions in private administration analyses and public administration statements, at least the prescriptions were prominent and, in many ways, productive. In February 1987 Bennett announced that SAT and ACT scores were on the rise in thirty-nine of the fifty states in 1984–85. The Department of Education's 1988 report *Making It Work* noted that since 1980, twenty-seven states had passed stricter admission requirements for teacher education programs, thirty-four had added minimum competency exams for new teachers, and twelve had established merit pay systems. The percentage of high school graduates taking a "minimal" academic program of four years of English, three years of social studies, and three years of science had increased from 13.4 percent in 1982 to 29.5 percent in 1987. While Bennett conceded the report's conclusion that "we are still at risk," he claimed that "the precipitous downward slide of previous decades has been arrested. . . . We are doing better than we were in 1983."[41]

The report's findings that from 1981 to 1986 per capita state spending for elementary and secondary education increased nationally by over 40 percent, that teachers' salaries climbed almost 21 percent, and that education became the largest budget item in all but two states belied the administration nostrum that "performance has gone down while dollars have gone up." But their inclusion signified progress in education rhetoric and reality. The *Washington Post* editorialized on the eve of the report's release that the five years since *A Nation at Risk* had seen "the longest sustained wave of school reform in recent memory. The first surge of energy went to raising standards—for teacher hiring, for high school graduation and promotion, for general accountability—and to mustering wide support." The *Post,* no friend of the Reagan administration, concluded of school reform, "It happened."[42]

It happened, ultimately, with the AFT and NEA aboard. Perhaps the most con-
spicuous shift in the education debate was the teachers' unions moving from
offense to defense, from feckless confrontation to guarded collaboration. The
Reagan era began with the AFT, the NEA, and the administration agreeing on very
little except that a Department of Education under Reagan might be worse than
no department at all. Linda Chavez was editor of the AFT's *American Teacher*
magazine, Mary Hatwood Futrell was the NEA's secretary-treasurer, and both
groups largely feared school reform. The era ended with all sides wedded to the
Department of Education; Chavez working for a president "sincerely" committed
to education; Futrell saluting that president for "elevating the conversation to
common standards, goals, and curriculum"; the AFT supporting a National
Teacher Examination; and the NEA not completely opposing merit pay.[43]

While politics played a substantial role in Reagan's attraction to the education
issue, he was not simply following the polls. Not only did unpopular budget
reductions, the authorization of the NCEE, and concepts such as "excellence,"
"math and science instruction," and "master teacher" precede *A Nation at Risk*
in private and public administration policies, but some distinctly apolitical
decisions by the president followed the report. Reagan advocated the NCEE call
for a longer school day and year, despite public opposition. His school discipline
initiatives arrived at a time when the issue was receding in the public mind. He
continued to resist the temptation to propose massive increases in federal education expenditures and taxes to pay for them. He failed to "go the extra mile" in
lobbying for the overwhelmingly popular school prayer amendment, which lost
in the Senate in the 1984 election year.[44]

If Congress ultimately determined how much money the federal government
would spend on public elementary and secondary education, the administration had a large say in how well the federal government would spend it. A 1983
General Accounting Office study recorded local officials' satisfaction with the
Reagan block grants. The 1988 Hawkins-Stafford amendments specified that 25
percent of bilingual education monies would fund "alternative instruction"
strategies, including English as a second language. The same law included the
unprecedented provision for NAEP direct evaluation of Chapter One.[45]

While Bell and others correctly faulted the administration for lacking a comprehensive strategy, the secretary did identify six major goals of the Reagan elementary and secondary education policy:

First, the President wanted to reduce substantially federal spending for education;
Second, he wanted to strengthen local and state control of education and to
reduce dramatically the federal responsibility in this area;
Third, the President wanted to maintain a limited federal role that would
build and enhance the capacity of the states to carry out their traditional
responsibilities;

Fourth, the President wanted to encourage the establishment of laws and rules that would offer greatly expanded parental choice and that would increase competition for students. . . .

Fifth, President Reagan wanted to encourage a substantial reduction in federal judicial activity in education; [and]

Finally, the President wanted to abolish the U.S. Department of Education.

Although Ronald Reagan achieved none of these objectives in the manner in which he had hoped in January 1981, he helped transform the education debate. For even though he failed in proving that public elementary and secondary education was not properly federal, he succeeded in proving, through his eloquence and energy, that it was properly national—in a way that it had not been for two decades.[46]

## George Bush

> Education is our most enduring legacy, . . . nothing less than the very heart of our civilization.
> —George Bush (1989)

At first glance, George Bush's four years in the White House from 1989 to 1993 looked very much like his four years in the House of Representatives from 1967 to 1971.[47] Foreign policy, dominated by an undeclared war, overshadowed domestic affairs. The Democratic Party controlled both houses of Congress. The president signed an unpopular tax increase. The ESEA withstood all challenges. And poverty amidst plenty defied all solutions.

But there were important differences. Ronald Reagan had seen to that. Yes, one-third of the nation's school population was still an undereducated underclass, but in Chester Finn's words, they had become "crisis two" for the newest self-proclaimed "Education President." The other two-thirds, underachieving middle- and upper-class children, were now "crisis one."[48]

If poverty ended all arguments over education in the 1960s, "competitiveness" began such debates in the 1990s. For if General Motors was to compete with Toyota, then Jennifer must compete with Kyoko. "The most important competitiveness program in the world," said President George Bush in his first address to Congress, "is one which improves education in America."[49]

And if education was to improve in the United States, the president must lead the way. Without federal control, of course. With the states and localities, certainly. With the teacher unions, hopefully. But with or without Congress. Although he "went out of his way to give the impression that he wanted a more civilized and less confrontational relationship with Congress," writes David Mervin, Bush was largely a "guardian in the White House" on domestic policy, "not attempting to advance any large programme of reform."[50]

If he did not try hard enough to advance reform, Bush nonetheless adopted it in his public elementary and secondary education politics and policies. In the end, however, Bush was the victim of the very movement he championed. For while he could justifiably blame the public education interests and their congressional allies for blocking many of his proposals, good intentions were no longer enough to win public approval in the federal aid to education wars. What really mattered, said the reformer in the White House, were outcomes.

## Bush and Education

George Herbert Walker Bush's formal education was that of a child of New England's elite. He attended Greenwich (Connecticut) Country Day School from the first through the ninth grades, Andover preparatory school from the tenth through the twelfth grades, and Yale University. In his two terms as a Texas congressman from 1967 to 1971, he did not show inordinate interest in education issues.

## The Education Excellence Act of 1989

"I wanted you to know that I meant it," the president-elect told a group of educators in the first event of the 1989 inaugural program. "Education will be on my desk and on my mind right from the start every day." As if to prove his point, Bush prominently included education in the list of goals that he presented to Congress a month later. Four principles—"excellence," "choice," "accountability," and "need"—would underscore Bush's school initiatives. In April, in his Educational Excellence Act of 1989, he added the specifics—"merit" schools, "magnet" schools, a federal assessment of accountability, and continued federal funding of programs for the disadvantaged, such as Chapter One of the ESEA.[51]

The public education interests demanded more money. "If we are calling for improved performance," NEA president Mary Hatwood Futrell responded, "then we are going to have to accept the responsibility of identifying the fiscal and physical resources to turn things around." Ernest Boyer, president of the Carnegie Foundation for the Advancement of Teaching, advocated a $12 billion "Marshall Plan" for education. Jonathan Wilson, chair of the Council of Urban Boards of Education, and James Oglesby, president of the National School Boards Association, advised Bush to "work with Congress for an increase of ten percent above inflation in the education budget—in addition to any new programs."[52]

But the administration displayed little enthusiasm for spending a lot of money or working with Congress. In February 1990, after two days of fierce debate over Title X (the financing of the National Board for Professional Teaching Standards), the Senate voted 92–8 in favor of a $414 million version of the $423 million Bush bill. Encouraged by more than twenty-five hundred telephone calls to the White House by private school and home school advocates, the administration had supported amendments by North Carolina Republican Jesse Helms to delete the offensive title and by Kansas Republican Nancy Kassebaum to amend it. When these efforts failed, Roger Porter wrote to Bush that the Senate measure "may well require a veto signal."[53]

In July, the House voted 350–25 for a $1.1 billion hybrid of the Bush bill and a Democratic alternative sponsored by Augustus Hawkins of California, chairman of the House Committee on Education and Labor. Three months later, as a conference committee prepared to reconcile the Senate and House measures, Education Secretary Lauro Cavazos transmitted the veto signal. "The House bill, especially, is a disappointment: a complex, unwieldy array of new programs, most of which are not needed, and undesirable amendments to current program statutes." At the urging of House bill cosponsor William Goodling, however, Porter finally joined the negotiations on October 18. When a compromise emerged from conference, the House approved it by voice vote, but Helms and other conservative Republicans helped prevent it from coming to the Senate floor before adjournment.[54]

## *The Education Summit of 1989*

Six months into the new administration, with the public disinterested and the Congress disenchanted, the Education Presidency looked to be over almost before it had begun. But the president and his associates acted to salvage it. Richard Thornburgh, chairman pro tempore of the Domestic Policy Council, organized a working group to "provide a forum to formulate and coordinate education policy." Bush urged the Business Roundtable, a seventeen-year-old association of the chief executive officers of two hundred large corporations, to join him in a "national crusade for excellence in education."[55]

And the president invited Terry Sanford to the White House. Sanford, a moderate Democratic senator from North Carolina, had distinguished himself on education issues as a governor and as president of Duke University. Assuring Bush that "there is not much that can be done, or should be done, by creating additional federal programs," Sanford mapped a six-pronged strategy for presidential leadership in education. First, he recommended that Bush appoint a "White House Board of Education," a bipartisan group of educators to advise the White House on school policy. Second, he urged Bush to become "Honorary Chairman" of the Education Commission of the States. Third, from this position, Bush could deliver an annual "Education Address" to chart educational progress and "stir up the troops." Fourth, the president could create Presidential Education Awards. Fifth, he could sponsor a White House conference on teaching. Sixth, he could establish a "Vocational and Technical Education Day." Sanford added that "the process of how a President becomes an Education President has probably not seriously been considered by previous Presidents. It is easier to become an Education Governor . . . because education is primarily a state and local function."[56]

So Bush would try being an Education Governor. On July 31 Bush told the annual meeting of the National Governors Association that he would hold an education "summit" with the governors in September. "He's trying to do the right thing," applauded Democratic governor Richard Celeste of Ohio. "He's light years better informed on the issues than his predecessor," cheered Democratic governor George Sinner of North Dakota. Bush is "moving closer and closer to the Democrats" in his concern for education, added Democratic governor Mario Cuomo of New York.[57]

But not too close. A week before the summit, a group of congressional Democrats presented their own education agenda: full funding of Head Start by 1995, federal efforts to improve minority student performance on standardized tests, and raising of enrollment and financial aid for minority college students.[58]

Nothing could upstage the summit, however. Bush told a group of NEA representatives on the eve of the conference, "That will be only the third time in history that a President has called together the Nation's governors to discuss a single issue." The summit, held outside of Washington in Charlottesville, Virginia, to emphasize state and local control of education, nonetheless produced a set of national goals related to "the readiness of children to start school; the performance of students on international achievement tests, especially in math and science; the reduction of the dropout rate and improvement of academic performance, especially among at-risk students; the functional literacy of adult Americans; the level of training necessary to guarantee a competitive work force; the supply of qualified teachers and up-to-date technology; and the establishment of safe, disciplined, and drug-free schools." The president and the governors called for educational "restructuring," defined as "find[ing] ways to deploy the resources we commit to education more effectively," and "accountability," to be ensured by "annual report cards on the progress of students, schools, the states, and the Federal Government." The federal role in education, they concluded, is "limited . . . yet still important" to "promote national education equity" and "to provide research and development."[59]

The response to the summit was overwhelmingly positive. Bush called it "historic," explaining that "we have never before worked together—President and principal, governor and teacher—to achieve results in education." Arkansas Democratic governor Bill Clinton agreed: "This is the first time in history that we have ever thought enough of education and ever understood its significance to our economic future enough to commit ourselves to national performance goals." The AFT claimed that the organization "definitely shared the limelight" at a summit to which it was not invited, noting that Shanker had coined the term "restructuring" two years earlier. Bush appointed Shanker and the NEA's Keith Geiger to his Education Policy Advisory Committee. The only discordant note from the summit came from drug czar and former Education secretary William Bennett, whose characterization of the proceedings as "standard

Democratic pap, . . . standard Republican pap, . . . and stuff that rhymes with pap" earned him a trip to the White House woodshed.[60]

The general goals outlined at the summit grew more specific in Bush's first State of the Union address in January 1990. Based on consultations with Democratic governors Clinton of Arkansas and Booth Gardner of Washington as well as Republican governors Terry Branstad of Iowa and Carroll Campbell of South Carolina, the president announced six education goals: "By the year 2000, every child must start school ready to learn; the United States must increase the high school graduation rate to no less than ninety-percent; at the 4th, 8th, and 12th grades, we must assess our students' performance; by the year 2000 U.S. students must be first in the world in math and science achievement; every American adult must be a skilled, literate worker and citizen; [and] every school must offer [a] disciplined environment and . . . must be drug-free."[61]

Then the virtual unanimity of agreement that followed Charlottesville gave way to dissension. The *Washington Post*'s David Broder, who had applauded the setting of national goals, now wondered "whether anything will be done to achieve them." The *Boston Globe*'s Anthony Flint wrote that "educators in Massachusetts and across the nation . . . criticized President Bush for not backing up far-reaching education goals in his State of the Union address with a clear strategy or increased federal funding." The AFT's Shanker discovered "a yawning gap between the rhetoric of President Bush's education speeches and the funding levels he offers in his budget." Governor Clinton called the most ambitious goal—that U.S. students lead the world in math and science achievement in ten years—neither "achievable" nor "valuable." Chester Finn concurred with Clinton, noting that to reach the math-science objective, "Lightning would have to strike." Of the 70 percent of Americans who supported national education goals, only 5 percent wanted the president to define them. Two-thirds of Americans believed that Bush had "mainly just talked" about education. Christopher Cross, assistant secretary of Education for research and improvement, conceded that he could find no example of a school district that had raised its graduation rate twenty points.[62]

There was much evidence to justify such skepticism. In January 1990 the NAEP released its report, mandated by the Hawkins-Stafford Act of 1988. The report showed that "reading and writing skills of American children improved only slightly during the late 1980's, despite the education reforms instituted by states and school districts." Another study, by the liberal Economic Policy Institute (EPI), claimed that the United States spent "relatively less on elementary and secondary education than do thirteen other industrial countries." A third report by the Carnegie Corporation concluded that because "most minority children are in schools that are separate and decidedly unequal," teachers in such institutions required "financial incentives."[63]

The administration accepted the NAEP findings, which according to Cavazos, showed that "there has been very little education progress in the United

States" since *A Nation at Risk,* the ballyhooed report by President Reagan's NCEE in 1983. But it challenged the EPI assumption that percent of national income was the best way to judge education spending, noting that Minnesota spent a smaller percentage, but a greater sum, of its income on education than did Mississippi. A better index of school expenditures, the Department of Education argued, would be spending per pupil, in which the United States was second only to Switzerland among the nations in the EPI study. As for the Carnegie report, Porter contended that the lack of progress in minority schools came despite a 30 percent rise in national education spending (after inflation) in the 1980s.[64]

Perhaps Senator Sanford's "White House Board of Education" could settle the controversy over the costs and benefits of national education policy. On July 31, 1990, Bush and the governors established the National Education Goals Panel proposed at the summit. It would consist of six governors (three from each party), four administration appointees, four ex officio congressional representatives (House Speaker and minority leaders, Senate majority and minority leaders) and a chairman appointed annually by the chairman of the National Governors Association. The panel would issue annual report cards on the progress of the education goals. To assuage Democrats who feared that the report cards would become administration press releases, a three-fourths vote would be necessary to reach any conclusion. To appease governors from education-poor states, the report cards would compare states not with each other but with their prior performances. And over the objections of Democratic Speaker of the House Thomas Foley of Washington and Democratic majority leader George Mitchell of Maine, no educators would serve on the panel.[65]

The panel moved slowly to fulfill its mandate. Porter reminded White House chief of staff John Sununu in December that the group's first report card was three months overdue: "Although there are encouraging reports that up to thirty-seven states have adopted the national goals, state goals, and/or are undertaking restructuring efforts," wrote Porter, "the governors have not yet issued a report as promised." When a preliminary assessment finally came two months later, the panel appeared to question the mission itself: "The story was told of a rancher weighing his sheep for market. The man comes to one sheep that does not weigh enough and puts it aside. After awhile he puts it back on the scale and is surprised that it weighs the same." The moral of the story, the report concluded, was that "weighing alone is not enough; we also need to feed the sheep."[66]

The administration predictably viewed things differently. When a *Washington Post* editorial echoed the panel's plea for more money, Kolb dismissed "the tired old theme." But Porter uncovered a silver lining: "One criticism repeatedly made of the panel is that elected officials will be anxious to show progress and not likely to present an objective picture of whether the Nation is on track in achieving its goals." The panelists may not be saying what the White House wants to hear, Porter noted, but at least they're not, well, a flock of sheep.[67]

## America 2000

The midpoint of any administration is a good time for taking stock of its pluses and minuses, and the first half of the Education Presidency received mixed reviews. "There is the perception that you care about education," Porter assured Bush in March 1991, citing the sixty-seven education-related events that Bush had attended. "But we need to do more," added the president. "There is a perception that we have talked more than we have done . . . coupled with the belief that we are opposed to spending more money on education," Porter conceded. The president had no comment.[68]

If the reviews for the president were mixed, the responses to his Education secretary were not. The Right accused him of being a tool of the teacher unions; the teacher unions wanted little to do with him. Appointed by Ronald Reagan in a gesture toward Hispanic voters, the former president of Texas Tech University had begun his term advocating more federal spending on public schools and opposing nonpublic school vouchers but had ended it attacking the former and supporting the latter. Perhaps his greatest sin was poor timing—he followed charismatic, controversial William Bennett, who had helped raise the profile of the office as well as the issue. Though Porter and Kolb had long since appropriated much of Cavazos's portfolio, the end came abruptly, when the administration made public an internal investigation of the nature of his wife Peggy Ann Cavazos's position at the department. After a December 11, 1990, meeting with Sununu, Cavazos drafted a curt resignation letter lacking the customary words of gratitude to the president for the opportunity to serve.[69]

If Cavazos exited amidst virtually universal disfavor, Lamar Alexander entered six days later to widespread acclaim. As Republican governor of Tennessee, Alexander had shepherded through a Democratic legislature an innovative merit pay scheme and a sales tax increase to help pay for it. "This nomination outshines any made in recent memory," cheered Chris Pipho, director of state relations for the Education Commission of the States. Only the NEA's Geiger among major education leaders withheld praise for the nomination, recalling that "we have not always seen eye to eye" on the issues, and preferring "someone with hands-on classroom experience" to the president of the University of Tennessee.[70]

The new secretary hit the ground running. On January 16, 1991, as U.S. warplanes dropped bombs on Baghdad, Alexander gathered his advisors in Tennessee to map the administration's new education strategy. "It was kind of surreal," Chester Finn, the former Moynihan and Bennett aide and now Alexander aide, said of the meeting that was in many ways a metaphor for the Bush legacy. "The substantive discussion of education was interspersed with tuning on CNN to watch the bombs fall."[71]

The blueprint that emerged from this meeting and the concurrent conference of the President's Education Policy Advisory Committee arrived on Bush's desk two months later. Dubbed "America 2000," the strategy comprised four major parts. The first was "creating better and more accountable schools for today's students" by allowing for nonpublic as well as public school choice, funding merit schools, rewarding math and science achievement, encouraging merit pay for teachers, and establishing national standards and voluntary national examinations for fourth-, eighth-, and twelfth-grade students to measure their performance against those standards in English, mathematics, science, history, and geography. The second was "creating a new generation of American schools for tomorrow's students" through establishment of a New American Schools Development Corporation, a research and development organization funded by private businesses; start-up federal funding for one "break-the-mold" New American School in each of the 535 congressional districts; and designation by the governors in their states of America 2000 communities that adopt, implement and measure the six goals of the 1989 summit, as well as prepare for a New American School. The third was "transforming America into a 'nation of students'" by enhancing "accountability and choice" in federal adult literacy programs and encouraging the establishment of "skill clinics" in businesses and communities to assist in job training and placement. The fourth was "making our communities places where learning will happen" by federal encouragement of parental involvement and program effectiveness in state and local education efforts.[72]

Alexander exhorted Bush to make a "significant contribution" to the strategy, defined as a prime-time, nationally televised speech, preceded by a day of briefings by the Bush cabinet and followed by two days of travel to education events. "Such an allocation of Presidential time is unusual," wrote the energetic new secretary, "but so is wanting to be the Education President. A priority must have priority time."[73]

The OMB found America 2000 too good to be true. Its analysis of the program complained that "the strategy does not make clear what various proposals will cost," warned that "reaching consensus" on national standards would be "difficult," noted that the "relationship to NAEP" of the proposed national examinations is "an important and undefined issue," added that the proposal to voucherize the popular Chapter One program "will generate unnecessary hostility," and asserted that the plan raises "philosophical issues" of a "federal curriculum."[74]

So the brochure accompanying the president's April 18 afternoon, untelevised address launching the initiative (the broadcast networks did not share Alexander's sense of proportion) included questions and answers intended to preempt such criticisms. The response to "How much will the America 2000 plan cost?" was "$690 million. . . . The answer does not lie in spending more money on old ways, but to redirect our resources and our energies to new approaches." To the question "Aren't the New American Schools going to be more expensive than today's schools?" came the reply, "No. It will be a requirement for the Research and Development Teams that the new schools they design can operate at costs no more than conventional schools." The question "Will the American Achievement Tests compete with the work of the National Education Goals Panel?" prompted the answer, "No, we expect to follow the Panel's lead in developing the New World Standards and the American Achievement Tests." To the question "Do national tests mean a national curriculum?" the brochure answered, "No, although surveys and polls indicate that most Americans have no objection to the idea of a national curriculum. The American Achievement Tests will examine the results of education." And finally, in answer to "What's the single most important part of the America 2000 strategy?" came the reply that "The most controversial may be school choice. . . . The knottiest is probably standards—and testing. . . . The most dramatic is the research and development for New American Schools. But the most important may be the America 2000 Communities."[75]

That took care of the critics—for now. "I think this is the first time the President of the United States said the federal government had a major role in improving elementary and secondary education," Shanker applauded. "I never remember any President doing a speech and laying out a long-range plan." Geiger added that "it's bold and far-reaching." John Chubb of the liberal Brookings Institute called America 2000 "the most encouraging education proposal to emerge from the federal government in a very long time." Denis Doyle of the conservative Hudson Institute praised Bush's "vision [as] at once bold, even daring," and said "that [it] recognized the national interest but does not compromise local initiative." The liberal *Philadelphia Inquirer* editorialized, "We see a lot to like in President Bush's strategy." The conservative *Wall Street Journal* called the plan "the most ambitious and comprehensive education agenda ever offered by a President." Porter wrote to Bush the day after the speech that "media coverage of yesterday's launch of your America 2000 Education Strategy has been extensive and impressively favorable. . . . The unveiling was the lead story on every major network during yesterday's evening news and received front page coverage in every major national newspaper."[76]

"We must follow up," Bush implored Alexander the day after the speech, and his cabinet did. Secretary of Agriculture Edward Madigan promoted nutrition education; Secretary of Commerce Robert Mossbacher stressed the need for a well-educated workforce; Secretary of Energy David Watkins established a National Science Board competition for high school students; Secretary of Health and Human Services Louis Sullivan delivered fourteen high school and college commencement addresses in the month of May; Secretary of Housing and Urban Development Jack Kemp was to speak on education at the American Academy of Achievement in July; Secretary of the Interior Manuel Lujan was working to achieve the National Education Goals at Indian schools; Secretary of

Labor Lynn Martin discussed the role of education in the workforce in many speeches; Secretary of Transportation Samuel Skinner highlighted America 2000 in meetings with students and alumni associations; Trade representative Carla Hills focused on adult learning in her speeches; Secretary of Veterans Affairs Edward Derwinski called for accountability in education in his addresses; Environmental Protection Agency chief William Reilly was promoting environmental education; and Attorney General William Barr even taught a class at a District of Columbia middle school.[77]

Following Alexander's counsel, in the two months after the unveiling of America 2000 the president himself took three trips to publicize it to St. Paul, Minnesota; Seaford, Delaware; and Grand Junction, Colorado. At his first stop, the Saturn School for Tomorrow, an experimental, high-technology magnet school in St. Paul, Bush promoted his plan with the garbled syntax that would become his trademark: "I don't imagine when this started that it had fantastic amounts of money to begin with, so what'll happen is we will inspire, as it's always happened in this country, good example will inspire others." Bush's "good example," he told the Saturn students, would include learning to use a computer.[78]

In June, Bush told the National Education Goals Panel that "we've seen our young people perform in the Persian Gulf, and we've seen what they can do. And they inspire us to reinvent our education system." He then established a commission to study the desirability of lengthening the academic year. At the White House in July, Bush launched the New American Schools Development Corporation, to be headed by former New Jersey chief state school officer Saul Cooperman. Later that month, at the urging of Republican House whip Newt Gingrich of Georgia, Bush held a White House signing ceremony for the National Literacy Act of 1991, which established a National Institute for Literacy and federal grant programs for state or regional literacy resource centers, national workforce literacy strategies, and literacy services for state prisoners. Bush said that the legislation would help attain the fifth of the National Education Goals: "By the year 2000 every adult American will be literate."[79]

By August, Alexander had peddled America 2000 in fourteen states. In September, Bush traveled to Maine, where he visited a high school and read a children's story to kindergarteners, then to Maryland, where he helped kick off that state's America 2000 campaign. He then signed the Carl Perkins Vocational and Applied Technology Act, which provided federal grants for vocational education. In April 1992 in Pennsylvania, the president observed the first anniversary of America 2000 by saluting the forty-three states and eleven hundred communities that had joined his crusade.[80]

The Bush presidency had achieved such a consensus on education, Alexander argued in April 1992, that he doubted it would be a major issue in the presidential campaign. Even Bush's defeat by Arkansas Democratic governor Bill Clinton in November was a victory of sorts for the Education President. "When the dust settles, and the history books are written, President Bush's leadership in education will be among his most significant contributions," the outgoing secretary told the Ohio School Boards Association. "He did what a President can do best— set a national agenda for change to make things happen. And because he did it in partnership with the nation's Governors, his contributions will be lasting. . . . One of the Governors who helped set that agenda is now President-elect."[81]

But the consensus that Alexander claimed had long since cracked. Conservatives who feared federal control joined liberals afraid of discrimination in opposing national testing. *National Review* editorialized in May 1991 that "national standards for math and science are not such a bad idea, but when you get to other subjects—history, literature, social studies—the likelihood is that national standards will translate into the 'curriculum of inclusion,' i.e. no standards at all." The conservative Citizens for Excellence in Education, wrote Bush aide Jonathan Levey in November 1991, believed "that the Federal government already controls testing, production of textbooks, and other materials. . . . America 2000 will only complete this domination." The following month the NEA Representative Assembly voted to oppose national testing. The National Center for Fair and Open Testing formed a coalition of school administrators and minority groups, including the National Parent Teachers Association, the National Association for the Advancement of Colored People, and the Mexican-American Legal Defense Fund, united behind the NEA position: "We don't believe there's any evidence that national testing will lead to better education."[82]

The cost of the Bush proposals also raised the hackles of the Right and the Left. The conservative journal *Human Events* worried that the substantial influence of former Moynihan aide Chester Finn would invite an expensive federal effort. Conservative outrage at Alexander's highlighting of the similarities between the Bush and Clinton education records helped prompt Porter to prepare this about-face for an interview with the secretary: "The best thing that Governor Clinton could do to help education in America is to get his business-as-usual friends in Congress moving on the President's education program." The liberal *New York Times* was calling Bush a "part-time Education President" who has "never seriously addressed costly problems such as overcrowded classes, deteriorating buildings and underpaid teachers." And the AFT, which had cheered Alexander's selection, booed the secretary when he appeared at its convention.[83]

## The Educational Excellence Act of 1991

The sternest test of America 2000 would come on Capitol Hill. In June, Bush sent Congress the Educational Excellence Act of 1991, calling for $180 million for New American Schools, $100 million for merit schools, $70 million for governors' academies for teachers, $22.5 million for governors' academies for school leaders, $25 million for alternative certification of teachers and principals, $200 million for parental choice programs, $30 million for parental choice programs "of national significance," and $38.2 million to develop standards and voluntary testing. In the Senate, in a remarkable demonstration of bipartisanship, Democrats Edward Kennedy of Massachusetts and Claiborne Pell of Rhode Island, chairmen of the Labor and Human Resources Committee and its education subcommittee, joined Orrin Hatch of Utah and Nancy Kassebaum of Kansas, the ranking Republicans on those panels, in introducing the Bush legislation. "I have some reservations about some parts of it, especially the plan to form the Chapter One program into a voucher and the creation of a choice program that includes private schools," said Kennedy. But "we need to put partisan differences aside and get on with the business of improving our schools." In the House, Pennsylvania's William Goodling, the ranking Republican on the Education and Labor Committee and Elementary and Secondary Education Subcommittee, introduced the bill, while the chairmen of those committees, Michigan Democrats William Ford and Dale Kildee, promised to consider it.[84]

But Congress remained unpersuaded. The House Education and Labor Committee reported a bill that Alexander called "not an acceptable alternative" because it left vouchers in state, rather than federal, hands. The Senate Labor and Human Resources Committee released a version which the OMB urged Bush to veto because it "unnecessarily constrains implementation of the new generation of 'break the mold schools,' [and] . . . includes . . . policy statements calling for excessive and unrealistic expansion of existing Federal programs." Negotiations between the administration and committee members failed to produce legislation before congressional adjournment in 1991.[85]

The Bush initiative went no further in 1992. When Kennedy's Neighborhood Schools Improvement Act emerged from the Labor and Public Resources Committee bearing little resemblance to the Education Excellence Act of 1991, Alexander vowed that "the President will keep fighting for more radical change in the American system." And when the House Education and Labor Committee reported Ford's Neighborhood Schools Improvement Act, Alexander called it "even worse than worse than awful." The conference committee's approval of an $800 million bill authorizing block grants to states and local education agencies, with no mention of national testing, school choice, or "break the mold" schools, the secretary lamented, "evidences the cozy relationship between the majority members of the education committees and entrenched education special interests that are most responsible for the current state of American schools." After the House adopted the conference report, a Senate cloture vote failed when Minnesota's David Durenburger refused to join forty fellow Republicans. Then the congressional session, and the Bush presidency, ended without a bill.[86]

## The Bush Record

"Can you tell us what President Bush will personally do for this populist crusade," a reporter asked Alexander at the introduction of America 2000, "other than learn how to run a computer?" The answer is that Bush would do a lot. He logged thousands of miles, gave numerous speeches, and authorized countless studies to help keep public elementary and secondary education high on the national agenda. Bush "felt very strongly about education," Porter would remember. He challenged the public education interests with innovation but treated them with conciliation. Bush "was more willing to meet with education groups" than Reagan, and there was "less bashing" of the teacher unions, Futrell would recall. By elevating the governors' visibility and influence, Bush rewarded them for the durability of the reforms of the 1980s and reminded Congress of the inevitability of the reforms of the 1990s. "He worked hard," Alexander would insist. "He was on his way to succeeding."[87]

Along the way, however, the elementary and secondary education politics and policies of George Bush underwent several dramatic transformations that invited skepticism and demanded explanations. The first change occurred on the campaign trail in 1988, when the candidate who had previously touted his extensive foreign policy résumé—the "President you won't have to train"—announced that he wanted to be the "Education President." Bush had headed the Republican National Committee and the Central Intelligence Agency, had represented the United States in China and at the United Nations, and had served two terms in Congress and two terms in the vice presidency. Except for opposing federal aid to education as an unsuccessful candidate for the House in 1964 and voting against the extension of the ESEA as a Texas representative in 1967, however, Bush's record, as *The New Republic* editorialized in May 1988, didn't show him to be "really very serious about education." So his election-year conversion seemed driven more by polls than principles—a whopping 78 percent of Americans expressed concern over "the quality of United States education."[88]

The second change was the transition from Reagan to Bush. As the first incumbent vice president since 1836 to succeed to the presidency by election, Bush shared with Martin Van Buren the luxury and the handicap of following a popular two-term president. But education was not an issue that Andrew Jackson had bequeathed to his successor. So Bush could look instead to the examples of Lyndon Johnson, who succeeded where his predecessor had failed, and Gerald Ford, who largely avoided what his predecessor had abandoned. Bush would follow both models. From his 1988 Republican Convention promise of a "kinder, gentler" presidency to his outreach to his congressional adversaries, Bush broke with Reagan in style. But in his frugal budget proposals and "read my lips" resistance to taxes (for his first two years), Bush emulated Reagan in substance.

The third metamorphosis was from good news to bad news. Reagan often told the story of the farmer who, upon finding his barn filled with manure, gleefully announced, "There must be a pony in there somewhere." While Reagan had presided over *A Nation at Risk*—the reality as well as the report—and Bennett could be as acerbic as he was astute, the prevalent tone at the end of their tenure was encouragement of the state and local reforms they had helped unleash and the public goodwill they had helped foster. But Bush and his lieutenants often acted as if they did not want to clean the barn. A 1988 Gallup Poll showed that Americans who believed that their schools had "gotten better" in the previous five years outnumbered by 10 percent (up from 3 percent the year before) those who believed the schools had "gotten worse," and 61 percent of the public believed that the president could "improve education standards." Yet Porter wrote to Bush, "Unfortunately, this satisfaction may make it more difficult to convince people that significant changes are needed." After California superintendent of schools Bill Honig claimed in the fall of 1990 that "the last six years have produced a rate of growth in student achievement that is as great [as] or greater than during the Sputnik-inspired education productivity burst of the late 1950's and 1960's," Porter's assistant Charles Kolb replied that although Scholastic Aptitude and Advanced Placement exam scores increased during the period identified by Honig, "scores have not changed greatly." Bush acknowledged in his 1988 campaign that "the last five years have witnessed the most far-reaching education reform movement in this century." Yet after the forward-looking Education Summit and America 2000 as well as the addition of the upbeat Alexander, Bush lamented, "Every day brings new evidence of crisis; our schools are in trouble." Bush complained in his 1992 campaign that in education, "We're just not performing as a nation."[89]

Bush's pessimism was neither extraordinary—only 21 percent of Americans awarded the nation's public schools an A or B—nor unfounded. He could always back it up. And herein lay a fourth change that undercut the Bush education record. The nation had, within a decade, gone from too few measurements of the education performance of its students and their public benefactors to too many. The statistics came fast and furious, and they seemed to prove anything—or nothing. "If all the national, state, and education reform reports that have been produced the past ten years about what American students don't know and can't do were laid out end to end . . . they would circle the nation at least once, if not twice," asserted a 1992 AFT background paper. "If we excluded anything that was incomprehensibly vague, we probably would be down to one zip code." There was the Education Department's "Education Performance Chart," not to be confused with its "Taking Stock of U.S. Education" report. There was the report of the National Governors Association Task Force on Education, which was not the National Assessment of Educational Progress. Then there was the National Education Goals Panel, the watchdog of America 2000, that concluded of goals two to six in its 1992 report that the high school graduation rate had stayed about the same; the number of students taking advanced placement exams had increased slightly; American students continued to be outperformed in mathematics and science by students in Korea, Taiwan,

Switzerland, France, and Hungary; the number of functionally illiterate adults remained "stagnant"; while student use of cocaine and alcohol increased, marijuana use remained steady; and incidents of violence increased. As for Goal One, "readiness for school," the panel apologized, "we do not yet have an assessment instrument."[90]

The administration's amply documented despair produced not only counterproductive politics but also contradictory policy, for Bush presided over a fifth transformation: the rhetorical leap from reform to revolution. "Business-as-usual is not getting us where we need to go," Bush proclaimed at the education summit. "The American people are ready for radical reforms. We must not disappoint them." In launching America 2000, Bush declared that "Our challenge amounts to nothing less than a revolution in American education, a battle for our future."[91]

Even if it were affordable, Bush's "revolution in a recession" seemed unrealistic. Although education spending would increase 22 percent after inflation during Bush's term, much of it came from congressional add-ons. The National Education Goals Panel, in its first "report card" in September 1991, admitted that Goal Four (American students first in the world in science and mathematics) would be "virtually impossible to reach." A 1991 Gallup Poll found the public more devoted to the six education goals but less confident of their fulfillment than in the previous year. And even if it were realistic, for the Bush program to be revolutionary it would have to be new. "The Presidential goals set out in 1990 would have been more defensible," wrote New York Democratic senator Daniel Patrick Moynihan, who had served in the Johnson and Nixon administrations, "were it not for the fact that in 1984 the preceding President set out substantially the same goals for 1990 [90 percent high school graduation rate, better SAT and ACT scores, competitive teacher salaries]." An internal administration memo went back much further: "The country's most famous magnet school, the Bronx High School of Science, was founded in 1938. . . . Alternative certification [of teachers occurred during] World War II [when] standards were dropped to allow individuals with little or no formal training to fill the vacant slots." Larry Lindsey concluded that in education, "The President should be aware that there aren't a lot of really new ideas to be tried."[92]

But there were new approaches to old ideas, and one of these comprised the sixth major shift of the Bush presidency—from "neopluralism" to "neocentralism." The terms, employed by David Boaz, executive vice president of the libertarian Cato Institute, described the former belief that "decisions about education should be made by parents, teachers, and principals [through] vouchers and tax credits" and the latter reliance on "strong leadership and comprehensive reforms drawn up by state or federal officials." Boaz explained that while the Reagan administration was largely a battleground between neopluralists and neocentralists, the Bush administration, with the Education Summit and America 2000, appeared to have settled on neocentralism.[93]

"Who is calling for an assertive national role in education in the 1990's? Who is calling for national standards? Who is putting local control, if not at risk, at least on notice? . . . Wonder of wonder, it is a conservative," wrote Denis Doyle of the conservative Hudson Institute after the announcement of America 2000. "The strongest aspect of America 2000 is its emphasis on standards and testing," editorialized the liberal *New Republic*, noting a switch from the "1970's and 80's [when] it was always Republicans who insisted education was a local rather than a federal concern." The AFT's Shanker, a long-time adherent of national standards, mused, "Maybe George Bush is a closet Progressive."[94]

One could understand this befuddlement at an upside-down Washington where Republicans were seeking to expand the power of the Department of Education and Democrats were backing block grants, because like the other transitions in the Bush presidency, this one was hardly smooth. Not only did the president embrace the neopluralist concept of nonpublic school vouchers at the same time he was spreading the neocentralist faith in national standards and testing, but he and his surrogates too often defended neocentralism in the language of neopluralism. "I think the President will be doing his best to fulfill his pledge to be the Education President," said Alexander in unveiling America 2000, "and not be trying to pull any tricks on the American people by saying, as a result of an action I took in Washington this year, your third-grader a few months later has seen a lot of difference." An April 1992 Bush campaign "fact sheet" blamed the Democrats for "the tired formula of federal mandates and bureaucratic management." Even today, Porter maintains, "Bush was not any more enamored of a Washington role [in education] than Reagan," while Alexander remarkably goes further: "It would be better for the federal Department [of Education] to withdraw—just give it to parents."[95]

This makes for a good sound bite, leading to a seventh transformation in the Bush presidency: from short-term to long-term planning. "Our biggest challenge," Alexander wrote to Bush the day after the inauguration of America 2000, is "to get a country which is accustomed to nine-second soundbites and a 100-hour war to think in terms of a nine-year crusade." Alexander might have added "four-year election cycles" to his list of contributors to the country's short attention span. "Suppose Bush has one term or two terms, how does the public measure the President's performance on education?" asked a reporter at Alexander's America 2000 press conference. "That's the way the world works," the secretary shrugged. Bush's far-reaching approach was in many ways statesmanlike, even apolitical—it seems ironic to blame a president who by his own admission lacked "the vision thing" for excessive vision. But the administration's foresight not only unsettled the pundits and the voters; it arrived in an atmosphere of annual reports and frequent demands, inside and outside the administration, for concrete improvements in American education. A further irony is that the administration's plea for patience was the product of its own impatience. "Eight years after the National Commission on Excellence in Education declared the nation at risk, we haven't turned the situation around," Alexander wrote to Bush in only his second month on the job.[96]

The "situation" to which Alexander alluded was the relatively stagnant performance of that two-thirds of the nation's schoolchildren identified by Finn. The eighth major change in the Bush presidency actually began during the Nixon administration, when Finn and the president realized that "the education equity issues of the 1960's and 1970's—extending education services to the disadvantaged, the handicapped, the non-English-speaking student—had overshadowed the issue of the quality of what students were learning." Twenty-five years after a Johnson administration task force awakened the nation to the educational deficiencies of the lower one-third, economically, of the nation's population, the country's leaders had largely refocused their attention on the upper two-thirds. "The math and science goal is critical," Marc Tucker, president of the National Center for Education and the Economy, said of Bush's fourth goal, "but reaching it with twenty percent of our kids living in poverty is ludicrous." Bush greatly increased Head Start funding, advocated nonpublic and public school vouchers for low-income students, and targeted three-fourths of the money for his New American Schools to the most needy districts. Alexander adds that the ESEA, with its Chapter One provisions for disadvantaged students, was not up for renewal during Bush's term.[97]

The word "excellence" nonetheless seemed to have replaced "equity," and "accountability" appeared to have removed "opportunity" from the political lexicon of the day. "Asked in a recent interview to name his most significant domestic initiatives, the President's very first response was 'I think clearly the education initiative,'" wrote Susan Chira of the *New York Times* near the end of the Bush presidency. "[But many] educators say there is little hope . . . until the Government also offers broader initiatives to counter the urban ills that so often lead to school failure." Kolb related to Porter that in 1990 "eight percent of urban junior and senior high school students miss at least one day a month because they are afraid to go." Chira told the story of three African American high school honor students struggling to excel in inner-city Memphis, Tennessee. "From what we see, people are dying every day," said one. "You don't know when you might go."[98]

Even if Bush's education agenda had paid closer attention to the underclass, it would have had to succeed on Capitol Hill, where a final metamorphosis was under way. Reagan arrived in Washington in 1981 with a mandate and a friendly Senate; Bush entered the White House in 1989 with neither. With a 55–45 Democratic majority in the Senate and a 260–175 Democratic margin in the House, but without Reagan's media skills, Bush faced an uphill battle on Capitol Hill. Unlike Reagan, who adopted a confrontational style yet was willing to compromise with Congress, Bush by most accounts adopted a conciliatory style toward legislators and lobbyists yet deferred compromise until the eleventh hour. Charles Tiefer, House general counsel during the Bush presidency, recalls that Porter devised a strategy by which Bush sent veto threats to Capitol Hill while bills were in committee. "One of Porter's major beliefs," Tiefer writes, "was that the veto should not always be considered at the end of a bill's evolution but only [as] part of an ongoing process of compromise." Yet Chira reported that "Democratic aides on Capitol Hill who negotiated with the Administration say officials essentially gave up on Congress when they realized they would have to compromise." Alexander virtually admitted as much, blaming the congressional committees for doing the bidding of the teacher unions.[99]

Finn defended Bush's relative absence from the legislative fray by calling the Educational Excellence Acts "a consciousness raising effort." Bush indeed raised consciousness about education and other issues, but he seldom passed legislation: by the end of his term, after additional Republican losses in the midterm elections, his veto strategy had produced not compromises but vetoes—forty-four, with only one overridden—and his rate of legislative success with Congress in 1992 stood at only 43 percent. Congress's failure to override Bush's vetoes was a record in futility unmatched since 1933, but Bush's fourth-year legislative score was the worst for a president since 1944.[100]

In keeping public schools in the forefront of national politics and policy, George Bush was an—if not the—Education President. But for virtually every positive aspect of the Bush record, there was a negative one. He raised expectations but expressed doubts. He mounted the bully pulpit, only to mix his message. He affirmed a federal presence, then attacked it. He offered an innovative program, but Congress would not pass it. For this Education President the glass was half full, but it was also half empty.

## Bill Clinton

> Now, looking ahead, the greatest step of all, the highest threshold of
> the future we must now cross, and my number one priority for the
> next four years is to ensure that all Americans have the best education
> in the world.
> —Bill Clinton (1997)

Since the advent of the ESEA of 1965, Washington had largely divided into two camps—those who argued for more federal money for education (Lyndon Johnson, Jimmy Carter, and most congressional Democrats), regardless of the effectiveness of the federal role, and those who argued for less federal money for education (Richard Nixon, Gerald Ford, Ronald Reagan, George Bush, and most congressional Republicans), regardless of the cost of federal reform.[101] Now, following the example of his governorship and the promise of his centrist

"New Democrat" presidential campaign, Bill Clinton prepared to enlarge and reform the federal role at the same time. "On one side," said Clinton, "is the old view that big, one-size-fits-all Government can provide the answer to all of our problems. On the other side is the view that Government is the source of all our problems. In the real world, that's a false choice."[102]

Instead, Clinton called for a "New Covenant" between the American people and their government to "create economic opportunity" as Johnson had attempted; to "enhance the security of the American people here at home, on our streets, in our schools, and abroad," as Nixon had sought to do; to "reform the National Government to make it smaller, less bureaucratic," as Reagan had tried to do; and to "help our people raise their education and skill levels so they can make the most of their own lives," as Bush had undertaken. Thus Clinton pledged to "reduce the education gap between rich and poor students by increasing Chapter One funding for low-income students" so as to "achieve the 1989 Education Summit's National Education Goals." In other words, in the thirty-year-old debate over federal aid to elementary and secondary education, Bill Clinton would find himself in a familiar position—on both sides.[103]

## Clinton and Education

Education has always been central to the Bill Clinton story. When Billy was seven, his family moved from Hope, Arkansas, to the larger city of Hot Springs, where he enrolled first in a parochial school and then a public school. Virginia Clinton constantly complained about the poor quality of her son's education in a state where public school teachers did not need college degrees. Yet Bill Clinton somehow overcame the death of his father two months before Bill's birth, an abusive stepfather, and a lower-middle-class upbringing to excel at Hot Springs High School, Georgetown University, Oxford University, and Yale University Law School.[104]

After losing his first race for a House seat from the Third District of Arkansas and serving two years as the state's attorney general, Clinton became the nation's youngest governor in 1978. Proclaiming education his top legislative priority, Governor Clinton proposed competency examinations for new teachers; mandatory achievement tests for third-, sixth-, and eighth-grade students; a consolidation of the state's school districts; a "fair dismissal" law to protect teachers from arbitrary removal; and higher teacher salaries. Clinton's introduction of new taxes to fund these programs, however, helped cost him reelection, as Republicans took over the White House, the Senate, and the Arkansas governorship.[105]

The failure of Ronald Reagan's across-the-board tax cuts to prevent the recession of 1982–83 helped return Clinton and his education reforms to Little Rock in 1983. In his second term as governor, Clinton tied his school consolidation plan to the creation of a fifteen-member commission to develop a new set of

minimum standards for Arkansas public schools. He required all school districts to offer kindergarten, allowed students to take up to half of their courses
in another school district if their district did not offer them, strengthened the
Teacher Fair Dismissal Act, resurrected his call for higher faculty salaries and
teacher and student competency testing, and advocated a tax increase to finance
his proposals. Clinton's initiatives became law over the bitter opposition of the
Arkansas Education Association (AEA, the state's NEA affiliate) to the teacher
testing provisions. "He came in the back door, walked directly to the stage, made
his speech, did not go up and down the aisle to visit with people, did not open
it to questions and answers and left by the same way," Clinton's mother would
recall of her son's speech to the AEA following the passage of his reforms in
November 1983. "But there was a professor behind me, or a teacher, so help me,
his words were, 'I ain't gonna take no damn test!' I turned around, and I said, 'sir,
that's a double negative and that means you will take the damn test.'"[106]

The governor's standards commission, chaired by his wife Hillary Rodham
Clinton, called for maximum class sizes of twenty in kindergarten to twenty-
eight in junior high and high school; high school graduation course requirements of four English, five mathematics and science, two social studies, one
practical arts, and one-half each of physical education, health education, and
fine arts; the lengthening of the school year from 175 to 180 days; and provision
of one counselor for every 450 high school students and every 600 elementary
school students. In the face of AEA objections that such change would be too
costly, the Arkansas Board of Education enacted the standards in February of
1984. Riding a wave of popularity due in no small measure to his education
reforms, Clinton would win the next four gubernatorial elections.[107]

## Government as Answer: Improving America's Schools Act

By the time the governor decided to run for president, however, the AEA and the
NEA were willing to forgive Clinton for his advocacy of teacher testing. AEA
executive director Lora McHenry said in 1991 that Clinton "had a vision for the
state, and I felt that he could do something for us; and I wholeheartedly supported him in almost all of his campaign [for education reform]." The governor,
for his part, was willing to forget about teacher testing. In the 1992 presidential
campaign Clinton supported greater funding for Chapter One of the ESEA,
smaller class sizes, alternative certification of teachers, and public school choice.
He endorsed national standards, goals, and examinations for students but not
for teachers. So the NEA endorsed Clinton.[108]

A decade after A Nation at Risk and the enactment of his own bold school
reforms in Arkansas, another "Education President" entered the White House amid
a whirlwind of bad news. The publication of liberal Jonathan Kozol's Savage
Inequalities: Children in America's Schools in 1991 had exposed the inequities inherent in funding public schools by property taxes, with which Governor Clinton had

successfully grappled in Arkansas. "I visited over thirty schools all over the nation," Kozol recalled. "Almost everywhere I went in inner-city schools, I saw good teachers overburdened with large classes, working with too few supplies, in physically repellent buildings, struggling against the odds of poverty in the streets and parsimony in school budgets, sometimes prevailing, sometimes drowning, sometimes simply holding on for sheer survival." Conservative Thomas Sowell's 1993 *Inside American Education: The Decline, The Deception, the Dogmas* observed that while SAT scores had fallen since the 1960s, grade point averages were rising. While public elementary and secondary schools suffer from lower standards and greater politicization, Sowell lamented, students learn to "feel good about themselves."[109]

The ability of the states or the federal government to address these concerns appeared to be limited. "The state of the states' fiscal health may have reached a new low-water mark," wrote Chris Pipho of the Education Commission of the States in February 1993. "In fiscal year 1992, thirty-one states reported that tax collections fell below the projections used to make up their budgets; twenty-nine states raised taxes last year; [and] thirty-five states cut spending below levels initially approved in 1992." The Commission on Chapter One (an independent committee of twenty-eight educators and policy makers), the first National Assessment of Chapter One (composed of Education Department staff members and other education analysts), and an independent review panel appointed by the National Assessment concurred that too little of Chapter One money reached students, especially secondary school pupils. In a nod to Kozol, the three groups recommended that "all schools should be improved, because no matter how good Chapter 1 programs were in individual schools the effort was wasted unless students attended schools undergoing improvements," and "the Federal Government should give additional money to Chapter One schools." Echoing Sowell, the reports added that "all students should be held to higher standards and be taught critical and analytical thinking skills," while Chapter One "should pay more attention to how well students are learning and adopt better ways to measure progress."[110]

"Every problem in American education has been solved by somebody, somewhere," said the newest Education President. "What we are not good at in American education is taking what works in one place and putting it in place in another." Nowhere was this adage more appropriate than the beleaguered ESEA of 1965, due for renewal in Clinton's first year in the White House. Despite the dismal record of Chapter One of the legislation, Clinton believed that there was nothing in the ESEA that some old-fashioned redistribution of wealth could not fix.[111]

Although Chapter One funds ostensibly targeted impoverished areas, some money reached virtually every school district, with only 10 percent of the total set aside as "concentration grants" for the poorest districts. The Clinton administration thus proposed to raise this percentage to 50 percent, transferring about $510 million from wealthier to poorer districts. It also sought to reduce the threshold by which a district received schoolwide Chapter One programs from 75 percent to 50 percent of pupils below the poverty line, thus increasing the number of school-wide programs from twelve thousand to twenty thousand. The proposal would require school districts to administer health and nutrition tests at elementary schools with more than 50 percent of their students below the poverty line, to dis-tribute Chapter One monies based on the poverty levels rather than the achieve-ment levels of its schools, and to allocate Chapter One funds to poorer schools before funding wealthier schools in the districts. In response to the three 1992 studies critical of Chapter One programs, the administration would require states to develop standards consistent with its Goals 2000 program as a condition for receiving Chapter One, would replace multiple-choice basic skills tests of Chapter One students with more sophisticated instruments, and would require a higher level of instruction to adapt students to these new tests. (Under the proposal, six-teen states would lose Chapter One funds, while New York, California, Texas, Mis-sissippi, and Louisiana would gain the most.)[112]

As if to burnish his liberal Democratic credentials, Clinton not only proposed to spend more on Chapter One—$7.1 billion compared to $6.7 billion in the final year of the Bush administration—but to restore its original name, Title I, and to eliminate Chapter Two, the $400 million block grant package added by the Reagan administration in 1981. Sounding like Lyndon Johnson, Secretary of Education Richard Riley called the nation's poverty rate for children "a national scandal," which required the federal government "sticking our necks out to help these children."[113]

Time-worn arguments accompanied the ESEA extension legislation to Capi-tol Hill, where the Elementary, Secondary, and Vocational Education Subcom-mittee of the Education and Labor Committee held hearings in the fall of 1993. "We think the argument for targeting is very, very strong," Undersecretary of Education Marshall Smith told the legislators. "There are lots of examples of schools with six and seven and four and five percent poverty getting Title I funds. And schools with 50, 55, and 60 percent poverty are not. And we think that is contrary to the intent." A 1998 General Accounting Office study would support Smith. It found that in the 1991–92 school year, state and federal money had eliminated funding gaps in sixteen of thirty-seven states, but two-thirds of poor children lived in the twenty-one states with inequitable spending. It also concluded, however, that the size of the state and federal grants was more important than the funding formula. Since more than half the students in schools with the highest concentration of poverty scored below the thirty-fifth percentile on standardized tests, test scores declined as student eligibility for free lunches increased, and the achievement level of students in schools with high poverty concentrations was lower than that of students in lower-poverty schools. Smith contended, "The real issue is serving poor kids the best we can possibly serve them—poor kids in high-poverty areas."[114]

But subcommittee chairman Dale Kildee, Democrat of Michigan, countered that poor children suffer wherever they live, and ranking Republican member William Goodling of Pennsylvania, echoing another General Accounting Office report, added that poor children in impoverished rural areas would be the big losers in the administration's numbers game. Michael Edwards, manager of federal relations for the NEA, argued that augmenting, not targeting, existing ESEA monies should be the primary concern of the legislators. "To target more is simply to say we're going to take from deserving schools and students and give to schools and students with greater needs," said Edwards. "It doesn't solve the need, and it's too much to ask."[115]

So, apparently, was action on the Clinton proposal in the first session of the 103rd Congress. The ESEA's institutionalized legislative oversight, Clinton's inexperience in the ways of Washington, and the low-key Riley's aversion to negotiating in the media helped postpone the bill's day of reckoning.[116]

When the subcommittee reported the ESEA extension largely along party lines on February 6, 1994, it rejected the Clinton redistribution formula, opting instead for an alternative devised by Kildee and Wisconsin Republican Tom Petri that allocated $6.3 billion under the existing formula and only $1.1 billion under a new plan tilted toward poorer districts. If subcommittee Republicans carried the day with the Kildee-Petri compromise, however, subcommittee Democrats killed Chapter Two, with the failure of a last-ditch effort by Goodling and Wisconsin Republican Steve Gunderson to earmark some of the open-ended block grants for computers, library materials, and "promising educational reform projects."[117]

When Education Department documents showed that as many as half of the committee members would lose money for their districts under the Clinton plan, the administration backpedaled, seeking a compromise closer to the existing Chapter One formula. When Secretary Riley's personal intervention failed to change enough votes, he settled for a slightly more equitable version of Kildee-Petri. To appease some Republicans, the committee restored the $435 million Chapter Two program, then reported the bill, 29–14. The House finally approved HR 6 on March 24 by a 289–128 vote, sending the bill to the Senate.[118]

A week-long floor debate ended on August 2, with a 94–6 vote for S.1513. The funding distribution adopted by the conference report was closer to the House than the Senate, and a far cry from the original Clinton proposal. The House passed the conference report 262–132 on September 30, and the Senate approved it (following a two-day Republican filibuster in favor of a school prayer amendment) by 77–20 on October 5.[119]

When President Clinton signed the legislation, dubbed the Improving America's Schools Act of 1994, it retained several provisions from his original proposal—schoolwide programs replacing "pullouts" of Chapter One students, state or district takeovers of failing schools rather than withdrawal of Chapter One monies from succeeding schools, and a greater latitude and higher standards for schools in spending Chapter One money. "For thirty years," said Clinton, "the Federal Government has shipped money to the states and the local school districts to try to help with problems . . . in ways that pre- scribed in a very detailed manner the rules and regulations . . . your States had to follow in applying for the money and in complying with it. . . . This bill changes all that." Clinton later added, "We overhauled the ESEA, and we redid Title I and . . . took out what was then in the law for Chapter 1, which was lower education expectations for poor children. It was an outrage, and we took it out of the law."[120]

But the biggest change of all sought by the president—a funding formula to address the "savage inequalities" of federal school finance—had fallen to the same constituency politics of which Title I was born decades earlier. The federal government would spend $60 billion over the next five years under the ESEA, and most of it would never reach the children who needed it the most.[121]

## Government as Problem: Goals 2000

"I didn't come to Washington to save the job of a bureaucrat or to defend old ways of doing business." The Education secretary who uttered those words was not William Bennett or Lamar Alexander but the former Democratic governor of South Carolina, Richard Riley. "There are still too many school districts spending way too much money on administration and too little money on edu- cation and instruction. We cannot ask the American people to spend more on education until we do a better job with the money we've got now." The president who spoke those words was not Ronald Reagan or George Bush, but the former Democratic governor of Arkansas, Bill Clinton.[122]

For the first time in the fifteen-year history of the modern Department of Education, former governors sat in both the secretary's and the president's chairs. When they arrived in Washington, they prepared to preside over a coun- try that had not elected a sitting member of Congress to the presidency since 1960, had chosen Republicans to a majority of governors' mansions, and was beginning a love affair with the Tenth Amendment. "Some people play favorites with the Bill of Rights," Garry Wills would write. "The favorite amendment of gangsters is the fifth (no self-incrimination), of liberals the first (free speech), of drug dealers the fourth (no unauthorized search), of gun fondlers the second (to bear arms). Now, many people have a new favorite, the long-neglected tenth (powers not specifically assigned to Washington are reserved to the states)." Jacob Weisberg would go even further in analyzing the Clinton presidency: "Coming to the White House from the governor's mansion in Little Rock, Clin- ton has recast the Presidency on the more modest model of his previous job. . . . A governor is expected to address whatever issues arise, from upgrading the skills of his state's work force to reducing traffic congestion on its highways. Financial constraints deny governors the possibilities of grander schemes.

Within the confines of balanced and limited budgets, however, they can distinguish themselves with creative social policy ideas."[123]

Goals 2000 was such an idea. In April 1993, following negotiations between the Department of Education, congressional Democrats, and the governors, Riley and Secretary of Labor Robert Reich unveiled a plan for "codifying into law" the National Education Goals established in 1990 by the president and the nation's governors; adopting national performance standards in such areas as science, math, history, English, and geography and supporting local reform efforts designed to meet those standards; strengthening and improving teacher training and instructional materials, technologies, and other school services to enable students to achieve higher goals; establishing a National Skills Standards Board to promote the development of occupational skills standards to ensure that American workers are better trained and internationally competitive; and increasing flexibility at the state and local levels by waiving rules and regulations that might impede reform and improvement. The cost of the program would be $420 million, considerably less than the $690 million requested by Bush to implement the national goals in 1990, and about the same as Bush's 1989 proposal, which many Democrats had derided as a "Band-Aid."[124]

"Everybody's for education. You ask anybody in the Congress, are you for education? They say, absolutely," Clinton mused. "But you've always got to ask the next question; the first question is never enough." Everybody was for educational standards, but it was not long before many began asking the "next questions." Bush administration Assistant Secretary of Education Diane Ravitch wondered why the National Education Standards and Improvement Council would be appointed by the president with no requirement for bipartisanship. Bush's deputy assistant Charles Kolb asked why his boss's National Council on Educational Standards, which became the National Education Standards and Assessment Council, would now be the National Education Standards and Improvement Council, if not to defer educational assessment until national uniformity of instructional materials and teacher-training techniques had occurred. University of North Carolina professor Svi Shapiro asked why, after a 1991 federal survey reported that one-fourth of all U.S. high school students had seriously contemplated suicide, the president had hopped aboard the "mindless" educational testing bandwagon, which made school even less meaningful than students already perceived it to be. William Ford, the Michigan Democrat who chaired the House Education and Labor Committee, asked why the Clinton plan didn't provide more money.[125]

The path navigated by Goals 2000 mirrored that taken by the ESEA. In the Elementary, Secondary, and Vocational Education Subcommittee on May 6, 1993, the Democrats added "opportunity-to-learn standards" on spending, teacher certification, and equipment as well as the provision that state performance standards not determine promotion or graduation for at least five years. On June 23 in the

Education and Labor Committee, the majority adopted an amendment, sponsored by Rhode Island representative Jack Reed and opposed by Clinton, the AFT,
and the Republicans, requiring that before receiving federal funds, a state must
not only set opportunity-to-learn standards but detail the "corrective action" that
is planned to attain those standards. A party-line 28–15 committee vote became a
bipartisan 307–118 floor vote on October 13, however, after the House unanimously adopted an amendment proposed by Pennsylvania Republican William
Goodling disavowing federal control over local educational issues. The bill then
sailed through the Senate Labor and Human Resources Committee, 14–3, on May
19, 1993, and the full Senate, 71–25, on February 8, 1994. The House passed the conference report, 306–121, and the Senate adopted it, 63–22. When the president
signed it on March 31, 1994, at the Zamorano Fine Arts Academy in San Diego,
California, it included two new goals ("teachers will have access to training programs to achieve their skills," and "every school will strive to increase parental
involvement in their children's education"), voluntary "opportunity to learn"
standards, and a $700 million price tag.[126]

Writing in Columbia University's *Teachers' College Record*, Peter Cookson
called Goals 2000 a "critical turning point in the history of American education. . . . Despite the fact that constitutionally the federal government has no
authority to regulate public education, the president and Congress, through the
Department of Education, established a set of educational objectives that, while
officially voluntary, essentially mandates a comprehensive educational reform
plan for the entire nation." AFT president Albert Shanker said the new law "will
bring us to a more systemic approach to education. What kids learn each year
will build on the last like building blocks." Clinton said, "This is a new and different approach for the national government [that] sets world-class education
standards for what every child at every American school should know in order
to win when he or she becomes an adult. Today we can say America is serious
about education." Within a year, forty-nine states had begun developing new
education standards.[127]

The enactment of Goals 2000 was also its high-water mark. Eight months after
Clinton affixed his signature to the bill, the Republican Party gained control of
both houses of Congress for the first time in the era of comprehensive federal aid
to elementary and secondary education. In 1995, Secretary Riley appeared before
the newly reconstituted Economic and Educational Opportunities Committee
(formerly Education and Labor) to stave off new calls for his department's termination, then watched Congress cut the Goals 2000 budget in half and the Senate
repudiate the proposed national history standards by a 99–1 vote. Two years after
Goals 2000 became law, the new Congress eliminated the National Education
Standards and Improvement Council, provisions governing the composition of
state and local education improvement panels, and the voluntary "opportunity to
learn" standards from the legislation. In March 1996, seven years after President

Bush convened the nation's governors at Charlottesville, the nation's governors and corporate leaders arranged their own education summit, then invited President Clinton. Admitting that "the effort to have national standards . . . has been less than successful," the president all but abdicated the federal role in Goals 2000. "We can only do better with tougher standards and better assessment," he told the governors, "and you should set the standards."[128]

In November 1996, the NAEP released its report on the achievement of U.S. thirteen- and seventeen-year-olds from the 1970s to 1994, which concluded that while "the trends in science and mathematics show early declines or relative stability followed by improved performance, reading and writing results show few indications of positive trends." In the same month, the report of the bipartisan National Education Goals Panel noted that because the nation had reached only five of twenty indicators measuring education performance, "we're not going to make it" to the eight national goals by the end of the decade. "There is absolutely no way we can be assured of annual progress toward reaching the goals," said Colorado Democratic governor Roy Romer, who would chair the panel in 1997, "until states and communities develop and use rigorous standards and design new forms of assessments."[129]

Yet buoyed by his landslide reelection victory over Kansas Republican senator Robert Dole, the latest in a series of turnabouts in the political career of the self-proclaimed "Comeback Kid," the president pressed forward in his quest for nationally directed school standards. With many Americans' attention diverted by the imminent verdict in the celebrated O. J. Simpson civil trial, Clinton presented his fourth State of the Union address on February 4, 1997. After introducing two eighth-grade students in the House gallery, the president called education "my number one priority for the next four years" and urged a "new nonpartisan commitment to education." He then recited ten principles that constituted a "call for action" for American education, a list headed by "a national crusade" for education standards. "To help schools meet the standards and measure their progress," Clinton announced, "we will lead an effort over the next two years to develop national tests of student achievement in reading and math. . . . By 1999 every state should test every fourth grader in reading and every eighth grader in math to make sure these standards were met." As a testament to a presidency at the height of its popularity, even the two eighth-graders applauded.[130]

If the Democratic president was riding high, the Republican Congress was lying low. Unaccustomed to being the majority party on Capitol Hill, the Republicans had found themselves winning the battle over issues, helping move Clinton to a balanced budget and welfare reform, yet losing the public relations war, being blamed for two partial government shutdowns in the winter of 1995–96, when Clinton adeptly took spending on education, health, and the environment off the table in budget reduction talks. "I don't want to spend more money on everything," the president said. "I want to spend more money on the right things," and most of the American people agreed that education was one of them. So after Clinton announced a 20 percent increase in funding for Goals 2000, Pennsylvania representative William Goodling, chair of the re-renamed House Education and the Workforce Committee, responded, "We should be able to reach across the aisle," and Vermont senator James Jeffords, chair of the Senate Labor and Human Resources Committee, pronounced himself in full accord with the administration's school aid proposals: "I'm going for everything." After the Republican Congress gave the Democratic president virtually all the spending he wanted in the FY 1998 Labor–Health and Human Services–Education appropriations, *Congressional Quarterly*'s Jackie Koszczuk wrote, "Nowadays, a conservative-led attack on big spending bills is a restrained affair among gentlemen and ladies. It's more polo than mud-wrestling and in the end nothing radically changes."[131]

But the good intentions on both ends of Pennsylvania Avenue could not bridge the ideological divide over Goals 2000. When Clinton announced that the Education Department would broaden the NAEP and the Third International Mathematics and Science Study (which tested random samples of students) to evaluate all students, many members of Congress argued that the development of the tests should occur outside of the administration. Clinton relented, compromising with the Senate to permit the National Assessment Governing Board, an independent entity that oversaw the NAEP, to formulate the tests. But an unusual alliance of conservative Republicans, who identified the tests with federal control of the schools, and liberal Democrats representing districts with large minority populations, joined to defund testing in the House. "We have plenty of testing," said Goodling. "Why have another measurement instrument to tell us what we already know?" Ruben Hinojosa, Democrat of Texas, argued that "standardized testing has a negative, disparate impact on poor and minority students. Equal opportunity in testing cannot be achieved given unequal education opportunity."[132]

Despite the 295–125 House vote, Clinton vowed to continue his campaign for national tests. "The same old forces that have resisted education reform over the past decade," the president lamented, "came together to defeat high national standards in the basics." A compromise among the Senate, House, and White House cut Goals 2000 spending by 15 percent but restored the tests, placing them under the authority of the National Assessment Government Board (NAGB), and imposing a one-year moratorium on national testing until the National Academy of Sciences had determined that existing tests could not substitute for new ones and the NAGB had assured that new tests would account for the needs of disadvantaged, disabled, and limited English-proficient students.[133]

While the politicians wrestled over new national tests, the news from existing evaluations of student performance was mixed. The College Board announced in August that while the nation's students slightly improved their math scores on the Scholastic Achievement (formerly Aptitude) Test, the reading scores remained the same as the previous year. The National Education Goals Panel announced similar results in November: math and science scores of high school seniors were up, but reading scores were down in many states. But compared to the rest of the industrialized world, even the math scores were not very promising. The Third International Mathematics and Sciences Study found American high school seniors behind their counterparts in eighteen of twenty-one nations, ahead of only Lithuania, Cyprus, and South Africa.[134]

No wonder the administration seemed to be losing its enthusiasm for national tests. In his January 29, 1998, State of the Union address, the president noted that "thanks to the actions of this Congress last year," the country would have its national tests. Gone, however, was the March 1999 deadline, replaced simply by the word "soon." Two weeks later, when the House voted 242–174 that Congress have final approval of any national test, Assistant Secretary of Education Marshall Smith said he "now thinks the tests will never be given." Clinton, addressing the nation's governors in March, continued to hedge his bets: "I think it is important that we say, whether we use national tests that are somehow evaluated by a national standard or state tests that are evaluated by national standards, that we do believe that learning the basics is the same in every state in America, and we want to raise the standards in America."[135]

In the president's quest for student accountability, the governors were starting without him. By July 1998, twenty-two states had instituted "high-stakes, must-pass-to-graduate" high school proficiency examinations. Massachusetts became the forty-fourth state to test its new teachers, 60 percent of whom scored below the passing grade of C in the state's first exam, creating what the *New York Times* called the "biggest fuss" over teacher testing "since Arkansas tried it under a young governor named Bill Clinton in 1985." In the wake of yet another study decrying the poor performance of American students (the Paris-based Organization for Economic Cooperation and Development found that there is nearly a four-year gap between the highest- and lowest-performing eighth-graders in the United States), the public was only half as concerned with standards for students, which the president had stressed, as with the quality of teachers, which the president had largely ignored. In a report issued by Clinton's own Education Department, only one in five public school teachers considered themselves well-qualified—a "wake-up call," in Secretary Riley's words, "to get serious about better preparing for and supporting our teachers in the classrooms."[136]

So in his 1999 State of the Union address the president reviewed the latest data on student performance: "You know, our children are doing better. SAT scores are up; math scores have risen in nearly all grades. But there's a problem. While our fourth graders outperform their peers in other countries in math and science, our eighth graders are around average, and our twelfth graders are near the bottom." He reiterated his advocacy of student testing: "With our support, nearly every state has set higher academic standards for public schools, and a voluntary national test is being developed to measure the progress of our students." But for the first time, he proposed that as a condition of receiving federal aid, "new teachers should be required to pass performance exams, and all teachers should know the subjects they're teaching." If Bill Clinton, twice the candidate of the NEA and the AFT, did not quite resemble the anticommunist Richard Nixon in China in 1972, he was sounding more like the proteacher Bill Clinton in Arkansas in 1983.[137]

## The Clinton Record

During the 1996 presidential campaign, Republican nominee Robert Dole derided Clinton's penchant for modest education initiatives such as school uniforms, teenage curfews, and "zero tolerance" for truancy, alongside the larger ESEA and Goals 2000 programs. "I haven't thought much about truancy," said Dole of the latest proposal. "It's probably a good idea," Dole quipped, adding that the president was "taking a lot of tough stands these days."[138]

There was indeed much about the Clinton era that bespoke a national consensus on public education not achieved since the passage of the ESEA of 1965. First, if the baby boom of the 1950s and the 1960s had created a national awareness of education, the "baby boomlet" of the 1980s and 1990s refocused national attention on the nation's schoolchildren. Forty-eight million students entered elementary and secondary schools in the fall of 1997, just below the all-time high of 48.7 million in 1970, and in 1999 as in 1965, Americans cited education as the nation's top priority. So political candidates such as Democratic novice Jay Johnson, running in an overwhelmingly Republican Wisconsin congressional district in 1996, stressed education—and won. "My political consultants told me that education would be a great problem-solving issue," Johnson explained.[139]

Second, if the escalation of the cold war had provided the impetus to enact federal aid to education, the end of the cold war offered the opportunity to fix it. "At the end of the cold war, at the beginning of this period of global economy, of the information age," said Clinton, "education is more important today to individual Americans, to families, to communities, and to our future than it has ever been in the history of the United States." More than two-thirds of Americans believed that the nation that overcame the Soviet Union could conquer its education problems as well. Third, if poverty amidst plenty was the rationale for federal aid, mediocrity amidst plenty was the justification for education reform. "The greatest blow for equity" that the federal government can administer, said Gerald Tirozzi, Clinton's assistant secretary for elementary and secondary education, "is high standards."[140]

Fourth, even if states and localities still accounted for 93 percent of education funding, the country now expected the White House to be a bully pulpit for education reform. Following in the footsteps of Ronald Reagan and George

Bush, Bill Clinton was visiting so many schools during his presidency that, in the words of Peter Applebome of the *New York Times*, "he seems to be running for P.T.A. president." Fifth, if political adolescence prevented an NEA-AFT merger and compelled the unions to settle for categorical aid in the 1960s, political obsolescence was enough of a threat to rekindle merger talks between the 2.3 million-member NEA and the 950,000-member AFT, influence both unions to accept peer review of teachers, and cause California's NEA affiliate to endorse Democrat Gray Davis for governor despite his support for teacher testing. "The fact is that in some instances we have used power to protect the narrow interests of our members," NEA president Bob Chase conceded in February 1998, "and not to advance the interests of our schools."[141]

Sixth, if efforts toward the establishment of a modern Department of Education began during the Johnson administration, calls for its abolition ended during the Clinton administration. During the 1996 presidential campaign, Republican pollsters discovered that 54 percent of registered Republicans, and a greater percentage of women, supported the Department of Education. "Now that Republican talk about abolishing entire federal departments (Education, Energy, Commerce) has proven to be empty bombast, is there *any* institution, or even any activity, of government your administration would terminate?" a frustrated conservative columnist George Will asked Republican presidential candidates in March 1999. "Now that Republicans regard education as among the most important federal issues, do you believe there is *any* sphere of American life that is none of the federal government's business?" Seventh, if the thinly disguised "targeting" of Title I to 95 percent of all school districts in 1965 muffled pleas for fairness from the Left and flexibility from the Right, the loosening of strings on $10 billion of non–Title I federal money under the Education Flexibility Partnership Act (which was supported by both teacher unions and all fifty governors, overwhelmingly passed by Congress, and signed by the president in April) quieted such voices in 1999.[142]

Eighth, if the failures of the states in addressing educational inequality led to the federal aid of the 1960s, the successes of the states in attacking educational inequality encouraged the federal reforms of the 1990s. Spurred by litigation, budget surpluses, and activist governors, sixteen states had gained control of more than 55 percent of their states' education funds; twenty-one approached the national average of 48 percent state, 45 percent local, and 7 percent federal; and only thirteen states still relied on more than 55 percent local funding. "What the states did in assuming greater responsibilities was mostly positive," Clinton concluded, adding that by assuming a greater role over their schools, the states had freed the federal government to be "more active in some areas than the Federal Government traditionally has been."[143]

Finally, just as a liberal Democratic Congress had successfully prodded a liberal Democratic president to spend more money on education in the 1960s, a moderate Democratic president was successfully persuading a conservative Republican Congress to spend more money on education in the 1990s. In October 1998, on the eve of the off-year election, Congress agreed to Clinton's plan to hire one hundred thousand new teachers over seven years to reduce class size to a national average of eighteen in grades one through three, with 80 percent of the monies to school districts based on need and 20 percent based on population. Former Nixon and Reagan aide Chester Finn, a liberal Democrat in the 1960s and a conservative Republican in the 1990s, provided a partial list of Clinton initiatives as of the fall of 1998: "subsidies for state academic standards, tax credits for school construction, paying for teachers to be appraised by a national standards board, hiring 100,000 teachers to shrink class size, ensuring 'equity' in textbooks, collecting gender-sensitive data on the pay of high school coaches, boosting the self-esteem of rural students, establishing a National Hawaiian Education Council, connecting every classroom to the Internet, developing before-and-after school programs, forging mentoring relationships between college students and middle schoolers, increasing the number of drug-prevention counselors, requiring school uniforms, and fostering character education."[144]

For their part, wrote Finn and Michael Petrilli, "Republicans in Congress have proposed . . . slashing class size, ending social promotion, legalizing school prayer, replacing textbooks with laptops, funding environmental education, paying for school metal detectors, and creating a new literacy program." Republicans have "increased the funding for education over the last three years," said the NEA's top lobbyist in July 1999, "far more than any Democrat ever did." No wonder Senator Dole had not found time to think about truancy.[145]

Although there was much upon which the nation could agree, several currents threatened to unravel this emerging unity in the same way that the 1965 consensus had come undone. First, of the near-record number of students in the nation's schools, an alarming one-third of fifteen- to seventeen-year-olds attended classes below their appropriate grade. Second, in the Gannett News Service poll that discovered great optimism among the nation's adults about American education, the least hopeful age group was those eighteen to twenty-four years old who had most recently gone to school. Third, sixteen years after *A Nation at Risk* and ten years after the first Education Summit, a federal government that had agreed on standards still had not tested them. "If national testing went down in flames," concluded Finn, "it would be because those on the right couldn't stand the word 'national,' and those on the left can't abide testing." Fourth, the bully pulpit of the White House is only as credible as the preacher, and Clinton's 1998 impeachment on charges of perjury and obstruction of justice in the Monica Lewinsky scandal undermined his frequent calls for "values," "responsibility," and "character education" while undercutting his political capital with both parties. As of July 1999, two-thirds of Americans had an unfavorable opinion of Bill Clinton the person.[146]

Fifth, the teacher unions revealed the limits of their openness to change when the NEA Representative Assembly rejected a merger with the AFT largely to fend off "right-wing groups and politicians promoting [nonpublic school] vouchers" and when both unions returned to their pre-1965 advocacy of federal spending for school construction. Sixth, the apparent death of the twenty-year-old movement to abolish the Department of Education threatened to perpetuate the agency's flaws as well as its feats. A September 1996 study by the National Commission on Teaching and America's Future found that 23 percent of all secondary teachers had not even minored in their specialty fields while in college. When asked what the Department of Education had done to address this problem, department spokesman Rick Miller replied, "There are not really any programs. We're not involved in the hiring of teachers. That's a state and local issue."[147]

Seventh, the bipartisan enactment of the Education Flexibility Partnership Act was as significant for what it excluded, Title I, as for what it included—just about everything else. Title I remained, as it had been from the beginning, a source of highly partisan strife. An amendment to the fiscal 1998 education appropriations bill by Washington Republican senator Slade Gorton that would block grant the $7 billion program while terminating Goals 2000 narrowly passed the Senate, only to succumb in the House-Senate conference committee to the threat of a Clinton veto. In 1999, with the ESEA again up for renewal, familiar actors recited familiar lines. William Goodling, now the chairman of the House Education and Workforce Committee, reappeared to argue for block grants: "For more than three decades, the Federal Government has been sending money to the states through scores of Washington-based programs. But all the studies, evaluations, and reports show little or no academic results from these programs." Dale Kildee, now the ranking minority member on the panel, returned to say that block grants would be a bad idea: "Governors like to spread the money around rather than target it. They would like the money to be left on a stump, and let them come and pick it up and spend it where they want." Marshall Smith, now acting deputy secretary of education, again pleaded for fair distribution of funds: "In this nation's brand of federalism, there is more disparity at the local level, less at the state level, and even less at the Federal level. The allocation of resources is fairer at the Federal level."[148]

Eighth, promising trends toward state control of local schools could only go so far if those schools had too many administrators, unqualified teachers, ill-equipped classrooms, deteriorating buildings, and impoverished students from broken homes. "With few exceptions among our 16,000 school systems," wrote conservative Chester Finn, "the norm is smug or timid administrators who may speak eloquently to the Rotary Club but who also twitch when the teachers' union tugs their chain, who churn out misleading press releases about the kids reading above grade level, who squander vast sums on bureaucratic overhead, and who conspire with the school board to shore up the monopoly." Liberal

Nicholas Lemann put it more succinctly: "American education is still local in one crucial way," he wrote. "Individual schools have the freedom to be bad."[149]

Finally, the sheer volume of proposals by "Education Governors," the "Education President," the "Education Congress," and the education interest groups was depriving the country of perhaps the most important debate of all: Which of these initiatives was the most urgent, demanding immediate attention and substantial federal resources? During his first two years, in an era of budget deficits and a friendly Congress, the president was pretty clear about his top priority: Goals 2000. But by 1995, seizing a political opportunity offered by an opposition Congress more intent on balancing the budget than rescuing education spending, Clinton astutely promised to do both. In the budget showdown that the president's pollsters invited, specific national goals gave way to broader "investment" and "values": "What we have to do is balance the budget and increase investment in education. . . . I have consistently said that if Congress sends me a budget that violates our values, I'll veto it." So he did, and he helped save his presidency.[150]

By his second term, vindicated for his defense of education expenditures and relieved of the "tough choices" of deficit spending, Bill Clinton had further modified the national dialogue on elementary and secondary education. Lyndon Johnson told the American people to judge him on how much money he spent. Ronald Reagan asked that he be judged on how well the money was spent. Bill Clinton began his presidency by agreeing with both Johnson and Reagan. But he was ending it by insisting that money was not really the issue at all. What really mattered to Bill Clinton were ideas—and, when it came to education, no one had more than he did. "No other President," boasted Tirozzi, "has devoted twenty-five percent of his State of the Union address to education," as Clinton did in 1997. In the next year's address, Clinton kept score: "Since then, this Congress and the American people have responded, in the most important year for education in a generation, by expanding public school choice, opening the way for 3000 charter schools, working to connect every classroom to the information superhighway, continuing to expand Head Start to one million children, launching America Reads, [and] send[ing] out thousands of college students into our schools to make sure every eight-year-old can read." Clinton was right—no president since Lyndon Johnson had enacted so many public school aid proposals in a single legislative session. But Johnson only served five years. Clinton was entering his sixth of eight years, with a lot more time for a lot more ideas.[151]

# CHAPTER 5

# School Desegregation
## 1981–2001

## Ronald Reagan

"When I arrived in Sacramento, it had been less than two years since a large portion of Los Angeles had gone up in smoke during the Watts riots," Ronald Reagan would remember of the years before his governorship began in 1967. "To understand more about the causes that had led to the rioting, I decided to visit families who lived in black neighborhoods around the state as well as the large Mexican-American barrios in East Los Angeles." From these secret visits Governor Reagan learned that "some blacks just hadn't had the opportunity to get the same kind of schooling as other Californians."[1]

The governor arrived in the minority communities of Los Angeles only a few years before the school buses did. In 1971, in *Swann v. Charlotte-Mecklenburg Board of Education,* the Supreme Court unanimously approved forced busing as a constitutional method of achieving school desegregation. By the last year of Reagan's governorship, however, the Supreme Court's *Milliken v. Bradley* decision of 1974 had outlawed forced busing across governmental jurisdictions, and President Richard Nixon had joined a majority of Americans in opposing this means of desegregating the nation's public schools. "A dwindling band of northern liberals found that they were defending a policy with no real constituency," write Thomas and Mary Edsall. "Poll after poll found white opposition to busing, and only lukewarm support in the black community, which was generally right down the middle on the issue."[2]

In 1976, for the first time, both major parties nominated antibusing presidential candidates, Democratic challenger Jimmy Carter and Republican incumbent Gerald Ford. Carter's victory hardly slowed the buses, however, as his Justice Department, led by Solicitor General Wade McCree and assistant attorney general for civil rights Drew Days, continued to defend busing in court. In two Ohio cases in 1979, the Supreme Court, in the words of Herman Schwartz, made it "relatively easy to show that [an] entire school system had been deliberately segregated and warranted a busing order."[3]

So although forced busing was uncommon, it remained unpopular. Republican presidential candidate Ronald Reagan therefore agreed with the "great majority of Americans in opposing forced busing.... It is time we removed control of our schools from the courts and the federal government, and returned it to the local school boards where it belongs." Reagan supported alternatives such as voluntary public magnet schools with specialized curricula and nonpublic school vouchers to promote racial integration and quality education.[4]

Though Reagan's busing rhetoric was not substantially different from that of the three presidents who immediately preceded him, the passion of many of his followers on this and other "social issues" was considerably deeper. In 1980 as in 1976, when he unsuccessfully challenged Ford for his party's nomination, candidate Reagan therefore criticized the sitting president for failing to match words with actions against busing. So by the time Reagan took the oath of office in 1981 in a city whose public schools were 96 percent black, his partisans had raised a higher standard by which he would be judged. He would have to stop the buses, and do it quickly.[5]

By the end of his two terms in the White House, Reagan had succeeded in stopping some buses. But he had moved belatedly against forced busing and feebly toward school desegregation. And these issues, which inflamed his most ardent supporters and his most fervent critics, hardly seemed to interest the president at all.

## Busing

CONTINUITY   When President John Kennedy appeared to have reneged on his pledge to end housing discrimination by the federal government by executive order, civil rights leaders deluged him with pens to remind him of his promise. Unfortunately for Ronald Reagan, he could not end court-ordered busing "with the stroke of a pen." But in the eyes of his backers, he could have done a lot more toward that end in the first three years of his presidency.

The first test of Reagan's antibusing stance was the Chicago school desegregation case that he inherited from the Carter administration. Following negotiations between the Justice Department and the Chicago Board of Education, the U.S. District Court for the Northern District of Illinois, on September 24, 1980, acknowledged "substantial racial isolation in Chicago schools" and mandated a plan to create "the greatest practicable number of stably desegregated schools" in order to provide "education and related programs for any Black and Hispanic schools remaining segregated" and to find "financial resources adequate for implementation" of the program. The court required "mandatory reassignment and transportation" of pupils "only to the extent that other techniques are insufficient" to achieve these goals. A March 1981 analysis of the Reagan administration's implementation of the consent decree for the city of Chicago concluded, however, that "the Justice Department is leaning hard on Chicago for prompt action on a busing proposal" over Mayor Jane Byrne's opposition. Richard Williamson of the Justice Department lamented, "It would appear that Justice is continuing to proceed in the framework of the Carter Administration as opposed to reflecting the President's views." In July the Justice Department pronounced Chicago's school desegregation "incomplete" and asked the federal judge in the case to require the city to submit a revised plan that "desegregates schools as much as possible by September 1982." Reagan aide David Waller complained, "In the continuing rift between career Civil Rights division attorneys and the Reagan appointees to that division," the Chicago case "would suggest that the career types are prevailing."[6]

Another holdover from the Carter era was the case of Port Arthur, Texas, where U.S. District Court judge Joseph Fisher sided with the state against the Reagan Justice Department in refusing to replace a 1970 voluntary school desegregation plan with forced busing. U.S. Supreme Court justice Lewis Powell rejected a plea by parents in Beaumont, Texas, to prevent implementation of a forced busing plan "neither supported nor opposed" by the Reagan Justice Department for the South Park Independent School District. The Reagan Justice Department's endorsement of the Seattle School Board's opposition to a statewide antibusing initiative prompted an angry letter from Washington's attorney general. "I enclose for your perusal a letter to me of August 4 from Ken Eikenberry," White House aide Lyn Nofziger wrote to Special Counsel Edwin Meese. "Not surprisingly, he, like 99.9 percent of the people who supported Ronald Reagan in the past, is at odds with mandatory school busing—as I think we all are. Surely if we are going to change the direction of this country, mandatory school busing is a place to make changes—as I thought we would do because I thought that was what the President wanted."[7]

Eikenberry was not the only Republican attorney general upset with the administration's course on school desegregation. On December 19, 1980, a district court ordered the state of Missouri to devise and largely finance a voluntary desegregation plan for the St. Louis public schools. When Missouri failed to comply, the court ordered the Justice Department to enter the case in March 1981. The resulting plan, subject to the approval of Judge William Hungate, provided for magnet schools, special interschool programs, and the "voluntary transfer of majority-race students to districts where they would be in the minority by providing all transfer students with one-half-year free tuition at a Missouri state school for each year of transfer study." Attorney General John Ashcroft of Missouri claimed that the plan would cost too much and would stigmatize those pupils not receiving college scholarships. Barbara Mueller, president of the St. Louis chapter of the antibusing National Association for Neighborhood Schools (NANS), found the "scheme of bribery, from the Justice Department, which would offer 'free' college tuition to students transferring to another school district to improve racial balance," nearly as distasteful as forced busing. Reagan aide James Medas wondered, "Isn't this a federally-mandated, unfunded program counter to Reagan Federalism?"[8]

Not only were Justice Department actions at odds with Reagan's campaign statements, but its words seemed to clash with the president's. In May 1981, in the administration's first statement on school desegregation, Attorney General William French Smith echoed Reagan in his promise to "vigorously prosecute any governmental attempts to foster desegregation" and his contention that "there is no inherent value in reaching a pre-determined racial mixture . . . in the schools; it[']s the quality of education itself that makes the difference." Smith's attack on forced busing, however, was somewhat less than Reaganesque. "The Justice Department is not expected to seek *widespread* busing of children to achieve racial integration in schools. . . . Busing efforts to date have been counterproductive in *most* areas. The Justice Department *will pursue* busing as a solution only where there is a proven relationship between busing of students and the quality of education in the schools affected."[9]

In a July memorandum, deputy assistant attorney general for civil rights Thomas D'Agostino, sounding like Reagan, criticized the "integrationist mindset" of the career lawyers in the Justice Department, but in September D'Agostino's boss, assistant attorney general for civil rights William Bradford Reynolds, repudiated the memo. Later that same month, Reynolds resembled Reagan: "This department is committed to the vigorous and forceful enforcement of laws in all civil rights areas, including school desegregation," yet "we will, in school cases as in all other areas handled by this division, refrain from seeking race-conscious or sex-conscious remedies solely for the purpose of achieving a particular balance in the classroom," and "mandatory transportation of students is not a remedy that the Department of Justice believes has addressed the above needs in a meaningful way in past years." But Reynolds also reinterpreted Reagan: "A number of school systems are now under court order to cure constitutional violations, and many of these orders require mandatory assignment of students to distant schools. In the absence of legislation, we would not anticipate routinely joining in requests to have such busing orders set aside. They may reflect unwise policy, but they are not per se unlawful."[10]

This ambivalence continued to alienate the administration's staunchest supporters. In his fourth letter to the president, Dan Seale of the board of directors of NANS reminded Reagan that "one of the reasons that you were elected President of the United States is because the people believed what you were saying. You stated your opposition to forced busing. The Republican platform has a plank that opposes forced busing. Yet your Department of Justice is continuing to seek system-wide busing." Neal Hammerstrom, a correspondent for Meese, noted that the Seale letter "is a good example of the kind of mail Mr. Meese has been receiving on this topic. The majority of people writing are urging action on a campaign promise that has not been fulfilled and voicing strong complaints over Justice Department activities that are contrary to President Reagan's beliefs about busing."[11]

Similar letters were piling up on Capitol Hill, where Congress rushed to fill the void of executive leadership. Democratic senator Bennett Johnston of Louisiana joined Republican senator Jesse Helms of North Carolina in resurrecting the antibusing amendment to the Justice Department appropriations bill that Carter had vetoed in the waning days of his administration. Although Meese was privately "delighted" when the Senate passed what the conservative journal *Human Events* called "the most effective anti-busing bill ever approved by either house of Congress," Smith was publicly disturbed. "Encouraging or permitting the routine opening of court decrees is not in harmony with the special interest recognized in the law in the finality of judgments," the attorney general wrote to House Judiciary Committee chairman Peter Rodino of New Jersey in May 1982 in objecting to the bill's prohibition of the busing of schoolchildren more than five miles or fifteen minutes from their homes. "To the extent that Congress does intend to effect a long-term substantive change in the law," Smith added, "the proper vehicle would seem to be permanent substantive legislation, not an authorization bill which must be reviewed annually by Congress and which becomes more difficult to enact." After reading a draft of Assistant Attorney General Theodore Olson's similar testimony before the House Judiciary Committee's Subcommittee on Courts, Civil Liberties, and the Administration of Justice, White House aide Morton Blackwell lamented, "This testimony could have been expected from the Justice Department during the Ford and Carter Administrations. . . . Foes of forced busing can only conclude upon reading Ted Olson's testimony that no leadership against forced busing will be coming from this Administration." Blackwell predicted that "we can expect the anti-busing leaders to become more vocal in their opinion that they wasted their time working the precincts for Ronald Reagan. In the meantime, there is little to be done, aside from a wholesale personnel change at the Justice Department." Without administration support, the Johnston-Helms measure died in the House.[12]

If the Reagan administration's devotion to the status quo disheartened its conservative supporters, it nonetheless failed to appease its liberal opponents. Despite the Justice Department's reluctance to oppose forced busing, "the professional civil rights extremists will still call us racists," Blackwell accurately observed. In February 1982 U.S. Civil Rights Commission chairman Arthur Flemming warned that "reduced resources, requirements, and leadership jeopardize voluntary civil rights compliance and civil rights enforcement in education." Flemming urged Reagan to "halt this abandonment of federal civil rights leadership and commit your Administration to carrying on the effort to banish illegal discrimination from this Nation's schools." Black civil rights activist Jesse Jackson claimed in March that the administration's antibusing rhetoric targeted "not the bus, but us." In October, the three Carter, one Ford, and one of two Reagan appointees on the

U.S. Civil Rights Commission reaffirmed their support for busing to coerce school desegregation; Chairman Clarence Pendleton, with whom Reagan had replaced Flemming, abstained from the vote.[13]

The administration nevertheless seemed more eager to placate its adversaries than its allies on school desegregation. In August 1982 the Justice Department for the first time asked a court to restrict an existing busing plan, arguing that a court order had induced substantial white flight from the East Baton Rouge, Louisiana, public schools. But after an alternative designed by Boston University scholar Christine Rossell to replace busing with magnet schools and transfer options met opposition within the Civil Rights Division of the Justice Department as well as the local school board, Reynolds abandoned the fight in February 1983. In September 1982 Reynolds announced that while the Justice Department would not "undo existing decrees, where a school board seeks to modify a busing plan that is not working and requests our support, we will of course give that request serious consideration." When the *Washington Post* reported that this position would lead to the reopening of desegregation cases in Boston, St. Louis, Cleveland, Memphis, Detroit, and Denver, moderate Republican representative Millicent Fenwick of New Jersey wrote to Reagan to express her apprehension that "the Justice Department may abandon its commitment to court-ordered busing in several major cities." So the administration retreated. A White House staff briefing for Reagan's September 28 press conference stated that "there is nothing new in this [*Post*] story. . . . The Administration is not going to try to undo what has already been done through four hundred to five hundred past court orders."[14]

In April 1983 the Justice Department objected to a revised plan for desegregating St. Louis schools, in part because it allowed for the imposition of forced busing after five years of voluntary measures. Three months later, however, when Judge Hungate accepted the plan over the opposition of Missouri attorney general Ashcroft and Republican governor Christopher Bond, the department refused to take a stand. In his May 17, 1983, press conference, Reagan praised Principal Adan Salgado for leading an educational renaissance at Albert Sidney Johnston High School in Austin, Texas. But when Salgado insisted that "it would have been most difficult, if not impossible, to get where we are now without court-ordered desegregation," the administration scrambled for a response. Within two months, White House aide Stephen Galebach had compiled a list of explanations for the school's improvement that included "requiring hard work and discipline," "setting clear-cut academic standards," and "putting in a school computer center." Although Galebach noted that "every one of these factors was provided by local initiative [and] most of them have nothing to do with increased spending," he conceded that "court-ordered busing may have been the catalyst that motivated the Austin school to begin an improved academic approach." In July, Smith boasted that the administration had filed "three school desegregation suits, as compared to two in the same period during the previous administration." Reynolds at the time was traveling the southern United States with Jesse Jackson to "convey to the public that we do care" about civil rights and "that our job of enforcement is one that is carried on as vigorously and rigorously as it has been in prior administrations." As for this administration's "image problem" in liberal circles, Reynolds added, "Whether it's fair or unfair . . . I certainly intend to the extent that I can to correct that."[15]

A month later, two years after his administration accepted a revised plan to desegregate Chicago's schools without forced busing but with racial quotas for magnet schools, Reagan vetoed a bill authorizing $250 million of Department of Education monies to help implement the plan. "The Constitution and its process of separated powers and checks and balances does not permit the judiciary to determine spending priorities or to reallocate funds appropriated by Congress," Reagan explained. Yet in September Congress passed a similar bill, and Reagan quietly signed it. A disappointed Nofziger admonished Reagan "imagemaker" Michael Deaver, "Frankly, I think that it would be helpful if the President were to get out in front a little more on social issues such as this [busing] that he campaigned on so heavily in 1976 and 1980." Reagan thus entered the final year of his first term having delivered only one major speech on civil rights (to the American Bar Association in August 1983) and having done little to end forced busing. "We are still awaiting an all-out effort on your part to get the necessary legislation to stop forced busing," NANS' Joyce Haws wrote to Reagan in March 1984, in another futile attempt at meeting with the president.[16]

CHANGE    By 1984, however, three major factors had produced the Reagan administration's belated break with its predecessors on forced busing and school desegregation. First, the surprisingly widespread resonance of the Department of Education's April 1983 *A Nation at Risk* report on the dismal state of American education heightened the visibility of the nation's schools. Thus Reagan, who had accorded other educational issues as little attention as school desegregation, suddenly emerged as the country's "Educator-in-Chief." From the issuance of the report to his reelection in November 1984, Reagan would discuss education in sixty-two addresses to colleges, high schools, elementary schools, meetings of teachers and school administrators, and his administration's National Forums on Excellence in Education. When Reagan told a group of African American members of his administration that he now placed education "at the top of the national agenda," he almost inevitably had to resurrect forced busing as a cause of public education's decline and public magnet schools and nonpublic school vouchers as keys to its reform.[17]

A second explanation for the change in the administration's school desegregation policies was election-year politics, which caused Reagan to rediscover his ideological base of support. In January 1984, when District Judge Edward Dean

Price approved the first desegregation plan begun and ended by the Reagan administration, Reynolds this time held his ground in the face of liberal criticism. Rather than succumb to the charges of the *New York Times,* Ralph Neas of the Leadership Conference on Civil Rights, and his predecessor Drew Days that the voluntary plan for the Bakersfield, California, schools was unworkable, the assistant attorney general for civil rights boldly declared it "a blueprint for desegregation in the future." The Justice Department moved from neutrality to opposition to the St. Louis busing order, and Reagan enacted the Magnet Schools Assistance Program, which allocated federal monies for voluntary desegregation. In August NANS president William D'Onofrio thus introduced Reynolds to his organization's members in Pittsburgh with words he had waited almost four years to utter: "For the first time, we have a Justice Department that does not go before the courts to support forced busing." In October, Reagan took his campaign to Charlotte, North Carolina, thirteen years after the landmark *Swann* ruling had forcibly desegregated that city's schools. "Busing takes innocent children out of the neighborhood school," said the Republican presidential nominee a month before his landslide reelection, "and makes them pawns in a social experiment which nobody wants"—and one that his administration was finally abandoning.[18]

The final catalyst for the administration's change of position was the change of personnel at the Justice Department, where the Carter administration holdovers, according to Reynolds, eventually "either left or got on board." While it fell short of the housecleaning advocated by Blackwell and other conservatives, this transformation began at the top. A month after the Reagan victory, Attorney General Smith resigned as quietly as he had served. Smith's more vocal and more ideological successor, former White House Counsel Edwin Meese, quickly served notice that Reagan's second term would begin differently from his first. In February 1985, after the Supreme Court refused to hear an appeal by the Chicago school board of the Justice Department's withholding of desegregation monies from the city, Reagan pronounced his administration firmly in favor of magnet schools. Such an approach, the president argued, "would permit students to avoid mandatory attendance in schools that were racially integrated by court order." In March, asserting that many of the reasons for segregated schools had been "corrected," Meese instructed Reynolds to encourage school districts under court orders to seek alternatives to forced busing. While Smith had kept Reynolds at a distance, Meese would work closely with his assistant to execute the department's new strategy. "If he's in by seven a.m.," said Reynolds about Meese, "generally I'm in by seven. If he's in at eight, I'm in at eight, and I see him from the beginning of the day on a whole raft of things. It really is a very close, one-to-one relationship."[19]

It would also be a productive one. In June 1986 Reynolds successfully backed the Norfolk, Virginia, school board, arguing in the Fourth Circuit Court that court-ordered busing should end because the city had met the criteria for a "unitary" school district as provided in the Supreme Court's 1968 *Green* decision—desegregation of students, faculty, and staff as well as equity in facilities, transportation, and extracurricular activities. Calling the Norfolk decision a "model for the future," Reynolds announced that the Justice Department would "assist other school boards that wanted to regain local control for color-blind policies." By the fall of 1987, with Meese immersed in the Iran-contra and Wedtech scandals, Reynolds effectively was leading the department in its advocacy of magnet schools and voluntary transfers as well as its assault on forced busing.[20]

In the final year of his presidency, Ronald Reagan reached the end of his administration's journey away from forced busing and toward voluntary school desegregation. Five years after inadvertently praising a school that had forcibly bused its pupils, Reagan visited a magnet school that he called "a great success story." Suitland High School was just outside of Washington, D.C. The president had not traveled very far.[21]

## *The Reagan Record*

As in so many other areas, Ronald Reagan's greatest influence on busing and school desegregation was in transforming the dialogue. Although he spoke infrequently against busing and less frequently for school desegregation, writes Steven Shull, Reagan "used strong rhetoric to rekindle and recast civil rights policy." Though more than six hundred school districts remained under federal court order at the end of his tenure, Reagan's ritualistic denunciation of forced busing had helped persuade a majority of blacks as well as whites, and school desegregation would not be an issue in the 1984 and 1988 presidential campaigns. The word "busing" even disappeared from the convention resolutions of the National Association for the Advancement of Colored People (NAACP), which in 1985 merely expressed the wish to "find a way to re-create the understanding that desegregation is important, and it works." Two years later, Meese omitted forced busing from his list of major issues tackled by the Reagan administration and the conservative movement. Today, Meese recalls that busing "wasn't much of an issue" in the Reagan administration.[22]

Beyond his rhetoric, Reagan was able to leave his imprint on school desegregation by appointing antibusing judges. When Reagan entered office in 1981, there were more than ninety vacancies on the federal bench and, for the first time in thirty years, a Republican Senate majority to confirm a Republican president's nominees. By the end of his presidency, Reagan had appointed nearly half of all lower-court judges and one-third of the justices of the Supreme Court. While the Reagan appointees' rulings did not constitute a "judicial revolution," they did, in David O'Brien's words, "reinvigorate traditional notions of judicial self-restraint." As a result, "you won't see Reagan's appointees taking over school systems," added University of Virginia law professor A. E. Dick Howard, "or ordering forced busing." Gary Orfield concludes that "when the federal courts allowed Norfolk, Virginia to return to segregated neighborhoods in 1986, the decision wrote into law conventional conservative criticisms of busing, blaming [it] for white flight and parental disengagement."[23]

If the Reagan administration had certified its resistance to forced busing, was it equally committed to school desegregation? Attorney General Smith thought so. "We pioneered desegregation plans that rely on the voluntary participation of students in magnet schools, outreach programs, or careful structuring of school-district zoning, and on sound long-range plans for school construction," he would write in his memoir. "In places as diverse as . . . Chicago, Illinois, and Bakersfield, California, these plans were put in place, and they work." Indeed, the *Chicago Tribune* claimed in July 1983 that the administration-backed magnet schools in that city "have lured students of all racial and ethnic groups into voluntary integrated schools without the whip of court-ordered busing." Raymond Wolters adds that "Bakersfield was a success. The Reagan administration rejected forced busing and developed an affirmative plan that satisfied the courts' requirements for numerical mixing while avoiding white flight and other damage to quality education." A 1984 Department of Education study found that in thirty-two of forty-five representative magnet schools, "positive racial integration is advanced." A 1987 study by the U.S. Commission on Civil Rights (at the time dominated by Reagan appointees) concluded that desegregation plans from 1967 to 1985 that "used pairing and clustering—particularly in combination with rezoning—had larger desegregative effects than busing plans."[24]

But these successes were incomplete. By 1988 white enrollment in Chicago's public schools had dropped to 12 percent (from 51 percent in 1967), 45 percent of the system's students did not graduate from high school, 93 percent scored below the national average on high school reading tests, and Secretary of Education William Bennett labeled these schools "the nation's worst." Most white families moving to Bakersfield settled outside of the boundaries of the desegregation plan, gangs appeared within the borders, and academic achievement stagnated. Studies of voluntary desegregation in Charlotte, North Carolina, and Montgomery and Prince George's Counties, Maryland, discovered that magnet schools had failed to stem the movement toward resegregation of those districts. And there were remarkably few assessments of the impact of voluntary desegregation. "Courts, policy-makers, and the press have trusted local school officials to make resegregated schools fair," Orfield writes. "Usually no one is required to show that the proposed program for equalizing segregated schools has worked anywhere, with no independent assessment of the results."[25]

In the absence of such evidence, mere perceptions of the administration's commitment to school desegregation often would have to suffice. Ronald Reagan "had been taught by his parents that racial intolerance was abhorrent," writes biographer Lou Cannon, "and the many people whom I interviewed who knew him as a young man were unanimous in believing that he absorbed those lessons." But Reagan's application of those lessons during his presidency was uneven at best. While he "took few legislative actions" on civil rights, Shull observes, Reagan's "executive actions were unparalleled"—and controversial. His Justice Department unsuccessfully petitioned the Supreme Court to restore tax-exempt status to racially discriminatory Christian schools in *Bob Jones University v. United States* and *Goldsboro Christian Schools v. United States* in 1983. He supported the 1984 Supreme Court decision in *Grove City v. Bell* that restricted antidiscrimination laws to specific programs receiving federal funds, not to the institution in which the discrimination had occurred, only to have Congress overcome his veto of a bill reversing the decision. He waited seven years to meet with civil rights groups, and he unsuccessfully proposed legislation to make bilingual education voluntary rather than mandatory for school districts. According to Shull, Reagan "requested the least increases in civil rights budgets" of presidents from Dwight Eisenhower to George Bush, and Congress virtually defunded the pro-Reagan U.S. Civil Rights Commission from 1986 to 1988. So even though the percentage of black high school graduates increased from 60 to 75 percent in the 1980s and the largest three-year decline in black poverty in two decades occurred from 1983 to 1986, seven of every ten African Americans believed that the Reagan administration was not doing enough to help blacks.[26]

Ronald Reagan thus presided over the troubled transition to a post–civil rights era. For most of his first term, conservatives battled moderates for control of the administration's school desegregation policy. The triumph of the conservatives by 1984 was a step back for forced busing. But it was hardly a step forward for school desegregation. "Even magnet schools and [public school] choice have not made inroads in some places," Meese concedes today, though he does not view school resegregation as a problem. "I don't like the term *de facto* segregation," says the former attorney general. "It is natural for people to go to school near where they want to live." Reynolds agrees: "People are living where they want to live. If as a consequence of that, you have one school district with a lot of minority students and one with a lot of majority students, I don't think we should change that. We should make damn sure students get a good education." For better or worse, by the end of the Reagan presidency, most Americans, black and white, were saying much the same thing.[27]

## George Bush

In 1986, Willie Horton, a convicted murderer on a weekend furlough granted by Massachusetts Democratic governor Michael Dukakis, raped a woman and tortured her fiancé. Two years later, seizing upon an issue introduced to the Demo-

cratic presidential primaries by Tennessee senator Al Gore, a George Bush supporter produced a television commercial showing a photograph of Willie Horton passing in and out of prison doors. Although the Bush camp called Horton
a symbol of Democratic nominee Dukakis's softness toward crime, critics
claimed that Horton's photograph was memorable less for his blue coveralls
than his black skin. The ad, they asserted, was racist.[28]

They stopped short of calling Bush a racist, however. After all, as an under-
graduate at Yale, Bush had led a drive for the United Negro College Fund. As a
Republican congressman from Texas, he had voted for the Fair Housing Act of
1968, taking on a group of angry white constituents in a meeting he later called
the most significant of his political life. As a presidential candidate two decades
later, he called on the country to "leave that tired old baggage of bigotry
behind." As president, he would appoint his friend Dr. Louis Sullivan, president
of predominantly black Morehouse College, as secretary of Health and Human
Services, and black conservative Clarence Thomas to succeed Thurgood Marshall on the Supreme Court. He would provide legal safeguards and compensation for minorities and women by signing the Americans with Disabilities Act in
1990 and the Civil Rights Act of 1991. He would reject a recommendation by
Deputy Undersecretary of Education Michael Williams to outlaw race-based
college scholarships.[29]

But in the eyes of his opponents, President Bush would never completely
exorcise the ghost of Willie Horton. By vetoing the Civil Rights Act of 1990 as a
"quota bill," trying unsuccessfully to appoint black conservative William Lucas
as assistant attorney general for civil rights, refusing to withdraw Thomas's
nomination amid charges of sexual harassment, and selecting relatively obscure
David Souter for the Supreme Court, Bush rekindled the ire of his adversaries.
And on an issue that still mattered to the civil rights community, the inconsistent Mr. Bush remained consistently "wrong." In word and deed, his administration opposed busing to coerce school desegregation.

## The Return of Busing

"For those who think busing is no longer a major issue in American education,"
wrote David Armor in February 1989, "look again." In the fall of 1988 federal circuit courts had overturned voluntary school desegregation plans in Oklahoma
City, Oklahoma; Topeka, Kansas; and DeKalb County, Georgia. Busing to coerce
school desegregation was returning, Armor contended, even though "racial-
balance programs have failed to achieve their ultimate educational goal—to
improve the academic performance of minority students." The new administration concurred. In a December 1989 reply to Rebecca Amerson, who protested
the DeKalb County decision, Acting Assistant Attorney General James Turner
asserted that "the Justice Department has favored whenever possible the use of
non-mandatory busing measures to achieve desegregation." When Bush

unveiled his America 2000 education reform proposal in April 1991, he called for voluntary desegregation through public magnet schools and nonpublic as well as public school vouchers.[30]

If the administration were to move toward voluntary school desegregation, however, it first would have to remove the vestiges of mandatory plans. In September 1990, when the Seattle school board voted to relax coercive desegregation in an attempt to stem "white flight," the Department of Education invoked Title VI of the Civil Rights Act of 1964 in withholding $3.2 million in matching funds for the city's magnet schools. Faced with "an economic gun to the board's head," in the words of member Michael Preston, the panel deferred its revised plan for a year. Five days later, the American Civil Liberties Union, the NAACP, and the Church Council of Greater Seattle joined in a lawsuit to eliminate the delayed program. The Seattle situation is "illustrative of the competing messages behind federal desegregation policy and school choice," wrote Doreen Torgerson of the Education Department. "It is unfortunate that federal financial incentives tied to old paradigm desegregation strategies (even those that include magnet schools) are working against Seattle's propensity for greater school choice. What do we do about this?"[31]

What the Bush administration could do was to seize an opportunity that its three immediate predecessors had not received. It could argue against mandatory school desegregation before the Supreme Court. The question before the Court in *Oklahoma City v. Dowell* in October 1990 was whether the city's schools, which five years earlier had abandoned mandatory busing from kindergarten to the fourth grade, should have to reinstate it. Solicitor General Kenneth Starr, siding with the defendant, contended that since a circuit court had declared Oklahoma City a "unitary" school district in 1977, the judiciary should relinquish its jurisdiction over the city's schools. But Julius Chambers of the NAACP, representing the plaintiffs, argued that Oklahoma City remained a "segregated community that the state helped create" before *Brown v. Board of Education.*[32]

Justice Thurgood Marshall challenged Starr, asking, "How is the school board injured by being required to operate the schools in conformity to the United States Constitution?" "With all due respect," the solicitor general replied, "that is not our position," asserting that demographics, not politics, had produced the city's largely segregated schools. When asked by Justice Sandra Day O'Connor if the courts should continue to operate the Oklahoma City schools even if segregated residential patterns were to remain for another century, Chambers simply replied, "Yes." Justice Antonin Scalia then lamented that "twenty-five years" of mandatory busing "has produced nothing."[33]

As the debate over busing revisited the Supreme Court, it also reappeared on the nation's editorial pages. Former civil rights commissioner Linda Chavez, noting in the *Dallas Times Herald* that since the advent of forced busing Oklahoma

City's public school enrollment had plunged from sixty-nine thousand to thirty-eight thousand and its African American school population had grown from 25 percent to 40 percent, concluded, "Ironically, busing itself has contributed heavily to the racial imbalance in some school districts by exacerbating white flight." Joan Beck of the *Chicago Tribune* concurred: "Once again, it's discomforting to consider how little academic improvement has been achieved by all the money, effort, time, energy, and high expectations put into desegregation efforts in the past decade." William Raspberry of the *Washington Post* opined, "It may be time for advocates of school integration to take another look at busing." William Murchison of the *Dallas Morning News* went even further: "Busing is the high court's illegitimate offspring. No blood test is needed to establish paternity. They're the ones—those people in black robes; and oh, what a mess they've made!"[34]

A rare exception to the chorus against mandatory busing came from Bonnie Erbe in the *Dallas Times Herald*. While conceding that "busing isn't the long-term solution to quality education for our children," Erbe nonetheless observed that since Oklahoma City had dropped its mandatory busing plan for kindergarten through fourth grade, its test scores, teacher performance, and facilities were "worse than the group of comparison schools," according to a report commissioned, then rejected, by the school board. Erbe warned that "black parents throughout the country fear a return to the days of separate-but-equal."[35]

Almost forgotten in the legal briefs and editorial opinions were the children and parents of Oklahoma City. At Creston Hills Elementary School, where the paint was peeling and the third-grade teacher was distributing grocery bags to pupils too poor to afford backpacks, all 235 students were black. "Black children don't have to sit next to white children to get a quality education," said Glendora Sykes, a former Parent Teacher Association president who sent her children to Creston Hills. But Clara Luper, whose daughter was an original plaintiff contesting the voluntary desegregation program, disagreed. "Unless you start at an early age, by the time a child gets to the fifth grade, that child is already formed in his mind—his ideas as far as race relations are concerned."[36]

The Supreme Court rendered its verdict in January 1991. In a 5–3 decision, the Court ruled in favor of the Oklahoma City School Board and the Bush administration. The majority opinion, authored by Chief Justice William Rehnquist and joined by Justices O'Connor, Scalia, Byron White, and Anthony Kennedy, noted that once school districts have taken all "practicable" steps to combat racial segregation, court-ordered busing may end. It added that residential segregation could not prolong the court order unless it was a remnant of the Jim Crow era. "A District Court need not accept at face value the profession of a school board which has intentionally discriminated that it will cease to do so in the future," wrote the chief justice. "But in deciding whether to modify or dissolve a desegregation decree, a School Board's compliance with previous court orders is obviously relevant." The dissenting opinion, written by Marshall and supported by

Justices Harry Blackmun and John Stevens, countered that the effect in Oklahoma City—segregated schools—was more significant than the cause. "The majority today suggests that thirteen years of desegregation was enough," wrote Marshall. "However, it . . . fails to recognize explicitly the threatened re-emergence of one-race schools as a relevant vestige of *de jure* segregation."[37]

A year later, the Bush administration could claim another victory. In *Freeman v. Pitts,* the Supreme Court ruled that the "root and branch" eradication of school segregation need not occur all at once, that a district could end a successful student desegregation plan before achieving desegregation of faculty or programs.[38]

## The Bush Record

In many ways, the Bush administration acknowledged the end of an era in school desegregation. In her study of Boston from 1984 to 1987, Boston University political scientist Christine Rossell concluded that with whites comprising 75 percent of the city's population but only 22 percent of its public school enrollment, mandatory busing "definitely led to white flight from public schools." William Clark, a geographer at the University of California at Los Angeles, discovered that only one of 228 families who relocated in Oklahoma City during a period of mandatory busing from 1974 to 1978 moved closer to the school where its children were being bused. A study by the Kentucky Commission on Human Rights determined that Louisville's busing plan had backfired, as many black families moved to predominantly white neighborhoods not to follow the school bus but to evade it. "Perhaps the hottest new idea" in education, NAACP president Benjamin Hooks summarized the antibusing scholarship, "is an old one—segregation."[39]

In challenging mandatory busing in court, Solicitor General Kenneth Starr thus returned to the language of "choice" and "neighborhood schools." With almost two-thirds of the public (and more than two-thirds of minorities) believing that parents should be able to choose their children's public schools, Secretary of Education Lamar Alexander concluded that "the country was fed up with busing." With a conservative Supreme Court and a civil rights movement weakened by its unpopular defense of busing, domestic policy advisor Roger Porter decided, "It was time to end it."[40]

But the Bush administration did not simply seek to rewind the clock. To do so would ignore a body of scholarship still committed to school desegregation. Dana Pearce, an authority on school and housing segregation, concluded from her study of twenty-five major American cities that residential desegregation stemmed from only two factors: the population growth of the cities and the racial mix of their schools. Robert Crain, a sociologist at Columbia University Teachers' College, found that black adults who had attended integrated schools in Hartford, Connecticut, were more likely to live in integrated neighborhoods and work in predominantly white occupations than those who had attended segregated schools. Gary Orfield, a political scientist at Harvard University, would contend after studying four decades of school desegregation that "although urban desegregation has never been popular among whites, it is viewed as a success by both the white and minority parents whose children have experienced it." With nine of every ten Americans professing support for racially integrated schools, NAACP assistant counsel Janelle Byrd asserted that despite her defeat in the *Dowell* case, "The arsenal of desegregation remains intact."[41]

And the Bush administration continued to tap it. In contesting the transfer of teachers to achieve racial balance in the Prince George's County, Maryland, public schools in 1990, the brief prepared by the Justice Department's Office of Civil Rights nonetheless suggested that the district's hiring decisions and transfers consider the race of teachers. In the *Dowell* case later that year, the Justice Department broke with Reagan administration precedent in contending that any examination of whether a court should relinquish control of a school district must study the residual effects of school segregation, including housing patterns. In its decision, the Supreme Court let the lower courts decide how and when such vestiges have disappeared. "The decision opened a new, but almost certainly not the last, chapter in the decades-long history of federal court efforts to dismantle the era of official segregation," wrote Linda Greenhouse of the *New York Times,* adding that "both the majority opinion and the dissenting opinion were notable for their moderate tone."[42]

The administration's proposed reform of the federal role in school desegregation to include public magnet schools and nonpublic school vouchers similarly looked forward. In an April 1989 letter to Pennsylvania Republican representative William Goodling, Porter explained that while "the Reagan budget already proposes $115 million for desegregation purposes, we want to go further and facilitate the development of magnet schools to enhance educational excellence in diverse settings." In May 1990 the House Republican Empowerment Task Force endorsed the Bush magnet school proposal. Citing a "sea change in public opinion in . . . race relations in the last twenty-five years," the group's chairman, Rep. Stephen Bartlett of Texas, wrote that "'choice' in the 1990's is not 'freedom of choice' of the 1960's." On the eve of the *Dowell* verdict, Doreen Torgerson wrote to Charles Kolb, "The Court's focus on the desegregation issue may provide an opportunity to highlight school choice as a new wave of desegregation policy (as opposed to mandatory busing)."[43]

In many ways the ambiguous record that George Bush brought to the White House, as well as the mixed messages of his administration, mirrored the uncertainty of an American public torn between its resistance to mandatory busing and its devotion to school desegregation. So despite his promise of a bully pulpit against racial injustice, the president's silence on *Oklahoma City v. Dowell, Freeman v. Pitts,* and the hundreds of other desegregation cases under review during his administration helped lower the profile of a volatile issue. "We were generally reluctant to have the White House involved in any specific case," Porter would recall. Busing was "not a huge issue, not high on my radar screen," Alexander would remember.[44]

"Most Americans, I'm convinced, believe that government can be an instrument of healing," Bush told the United Negro College Fund early in his administration. "There are times when government must step in where others fear to tread." Not surprisingly, given his preference for foreign policy, the most daring example of federal intervention during his administration was the deployment of troops in Iraq in January 1991. But the most desperate was the extension of emergency aid to South Central Los Angeles following the race riots of April 1992. In the Persian Gulf War, Bush thus went a long way toward healing the wounds opened by the Vietnam War. But on the battlefield of school desegregation, where Bush succeeded in slowing court orders and buses but failed in funding magnet schools and vouchers, the healing had only begun.[45]

## Bill Clinton

Americans can be good at talking about race. The most-quoted phrase of the Declaration of Independence is not the statement regarding independence but "all men are created equal." Abraham Lincoln's most famous legacy is not the war he successfully commanded but the Emancipation Proclamation that ultimately justified it. Martin Luther King led marches, boycotts, and protests that landed him in jail and ultimately cost him his life, but his "I Have a Dream" speech made him an American icon.

Actions have been more difficult. Thomas Jefferson, the author of the Declaration of Independence, was not only the owner of many slaves but the father of a few. The Emancipation Proclamation was purely symbolic, lacking the legal jurisdiction to free the slaves in the Confederate States of America, and lacking the political backbone to free the slaves in the loyal border states. Dr. King's exhortation that Americans "not be judged by the color of their skin, but by the content of their character," laid the rhetorical foundation for the Civil Rights Act of 1964, only to be manipulated by both sides of the affirmative action debate that followed.

Bill Clinton, child of Jim Crow Arkansas, began his presidency with a plea for less talk about the country's stubborn racial maladies. "There seems to me to be four things we can do," said the new president on the fortieth anniversary of the landmark May 17, 1954, *Brown v. Board of Education* decision by which the Supreme Court unanimously repudiated de jure school segregation. "One is, we can . . . talk about how wonderful *Brown* was and preach until the day we die and not do anything to deal with the problems of this time . . . [or] you can say the wrong things and reject the spirit of *Brown* and do nothing but cash in, and that's wrong. Or you can do what's disturbingly working: You can say the wrong things, you can preach division." Instead, the president pledged to act: "People desperately wish their lives to change. They want to do something that will make a difference. They want safer streets, not nice talk. They want schools that work, not nice talk. They want children to be raised by caring parents, not nice talk."[46]

Yet by his second term, the president was appealing for more talk. "Of all the questions of discrimination and prejudice that still exist in our society," the president told the graduating class at the University of California, San Diego, in June 1997, "the most perplexing one is the oldest, and in some ways today, the newest: the problem of race." He then announced, "I want to lead the American people in a great and unprecedented conversation about race." A seven-person panel, headed by Duke University historian John Hope Franklin, would lead this new national dialogue.[47]

The history of federal aid to elementary and secondary education had shown that a president's words could be almost as powerful as his actions. The experience of Ronald Reagan, who tried to reduce the federal role in the nation's schools before promoting a national dialogue on education, had proved that a president could succeed with an act first, talk later strategy. But as Bill Clinton conceded, he was testing this strategy on the "most perplexing" issue of all, which, unlike education, did not come equipped with all the answers. Despite being the best-prepared president, by background and conviction, to address school desegregation since Lyndon Johnson, even Bill Clinton was largely venturing into the unknown.

## Action

"On September 4, 1957, Elizabeth Eckford . . . was turned away by people who were afraid of change, instructed by ignorance, hating what they simply could not understand," Bill Clinton would recall of that historic day in his home state. "And America saw her, haunted and taunted for the simple color of her skin, and in the image we caught a very disturbing image of ourselves." This was not the image that the black customers at his grandfather's grocery store or the black patients of his grandmother the nurse had implanted in eleven-year-old Billy's mind. So he cheered President Dwight Eisenhower's dispatch of federal troops to ensure safe passage to Central High School for Elizabeth Eckford and the rest of the Little Rock Nine.[48]

This president intended to be just as committed, if less dramatically, to school desegregation. Within a year, his assistant secretary of education for civil rights, Norma Cantu, had issued a sweeping set of regulations to combat racial, sexual, and age discrimination in the classroom. She had mandated that her ten regional offices hire more bilingual employees and double the number of investigations of civil rights complaints. Though she would prefer to settle disputes out of court, Cantu, a former attorney for the Mexican American Legal Defense and Educational Fund, admitted, "We are spending a lot of money in adversarial proceedings." Janell Byrd, assistant counsel for the Legal Defense and Educational Fund of the liberal NAACP, applauded the changes that Cantu brought to her office: "What was so disheartening was [that] the focus seemed to be that the greatest civil rights problems we had were those relating to the discrimination of whites. I get the sense that the department is more in sync with reality now than it was under the Reagan and Bush Administrations." But Clint Bolick, litigation director for the conservative Institute for Justice, argued that Cantu was "too anxious to go to court, a legacy of her advocacy in the previous decade of social engineering schemes like busing."[49]

While Clinton opposed busing, he did not want to see its abandonment spell the end of school desegregation. "I think that racially balanced schools or racially diverse schools are good for the students," the president said in May 1994. This integrationist philosophy was behind his efforts to redistribute Elementary and Secondary Education Act Title I monies to the neediest school districts: "Very often that [redistributing] means a more racially diverse population." So when presented with the opportunities to replace Justices Harry Blackmun and Byron White on the Supreme Court, he chose the more liberal Ruth Bader Ginsburg and Stephen Breyer.[50]

In 1995, by a 5–4 majority in *Missouri v. Jenkins,* the Court relieved the State of Missouri of the costs of court-ordered desegregation alternatives to busing in Kansas City, even though only about one-fourth of the city's schools had achieved the federal court's recommendation that enrollment be 65 percent minority and 35 percent white. Chief Justice William Rehnquist, writing for the majority, held that the $1.3 billion magnet school plan, in calling for air-conditioned classrooms, computers, a planetarium, a twenty-five-acre farm, a model United Nations, an art gallery, and swimming pools, was so attractive that it had gone from a court-mandated plan to desegregate the Kansas City school district to an interdistrict plan in violation of the 1974 *Milliken v. Bradley* decision. But Bush appointee David Souter, joined in his dissent by Ford appointee John Paul Stevens and the two Clinton choices, Ruth Bader Ginsburg and Stephen Breyer, invoked the 1976 *Hills v. Gautreaux* case in arguing that the Missouri remedies did not "consolidate or in any way restructure" the suburban school districts, implicating "only . . . the operation and quality of schools within Kansas City," so "[their] burden . . . accordingly falls only on the two constitutional wrongdoers in this case, the [Kansas City school district] and the State." In an amicus brief, the American Civil Liberties Union supported the position of Souter, Stevens, Ginsburg, and Breyer in assailing Missouri's (and the majority's) argument "that any remedy that has any effect on any person beyond the school district at issue is by definition an interdistrict remedy."[51]

*Missouri v. Jenkins* confirmed the worst fears of the Clinton White House: that the country was moving beyond condemning forced busing and was beginning to reject *any* mandatory desegregation remedy. Even magnet schools, the favorite desegregation strategy of the Reagan, Bush, and Clinton administrations, had become suspect if dictated by a court. As a result, the nation continued its path to school resegregation. A 1993 Harvard study conducted for the National School Boards Association found that in the nation's large inner cities, "fifteen of every sixteen African-American and Latino students are in schools where most of the students are non-white." In medium-size cities, "sixty-three percent of African-American and seventy percent of Latinos attend such schools."[52]

Black sociologist Kenneth Clark, who helped prepare the appendix to the appellants' brief in *Brown v. Board of Education,* pronounced himself "embarrassed" about four decades of "failure to desegregate." Black professor Roger Wilkins, who "started my education fifty-seven years ago in a one-room segregated schoolhouse in Kansas City, Missouri," lamented that in the forty years after the *Brown* decision, "We've only had something else that sure as heck is not equality." Kenneth Jenkins, president of the Yonkers, New York, branch of the NAACP, sacrificed his position by claiming that contrary to his organization's stance, "busing may have outlived its usefulness," only to have NAACP president Kweisi Mfume say much the same thing two years later. Courts in Wilmington, Delaware, and in Indianapolis, Denver, Norfolk, Nashville, and Cleveland appeared to agree, as they released those school districts from busing plans. Janet Schofield, a scholar on education and race at the University of Pittsburgh, concluded that while desegregation had helped blacks into more schools and colleges, it had not substantially improved African American academic achievement.[53]

The administration reluctantly acknowledged this new, old climate. In 1988, Connecticut education commissioner Gerald Tirozzi, calling school segregation "educationally, morally, and legally wrong," had advocated a voluntary, and if necessary, mandatory desegregation plan for the state. Less than a decade later, Tirozzi, now Clinton's assistant secretary for elementary and secondary education, admitted that "busing is not a political issue" and could not recall the president ever discussing it. In January 1999 the Clinton Justice Department would broker a deal in St. Louis that replaced a twenty-seven-year-old court order for mandatory busing with a plan for magnet schools, limits on class size, accountability standards, and voluntary busing. Clinton lamented at the end of his first term that forty years after Little Rock, "too many Americans of all races have actually begun to give up on the idea of integration and the search for common ground. For the first time since the 1950's, our schools in America are resegregating."[54]

## Talk

Having acted against school segregation, Clinton set out to talk about race relations. "Anybody who looks at my public life can see that it's been dominated by three things: economics, education, and race. If there is any issue I ought to have credibility on, it is this one, because it is a part of who I am and what I've done," explained the president. "I think all you have to do is look at the way I constitute my administration, look at the way that we've changed the federal bench, and look at the policies I've advocated." Clinton biographer David Maraniss agrees that few could address the thorny issue of race with more genuine passion. While "it was not difficult to find the darker corners of Clinton's life," Maraniss writes, "the forces of light often prevailed when he dealt with African-Americans and other minorities." Maraniss relates that as a young law professor at the University of Arkansas, Clinton was so solicitous of the school's first wave of black students that they dubbed him "Wonder Boy." Though he did not enact a civil rights law in his twelve years as governor of Arkansas, Clinton appointed more African Americans to state boards and commissions than all his predecessors combined, selected the first black member of the state supreme court, and sent his daughter to a majority black public school. "Racial equality," writes Clinton's assistant Sidney Blumenthal, was Clinton's "earliest and most passionate motivation in politics."[55]

Despite having established his credentials on the issue before and during his presidency, Clinton would find his race panel mired in controversy almost from its inception in June 1997. Political pundits minimized it as a feeble attempt at "legacy building," while conservatives, Hispanics, and Native Americans decried their exclusion from the board. "Critics have claimed that we did not have enough disparate voices at our meetings, or that we were simply preaching to the choir," the panel's chairman, John Hope Franklin, acknowledged after a year of public meetings. "From the beginning, our interest was in promoting constructive dialogue, not in polarizing the debate. We have made every effort to include the full diversity of racial and political viewpoints."[56]

By the time the panel's fifteen-month nationwide tour had ended, however, the country had turned to other things. Steven Holmes of the *New York Times,* reporting on Clinton's acceptance of the panel's final report, wrote that "President Clinton focused his attention on an area where he has displayed comfort, as well as intellectual and political surefootedness: race." The small article, which appeared during the time of the impeachment hearings in the House Judiciary Committee, was relegated to the bottom of page seven. In addition to endorsing administration initiatives such as money for school construction in minority areas, the report established a permanent Presidential Council on Race to recommend federal policies for improving the country's racial climate. Speaking before an audience which included such civil rights luminaries as Rosa Parks and John Lewis, Clinton defended the need for talk for a final time. Racial progress "comes from[,] yes, opportunity; it comes from[,] yes, learning; it comes from, yes, the absence of discrimination," the president conceded. "But it also has to come from the presence of reconciliation, from a turning away from the madness that life only matters if there is someone we can demean, destroy, or put down."[57]

## The Clinton Record

"I went to segregated schools, segregated public pools, sat in all-white sections at the movies, and traveled through small towns in my state that still marked restrooms and water fountains 'white' and 'colored,'" Bill Clinton recalled in June of 1997. The public could rejoice that the nation would never return to these days of de jure racial segregation. They could applaud the rise in the percentage of black high school graduates from 50 percent in 1973 to almost 90 percent in 1997; the improvement in black elementary school students' standardized test scores in reading from 170 points in 1971 to 190 points in 1996 and in math from 220 points in 1973 to 250 points in 1996; and the increase from 14.5 percent of twenty-five- to twenty-nine-year-old black women completing high school and four or more years of college in 1981 to 18.5 percent in 1997. They could cheer that under the president who had so closely linked school to work, black income was higher and black unemployment was lower than they had been in the previous twenty-five years.[58]

But they could also lament that in all of these categories, blacks lagged behind whites. They could bemoan the increase in the percentage of black high school dropouts, from 6 percent of tenth-, eleventh-, and twelfth-graders in 1991 to 6.7 percent in 1996, and the decrease in college attendance among black males, from 15.4 percent of twenty-five- to twenty-nine-year-olds who completed high school and four or more years of college in 1981 to 13.7 percent in 1997. They could regret that under a president deeply troubled by residential segregation, black home ownership was up only 1 percent since 1983.[59]

Although there were no longer any laws making it so, Bill Clinton's United States in 1997 in one way resembled Bill Clinton's Arkansas in 1957. "That's really a question to be solved on a State-by-State basis," said Clinton about school segregation, sounding a bit like Arkansas segregationist governor Orval Faubus from four decades earlier. "Redistributing Title I monies and enforcing civil rights laws," Clinton added, "is about all we can do at the national level"—and about all his administration did, besides talk. Meanwhile, the country continued its drift away from school desegregation. In 1972, 44 percent of African American children attended desegregated schools. In 1995, one-third of Hispanic and African American children were attending schools with over 90 percent minority enrollment. "The separation of black children in America's schools is on the rise," wrote James Kumen in 1996, "and is in fact approaching the levels of 1970, before the first school bus rolled at the order of the court."[60]

"We are clearly in a period when many policy-makers, courts and opinion-makers assume that desegregation is no longer necessary, or that it will be accomplished somehow without need of any deliberate plan," claimed Harvard's

Gary Orfield and John Yun about the years 1980–96. In July 1999, a month after the release of the Harvard study, the Boston School Committee abandoned the busing plan that Judge Arthur Garrity had imposed over violent resistance twenty-five years earlier. "Well-intentioned," wrote Tamar Jacoby, whose 1998 book *Someone Else's House* documented resegregation in New York, Detroit, and Atlanta, "is almost a dirty word today."[61]

Almost. "Racial integration is unquestionably a social good," the *New York Times* editorialized in the wake of the Boston decision, calling upon the city to "keep its pledge to build new schools in crowded minority districts and raise the level of instruction throughout the city." Bill Clinton probably would have said much the same thing. But in this postbusing, postintegration era, nobody thought to ask him.[62]

CHAPTER 6

# Nonpublic School Aid
## 1981–2001

### Ronald Reagan

In October 1976, Democratic Party presidential candidate Jimmy Carter had assured the Chief Administrators of Catholic Education that he was "firmly committed to conducting a systematic and continuing search for constitutionally acceptable methods of providing aid to parents whose children attend nonsegregated private schools." In October 1980, Republican Party presidential candidate Ronald Reagan reminded the Chief Administrators of Catholic Education of Carter's campaign promise. "Not only did Mr. Carter refuse to help parents [of private and parochial elementary and secondary school pupils]," said Reagan, "but he played a major role in defeating the tuition tax credit bill when it was before the Senate." Quoting his party's platform, Reagan pledged that "Next year, a Republican White House will assist, not sabotage, Congressional efforts to enact tuition tax relief into law." In part because of his openness to nonpublic school aid, Reagan received 51 percent of Catholics' votes in his narrow election victory over incumbent Democratic president Jimmy Carter. Yet in November 1983, by a vote of 59–38, the Senate would delete from a bill an amendment, supported by Democrat Daniel Patrick Moynihan of New York and Republican Robert Packwood of Oregon, that would have provided federal tuition tax credits for parents of nonpublic school children. President Ronald Reagan had led the unsuccessful campaign for the bill.[1]

Why did Reagan's support for tuition tax credits lead to the identical outcome as Carter's resistance? Why did Reagan's apparent allegiance to his campaign promise achieve the same result as Carter's apparent betrayal? The answer lies less in *what* the ultimate fate of tuition tax credit legislation was than in the *when* and *how* of Reagan's impact upon that fate. At the party for advocates of nonpublic school tuition tax credits, the honored guest arrived late and left early.

### Late: The Ninety-seventh Congress

Two weeks after Reagan's election, Rev. Thomas Gallagher of the Education Department of the United States Catholic Conference (USCC) pronounced himself "quite optimistic" about the prospects for such legislation. In its December 13 issue, the Jesuit periodical *America* editorialized, "Never before has the political environment been better for the passage of a tuition tax credit." On February 24, 1981, asserting that "there has never been a better political climate for the passage of a tuition tax credit bill," Moynihan, Packwood, and Delaware Republican senator William Roth reintroduced 1978's failed initiative.[2]

On August 13, Reagan signed the Economic Recovery Act of 1981, which authorized a three-year, 25 percent personal income tax reduction. So the USCC vowed to increase the pressure on the president for tuition tax credits. Msgr. Thomas Leonard wrote on August 21, "We have . . . agreed to the Administration's strategy of not including tuition tax credits in the first tax proposal made to Congress. Now that this proposal has been accepted by Congress, it is time for the President to live up to his campaign promises." Two weeks later the USCC Office for Educational Assistance authorized "an immediate letter-writing campaign directed toward Congress on a massive scale." In an October 13 statement to the Chief Administrators of Catholic Education, Reagan reiterated his dedication to tuition tax credits. He added, however, that "due to the difficult budget pressures we will face in the months to come, and given our determination to address immediate and severe problems facing the nation's economy, my commitment to work with Congress to construct a tuition tax credit bill will necessarily require that we initiate our efforts later in the Ninety-Seventh Congress."[3]

If initiated at all. On November 15 Deputy Treasury Secretary R. Tim McNamar told Owen Ullman of the Associated Press that "he and a number of Justice Department officials had serious reservations about whether the First Amendment's separation of church and state would be violated" by tuition tax credits. In its December 1981 annual report, the independent Federal Advisory Panel on Financing Elementary and Secondary Education—established by the Elementary and Secondary Education Act (ESEA) Amendments of 1978—was noncommittal on nonpublic school aid. On April 12, 1982, Dole pronounced himself still opposed to tuition tax credits. "We're pushing pretty hard to raise revenues," he insisted. "I don't know whether we can spend any."[4]

Three days later, however, claiming that "we're a bunch of radicals [who] . . . really intend to keep our promises," Reagan unveiled the Educational Opportunity and Equity Act of 1982, which included nonpublic elementary and secondary education tuition tax credits of up to five hundred dollars per child. He fired tuition tax credit opponent Undersecretary of Education William Clohan. He dispatched White House counselor Edwin Meese to persuade tuition tax credit partisans of the depth of his devotion to their cause. And he promised that this tuition tax credit would be part of the administration's second major revenue measure.[5]

By July 1, however, the administration had reversed itself. Because of the deepening recession, Chapoton told the Senate Finance Committee that the revenue bill should not contain Reagan's Educational Opportunity and Equity Act of 1982. Calling the decision a "major setback in our efforts to ensure Congressional approval of tuition tax credits," USCC legislative director Frank Monahan urged the Catholic bishops to "confront the Administration in the strongest terms and at the highest levels." Monahan concluded that "Under any circumstances, the prospects for success have greatly diminished."[6]

And by the end of the Ninety-seventh Congress, they had disappeared. On August 2 the leaders of the coalition formed by the administration to press for tuition tax credits received a promise from Dole that his committee would mark up the Reagan bill within a week. On August 4, after returning from a speech to the Knights of Columbus, Reagan sent each member of the Finance Committee a personal letter requesting support for tuition tax credits. On August 9 Reagan met with selected committee members from both parties. The committee reported the bill, 16–7, on September 16, but the Senate recessed on October 1 for the midterm election campaigns, before a floor vote on the Reagan bill.[7]

## Late: The Ninety-eighth Congress

At the January 19, 1983, meeting of the USCC Committee on Public Policy and Catholic Schools, Anthony cited three prerequisites for passage of tuition tax credits in the new Congress: mention of credits in Reagan's State of the Union address, provision for the potential revenue loss in Reagan's budget message, and early introduction of a bill. In his State of the Union address on January 25, Reagan called for "passage of tuition tax credits for parents who want to send their children to private or religiously affiliated schools." In his budget message on January 31, Reagan boasted of having reduced federal education spending by $1 billion from 1981 to 1982 and pledged to "stabilize" such expenditures at $13.1 billion, including the addition of tuition tax credits. Then on February 16, after meeting with cabinet members, congresspersons, and interest group representatives, Reagan submitted another tuition tax credit bill to Congress. Under the measure, tax credits would cover up to 50 percent of tuition and would come in three phases: $100 in 1983, $200 in 1984, and $300 in 1985, for parents with incomes under $40,000. Parents earning more than $40,000 would receive smaller credits. The loss to the treasury would be $200 million in 1984 and $800 million by fiscal 1986.[8]

Having followed the USCC's blueprint for success, Reagan assured the organization of his determination to implement it. "Because as I mentioned in my State of the Union Address I consider this legislation to be of the highest priority, it is the first piece of legislation other than the budget which I have sent to Capitol Hill," the president wrote to the bishops on March 1. "I have met with Senator Dole and other key members of Congress to ask their cooperation in having the bill acted upon as quickly as possible." Ohio Republican representative Willis Gradison, who attended the White House ceremony introducing the bill, noted approvingly that the president "didn't give us some formal statement about tuition tax credits. He stayed and talked at length about an independent school on the South Side of Chicago (Providence-St. Mel, a mostly black Catholic school)." The Senate majority leader, Republican Howard Baker of Tennessee, announced, "We told the [White House] legislative office that when they finish with the budget and Social Security, the first thing on the plate is tuition tax credits." The American Federation of Teachers (AFT) urged its members to oppose this "legislation of critical importance." National Education Association (NEA) president Willard McGuire concurred, calling the Reagan proposal "bad public policy no matter how you cut it."[9]

The Senate Finance Committee reported the Reagan bill, S.528, on May 24, with Democrats Moynihan, Russell Long of Louisiana, and Bill Bradley of New Jersey joining Republicans Dole, Packwood, Roth, John Danforth of Missouri, William Armstrong of Colorado, David Durenberger of Minnesota, Steve Symms of Idaho, and Charles Grassley of Iowa in the majority. But Oklahoma Democrat David Boren promised to lead a filibuster against the "single most damaging legislative program I have ever viewed." On June 2, when Reagan reversed his opposition to repeal of the 10 percent tax withholding on interest and dividend income, he appeared to clear the way for attaching tuition tax credits to a conference report that had overwhelmingly passed both houses of Congress. Dole had attempted to block the legislation, however, by burdening the tax withholding repeal bill with multiple amendments. He was therefore opposed to attaching an amendment he could support to a bill he was trying to kill. So the administration abandoned the strategy.[10]

Just as the legislative outlook for tuition tax credits was again growing dim, the judicial climate appeared to brighten. On June 29 in *Mueller v. Allen,* the Supreme Court upheld a Minnesota statute permitting a state income tax deduction for education expenses. The Reagan proposal differed from the Minnesota statute, however, by offering credits rather than deductions, covering tuition but not textbooks or transportation, and targeting parents of nonpublic but not public school children. So tuition tax credit opponents Edwin Dorn and Mary Frances Berry argued that "in order to survive the court's scrutiny, the Reagan plan would have to be revised to allow parents of all schoolchildren to obtain tax benefits. . . . When one adds up all the potential deductions or credits for all of the nation's fifty million students, the losses to the U.S. Treasury could become astronomical."[11]

The Reagan administration thus sought to prevent a favorable development from turning unfavorable. On July 22 Reagan's deputy assistant director for legal policy William Barr told the administration's Coalition for Tuition Tax Credits that the Reagan bill "is constitutional, and that no changes should be made on that [legal] basis." The new administration strategy was to attach the tuition tax credit bill to popular railroad retirement benefits legislation, forcing the House to act on the entire measure. Barr did allow, however, that "if it becomes feasible," the administration would "give in" to adding public school parents to the bill.[12]

The process never went that far. The railroad bill passed both houses of Congress in time for the August recess, but without the tuition tax credit amendment. Reagan convened the Coalition for Tuition Tax Credits on September 16 to inform them of his newest plan: to add the credits to a House revenue bill. An October 25 *Washington Post* article, subtitled "Meanwhile, on the Titanic," reported that the president had again changed his mind, preferring a $425 million mathematics and science education bill as the vehicle for tuition tax credits. Such an amendment "could raise basic procedural questions," the *Post's* Felicity Barringer warned, "[because] one bill [tuition tax credits] is a revenue measure; the other [math-science education] is not."[13]

The administration heeded the warning. Explaining that the addition of a revenue bill to a nonrevenue bill might prompt a "point of order," Baker, the majority leader, announced on the floor of the Senate his intention to attach tuition tax credits to the Women's Pension Equity Act. When opposition to that approach arose, Baker selected an Olympic funding bill. Climaxing a week-long USCC mailgram lobbying effort, Baker requested a motion to proceed with the Olympic bill on November 14. As promised, Boren and others responded with a filibuster, but the following day the filibusterers relented to allow consideration of the bill on the Senate floor. On November 16, Dole offered S.528 as a rider to the legislation, and, after an hour of debate, the Senate voted 59–38 to table the amendment. Thirty-five Democrats and twenty-four Republicans were in the majority, with nine Democrats and twenty-nine Republicans in the minority. Ten Catholic Senators from both parties voted to table S.528.[14]

## Never: The Ninety-ninth and 100th Congresses

At their December 1983 meeting, the USCC's three Tuition Tax Credit Advisory Committees agreed that "no substantive action" should be taken on tuition tax credits for six to eight months, that any move toward a House vote "should be opposed," and that the bishops should pursue a "selective approach to find out why the Senators took the stand they took." The committee members, calling for "different strategies," wondered, "If tuition tax credits aren't to be, what are our options?"[15]

Tuition tax credits were not to be. Though education was a major issue in Reagan's 1984 election race against former vice president Walter Mondale, tuition tax credits were conspicuously absent from the Republican candidate's six steps "to turn our schools around and return excellence to American education." While Reagan mentioned tuition tax credits in his February 1985 State of the Union address, his Department of Education omitted them from that year's legislative agenda. Reagan included tuition tax credits and vouchers in his February 1986 "Message to the Congress on America's Agenda for the Future," but he merely urged Congress and the states "to enact proposals" providing parents "a broad array of educational options" in his July 1987 "Economic Bill of Rights." A 1987 Gallup Poll found 71 percent of the public in favor of "parental choice" in education, but in September of that year, when Secretary of Education William Bennett advocated a "distinctive, tough-minded, and positive" agenda for education, he left tuition tax credits off it. In his January 1988 "Legislative and Administrative Message" Reagan proposed vouchers but gave up hope that Congress would enact them, calling instead for the states to implement "model legislation" devised by his Department of Education.[16]

## The Reagan Record

Several obstacles combined to derail and defeat nonpublic elementary and secondary school tuition tax credits during the Reagan presidency. First, the parts of such legislation too often overshadowed its sum. In January 1982 the Justice and Treasury Departments announced that in cases before the Supreme Court, the Reagan administration would side with Goldsboro Christian Schools of Goldsboro, North Carolina, and Bob Jones University of Greenville, South Carolina, in their challenges to the Internal Revenue Service (IRS) policy of denying tax exemptions to racially discriminatory nonpublic schools and colleges. Contending that the IRS had been acting without explicit authority, the administration called for legislation to codify the ban. On May 24, 1983, the Supreme Court upheld the IRS policy and rejected the administration's position.[17]

In the meantime, the administration posture sowed mistrust among many tuition tax credit advocates. On August 13, 1982, Moynihan privately notified the USCC that tuition tax credit supporter Democratic senator Bill Bradley of New Jersey intended to offer amendments strengthening the antidiscrimination language of S.528. White House counsel William Barr and Senator Dole failed to reach a compromise with Bradley, who introduced his amendments to the Senate Finance Committee. Moynihan then attacked the Justice Department for failing to appear at the committee hearings to defend the original antidiscrimination language, and he and Packwood endorsed the Bradley amendments. Because the hearings produced "no consensus on the anti-discrimination language" of the bill, wrote the USCC's Monahan, "the political climate had radically altered." By the time the White House and Bradley finally reached an accommodation during the Labor Day congressional recess, the legislation had suffered irreparable harm.[18]

This resolution of one legal wrangle only led to the creation of another, further endangering tuition tax credits. When the USCC and the White House found themselves on opposite sides in their interpretations of the June 1983 *Mueller* decision, Gallagher worried that the bishops appeared "more interested in getting the [Reagan] bill amended to broaden the class [to include public school parents] then we were to get the legislative process going to pass the bill."

On the morning of October 24, 1983, Secretary of Education Terrel Bell told the American Council for Private Education that such broadening "might not be a bad idea" and might increase support in the Senate for tuition tax credits. But in the afternoon, Steve Galebach, Robert Cable, and Linas Kojelis of the White House staff told the same audience that the administration opposed this change. So until the administration finally acceded to the inclusion of public school parents in the tuition tax credit bill, the legislation, in the words of the USCC's Hoye, "wasn't going anywhere."[19]

The proposals for tougher antidiscrimination language and broader inclusion of beneficiaries not only postponed tuition tax credits but exposed a second obstacle in their path: the fragility of the coalition supporting such legislation. To Sr. Renee Oliver, president of the Catholic lobby Citizens for Educational Freedom (CEF), Moynihan and Packwood were merely grandstanding in their backing of the antidiscrimination amendments, and Bradley was "another friend [who] stabs us in the back." While the USCC elected neither to oppose nor support the Bradley effort, Robert Baldwin, chief lobbyist for Christian fundamentalist schools, denounced the "killer amendments" for giving the IRS "an iron boot . . . to tramp over schools and parents." The rift between the bishops and the fundamentalists became so wide that the CEF's Marilyn Lundy offered to mediate.[20]

The USCC position in favor of including public school beneficiaries in S.528 created similar friction with the lay Catholic organization the Knights of Columbus, whose leader Virgil Dechant emerged from a stormy meeting of tuition tax credit advocates with the warning that if the bishops did not "get back . . . with the word that the coalition was united," then the erstwhile allies should consider "folding our tent and giving up on tax credits." USCC opposition to Reagan education budget reductions caused Alan Davitt of its Federal Assistance Advisory Commission to worry that the bishops' "overidentification with the Democrats" would mean "we cannot get to first base with the Administration" on tuition tax credits.[21]

Such division sharply contrasted with the unusual unity evinced by tuition tax credit opponents. *Church and State* counted twenty-four major newspapers, including the *New York Times, Washington Post,* and *Wall Street Journal,* against credits, with only four in favor. AFT chief lobbyist Greg Humphrey quipped that the turmoil caused by Christian fundamentalist opposition to the Bradley amendments "couldn't happen to a nicer bunch of people," and AFT director of political education Rachelle Horowitz warned that in the 1982 congressional elections, "A candidate who supports tuition tax credits will not get AFT backing." NEA president Willard McGuire attacked the Reagan bill's "gross misdirection of financial resources," and his organization committed record sums to the fall campaign. The rival unions collaborated in what *Education USA* called "unprecedented" joint statements and press conferences attacking the 1982 Reagan bill, then joined forty other tuition tax credit adversaries in the National Coalition for Public Education. By March of 1983 the coalition had produced ten times as many letters to Congress as the Reagan forces to help ensure what Packwood called "uniform liberal opposition" to S.528.[22]

The tuition tax credit proponents often seemed envious and even solicitous of their adversaries, thus undermining their own credibility. In January 1981, Rev. Virgil Blum, president of the Catholic League for Religious and Civil Rights and veteran of the education wars, warned that "the National Education Association is now recognized as being the most powerful lobby on Capitol Hill." In July 1981 Moynihan, recalling the dialogue between nonpublic and public school interests that helped produce the ESEA in 1965, asked wistfully, "Can't we try again?" Two years later, the USCC's Richard Duffy suggested that the bishops "score some points with the public school community" by opposing vouchers. At the end of 1983's failed effort, a group of liberal Republican congresspersons lamented that if they vote for tuition tax credits, "the NEA is offended." If they vote against them, "the clergy back home will be up in arms." The solution? "Not to have to vote at all."[23]

A third obstruction to tuition tax credits was the divided attention of the Reagan administration. Not only did the nuclear arms race, Lebanon, Grenada, Iran-contra, and, especially, the economy relegate tuition tax credits to a secondary role in the Reagan administration, but other education issues often took precedence. In 1981, to the delight of the USCC, the administration and Congress expanded coverage of nonpublic school students in the ESEA. In 1983, to the dismay of the USCC, the National Commission on Excellence in Education (NCEE) overlooked nonpublic schools in *A Nation at Risk,* the celebrated report on the dismal state of the country's school system. And beyond 1983, to the bewilderment of the USCC, the administration gradually abandoned tuition tax credits, about which the bishops were enthusiastic, in favor of nonpublic elementary and secondary school vouchers, of which they were unsure.[24]

The consequences of tuition tax credits' diminishing status were more comfort for their enemies and more confusion among their allies. Speaking on NBC-TV's "Meet the Press" in May 1983, AFT president Albert Shanker noted that of the "outstanding businessmen and governors" on the NCEE, "not one . . . has come out in favor of prayer [in public schools] or tuition tax credit[s] or vouchers." Addressing a group of *Wall Street Journal* executives in February 1985, Reagan defended tuition tax credits "based on fairness in the country," only to conclude that "the ultimate fairness would be educational vouchers."[25]

A fourth impediment to tuition tax credits was Reagan's conception of the presidency. Consistent with his leisurely work habits, limited curiosity, and brilliant communication skills, President Reagan became in many ways the antithesis of President Carter. Where Carter had drowned in detail, Reagan savored simplicity. While Carter largely failed to prevent new problems (energy crisis,

North-South relations), Reagan largely succeeded in solving old ones (inflation, East-West relations). Carter spoke feebly but acted often; Reagan spoke force-fully but acted infrequently. Carter dominated; Reagan delegated.

"The strategy was as simple as the agenda was short," write Bob Schieffer and Gary Paul Gates of the Reagan presidency. "The rest of the campaign promises would be put on hold, and nothing would be allowed to interfere with the twin goals: build up defense, cut taxes." In April 1981 the USCC's Frank Monahan lamented that the tuition tax credit campaign "is not happening." Garry Wills concludes that Reagan's "was the politics of immediate, not deferred gratifica-tion. If Reagan had felt a [strong enough] commitment to the difficult parts of his moral program—e.g. to the social agenda of the New Right—he might have spent his early days of popularity working for them. But he made his first assignment the inflation that had plagued Carter." In May 1982, at the first White House meeting of the tuition tax credit coalition, Monahan reported that "Leg-islative strategies were discussed, but it appeared none had been thought through." Robert Dallek observes, "In contrast to the tax cut, his [Reagan's] backing of the New Right social agenda [including tuition tax credits] was more symbol than substance." In December 1982 Monahan attributed the delay in passing tuition tax credits in part to the administration's failure to consult with the Senate Finance Committee in the previous congressional session.[26]

Alonzo Hamby calls Reagan "ineffective in genuinely extemporaneous situa-tions" and "not an intellectual in the strict sense of the word." So before he effec-tively deserted the campaign for tuition tax credits, Reagan had largely delegated it. But Reagan's point persons on tuition tax credits—Treasury secretary Donald Regan and congressional liaison Kenneth Duberstein—were unenthusiastic about the potential revenue loss and arduous legislative effort that they would require. Regan never met with the president privately while at the Treasury Department, and he considered Congress, in the words of Nevada Republican senator and Reagan confidant Paul Laxalt, "a damn nuisance." Duberstein's deci-sion not to attach S.528 to the railroad retirement benefits bill (which would pass easily) prompted the *Washington Times* to observe that "it is Duberstein's job to sell Reagan policy on Capitol Hill, but in this case it was the other way around." So when the tuition tax credit coalition met with Reagan shortly afterward, the USCC's Rev. Thomas Gallagher reported that the president forced Duberstein to "acknowledge that he had received his marching orders on this issue."[27]

The final barrier to tuition tax credits was the growing skepticism surround-ing the issue. Moynihan told the *Washington Post* as early as May 1981 that Rea-gan education budget reductions and block grant proposals had helped create "an unstable environment" for passage of tuition tax credits. Two months later, the New York senator wrote to the USCC's Bishop Kelly, "I continue to support tuition tax credits, but in all candor the legislation appears doomed for this Congress and perhaps beyond, unless the Administration decides actively to press Congress to enact it." In January of the following year the USCC's James Robinson told Terence Cardinal Cooke of New York that "most members of Congress that we have talked with in recent weeks simply do not believe the Reagan administration can be serious about recommending a tuition tax credit program in 1982." When Reagan did just that, Colorado Republican senator and Finance Committee member William Armstrong called the proposal "a good idea, but it's bad timing"; Moynihan lamented, "The Administration has waited so long to make its intentions known, it may prove to be impossible for this Congress to deal with this issue in the time remaining"; and the *New York Times'* Steven Roberts concluded that "most lawmakers in both parties" saw "virtually no chance" of passing tuition tax credits in the Ninety-seventh Congress. The conservative Catholic journal *The Wanderer* was more direct: "The President's gesture would have been more believable if it had been proposed on April 15, 1981, or even January 1982. But April 1982? Come on!"[28]

In December 1983 Moynihan contrasted his just-concluded fight for tuition tax credits with the failed effort five years earlier. In 1978, "there was some constitutional doubt, the President was opposed, and there was lots of money for public schools." In 1983, "the constitutional question is resolved, the President is in favor, but the public perception is that it [tuition tax credits] would do bad things to public schools, especially given the tight economy." Democratic senator Ernest Hollings of South Carolina succinctly summarized this perception: "The tuition tax cut proposal would turn our nation's education policy on its head, benefit the few at the expense of the many, proliferate substandard segregationist academies, add a sea of red ink to the federal deficit . . . and destroy the genius and diversity of public education." While each of these assertions was open to challenge, the broad viewpoint would carry the day. In an era in which perception often became reality, Ronald Reagan would lose at his own game.[29]

Like Jimmy Carter, then-candidate Ronald Reagan had offered the nation a clear vision in his education policies: a smaller federal role in public school aid and school desegregation and a larger federal role in nonpublic school aid. Like Carter, President Ronald Reagan to a large extent reneged on his campaign promises: retaining the Department of Education, increasing public school aid, moving cautiously to end busing and failing to enact tuition tax credits. But unlike Carter, Reagan found consistency amidst confusion by deploying the weapon of his adversaries, the federal government, to fight the battle he had long championed, public school reform. And unlike Carter, Reagan knew how to lead.

## George Bush

As third-party candidate Ross Perot launched into a lengthy answer in the first 1992 presidential debate, George Bush glanced at his watch. In an unlucky snapshot of an unlucky administration, a national television camera recorded Bush's apparent disdain for the proceedings. Several pundits, and perhaps many voters, decided then that it was time for the incumbent to go home.

It was perhaps fitting that this itinerant politician, born in Massachusetts and raised in Connecticut with residences in Houston and Kennebunkport and stops in New York and Beijing, not stay in Washington for too long. His popularity had peaked almost two years earlier after the end of the cold war, during the triumph of the Persian Gulf War, and before the deepening of the economic recession. "Read my lips, no new taxes," Bush had promised at the 1988 Republican National Convention, so it did not seem to matter that his violation of that pledge in 1990 came only when the Democratic Congress refused to significantly reduce domestic spending. A promise, after all, is a promise.

With considerably less fanfare, candidate Bush had also promised in 1988 to support federal tuition tax credits or vouchers for parents of nonpublic school children. He would quickly break that pledge too, for the same reason—the deficit. Though he would ultimately redeem this promise, he would not fulfill it. For just as nonpublic school voucher legislation appeared imminent, George Bush ran out of time.

## A Promise Broken

The initial erosion of Bush's position came even before he had taken the oath of office. A White House Workshop on Choice in Education held ten days before the end of the Reagan presidency narrowed the definition of "choice" to public schools. Neither President Reagan nor President-elect Bush addressed the gathering. Secretary of Education Lauro Cavazos replaced a speech advocating nonpublic school vouchers, which had been written for him by Assistant Secretary of Education Patricia Hines, with one opposing such aid.[30]

Two months later the breach of promise was complete. On March 14, over the bipartisan objections of ninety members of the House of Representatives, Cavazos fired Hines. "Experience shows that choice works," Cavazos wrote on March 21, citing dramatic increases in reading proficiency among the school populations of East Harlem, New York, and Montclair, New Jersey, where public school choice experiments were under way. "Research shows that choice encourages differentiation among schools, reduces dropout rates, increases teacher satisfaction, and encourages parental involvement." On March 29, at a White House question-and-answer session with high school students, a private school pupil asked the new president if his parents should receive a tax break for tuition. "No, they shouldn't," Bush replied. "Everybody should support the public school system and then, if on top of that your parents think that they want to shell out, in addition to the tax money, tuition money, that's their right. But I don't think they should get a break for that."[31]

"Choice in education" in the Bush administration, therefore, was to mean choices for parents to send their children to public schools. Bush's Educational

Excellence Act of 1989, submitted to Congress in April, included a provision for specialized magnet schools to which parents could send their public school children. In May, Cavazos released two reports employing this definition: a guide for parents, "Choosing a School for Your Child," and a summary of state programs, "Progress, Problems, and Prospects of State Education Choice Plans." The secretary addressed the Education Press Association on the subject and convened four regional conferences of governors, legislators, and educators "to develop innovations to promote choice in their respective areas."[32]

The administration's change of heart predictably unsettled the nonpublic school interests. To preempt such criticism, Bush met with a group of Catholic lay educators at the White House in March. "I know education is as important to you as it is to me," the president told his visitors. "In a few days I will be introducing my new legislative package on education. I'm counting on you to help us make America's schools number one again." But when the Educational Excellence Act of 1989 omitted nonpublic school aid, Catholic school representatives reloaded. "Most Roman Catholic bishops were quite dismayed when they first heard of President Bush's public reservations about tuition tax credits," Rev. Robert Lynch, general secretary of the USCC, wrote to White House chief of staff John Sununu in April. "Such an opinion conflicts with statements made during the recent political campaign which led many in the Catholic Church to believe that the President was indeed in favor of tuition tax credits." National Catholic Education Association (NCEA) president Sr. Catherine McNamee expressed similar concerns to Bush in May.[33]

The White House then moved to reassure its friends without changing its position. Deputy assistant to the president William Roper wrote to Lynch and McNamee that while Bush was "clearly in favor of the idea of tuition tax credits," he would not be "seeking legislation at this time due to fiscal restraints." The strategy succeeded. Lynch emerged from a meeting with Roper conceding that "a major, tax-based program of relief for parents and children in non-public schools may well await partial resolution of the deficit challenge." McNamee needed only five minutes with the president in June to conclude, "The message we delivered to the President—calling for a public statement on parental choice for all Americans—was heard, and it's a good beginning." But no such statement would be forthcoming in 1989, and the day after their meeting, Bush could not even remember McNamee's name.[34]

If the administration had bought time with its natural allies, however, its endorsement of public magnet schools hardly appeased its erstwhile adversaries in the public education community. While National Parent and Teachers Association president Manya Unger telegraphed Bush, "We applaud your decision to remove tuition tax credits off of the White House education policy agenda," NEA president Mary Hatwood Futrell warned that public school choice "is not a panacea." While Americans United for Separation of Church and State opposed nonpublic school choice, they nonetheless criticized Bush's proposals for merit schools and Presidential Awards as violations of the First Amendment establishment clause. Although the leaders of the National School Boards Association told domestic policy advisor Roger Porter that their organization supported public school choice, they added, "Many members believe . . . it should be the object of debate, rather than presented as a solution." And despite the acknowledgment from Pennsylvania Republican William Goodling, chief House sponsor of Bush's Education Excellence Act of 1989, that the NEA considered it "such a joy under this Administration to have access to the Secretary of Education's ear after many years of not having that opportunity," a collision between the organization and the administration over a teacher certification title helped prevent the bill's passage.[35]

Bush's delicate balance was therefore doomed to fail. The vision of the nonpublic school interests was narrow, and their patience was finite. Mae Duggan, president of Catholic CEF, wrote to Bush in September asking him to include nonpublic school choice among the goals of his impending Education Summit. The vision of the public school forces was broad, and their influence was substantial. "It was not as high a priority for Catholic forces to get it [nonpublic school aid]," recalls former Republican senator Robert Packwood of Oregon, a staunch supporter of nonpublic school aid, "as it was for public school forces to stop it." The best course for the administration, therefore, would be to abandon its ambivalence. "As the education issues rises [sic] on the national agenda, it may be increasingly advantageous to communicate the Administration's message clearly and on many different levels," counseled Assistant Secretary of Education Rae Nelson in her year-end review of the Bush policies. "The choice message, for example, could be refined and targeted."[36]

It would not be. Cavazos cautioned that "those of us who are responsible for providing leadership have a special duty to continue to fuel that process with good information, research, evaluation, and professional support." Bush then resubmitted his Educational Excellence Act to Congress without any major changes. Yet even as the administration's deeds excluded nonpublic school choice, its words continued to include it. A trip to Milwaukee in June 1990 provided the president with a glimpse of the nation's first long-term nonpublic school choice program, championed by state representative Polly Williams, former Wisconsin campaign manager for liberal Democratic presidential candidate Jesse Jackson. "Thanks to your courage, leadership, and long-term commitment to the belief that parents—all parents—care and have a right to choose the best education possible for their children," the white Republican president told the black former welfare recipient, "that experiment is now resulting in new opportunities for one hundred Milwaukee children." In November the Department of Education sponsored a debate on nonpublic school choice between Delaware Republican governor Pierre DuPont and NEA president Keith Geiger. After he elicited Geiger's admission that under the Williams plan Milwaukee children had "escaped" the public schools, DuPont received a letter of congratulations from Porter. "Beyond his support of improving schools through public school choice programs," Special Advisor Jack Klenk wrote in promoting the Department of Education's new Center for Choice in Education in February 1991, "the President . . . has long favored tuition tax credits and hope[s] to see them in place as soon as possible."[37]

Once again, the education interests assumed their positions in the battle over nonpublic school choice. In June 1990 the NCEA issued a study titled "United States Elementary Schools and Their Finances, 1989," which concluded that although Catholic school per-pupil costs were less than half those of public schools, Catholic school students outperformed their public school counterparts in government-sponsored mathematics, science, and reading exams. The NEA's Geiger was unimpressed. "Free market economics works well for breakfast cereal, but not for schools in a democratic society," he wrote in September. "Market-driven school choice would create an inequitable elitist education system." And the public school forces remained stronger than their nonpublic school counterparts, as the Bush education legislation foundered a second time on the issue of teacher certification. The NEA exhibited "an enormous amount of influence on education policy," Porter would recall. "They're in all 435 Congressional districts and all fifty states." The public school lobbies had concluded, Porter wrote in March 1991, "that we have a single new idea—[public school] choice—and that we believe it will solve everything."[38]

## A Promise Redeemed

The public school representatives would not change their minds, but the president would change his plan. On April 18, 1991, when Bush introduced America 2000, he redefined "choice" to include nonpublic schools. "We can encourage educational excellence by encouraging parental choice," said the president. "It's time parents were free to choose the schools that their children attend. This approach will create the competitive climate that stimulates excellence in our private and parochial schools as well." The nonpublic school interests welcomed the overdue payment of a political debt. Paul Mecklenburg, chairman of the board of CEF, called Bush "a forceful advocate for choice and competition in education." The USCC's president, Archbishop Daniel Pilarczyk of Cincinnati, praised Bush for his "welcome intention to expand the notion of educational choice to include all parents, including those in private and parochial schools." A statement by the Institute of Public Affairs of the Union of Orthodox Jewish Congregations of America noted, "The concept of education choice is one that is long overdue, given the success such programs have had in areas across the country."[39]

While lauding America 2000's emphasis on national standards and educational excellence, the AFT's Albert Shanker and the NEA's Geiger criticized the choice component, which they viewed as the heart of the proposal. Bush "has started a war with everyone in the school system over the issue of private and religious versus public schools," said Shanker. "It's true that all public schools are not equal," added Geiger. "But the solution to funding social inequities that condemn children in inner cities and other impoverished communities to inferior schools is not to encourage the flight of the most promising students."[40]

Bush had long disagreed with this view, and his belated decision to join politics with policy was the product of several major factors. First, it is philosophically more comfortable to return to a position than to retreat from one, and the prospect of recovering his base was inviting after his party had lost nine House seats in the recent midterm elections. In Bush's first year, Porter had encouraged him to meet with the USCC "to solidify the President's support in the Catholic community." Two years later, in answer to whether the Catholic schools could "do it better" than public schools, Sam Allis of *Time* responded "yes," with "money, more selectiveness, and rigor" and despite "losing half their students and 2500 of their schools during the past twenty-five years." So Bush decided that he had jeopardized Catholic support long enough.[41]

Second, two years of fighting the NEA over education budgets and alternative teacher certification had shown Bush the limited political and policy benefits for a Republican president reaching out to groups that he considered "an arm of the opposition party." Bush told the Association of Christian Schools International Convention in November 1991, "I thank you for your support of choice. I will promote it *regardless* of the demogoguery of the NEA."[42]

Third, the change in style as well as substance accompanying Lamar Alexander's replacement of Lauro Cavazos at the Department of Education proved contagious at the White House, where the president seized the secretary's rhetoric of revolution. "It's not a program, it's a crusade," said Alexander of America 2000. "The President is more of a movement leader than a program proposer." And what could be more revolutionary than a federal nonpublic school choice program? Bush "wasn't hostile to it at the beginning," Porter would remember of the president's stance toward nonpublic school choice. "He was more inclined to say, 'I'm in favor of choice, but leave it up to localities, private or public.'" But a "movement leader" would have to be more active than that.[43]

Fourth, Bush began to see nonpublic school choice in a new light—not only as a lifesaver for financially plagued Catholic schools, but as an antipoverty program for minority children. If the face of nonpublic school tuition tax credits in the 1970s and 1980s was a middle-aged white male archbishop, the face of nonpublic school vouchers in the 1990s would be Polly Williams. "Choice is an effective desegregation strategy resulting in more interracial exposure among students, more community stability, less white flight, and better student achievement," concluded the House Republican Research Committee's Empowerment Task Force in a report sent to Bush in May of 1990. "Choice and magnet programs can foster diversity, enrich curricula, increase parental involvement, and expand educational opportunities for disadvantaged children," wrote school desegregation authority David Armor.[44]

"Our critics claim choice will *resegregate* the schools," Kolb wrote to Torgerson after reading the Armor article in September of that year. "This, of course, is nonsense. We should look for coherent, convincing evidence as to why choice can *help* desegregate." Torgerson replied, "We know what Polly Williams would say." Bush would employ this argument two years later in his first presidential debate with Bill Clinton and Ross Perot. "So let the liberal Democrats dream," said the president, "but strengthening family, not through legislation but through education, teaching discipline, teaching respect for the law, supporting law enforcement people, choice in child care, choice in education, all of these things will strengthen the family. As that happens we overcome the threshold of discrimination."[45]

Fifth, school choice had moved from abstraction to reality. "None of the arguments have changed," Kolb noted after reviewing the voucher experiment by President Nixon's Office of Economic Opportunity, but "in the meantime, since 1972 we have considerably more evidence that these ideas do, in fact, work." By June 1991, fourteen states already offered public school choice plans, twelve states were about to consider them, and one city—Milwaukee—was testing nonpublic school choice. Bush cited similar numbers in a letter to Representative Goodling defending his change of position. Bush could therefore point to the Milwaukee program in June 1990 as one of the most interesting experiments in education reform: "I think we will see that when schools compete to attract students, that can't help but raise the overall level of education."[46]

The sixth, and most powerful stimulant for Bush's policy change was public opinion. With each succeeding year, nonpublic school choice was becoming more popular. "Over the years, vouchers have never been particularly popular in the Gallup/Phi Delta Kappa polls," wrote Mary Farrell to Roger Porter in August 1991. "This year, though, fifty percent of the public say that they approve of school vouchers, while thirty-nine percent oppose them." In the two months after the announcement of America 2000, Alexander reported receiving twelve hundred letters a week. "The mail is overwhelmingly positive," the secretary assured the president, "and the largest single category favors school choice."[47]

## A Promise Unfulfilled

Bush's return to his campaign stance on school choice offered considerable cause for optimism. "[There is] the general expectation that the Administration will get much of the program [America 2000] enacted, a rare prospect for the Administration's domestic proposals," wrote the *New York Times'* Adam Clymer in April 1991. Six months later, after aggressive intervention by White House Chief of Staff John Sununu and Goodling, the House Education and Labor Committee passed a compromise version of the Bush plan, HR 3320, leaving public and nonpublic school choice at the discretion of local school districts and in conformity with state constitutions. "Any bill that includes a choice element in it and at least does not prohibit the participation of private schools is all to the good," applauded NCEA president Sr. Catherine McNamee. "We have a fundamental difference in strategy. We would argue for taking a strong position [against nonpublic school choice] and falling back," lamented NEA legislative director Michael Edwards. Education Subcommittee chairman Dale Kildee acknowledged the administration lobbying effort: "I think the factor that has changed is the strength the White House has been able to exert." Edward Kealy, director of federal programs for the National School Boards Association, viewed the vote as the culmination of "ten years of advocacy by the Bush and Reagan Administrations."[48]

The victory would be short-lived, however. The Senate Labor and Human Resources Committee reported S.2, sponsored by Massachusetts Democrat Edward Kennedy and limiting choice to public schools. After neither HR 3320 nor S.2 came to a floor vote in 1991, the chairman of the House Education and Labor Committee, Michigan Democrat William Ford, opened the 1992 session by proposing HR 4323, a public-school-only choice proposal backed by the NEA and AFT. Committee Democrats explained that they had supported the previous compromise only for fear of greater concessions to nonpublic schools, and before the Senate adoption of its public school–only bill. After a party-line vote released the bill from committee, the House passed it, 279–124, on August 12. In the Senate, Kennedy resurrected S.2, which won in committee and on the floor.

A 36–57 vote on January 23 rejected an amendment sponsored by Utah Republican Orrin Hatch and supported by the White House that would have established six demonstration projects in which federal monies would finance nonpublic school choice. "What have we heard on the floor these last three days?" asked Kennedy, his voice growing increasingly hoarse during the debate on his bill. "New schools, new schools, new schools," he answered. "What are we hearing tonight?" he protested before the vote on the Hatch amendment, pounding the lectern. "Private schools, private schools, private schools." When the amendment failed, Alexander conveyed his disappointment. "It is astonishing to me that the Senate could not bring itself to support even a demonstration project to determine what might happen if poor families are given more of the same choice of all schools that wealthy families already have." By voice vote, the House and Senate conferees agreed to a bill with provisions for neither public nor nonpublic school choice. The House approved the conference report, but the measure died in the Senate following a failed Republican cloture vote.[49]

If Congress was unwilling to agree even to the meager provisions of HR 3320 or the Hatch amendment to S.2, then surely it would not accede to more expansive, more expensive nonpublic school choice legislation completely separate from the more salient components of the Educational Excellence Act. But 70 percent of Americans now favored nonpublic school choice, and it was a presidential election year. So in June 1992 Bush proposed the $500 million GI Bill for Children, inspired by Franklin Roosevelt's 1944 legislation that provided veterans of World War II and subsequent conflicts with free higher education at the public or nonpublic institution of their choice. Citing Milwaukee as a model and invoking the names of Polly Williams and Wisconsin Republican governor Tommy Thompson, Bush introduced a four-year competitive grant program by which any state and locality could apply for enough federal funds to give each child of a middle- or low-income family a $1,000 annual scholarship to be used at any school or other academic program, public or nonpublic. Jonathan Kozol, author of the 1991 book *Savage Inequalities,* which exposed disparities between wealthy and impoverished school districts, called the Bush proposal "pure politics," adding "what can you buy with $1000?"[50]

"There are risks," the president conceded in unveiling his plan, "but we need revolutions, and revolutions carry with them risks." So do elections. The GI Bill for Children went nowhere on Capitol Hill, and Bush lost in November to nonpublic school choice opponent Bill Clinton.[51]

## The Bush Record

"For the first time in recent memory," Julie Miller wrote in *Education Week* in November 1991, "it is conceivable to think that the Congress might even . . . agree to fund choice plans that help parents send their children to private schools." Bush told his Domestic Policy Council a month later that "The momentum on school choice is moving in the direction we proposed—to the entire marketplace of public and private schools to benefit all families." This unlikely prospect was in many ways a tribute to George Bush's leadership of public opinion and his administration's lobbying of Congress. Bush worked harder and longer for federal aid to nonpublic elementary and secondary schools than any president since the church-state compromises of Lyndon Johnson's ESEA of 1965. Yet like all of his predecessors since Johnson, he ultimately failed to deliver on his promise of substantial nonpublic school assistance.[52]

Bush's defeat revealed that the costs of his midcourse correction on nonpublic school choice had come to outweigh its benefits. First, the comfort of Bush's retreat to his original position could not erase the discomfort of having to explain it. The result was a clumsy attempt to find continuity amidst change. When asked in the second presidential debate for his views on nonpublic school tuition tax credits, Bush reverted to his pre-1991 stance that "tax credits is a good idea, but . . . there isn't enough money around when we're operating at these enormous deficits to do that." Yet he adopted his post-1991 advocacy of nonpublic school vouchers to "supplement your family income to permit them to go to this school that you've already chosen." Not only did Bush fail to explain how tax credits would increase the deficit though vouchers would not, but he reduced his "revolutionary" GI Bill for Children to a consolation prize: "I don't think I can offer more than this 'G.I. Bill' for people that choose."[53]

Second, Bush's decision to call off his truce with the NEA and AFT may have acknowledged political reality, but it tempted political fate. In 1965, with the post–World War II era's largest coalition between Capitol Hill and the White House and before the NEA's decision to endorse congressional and presidential candidates, the Democratic Congress and president largely dictated to the public school interests. In 1991, however, with a Republican president, a Democratic Congress, and a politically mature NEA, the public school interests largely dictated to Congress and the president. "I'll be honest with you, we're moving into a very political environment in Washington, and I don't know whether this Congress is going to take up this legislation or not," Bush conceded of his GI Bill for Children in July 1992.[54]

Third, Bush's selection of Alexander, as well as Alexander's choices of Xerox chairman David Kearns and Columbia University education professor Diane Ravitch as his deputies, may have excited the mainstream media and energized the Department of Education, but they engendered suspicions among many advocates of nonpublic school choice. On his first day on the job, Alexander called for a "redefinition" of public schools, to include private schools and schools run by businesses or institutions. While not explicitly excluding vouchers for parochial schools, the new secretary asserted, "As you get down the continuum, it gets more difficult" to include such schools. A year later, William McGurn of *National Review* accused Alexander of seeking to "tone down" defenses of nonpublic school choice in a Bush speech and of bargaining away vouchers in negotiations with Congress over Bush's Educational Excellence Act of 1991. Kearns had coauthored (with Denis Doyle of the Hudson Institute) a 1988 book that opposed nonpublic school choice, a point raised by Senator Kennedy in the deputy undersecretary's confirmation hearings. Kearns replied that he had since reversed his position because there was broader support for the idea. Even if the Republicans inside the administration had joined the school choice bandwagon, many on Capitol Hill had not. Six Republicans were in the majority that killed the Hatch amendment in January 1992, and more than half the House Republicans helped defeat a school choice amendment sponsored by Texas Rep. Richard Armey in August.[55]

Fourth, Bush's attraction to nonpublic school choice as a civil rights issue may have defied conventional wisdom, but it could not upset traditional alliances. "Education is a key factor in lifting individuals from poverty," Senator Hatch said, echoing Lyndon Johnson, in defending his nonpublic school choice amendment to the Kennedy education bill in January 1992. "Once we pass this, the door is open to further and further aid," liberal Democratic senator Howard Metzenbaum of Ohio replied, sounding very much like a 1960s conservative

Republican wary of the "camel's nose" of federal aid to education. But if the preachers seemed to be singing each other's hymns, they did not seem to be converting each other's congregations. The faces of nonpublic school choice in Milwaukee may have been black, but so were those of its opponents, as the National Association for the Advancement of Colored People (NAACP) joined a suit in the Wisconsin Supreme Court to stop the program because it violated the "public purpose standard of the state constitution." Bush may have scored rhetorical points in embracing nonpublic school vouchers, but more than eight of every ten African American voters would support Bill Clinton in November 1992.[56]

Fifth, the metamorphosis of nonpublic school choice from abstraction to reality not only offered models that Bush could laud but targets that his opponents could assault. And there seemed to be fewer of the former than the latter. In the second presidential debate in October 1992, Bush claimed that "there's plenty of examples" of nonpublic school choice. But he could name only two—Milwaukee (in 1992) and Rochester, New York (in 1972). In the same month, a report by the Carnegie Foundation for the Advancement of Teaching reviewed all existing choice programs, public as well as nonpublic. It discovered that fewer than 2 percent of students availed themselves of such opportunities and that none of the choice plans met the "essential preconditions" of paying transportation, providing sufficient information to parents, or addressing the spending disparities between wealthy and impoverished school districts. "By these yardsticks, we concluded that responsible and effective statewide school choice does not exist in America today," the report decided.[57]

Sixth, even if Bush had the ultimate trump card—public opinion—on his side in the debate over nonpublic school vouchers, he was not quite sure how and when to play it. Initially, for fear of the public school teacher unions and their congressional allies, he tried to hide it amidst the even more popular components of his America 2000 plan. But the public school interests exposed it, and the best the administration could achieve was a compromise in the education committee of one house, so tautly worded as to exclude forty-eight states from experimenting with nonpublic school choice, and permit the same committee to report essentially the same bill without nonpublic school choice the following session. Then Bush allowed nonpublic school choice to stand—and fall—on its own, the victim of election-year gridlock and a flawed salesman. "President Ronald Reagan approached divided government by appeal[ing] directly to the American people to show their support for his policies by lobbying their representatives on his behalf," writes Charles Tiefer, counsel to the House of Representatives during the Reagan and Bush administrations. Bush's "rhetorical skills . . . pale, by contrast, however, with those of his immediate predecessor, whose dramatic talents were honed over a lifetime." The self-effacing Bush acknowledged his uphill battle to sell nonpublic school choice in a July

1992 campaign appearance: "I don't think every American is thinking, am I for the 'G.I. Bill' or not? I've got to do a better job of making them know that this is an issue."[58]

Federal aid to nonpublic schools became more of an issue than it had been in twenty-five years, and George Bush earned much of the credit for this achievement. But it did not become a successful one, and Bush deserves considerable blame for this setback. Seven years later, players on both sides of the issues would largely agree that nonpublic school choice had become an irresistible force, but a divided federal government had become an immovable object. After his failures to follow executive resolve with legislative success in the areas of public school reform, school desegregation, and nonpublic school aid, George Bush could have told them that.

## Bill Clinton

Consistency is a stranger to many politicians. During the final years of the Reagan administration, conservatives realized that the term "vouchers" was not selling their plan for public monies for parents of nonpublic school children. Emphasizing that such payments would offer parents the option of sending their children to public or nonpublic schools, they now pronounced themselves in favor of choice. To their ideological adversaries, however, "choice" was shorthand for "a woman's right to choose" abortion, which the conservatives opposed. So for the next decade, conservatives would argue in favor of choice in education but against it on abortion, while liberals would argue the opposite, with each side accusing the other of being inconsistent. Bill Clinton, on the liberal side of both arguments, would be consistently inconsistent.

During the 1992 presidential campaign, Clinton contended that nonpublic school choice would simply transfer badly needed federal funds from public schools to nonpublic schools. "It is crazy when some big-city schools don't work and people don't want to be in them," candidate Clinton told workers in Toledo, Ohio, in October. "And then I go to a place like Chicago and go into an area with the highest murder rate in Illinois to a junior high school that has a dress code, seventy-five fathers in the school every week, and 150 mothers in the school every week, no dropout rate, no violence, no problems, top ten percent in test scores in the state every year. If one person can do it, why can't they do it everywhere?"[59]

"Everywhere" apparently did not include Washington, D.C. Two weeks before taking office, President-elect Clinton announced that his twelve-year-old daughter Chelsea, then enrolled in a Little Rock public school, would attend Sidwell Friends, a $7,700-a-year Quaker school in the nation's capital. "They didn't reject public schools," spokesman George Stephanopolous said of Bill and Hillary Rodham Clinton's decision. "The schools in the District of Columbia and across the country are good schools, and Governor Clinton supports the public school system, as he has throughout his term as Governor and will continue as President. What they did was choose as a family Sidwell Friends." Then he uttered the words conservatives were waiting to hear: "it's a good choice."[60]

If the Clinton family's decision undercut the new president's primary argument, court decisions undermined his second case against nonpublic school vouchers—that they would violate the First Amendment's separation of church and state. "When I was a little boy, when I went to a Catholic school, when my folks moved from one place to another, and we lived way out in the country, and didn't know much about the schools in the new area where we were," Clinton recalled, "no one ever thought that the church would want more money from the taxpayers to run their schools. In fact, they said just the opposite, 'We don't want to be involved in that.' That's what the First Amendment is all about."[61]

Six months into the new administration, however, the Supreme Court ruled unanimously in *Jones v. Clear Creek Independent School District* that public school systems that open their doors to after-school community organizations must admit religious groups as well, effectively overturning a New York state law banning the use of public school property for any religious purpose. In the Court's majority opinion, signed by six justices, Byron White wrote that the refusal by the Center Moriches, Long Island, school district to admit religious groups to its high school did not violate the three-pronged test established by the court in the *Lemon* decision of 1971: that the aid to a religious institution "has a secular purpose, does not advance or inhibit religion as its principal effect, and does not foster an excessive entanglement with religion." The Court stopped short, however, of overturning *Lemon*, which Antonin Scalia, in a separate opinion joined by Clarence Thomas, likened to a "ghoul in a late-night horror movie," and which Anthony Kennedy criticized more temperately in his separate opinion.[62]

Later in the same term, the Court ruled 5–4 in *Zobrest v. Catalina School District* that a sign-language interpreter paid by the Tucson, Arizona, school district may accompany a deaf child into a Catholic high school. Citing the "child-benefit" precedent established in the 1947 *Everson* case, Chief Justice William Rehnquist argued for the majority: "If the Establishment Clause [of the First Amendment] did bar religious groups from receiving general government benefits, then a church could not be protected by the police and fire departments, or have its public sidewalk kept in repair."[63]

Encouraged by these two decisions, the USCC filed an amicus brief on behalf of the petitioners in *Board of Education v. Grumet*, who argued in favor of a special public school district created by the State of New York to accommodate the special education of children in Kiryas Joel, an incorporated Hasidic Jewish village in

Orange County. The parents of these children, the USCC contended in its brief, "have been forced into a 'cruel choice' between their religious faith and their children's education," the same "cruel choice" that vouchers would help remove. The First Amendment's free exercise clause "encourages" legislatures to avoid such choices "not as a protection from religion, but rather as a protection for religion." On the state level, the Vermont Supreme Court upheld a plan by which nonpublic school students would receive part of their tuition from public sources because "the reimbursement went to the parents, not the schools; the program did not distinguish between private and public school students; sectarian reasons did not motivate the awarding of vouchers; no substantial number of students were sent to private sectarian schools under the program; state regulation of sectarian schools was minimal; and the scheme did not operate to promote sectarian education."[64]

President Clinton himself may have unwittingly abetted the school choice movement by signing the Religious Freedom Restoration Act of 1993. The act provided that a government must show a "compelling governmental interest" that its interference with religion is the "least restrictive means" for advancing that interest before intruding upon religion. Frank Kemerer and Kimi King of the University of North Texas argued that the law "affects state voucher schemes because it requires such a heavy justification for the government to interfere with the exercise of religion that it could limit a state's ability to impose restrictions on parents who want to use a voucher to send their child to a religious school."[65]

The momentum for nonpublic school choice would not last, however. In November 1993 California voters overwhelmingly rejected a nonpublic school voucher initiative despite the support of the state's Republican governor, Pete Wilson. In June 1994 the Supreme Court ruled against the State of New York in abolishing the separate Kiryas Joel school district as a violation of the establishment clause of the First Amendment. The majority opinion, authored by Justice David Souter, argued that the law creating the special district had transcended the constitutional guarantee that religious communities can "pursue their own interests free from governmental interference." Justice Scalia's dissenting opinion lamented that the decision "takes to new extremes a recent tendency in the opinions of this court to turn the Establishment Clause into a repealer of our nation's tradition of religious toleration."[66]

In the same year, the Supreme Court of the Commonwealth of Puerto Rico struck down a plan by which low-income parents of children in nonpublic schools would receive from the island's education department a $1,500 voucher for reimbursement of educational costs. While a private school deserves police and fire protection, the court ruled, the Puerto Rican constitution's prohibition of public funds to support nonpublic schools applied to "public services or assistance that support its educational mission." The year ended with the 103rd

Congress having defeated nonpublic school vouchers, when amendments to Clinton's "Goals 2000: Educate America Act" failed by a 300–130 House vote in 1993 and a 52–41 Senate vote in 1994. Bishop Robert Banks of Green Bay, Wisconsin, chairman of the USCC Education Committee, said of nonpublic school choice that "the message was it was not to be discussed."[67]

The Republican ascendancy on Capitol Hill offered nonpublic school advocates new hope for federal school choice legislation. But a 7–7 vote in 1995 killed an amendment to the Department of Education appropriations bill, proposed by House Republican Frank Riggs in the Early Childhood, Youth, and Family and Educational Opportunities Committee, that would have transferred $30 million of ESEA Title I money to a three-year school choice demonstration project for low-income parents. In 1996 two Senate floor votes, 54–44 and 52–42, sank an aid package for the District of Columbia that would have allowed the city council to vote for nonpublic school vouchers.[68]

While nonpublic school vouchers met roadblocks on Capitol Hill, they continued to make inroads in the states. In August the Ohio Court of Appeals upheld a Cleveland school choice program enacted by the state legislature and Republican governor George Voinovich that provided fifteen hundred nonpublic school vouchers of $2,250 each to parents of disadvantaged children. At the same time, a study conducted by researchers from Harvard and the University of Houston found that participants in Milwaukee's pioneer nonpublic school choice program scored as many as eleven percentage points higher in math and five percentage points higher in reading than their public school counterparts. "What made the results valuable as well as impressive was the fact that the comparison was made among children with similar demographics, students who had not been selected in the lottery for the limited vouchers available," wrote Sharon Brooks Hodge in *Headway.* "By contrast, a study two years into the program [by John Witte of the University of Wisconsin, Madison] compared the choice students with the general student population of Milwaukee Public Schools, but found the vouchers didn't improve test scores." Hodge concluded that "It was important to compare apples to apples."[69]

*U.S. News and World Report* noted, however, that 27 percent of the students enrolled in the Cleveland program were already in nonpublic schools, and three of the seventeen schools in the Milwaukee plan had folded for financial reasons, with directors of two of them facing fraud charges. Alex Molnar, Marty Sapp, and Walter J. Farrell of the University of Wisconsin, Milwaukee, and James Johnson of the University of North Carolina, Chapel Hill, added that the Harvard-Houston conclusions were inconsistent with the study's own data, which showed that when adjusted for the students' gender, family income, and mothers' education, the choice and nonchoice groups showed "no statistically significant differences . . . in the performance of the two groups in reading or math for any year studied."[70]

The voucher debate reached the 1996 presidential campaign when former Kansas senator and Republican nominee Robert Dole proposed a four-year, $15 billion school choice plan that would fund voucher programs in up to fifteen states. Recognizing the increasing popularity of vouchers outside the Washington Beltway and desperate for a defining issue in his uphill battle with the incumbent, Dole seized school choice in his first debate with the president—and would not let go. "So it seems to me that we ought to take that money we can save from the Department of Education, put it into opportunity scholarships and tell little Landel Shakespeare out in Cleveland, Ohio, and tell your mother and father you're going to get to go to school," said Dole, "because we're going to match what the state puts up, and you're going to get to go to the school of your choice." Clinton responded that "I'm all for students having more choices," which he then defined as "public school choice" and charter schools. "What I'm against," the president continued, "is Senator Dole's plan to take money away from all of the children we now help with limited Federal funds, and help far fewer."[71]

Then, as if to try to change the subject, Clinton for the first time nodded in the direction of nonpublic school choice: "If we're going to have a private voucher plan, that ought to be done at the local level or state level." But Dole would not relent: "Let's turn the schools back to the parents and take it away from the National Education Association." Clinton, uncharacteristically off-balance from Dole's withering attack, repeated, "If you're going to have a private voucher plan, that ought to be determined by States and localities where they're raising and spending most of the money." To Dole's oft-stated assertion that Clinton was merely doing the bidding of the NEA in his opposition to nonpublic school choice, the president bristled, "And Senator, I remind you that a few years ago, when I supported a teacher testing law in my home state, I was pretty well lambasted by the teachers' association." Undeterred, Dole returned a final time to nonpublic school choice: "If a local school district in Cleveland or anyplace else wants to have a private school choice plan like Milwaukee did, let them have at it." As if to soften his assault on the president, Dole made a concession of his own, that "the results" of such programs "are highly ambiguous," before concluding with an upbeat "But I want to get out there and give a better educational opportunity to all our children."[72]

The verbal sparring did little to lift the Dole campaign, which fell to peace, prosperity, and the personal popularity of the president in November. It did, however, provoke an awkward moment for Clinton at his first postelection news conference. "Mr. President, when you begin your campaign to improve public education in this country, are you going to follow up on a suggestion that you made in the first Presidential debate," asked a reporter, "which is to encourage States and cities to offer vouchers for private school choice?" Clinton replied, "I don't believe I made that suggestion." Reminiscent of Senator Dole, the reporter persisted: "You said the states and cities should be allowed to do it." So Clinton corrected himself, "No—well, I've always thought they should be allowed to do it. I supported Milwaukee's right to do it. But I'm not going to encourage or discourage. . . . I am opposed to the Federal Government doing it. . . . At the State and local level, I would not be in favor of it because . . . the schools are underfunded." Clinton completed the circle by asserting that "they have the legal right to do it, and I don't support any action to take that legal right away from them. And if they think the situation is totally out of hand and they want to try what they did in Milwaukee . . . they ought to have the right to do it."[73]

The election had been over for a month, but the president was still campaigning, trying to be all things to all people on the school choice issue. But the newly restored Republican majority in Congress vowed to force the president to take a stand. In September 1997 Senate Republicans resurrected their proposal for a voucher plan in the District of Columbia. "Anyone who is going to oppose this ought to take their children and put them in the worst school in the city for a year," Speaker of the House Newt Gingrich of Georgia addressed school choice opponents in the upper chamber, where half of the parents of school-age children sent them to private schools. "Public schools are the cornerstone of our democracy," Clinton responded, in returning to his precampaign position. "We have always recognized our common responsibility for preparing all our young children for the challenge of the future." The president then urged the legislators to reject the measure: "I call upon Congress to challenge our public schools, but not to walk away from them." The bill's supporters then failed to obtain the sixty votes needed to forestall a Democratic filibuster.[74]

In the wake of a third study of the Milwaukee voucher program, which favorably compared "choice" to "nonchoice" students, and "choice" students after several years in the program to the same students when they entered, several other proposals appeared on Capitol Hill. The most prominent bill, cosponsored by Republican senator Paul Coverdell of Georgia and Democratic senator Robert Torricelli of New Jersey, would allow parents to create tax-free individual retirement accounts, from which they could withdraw up to $2,500 per year for education-related expenses such as tuition. The Coverdell-Torricelli bill passed the Senate, 57–41, but failed in the House-Senate conference committee when Clinton threatened to veto the larger tax legislation of which it was a part. Secretary Riley explained that the administration opposed the bill as a windfall for the rich; by his calculation, a family with an annual income of $25,000 who saved $200 a year at 8 percent interest would earn only $16 and a tax break of $2.50.[75]

If the Clinton administration continued to disapprove of the contents of nonpublic school vouchers, it nonetheless admired the packaging. Sounding very much like one of his Republican adversaries, the president in September 1997 announced the awarding of more than $40 million in federal grants for independent-minded schools that operate without many of the regulations imposed upon the public schools. "Every state should give parents the power to choose," said the president. "Their right to choose will foster competition and innovation that can make public schools even better." Parents would not be choosing nonpublic schools, however, but the next-best thing: publicly funded "charter schools," over seven hundred of which had already opened.[76]

The fortunes of nonpublic school advocates continued their ebb and flow during the following two years. The Supreme Court's 5–4 decision in *Agostini v. Felton* in June 1997 effectively overturned its 1985 *Aguilar v. Felton* and *Grand Rapids v. Ball* verdicts by permitting "the on-site delivery of [ESEA] Title I services for students enrolled in religiously affiliated schools." Citing the *Zobrest* decision, Justice Sandra Day O'Connor's majority opinion asserted that "we have abandoned the presumption in *Meek* [*v. Pittenger*] and [*Grand Rapids v.*] *Ball* that the placement of public employees on parochial school grounds, inevitably results in state-sponsored indoctrination or a symbolic union between government and religion." Echoing his three immediate predecessors, Secretary Riley hailed the decision as "a positive step forward for American education."[77]

In September 1997, the first study of the Cleveland voucher program showed improvement by those participants tested after their first year. In December 1997, however, a second study of the program tested the "choice" students and found them no better off than their peers outside the program. In May 1998, the District of Columbia voucher plan finally passed both houses of Congress, only to have the president finally act on his threat to veto it. In June 1998, the Wisconsin State Supreme Court ruled that the expansion of Milwaukee's nonpublic school choice to religious schools passed the *Lemon* test: "because it has a secular purpose, it will not have the primary effect of advancing religion, and it will not lead to excessive entanglement between the State and participating sectarian schools." But Wisconsin Republican governor and voucher advocate Tommy Thompson opposed extending it to other parts of the state because "it's going to take some time to evaluate."[78]

For the first time, the Gallup Poll found a majority of Americans in favor of nonpublic school choice. Yet from 1991 to 1998, voters rejected nonpublic school vouchers in four states. In August 1999, on the eve of the first week of school, Judge Solomon Oliver of the Federal District Court in Cleveland allowed that city's voucher students to attend classes, but only for a semester, pending a review of the program's constitutionality under the First Amendment.[79]

## The Clinton Record

For advocates of nonpublic school choice, the Clinton era was, in Charles Dickens's oft-quoted words, "the best of times, . . . the worst of times." Several new developments augured well for partisans of nonpublic school vouchers. First, not only did a majority of Americans support nonpublic school choice by 1998, but a greater proportion of African Americans than whites now backed vouchers. In announcing his organization's support for a statewide voucher scheme enacted in June 1999 by Florida's Republican legislature and Governor Jeb Bush (son of the former president), T. Willard Fair, president of the Greater Miami Urban League, asserted that "We are not bound by color the way we used to be bound where people said, 'You can't think that way because you're black.'"[80]

Second, while the Supreme Court had yet to rule on nonpublic school choice, voucher proponents interpreted the Court's inaction as a positive sign. In November 1998, the Supreme Court refused to intervene in *Jackson v. Benson,* which would have tested the Milwaukee program. Clint Bolick, director of the provoucher Institute for Justice, while admitting that the Court's evasion "was not an explicit endorsement of the Milwaukee program," nonetheless cheered that "it means that the highest court ruling on this is the Wisconsin Supreme Court, which held that Milwaukee's voucher program did not violate either the state or Federal constitutions." Court watchers believed that if and when the Court decided a voucher case, Justice Sandra Day O'Connor would tip the balance either way.[81]

Third, though the teacher unions remained strongly opposed to nonpublic school choice, they had also previously resisted public school choice, which they were now embracing. As late as 1992, the NEA informed Congress that the organization was "unalterably opposed" to using federal funds for charter schools. By 1996, however, the NEA announced that it was allocating $1.5 million to help its members open charter schools. An April 1998 *NEA Today* article wondered how a union could support charter schools. Quoting Jan Noble, president of the association's Colorado Springs affiliate, the article answered that this position was a chance for educators "to use energy and innovation to get the taxpayers on our side. We have to prove public education is the best game in town." Citing AFT president Sandra Feldman's similar declaration that charters could help improve failing public schools in Washington, D.C., *Washington Post* columnist William Raspberry remarked, "Feldman won't like this, but her proposal, and the self-confidence behind it, echo the conclusion that is driving the growing support of charter schools and vouchers: if the public schools aren't getting it done, many parents are saying, then give us the authority (charters) or the money (vouchers) to do it ourselves."[82]

Finally, if the chances for nonpublic school choice remained remote as long as there was a Democrat in the White House, the early presidential polls showed a Republican voucher proponent, Governor George W. Bush of Texas, brother of the Florida governor and son of the former president, comfortably ahead of voucher opponent Vice President Albert Gore. If Bush or another provoucher Republican were elected to the White House in 2000, and the Republican majority returned to Capitol Hill, it would mark the first time since the enactment of the ESEA that nonpublic school aid advocates predominated on both ends of Pennsylvania Avenue.

Supporters of nonpublic school aid knew better than to become too sanguine about the prospects for vouchers, however. First, despite the swing in public opinion toward vouchers, especially among blacks, the minority "establishment" largely continued to oppose them. In backing the Florida voucher plan, the Greater Miami Urban League was not only taking on the NAACP but the national Urban League as well. All but one (Republican voucher proponent Rep. J. C. Watts of Oklahoma) of the African American members of Congress were Democrats, and all but one (Rep. Floyd Flake of New York) of those Democrats opposed nonpublic school choice.[83]

Second, if the Supreme Court had not moved against nonpublic school choice, it also had not, despite the presence of seven justices appointed by Republican presidents, acted affirmatively on the question. Church-state separationists applauded as the Rehnquist Court struck down prayer at high school graduations and the Religious Freedom Restoration Act of 1993. "The court is trying to come up with kind of an even-handed treatment of religion that doesn't discriminate against religion," explained Marquette University constitutional law expert Christopher Wolfe of an approach that offered no guarantees to either side of the school choice debate.[84]

Third, despite the considerable strides taken toward educational reform by the AFT and the NEA, the teacher unions remained steadfast in their opposition to vouchers. NEA president Bob Chase, a reformer whom conservative critic Chester Finn saluted as the "Mikhail Gorbachev of the NEA," nonetheless elicited a standing ovation at his organization's 1999 convention when he likened vouchers' potential impact on the public schools to "applying leeches and bleeding a patient to death." The fervor of the unions' opposition to vouchers continued to translate into dollars: in the 1996 election campaign, the AFT and the NEA contributed nearly $5 million to political candidates who shared their views, with 98 percent of the sum going to Democrats. In 1999, the NEA spent $25,000 to help elect voucher opponents to the Milwaukee school board and planned to spend $30 million in the next two years to combat "threats to public education." At the 1999 NEA Convention, the union's leadership ruled out of order a proposal by a member of its Representative Assembly to "allow members to designate where the political contribution portion of their dues money is allocated," because in the leaders' words, "no dues money is used for that purpose."[85]

Finally, even if all of the pieces fell into place for nonpublic school choice advocates—a Republican president selecting conservative federal judges, a Republican Senate confirming them, and a Republican House of Representatives paying their salaries—there remained grounds for considerable skepticism. For if choice supporters had unfairly branded the Democratic Party as an antivoucher monolith, their adversaries had been inaccurate in ascribing unity to voucher supporters. During the 1992 presidential campaign, the conservative Heritage Foundation warned that nonpublic school choice "has the potential to backfire. It could easily lead to onerous regulation of private schools." A House Republican amendment to the FY 1998 education appropriation permitting states to earmark 25 percent of their ESEA Title VI funds for public and non-public school choice programs authorized by state law failed when thirty-five Republicans joined the opposition. The familiar argument from an unfamiliar source, Republican representative Marge Roukema of New Jersey, was "Ulti-mately these vouchers will result in gutting the public school system."[86]

The USCC's consistent stand in favor of nonpublic school choice similarly spurred dissension in the Church's ranks. For the first time in three decades, national Catholic elementary and secondary school enrollment had stabilized, undercutting the traditional "save our schools" argument of advocates of federal aid to parochial education. USCC secretary of education Monsignor Thomas McDade admitted that while the USCC had filed an amicus brief in the Mil-waukee case, he was unaware of any formal statement by the bishops in favor of equalized funding of public schools. University of Notre Dame professor Jay Dolan, an authority on U.S. Catholic history, lamented, "Since public schools serve the vast majority of children, the failure of the Church to speak out on their behalf should give us all pause." In a letter to the *National Catholic Reporter*, Edd Doerr, the non-Catholic president of the antivoucher group Americans for Religious Liberty, observed that "Catholic bishops seem far more concerned about the twenty-one percent of Catholic children in parochial schools than the seventy-nine percent who attend often underfunded or inequitably funded public schools."[87]

Despite their differences, voucher proponents and opponents could agree on one point: nonpublic school choice would not come cheaply. Under the Mil-waukee plan, students receive taxpayer-financed vouchers that are used at non-public schools. The Milwaukee public school system, however, is able to count voucher recipients as part of its student population when it receives state aid. As a result, wrote Joe Williams of the *Milwaukee Journal-Sentinel* in October 1998, "state taxpayers will begin pumping more money than ever before into educa-tion in Milwaukee." Under the choice proposal for Washington, D.C., that was vetoed by President Clinton, $10 million would have financed $3,200 "opportu-nity scholarships" for about two thousand schoolchildren in a city in which Catholic elementary school tuition averaged $2,131 and Catholic high school tuition began at $4,200. Even "compassionate conservatives," as George W. Bush likes to call himself, would have a difficult time financing a federal voucher pro-gram of considerable scope, especially if the budget surpluses projected by the Clinton administration should begin to disappear as they did three decades ear-lier, when the Democratic "Education President" transferred power to the first

Republican president to experiment with federal nonpublic school vouchers. The experiment ended abruptly, never to return.[88]

In his 1996 reelection campaign, President Bill Clinton proposed to erect a "bridge to the twenty-first century." In the areas of public school reform and school desegregation, however, he never specified what he would be transporting across the bridge. In the area of nonpublic school aid, he specified what he would not. By the end of the Clinton presidency, as the considerable promise of his first term yielded to the incrementalism and scandal of his second, the bridge remained under construction.

CONCLUSION

# The Era of Education

This study has endeavored to fill a significant void in the scholarly appraisals of late-twentieth-century U.S. political history: while many have written about the presidents and many others have written about the schools, virtually no one (with the exception of the enactment of the Elementary and Secondary Education Act during the Johnson administration) has connected the two. While the connection can certainly be overstated (presidents do not educate children, schools do), it instead has been remarkably understated despite its prominence in presidential politics and policies. Scholars continue to exhaustively address the domestic policy legacies of the recent presidents and the outcomes of public school aid, school desegregation, and nonpublic school aid, yet they largely overlook the impacts of elementary and secondary education on those legacies and of the presidents on those outcomes.

## The Schools

### Public School Aid

Like the assessments of the presidents themselves, evaluations of the impacts of their policies on the nation's elementary and secondary schools are ongoing, incomplete, and highly contentious. Though the federal role in education remains relatively small, the number of scholarly appraisals of that role is voluminous, further certifying the public's intense interest in the subject.

As has been documented, the primary mission of the federal government during the first two decades under the Elementary and Secondary Education Act (ESEA) was to help states and localities achieve equity among their schools. The major burden of this effort continues to fall on Title I, the most expensive and most controversial piece of the ESEA, sending $8 billion annually to forty-five thousand schools in more than thirteen thousand local school districts in 2000.[1]

The congressionally mandated study of Title I in 1997, *Prospects: Student Outcomes,* collected data from representative samples of first-, third-, and seventh-graders from four hundred schools nationwide. It concluded that Title I aid was helpful to disadvantaged pupils in those high-poverty schools with greater use of academic tracking, more experienced principals, a balance between remediation and higher-order critical thinking in classroom instruction, and higher levels of teacher, parent and community involvement in the schools. The study nonetheless concluded that Title I assistance to these schools "was insufficient to close the achievement gap" with students from low-poverty schools. "Data from the *Prospects* study," the researchers wrote, echoing the Coleman Report of 1966, "support earlier research findings that the characteristics of the individual student and family account for the largest part of the variation in student achievement measured by test scores, but that schools do make an important contribution that can be enhanced."[2]

Like the debate over equity, the dispute over the movement toward excellence was one of means, not ends. The primary method adopted by presidents, superintendents, and principals to address this new emphasis on academic standards is an old one: testing. The proliferation of so-called high-stakes testing, all in the name of raising academic standards, has evoked a furious exchange within the educational community. Largely in response to *A Nation at Risk,* by the 1987–88 school year forty-five states and the District of Columbia were using some kind of standardized test. By 1993, the federal government was spending $10 million on developing national content standards in other core academic subjects. By 1995, forty-nine states were developing content standards in core academic subjects.[3]

Testing advocates can point to many successes of the standards movement. A 2000 Heritage Foundation study of twenty-one high-poverty nonpublic and public schools found that they had achieved median scores above the sixty-fifth percentile on national academic achievement tests by stressing high academic standards. Scholastic Achievement Test mathematics scores in 2000 reached their highest level in thirty years, and verbal scores remained stable for the fifth consecutive year.[4]

Not only are teachers tailoring their instruction to the tests, critics counter, but the tests themselves are flawed. Because of the successful resistance to national testing, the individual states devise uneven assessments that produce uneven results. The examination can be either too easy, rendering it virtually meaningless, or too hard, inviting a revolt by students, teachers, and parents. In Ohio in 2001, 98 percent of the state's high school seniors passed the graduation exam. In California, less than half passed. In Massachusetts, California, Washington, and Oregon, parents refused to send their children to school to take the tests. In Wisconsin, the legislature responded to parent resistance by killing the test.[5]

As a result, the critics maintain, the standards movement is not adequately addressing the educational "crisis" identified by *A Nation at Risk.* In 1999 the National Education Goals Panel reluctantly concurred, noting that of the eight national objectives embodied in President Bush's America 2000 and President Clinton's Goals 2000, the country was making significant progress on only one: "All children will enter school ready to learn." On the others, the high school graduation rate remained four points below the 90 percent target; National Assessment of Educational Progress (NAEP) scores for reading, writing, history, geography, and prose literature generally improved yet nonetheless fell short of the "demonstrated competency" mark; high school seniors remained far behind the "first in the world" plateau in eighth- and twelfth-grade mathematics and science examinations; and drug use and violence increased in the schools.[6]

If they pause from attacking each other, the two sides of the public school aid divide can realize that they agree more than they disagree. Both seek reform of the education system, both acknowledge shortcomings in Title I and Goals 2000, and both want more money, whether for more teachers or more testing, to address them. Both cite the same data to draw different conclusions: student test scores either validate or discredit Title I and Goals 2000. Despite their different emphases, both groups value equity as well as excellence. And although they often talk past one another, the emergence of education as a prominent national political issue has ensured that in legislatures and courts as well as on campuses and in the media, the nation is listening. "It is evident that the presence of high-stakes tests has at least served as a conversation starter," writes Gregory Cizek. It is a conversation well worth having.[7]

## School Desegregation

"An American Dilemma," Gunnar Myrdal famously called the race issue in 1944, and it remains so half a century later. Just as the federal role in education has become entrenched, the federal role in desegregation is becoming extinct. Predictably, this development is good news to some observers, bad news to others.

Virtually all commentators agree that school desegregation deserved its moment in history. If desegregation, at least in the long term, has received virtually universal support in the scholarly community, busing to coerce desegregation is quite another matter. "When fully and carefully carried out, mandatory desegregation reduces racial isolation, enhances minority achievement, improves race relations, promotes educational equality, opens new opportunities, and maintains citizen support," writes Jennifer Hochschild. "If the United States remains a racially segregated country, the problem is not that the techniques failed," Joseph Watras concludes. "The techniques have not worked because people do not know why they should value racial integration."[8]

Other scholars, however, join the majority of Americans in valuing racial integration yet rejecting the technique of forced busing. From her study of magnet schools in twenty large urban districts, Christine Rossell concludes that voluntary desegregation is more effective than mandatory mixing. David Armor calls for "equity choice" plans that allow students to transfer from mediocre to excellent schools. "Whatever the educational benefits of desegregation, mandatory busing to non-neighboring schools is highly controversial and often leads to loss of white or middle-class populations," writes Armor. "Moreover, mandatory busing plans over the long run have proven no more effective than comprehensive voluntary plans in promoting interracial contact."[9]

Regardless of the merits of busing to coerce school desegregation, both sides accept the political reality that its time is quickly passing. Busing opponent Rossell wrote in 1990 that "I know of no mandatory reassignment plan implemented in the North since 1981, and only two implemented in the South since 1981." Busing advocates Amy Stuart Wells and Robert Crain agreed in 1997 that "since 1991, the U.S. Supreme Court appears to be moving in favor of ending federal school desegregation orders in districts that prove they have removed the vestiges of segregation 'to the extent practicable.'"[10]

With the decline of forced busing has come the variety of voluntary desegregation measures—magnet schools, charter schools, nonpublic and public school choice—advocated by Presidents Reagan, Bush, and/or Clinton. Here, too, the quest for equity is giving way to the pursuit of excellence. A 1998 Public Agenda Poll found that 82 percent of black parents valued "raising academic standards" over "more diversity and integration" in their children's schools.[11]

As the battle continues to rage over whether the schools are getting better, there is little question that they are becoming more segregated. In its 2001 report, "Schools More Separate: Consequences of a Decade of Resegregation," Harvard University's Civil Rights Project found that 70 percent of black children attended predominantly minority schools in the 1998–99 academic year, up from 66 percent in 1991–92 and 63 percent in 1980–81. Most alarmingly, predominately African American or Hispanic schools continue to be largely high-poverty schools.[12]

While there is little likelihood that the buses will roll again anytime soon, there is a real possibility that Americans of all races will rededicate their efforts toward school desegregation. For the moment, however, regardless of who the president is, such endeavors seem relics of a bygone era.

### Nonpublic School Aid

While public school aid was ascending and school desegregation was declining, nonpublic school choice was just arriving as the era of education came to a close. At the outset of the twenty-first century, eighteen states permitted public loans of textbooks, twenty-six allowed public transportation, and twenty-eight authorized public auxiliary services to nonpublic schools. Five states—Florida, Maine, Vermont, Ohio, and Wisconsin—had enacted nonpublic school voucher programs. Twenty-one governors and the new president, Republican George W. Bush, were open to some form of nonpublic school choice. The private Children's Scholarship Fund had distributed vouchers to forty thousand underprivileged students in forty-eight states. The Black Alliance for Educational Options launched a $3 million television campaign in the nation's capital to extol the virtues of nonpublic school vouchers for minority students.[13]

It was not clear, however, whether these developments marked the genesis or the apogee of the nonpublic school choice movement. The reviews of the few existing voucher programs remained decidedly mixed. An August 2000 study by Harvard's Program on Education Policy and Governance, chaired by Paul Peterson, concluded that African American voucher students in New York City, Dayton, Ohio, and Washington, D.C., improved their average test scores after two years in nonpublic schools—four points in New York, six points in Dayton, and nine points in Washington, D.C. A February 2001 study by Jay Greene of the Manhattan Institute found that seventy-six public schools that had received failing scores on Florida's achievement test once and would have lost students to nonpublic schools under the state's voucher law if they failed a second time, all improved enough to remove themselves from the list of failing schools in their second year. An April 2001 report by Harvard's Caroline Hoxby concluded that those Milwaukee public elementary schools where nonpublic school vouchers were readily accessible improved more rapidly between the 1996–97 and 1999–2000 academic years than did those public schools where vouchers were hard to obtain.[14]

Each of these studies drew criticism, however. People for the American Way claimed that the Peterson study "improperly compares two dramatically different groups and may well reflect private school screening out of the most at-risk students," while Mathematica Policy Research asserted that the New York results were not consistent across grade levels and that only sixth-graders achieved significant gains. The National Education Association (NEA) criticized the Greene conclusions for excluding "any other potential explanations for the results except for vouchers, cheating, or chance," adding that "the efforts that were made in those schools, not the vouchers," rescued the failing schools. Stanford's Martin Carnoy similarly observed that while Hoxby proved that the public schools she studied improved during the existence of the nonpublic school choice program, she did not show cause and effect.[15]

Such conflicting studies have helped create an increasingly skeptical public. In the same 2000 election in which voucher proponent Bush narrowly defeated voucher opponent Al Gore, nonpublic school choice referenda lost in Michigan and California. A Gallup Poll found black support for vouchers down from 72 percent in 1997 to 30 percent in 2001, with overall public endorsement of nonpublic school choice down to 34 percent. As if to acknowledge such sentiment, President George W. Bush, like his father, jettisoned nonpublic school choice to help pass education legislation in the early days of his administration.[16]

Public school teacher unions remained powerful obstacles to nonpublic school choice. Yet voucher advocates in many ways remained their own worst enemies. Not only was their advocate in the White House again turning his back on them, but their own arguments, like those of their adversaries, were colliding with one another. Many of the same voices who back vouchers are staunch supporters of the standards movement in public education. But the salience of the former may rely on the deficiencies of the latter. As the Florida study shows, one of the professed goals of vouchers is to improve public schools by at least the threat of competition from nonpublic schools. If the standards movement succeeds in radically improving public schools, there is presumably little need for vouchers. In the same 2001 Gallup Poll that showed declining public support for vouchers, two-thirds of Americans expressed support for at least as much testing of their children as presently occurs and, for the first time in the thirty-three-year history of the survey, a majority accorded their public schools grades of A or B. Unless grade inflation is as rampant outside the schools as it is inside, this overwhelming good news for academic standards could be an equally bad omen for nonpublic school choice.[17]

Nonpublic school aid proponents are in much the same position as mandatory desegregation advocates were three decades earlier, fending off academic challenges to their credibility and political assaults on their relevance. But while the federal courts offered cover for busing advocates in the 1970s and 1980s, they afforded no such undergirding for the similar arguments of nonpublic school choice partisans in the 1990s. When the U.S. Supreme Court finally heard a voucher case in June 2002, an appeal of the District Court's rejection of the Cleveland program, even the favorable 5–4 decision in *Zelman v. Simmons-Harris* may have come too late for nonpublic school aid supporters, for whom the era of education was more potential than real.[18]

## The Presidents and the Schools

A popular television commercial for a hotel chain that ran during the middle years of the Clinton presidency showed the leader of an education interest group struggling to make a speech. He posits that there are two major solutions to the country's ills. The first, he recites, is that governments should spend more money on schools. When he comes to the second, his mind draws a blank. "Never underestimate," goes the tag line at the end of the ad, "the importance of a good night's rest."

In the first two decades under the ESEA, dollars and cents dominated the discourse on the federal role in education. Lyndon Johnson and Jimmy Carter could boast that they had spent more money on education than their predecessors. Richard Nixon, Gerald Ford, and Ronald Reagan in his first three years could claim to have tried, albeit without much success, to spend less. Yet despite Carter's reopening of the Department of Education and Reagan's failed attempt to close it, federal expenditures as a percentage of the national education budget changed very little. And except for Nixon's disappointing National Institute of Education and Reagan's diluted Chapter Two block grants, there was little attention paid to how well the federal government was spending. As a result, the education interests and their allies on Capitol Hill, like the speaker in the commercial, placed more money at the top of their agenda. When trying to remember to seek quality as well as quantity, they too often seemed in need of a good night's rest.

Then came *A Nation at Risk* in 1983. The education interests and their advocates suddenly remembered their lines. "We got quite excited about educational innovation after the Russians sent up Sputnik in 1957, but the American people displayed a short attention span and the excitement lasted only eight years," John Gardner, Lyndon Johnson's secretary of Health, Education, and Welfare, would recall almost forty years later. The excitement died for almost two decades, said Gardner, until *A Nation at Risk*. "We're beginning to see some very good spurts of progress, and there are no signs that the impulse that began in 1983 is diminishing," Gardner asserted in the third year of the George H. W. Bush administration. "Good things are swelling up from the grassroots, and this is more hopeful than some national solution or some big formula program from the federal government."[19]

Just as liberals such as Gardner were rediscovering the tradition of local control of education, conservatives such as Chester Finn of the Nixon, Reagan, and Bush administrations were acknowledging an important role for the federal government in reforming education. A discouraged Professor Finn wrote from Vanderbilt University in 1983, on the eve of *A Nation at Risk*, that President Reagan "has paid little attention to education issues, and if there is a fount of informed intelligence and thoughtful planning about matters to be found elsewhere in the White House, it must be bubbling very quietly indeed." Yet five years later, Assistant Secretary Finn wrote to his boss, Secretary of Education William Bennett, that due to the Reagan administration's focus of national attention on education reform, "The NEA is now at least going through the motions of taking Republicans seriously." The following year, back on the outside looking in at the Bush administration, Finn, like the NEA, was requesting more money. In his capacity as chairman of the National Assessment Governing Board, Finn wrote to Secretary of Education Lauro Cavazos asking for $1.9 million to fund the NAEP tests, $700,000 more than the "inadequate" figure in the Bush FY 1990 budget.[20]

So after more than three decades and $120 billion of warfare between "cost-quality" and "social context," "equity" and "excellence," and inputs and outcomes, the country was closer to a consensus on federal elementary and secondary education policy than at any time since 1965. It was somehow appropriate that a "New Democrat" from the "New South" was implementing this new paradigm. Clinton's "neoliberal educational policy proposals are likely to confuse many," Frances Fowler prophesied in 1995. "At times, they will superficially resemble Bush and Reagan programs; at other times, they will be reminiscent of the Great Society or New Deal; at still other times, they will seem alien, as if they do not belong on the American political landscape." Indeed, Goals

2000 emulated Bush and Reagan, the Title I redistribution formula echoed the Great Society or the New Deal, and the piecemeal initiatives on guns, drugs, school uniforms, curfews, and truancy seemed a bit strange coming from the proverbial "most powerful person on earth," who presumably had more important matters to address.[21]

Such as poverty. Lyndon Johnson's "other" war, thirty-five years later, looked not so much futile as forgotten. Robert Wood, Johnson's undersecretary of Housing and Urban Development and later superintendent of the Boston public schools, still considers the urban poor the most pressing education issue, but he has very little company. Michael Harrington's "Other America" of 1962, later Kenneth Auletta's "Underclass" in 1982, became simply "those left behind" in the prosperity of the late 1990s. "Do you realize that the average 'A' student in an inner-city school," asks Urban League president Hugh Price, "knows about as much as the typical 'C' student in the suburbs?" Yet Minnesota Democratic senator Paul Wellstone took a "poverty tour" of the country in 1998 as a possible springboard for a presidential candidacy, then decided not to run. Bill Clinton, no child of privilege, made his own visit through the nation's "pockets of poverty" the following year. He talked a little about education and a lot about business tax credits.[22]

As the richest decade of the "American Century" came to a close, conservatives seemed to be talking more than liberals about the poor, but neither seemed to really know how to better educate them, beyond spouting middle-class nostrums such as "accountability," "responsibility," and "choice." Lyndon Johnson had wanted to pay the poor; Bill Clinton wanted to test them.

So despite the alarms sounded on the far Right about a *national* curriculum and on the far Left about a *national* religion, the new consensus for more dollars and more tests, which would culminate in President George W. Bush's bipartisan No Child Left Behind Act of 2001, had not overcome the socioeconomic divisions in the nation's schools. Neither the liberal panacea of property tax equalization, the conservative elixir of nonpublic school vouchers, nor the universally popular charter and magnet schools had yet moved conclusively toward bridging the yawning gap between the haves and have-nots in public elementary and secondary schools. The experts remained more adept at diagnosing the illnesses than finding cures for what ails underprivileged students. The politicians seemed increasingly to have stopped looking.[23]

Of the presidents in this "era of education," the first and last—Lyndon Johnson and Bill Clinton—probably cared the most about the nation's elementary and secondary schools. If one listened closely to Clinton, one could almost hear Johnson: Johnson enacted the ESEA, Clinton expanded it; both presidents increased federal education expenditures to 7 percent of the nation's school budget and withstood Republican challenges to reduce them through state and local block grants; both Presidents supported school desegregation yet opposed mandatory busing to achieve it; and both placed primacy on education within a balanced federal budget. But the similarities in their outputs could not obscure the differences in their objectives. Johnson saw education as a way for disadvantaged Americans to compete with more affluent Americans, while Clinton viewed education as a way for Americans to compete with their counterparts from other nations. Johnson resisted national standards, yet Clinton embraced them. Johnson confronted an officially nonpartisan and politically weak NEA by opposing federal funds for school construction and teacher salaries; Clinton joined an officially partisan and politically potent NEA in supporting them. Johnson fought de jure segregation but said little about de facto school segregation; Clinton declared victory over the former and said a lot about the latter. Johnson opened the door to federal aid to nonpublic schools; Clinton closed it.

It is ironic, however, that the president of this era who may have cared the least about education, Ronald Reagan, might, as Gardner and Finn acknowledged, have done the most to ensure a permanent and significant place for elementary and secondary schools in national politics and policy. He inadvertently saved the Department of Education, approved the rare national commission that actually makes a lasting impact, and through school visits, wall charts, and other manifestations of the bully pulpit of the presidency helped transform education into a potent political issue that attracted the attention of the media and the electorate as never before. If Ronald Reagan owes a debt to Lyndon Johnson for boldly ushering in the "era of education," Bill Clinton owes a debt to Ronald Reagan for effectively advertising it. Reagan not only proposed "what works" in education policy; he demonstrated what works in education politics.

In the end, however, as "accountability" supplanted "opportunity" as the major buzzword of school policy, and as the middle class displaced the lower class as the primary targets of school politics, not all that much had changed. The schools receiving assistance from Southern Democrat Bill Clinton looked remarkably similar to those aided by Southern Democrat Lyndon Johnson: public (with minimal federal monies for nonpublic schools), largely dependent on state and local funding (with less than ten percent from the federal government), racially divided (with de facto segregation having replaced de jure segregation), long on promise (in 1999 as in 1965, Americans identified education as their primary domestic concern), yet short on performance (Title I has been inadequate, Goals 2000 have proven unattainable). Thanks largely to the efforts of the seven presidents from 1965 to 2001, a small piece of federal policy has remained a large part of national politics.[24]

## NOTES

## Introduction

1. Adrienne Koch, ed., *Notes of Debates in the Federal Convention of 1787, Reported by James Madison 1787* (New York: Norton, 1987). President George Washington, in his first message to Congress in 1790, would propose the creation of a national university, but a bill for this purpose died in Congress in 1796. Jefferson himself tried unsuccessfully to divert federal funds to education. In 1809, the House of Representatives defeated a bill that would have channeled profits from a national banking system into education, as did the Senate in 1827; and in 1833 both houses of Congress passed, but President Andrew Jackson vetoed, a bill directing the revenue from public lands to education. See Lawrence McAndrews, *Broken Ground: John F. Kennedy and the Politics of Education* (New York: Garland, 1991), p. 11.

2. There is no other study of this kind, and except for the Elementary and Secondary Education Act of 1965 and the re-creation of the Department of Education in 1979, U.S. history textbooks seldom mention the education policies of presidents Johnson through Clinton.

3. Joel Spring, *The American School, 1642–1985* (New York: Longman, 1986), p. 14.

4. McAndrews, *Broken Ground*, p. 14.

5. Ibid., p. 10.

6. Davison Douglas, ed., *School Busing: Constitutional and Political Developments*, Vol. 1 (New York: Garland, 1994), p. ix.

7. McAndrews, *Broken Ground*, p. 27.

8. Timothy Boggs, "An Analysis of the Opinions in the United States Supreme Court Decisions on Religion and Education from 1948 through 1972," unpublished EdD diss. (University of Colorado, 1973), pp. 43, 80.

9. *Engel v. Vitale* (1962) outlawed official prayers, and *Abingdon Township v. Schempp* (1963) outlawed Bible readings. See Neil G. McCluskey, "Aid to Nonpublic Schools: Historical and Social Perspectives," *Current History*, June 1972, p. 303; McAndrews, *Broken Ground*, p. 161.

## Chapter 1: Public School Aid, 1965–81

1. The epigraph is from Lyndon Johnson, "Statement by the President Following House Action on the Education Bill," March 27, 1965, *Public Papers of the Presidents of the United States: Lyndon B. Johnson, Book 1, 1965* (Washington, D.C.: U.S. Government Printing Office, 1966), p. 1335.

2. Interview of Francis Keppel by Joe Frantz, August 17, 1972, Tape 2, Lyndon B. Johnson Presidential Library, Austin Texas, p. 7.

3. Lawrence McAndrews, *Broken Ground: John F. Kennedy and the Politics of Education* (New York: Garland, 1991), p. 219; "Elementary and Secondary Education Expanded," *Congressional Quarterly Almanac,* 89th Cong., 2nd sess., 1966 (Washington, D.C., 1967), p. 289.

4. McAndrews, *Broken Ground,* pp. 161, 166, 174.

5. Ibid., pp. 16, 21.

6. Ibid., p. 168.

7. For accounts of the passage of the ESEA, see Stephen Bailey and Edith Mosher, *ESEA: The Office of Education Administers a Law* (Syracuse: Syracuse University Press, 1968); Eugene Eidenberg and Roy D. Morey, *An Act of Congress: The Legislative Process and the Making of Education Policy* (New York: Norton, 1969); Hugh Davis Graham, *The Uncertain Triumph: Federal Education Policy in the Kennedy and Johnson Years* (Chapel Hill: University of North Carolina Press, 1984); Philip Meranto, *The Politics of Federal Aid to Education in 1965* (Syracuse: Syracuse University Press, 1967); McAndrews, *Broken Ground,* p. 173; Letter from Samuel Halperin to Frank Munger, n.d., White House Central Files, Box 246, Folder FG 165-4 9/1/66–1/24/67, Lyndon Baines Johnson Presidential Library, Austin, Texas [hereafter LBJPL]; Interview of Keppel by Frantz, August 17, 1972, Tape 1, LBJPL, p. 7.

8. Interview of Edith Green by Janet Kerr-Tener, August 23, 1985, Tape 1, LBJPL, p. 66.

9. "House Votes" and "Senate Votes," *Congressional Roll Call* (Washington, D.C.: Congressional Quarterly, 1966), pp. H-170, S-76; "President Johnson's Education Message," *Scholastic Teacher,* March 17, 1967, p. 4.

10. "Teachers' Role in Federal Aid," *Scholastic Teacher,* October 21, 1966, p. 1; "President's Budget: Education," *Scholastic Teacher,* February 11, 1966, p. 1; "Elementary and Secondary Education Expanded," p. 290.

11. Letter from Sidney Marland to William Cannon, January 6, 1967, Douglass Cater Files, Box 37, Folder Cater, Douglass: Material on Task Force on Education (2), LBJPL, p. 3; "Task Force Meeting," January 28, 1967, Douglass Cater Files, Box 37, Folder Cater, Douglass: Material on Task Force on Education (2), LBJPL, p. 13; Memorandum from John Gardner to Douglass Cater, William Cannon, and Herbert Jasper, February 13, 1967, White House Central Files, Box 6, Folder FA 2 12/1/66–4/15/67, LBJPL.

12. "Johnson Makes Minimal Cuts in 1967 ESEA Budget," *Library Journal,* February 15, 1967, p. 829; "Two-Year Elementary School Aid Bill Enacted," *Congressional Quarterly Almanac,* 90th Cong., 1st sess., 1967 (Washington, D.C., 1967), p. 616.

13. "Two-Year Elementary School Aid Bill Enacted," pp. 616, 621.

14. "A Gadfly to Democrats," *New York Times,* May 25, 1965, p. A33; *Congressional Record,* April 26, 1967, pp. 10828–10829; "Promises and Performance: The Quie Bill Is Not General Aid," n.d., Joseph Califano Files, Box 12, Folder Califano: ESEA Act Fight 4/67–5/67, LBJPL; Associated Press release, April 2, 1967, White House Central Files, Box 6, Folder FA 2 4/16/67–6/24/67, LBJPL.

15. Letter from Joseph Califano to John Kenneth Galbraith, April 25, 1967, Joseph Califano Files, Box 8, Folder School Desegregation, LBJPL; "Commissioner Howe on Quie Substitute," April 24, 1967, Irving Sprague Files, Box 1, Folder Sprague: Elementary and Secondary Education, LBJPL, pp. 1–2; "Statement of the President on the ESEA and the Proposed Quie Substitute," April 27, 1967, Mike Manatos Files, Box 7, Folder Manatos: Education Legislation, 1966–67, LBJPL.

16. "Some HEW Activities in Support of the Administration's Elementary and Secondary Education Act," May 1, 1967, Irving Sprague Files, Box 1, Folder Sprague: Elemen-

tary and Secondary Education, LBJPL; Memorandum from Douglass Cater to the President, May 16, 1967, White House Central Files, Box 6, Folder FA 2 4/16/67–6/24/67, LBJPL; Memorandum from Irving Sprague to Henry Wilson, May 4, 1967, Irving Sprague Files, Box 1, Folder Sprague: Elementary and Secondary Education, LBJPL; Letter from Roy Wilkins to "Dear Congressman," May 22, 1967, Irving Sprague Files, Box 1, Folder Sprague: Elementary and Secondary Education, LBJPL; Memorandum from Charles Roche to Henry Wilson, May 3, 1967, Irving Sprague Files, Box 1, Folder Sprague: Elementary and Secondary Education, LBJPL, p. 7; Cater to the President, May 16, 1967, LBJPL.

17. Interview of Green, p. 36; "Church-State Implications of Green Amendment to Title III of the Elementary and Secondary Education Act of 1965," Irving Sprague Files, Box 1, Folder Sprague: Elementary and Secondary Education, LBJPL, pp. 1–2; Letter from John Gardner to John McCormack, May 23, 1967, Irving Sprague Files, Box 1, Folder Sprague: Elementary and Secondary Education, LBJPL, pp. 1–2; Memorandum from Douglass Cater to the President, May 1, 1967, White House Central Files, Box 247, Folder FA 165-4-1 2/22/67–12/31/67, LBJPL.

18. "Two-Year Elementary School Aid Bill Enacted," p. 626.

19. Memorandum from Douglass Cater to the President, November 22, 1967, White House Central Files, Box 246, Folder FG 165-4, 10/31/67–5/10/68, LBJPL; Letter from Lyndon Johnson to Carl Perkins, December 18, 1967, White House Central Files, Box 7, Folder FA 2 12/2/67–1/18/68, LBJPL.

20. Memorandum from Wayne Reed to Harold Howe, May 19, 1967, White House Central Files, Box 6, Folder FA 2 4/16/67–6/24/67, LBJPL.

21. Memorandum from Francis Keppel to Joseph Califano, August 10, 1965, Joseph Califano Files, Box 8, Folder School Desegregation, LBJPL, p. 3; Memorandum from Douglass Cater to the President, September 2, 1965, White House Central Files, Box 15, Folder ED/MC 7/29/65–9/26/66, LBJPL; Memorandum from Ralph Huitt to Douglass Cater, August 9, 1966, Henry Wilson Files, Box 13, Folder Wilson: Education, LBJPL; Memorandum from Harold Howe, White House Central Files, Box 4, Folder ED 8/25/67–11/17/67, LBJPL; Memorandum from Ben Wattenberg to Central Files, December 4, 1968, White House Central Files, Box 6, Folder ED 11/1/68, LBJPL; "Two-Year Elementary School Aid Bill Enacted," pp. 622, 611.

22. "Johnson's Education Message," p. 4; "Transcript of the President's Speech to the Junior Chamber of Commerce in Baltimore," *New York Times,* June 28, 1967, p. A24.

23. "American Federation of Teachers' Position Paper," *School and Society,* February 14, 1967, p. 8 (emphasis in original); Memorandum from Douglass Cater to the President, July 18, 1967, White House Central Files, Box 4, Folder ED 7/18/67–8/24/67, LBJPL, p. 3; Letter from Sam Lambert to the *New York Times,* August 22, 1967, p. A43; "School Aid Plan Is Asked by Union," *New York Times,* August 22, 1967, p. A43.

24. Memorandum from Harold Howe to John Gardner, July 24, 1967, White House Central Files, Box 7, Folder FA 2 6/25/67–9/9/67, LBJPL, p. 2; Marjorie Hunter, "Panel on Schools Wants U.S. Funds Focused on Poor," *New York Times,* August 19, 1967, p. A1; Exchange of Letters between Charles Cogen and Harold Howe, October 6 and 10, 1967, American Federation of Teachers Office of the President, Box 6, Folder 6-33, U.S. Office of Education (H. Howe II), Correspondence 1967–71, 2 of 2, American Federation of Teachers Papers, Walter Reuther Library, Detroit, Michigan [hereafter AFTP], p. 2; "Text of President's Message to Congress on Budget for Fiscal Year 1969," *New York Times,* January

30, 1968, sec. A, p. 19; Memorandum from Wilbur Cohen to the President, March 14, 1968, White House Central Files, Box 246, Folder FG 165-4, 10/31/67–5/10/68, LBJPL.

25. Keppel to Califano, August 10, 1965; "Elementary and Secondary Education Expanded," p. 292; "Excerpts from the President's Special Message to Congress on Health and Education," *New York Times,* March 1, 1967, p. A26.

26. "Elementary and Secondary Education Expanded," p. 290; Memorandum from Donald Furtado to Harry McPherson, September 27, 1967, White House Central Files, Box 4, Folder ED 8/25/67–11/17/67, LBJPL; "What Are Americans Receiving in Return for Their Heavy Investment in Education?" *American Education,* November 1966, p. 25; "Task Force Meeting," pp. 4, 7; Daniel Patrick Moynihan, *Toward Equality as a Fact and a Result* (New York: Carnegie Corporation, 1967), p. 46; Cater to the President, May 16, 1967; Joseph Justman, "The Government and the Schools," *School and Society,* February 4, 1967, p. 75.

27. The epigraph is from Memorandum from Richard Nixon to Robert Finch, January 30, 1969, White House Central Files, Subject file Education, Box 1, Folder FG 23-26, Office of Education, Richard M. Nixon Presidential Papers, College Park, Maryland [hereafter RMNPP], p. 3.

28. Richard Nixon, *RN: The Memoirs of Richard Nixon* (New York: Grosset and Dunlop, 1978), p. 13; John Muncie, "The Struggle to Obtain Federal Aid for Elementary and Secondary Schools, 1940–1965," unpublished PhD diss. (Kent State University, 1969), p. 302.

29. Muncie, pp. 302, 232; Henry Citron, "The Study of the Arguments of Interest Groups Which Opposed Federal Aid to Education," unpublished PhD diss. (New York University, 1977), p. 104.

30. McAndrews, *Broken Ground,* p. 30.

31. "Statements on Education by Democratic and Republican Presidential Candidates," *NEA Journal,* October 1968, p. 14; "Report of the Task Force on Education," January 3, 1969, White House Central Files, Box 8, Folder FG 23-26; Office of Education, RMNPP, p. 1.

32. Richard Nixon, "Statement on Signing Bill Extending Assistance Programs for Elementary and Secondary Education," April 13, 1970, *Public Papers of the Presidents of the United States: Richard M. Nixon, 1970* (Washington, D.C.: U.S. Government Printing Office, 1971), pp. 352–53; Memorandum from Arthur Burns to the President, August 18, 1969, White House Central Files, Subject file Education, Box 1, Folder EX ED 6/1/69–8/31/69, RMNPP, p. 1; "Minutes, Council for Urban Affairs," August 25, 1969, President's Office Files, Box 79, Folder Memoranda for the President, August 3, 1969-December 28, 1969, RMNPP, p. 17.

33. "Statement by George D. Fischer, National Education Association President, News Conference," November 12, 1969, White House Central Files, Subject file Education, Box 10, Folder EX ED 1 Buildings, Grounds, Facilities 1/23/69–12/14/76, RMNPP, pp. 1–2; Memorandum from Daniel Patrick Moynihan to John Ehrlichman, November 26, 1969, White House Central Files, Subject file Education, Box 10, Folder EX ED 1 Buildings, Grounds, Facilities 1/23/69–12/14/70, RMNPP, pp. 1–2; Memorandum from Chester Finn to Edward Morgan, October 29, 1969, White House Central Files, Subject file Education, Box 1, Folder EX ED 5/31/69 to 3/31/69–3/31/70, RMNPP, pp. 1–2.

34. John Ehrlichman Notes, October 8, 1969, White House Special Files, John Ehrlichman Files, Box 3, Folder Notes of Meetings with the President, 1969 [2 of 4], RMNPP, p. 3; John Ehrlichman Notes, December 20, 1969, White House Special Files, John Ehrlichman File, Box 3, Folder Notes of Meetings with the President, 1969 [2 of 4], RMNPP; Robert

Semple, "President on TV, Vetoes School Aid as Inflationary," *New York Times*, January 27, 1970, p. A1; Chester Finn Diary, March 6, 1970, Box 23, Chester Finn Papers, Hoover Institution on War, Revolution, and Peace, Stanford, Calif.

35. "Statement on Education Message of President Richard M. Nixon, Adopted by American Federation of Teachers Executive Council, Pittsburgh, PA," March 7, 1970, American Federation of Teachers Office of the President, Box 4, Folder 4-22, U.S. Commissioner of Education—James Allen Jr., AFTP, pp. 1–4; Letter from James Allen to American Federation of Teachers Executive Council, March 10, 1970, ibid., p. 2.

36. "NEA's Concerns in the New Congress," *Today's Education/NEA Journal*, January 1971, p. 33; "Keyserling Goads Feds for Spending Boost," n.d., American Federation of Teachers Office of the President, Box 5, Folder 5-14, Committee on School Desegregation, 1969–70 [2 of 2], AFTP; Memorandum from Patrick Buchanan to the President, August 11, 1970, President's Office Files, Box 81, Folder Memoranda for the President, June 7, 1970–August 15, 1970, RMNPP, pp. 1–4; "Key Votes on Crucial Measures," American Federation of Teachers Office of the President, Box 38, Folder 38-2, Legislative Department 1973, p. 2.

37. "Reaction to President Nixon's Veto of the Education Appropriation Bill by President Selden," August 12, 1970, American Federation of Teachers Office of the President, Box 6, Folder 6-32, U.S. Office of Education (Harold Howe II), 1967–71 [1 of 2], AFTP; Memorandum from Charles Colson to John Dean, August 2, 1970, White House Central Files, Box 10, Folder EX ED 1, Buildings, Grounds, Facilities, 1/23/69–12/14/70, RMNPP; John Herbers, "President Signs $5.15 Billion Bill to Aid Education," *New York Times*, July 12, 1971, p. A1.

38. Memorandum from Caspar Weinberger to the President, June 26, 1972, White House Central Files, Subject file Education, Box 8, Folder FG 23-6 Office of Education, RMNPP, pp. 1–4.

39. E. W. Kenworthy, "Nixon Vetoes H.E.W. Bill; Cites 'Reckless Spending,'" *New York Times*, August 17, 1972, p. A1; "Educators for McGovern-Shriver," September 13, 1972, American Federation of Teachers Office of the President, Box 6, Folder 6-41, Educators for McGovern-Shriver, 1972, AFTP.

40. "Statement on Education by Democratic and Republican Presidential Candidates," p. 14; "Nixon Plans Total Overhaul of School Laws," *Education USA*, November 23, 1970, p. 67; "Nixon Discloses School Funding Plans for '72," *Education USA/Washington Monitor*, February 8, 1971, pp. 125–26.

41. Memorandum from Roy Morey to John Ehrlichman, January 31, 1972, White House Central Files, Subject file Education, Box 3, Folder EX ED 1/1/72–12/29/72, RMNPP; "Proposed AFT Policy Statement on Revenue-Sharing," April 29, 1975, American Federation of Teachers Office of the President, Box 81, Folder Executive Council Reports, April 29, 1975, AFTP, p. 1.

42. Richard Nixon, "Inaugural Address," January 20, 1969, *Public Papers of the Presidents of the United States: Richard M. Nixon, 1969* (Washington, D.C.: U.S. Government Printing Office, 1971), pp. 1, 4; Chester Finn, "On the National Institute of Education," *Yale Review*, March 1975, pp. 477–78.

43. Jonathan Spivak, "City Schools Need Extensive Reformation, New Education Commissioner Asserts," *Wall Street Journal*, May 9, 1969, p. A8; "U.S. Department of Education, Office of Education, Washington, DC," August 22, 1969, American Federation of

Teachers Office of the President, Box 4, Folder 4-22, U.S. Commissioner of Education James Allen Jr., AFTP, pp. 1–3.

44. "Statement by the Hon. Robert H. Finch, Secretary of Health, Education, and Welfare before the Subcommittee on Education of the Senate Committee on Labor and Public Welfare, Ninety-First Congress, First Session," June 11, 1969 (Washington, D.C.: U.S. Government Printing Office, 1969), p. 1; Memorandum from Daniel Patrick Moynihan to Robert Finch, March 11, 1969, White House Central Files, Subject file Education, Box 1, Folder EX ED 1/20/69 to 5/31/69, RMNPP, pp. 1–3; Memorandum from Chester Finn to D. Patrick Moynihan, October 16, 1969, Box 1, Folder EX ED 10/1/69–11/20/69, RMNPP; James Allen, "Goals for the Office of Education in the 1970's—A Framework of Priorities," American Federation of Teachers Office of the President, Box 4, Folder 4-22, U.S. Commissioner of Education James Allen Jr., AFTP, p. 3; Memorandum from Sam Hughes, Bryce Harlow, and Bud Wilkinson to the President, White House Central Files, Subject file Education, Box 1, Folder EX ED 10/1/69–11/20/69, RMNPP.

45. Memorandum from Bob Bhaerman to David Selden, February 17, 1970, American Federation of Teachers Office of the President, Box 6, Folder 6-32, U.S. Office of Education (H. Howe II), 1967–71 [1 of 2], p. 1; "Cheating the Disadvantaged," *Washington Post,* December 5, 1969, p. A26; "Urban School Crises: The Problems and Solutions Proposed by the HEW Education Task Force," January 5, 1970, Carl Megel Collection, Box 16, Folder 16-14, Urban Education, Report of, AFTP, p. 59; "Task Force for Self-Improvement Review of Title I," American Federation of Teachers Office of the President, Box 6, Folder 6-32, U.S. Office of Education (Harold Howe II), 1967–71 [1 of 2], AFTP, p. 2.

46. Memorandum from Robert Finch and D. Patrick Moynihan to the President, October 10, 1969, White House Central Files, Subject file Education, Box 1, Folder EX ED 10/1/69–11/20/69, RMNPP, pp. 2–3.

47. Memorandum from Chester Finn to Lew Butler, October 21, 1969, White House Central Files, Subject file Education, Box 1, Folder EX ED 10/1/69–11/20/69, RMNPP.

48. Richard Nixon, "Special Message to Congress on Education Reform," March 3, 1970, *Public Papers of the Presidents of the United States: Richard M. Nixon, 1970* (Washington, D.C.: U.S. Government Printing Office, 1971), pp. 228–38; Richard Nixon, "Special Message to Congress on Special Revenue Sharing for Education," April 6, 1971, *Public Papers of the Presidents of the United States: Richard M. Nixon, 1971* (Washington, D.C.: U.S. Government Printing Office, 1972), pp. 501–7; Richard Nixon, "Annual Message to the Congress on the State of the Union," January 20, 1972, *Public Papers of the Presidents of the United States: Richard M. Nixon, 1972* (Washington, D.C.: U.S. Government Printing Office, 1974), p. 68.

49. "Statement on Education Message of Richard M. Nixon," pp. 2, 4; telephone interview of Helen Bain by author, March 25, 1994; "Nixon Discloses School Funding Plans for '72," pp. 125–26.

50. Finn, "On the National Institute of Education," pp. 227–43.

51. "NEA's Concerns in the New Congress," p. 33; "Five Billion Dollar Education Bill Approved," *Education USA/Washington Monitor,* February 8, 1971, p. 125; Finn, "On the National Institute of Education," p. 477; Memorandum from Lew Engman to the President, March 6, 1972, White House Central Files, Subject file Education, Box 3, Folder EX ED 1/1/72–12/29/72, RMNPP.

52. Letter from D. Patrick Moynihan to Eliot Richardson, November 16, 1970, White House Central Files, Subject file Education, Box 8, Folder FG 23-6, Office of Education,

RMNPP, p. 3; Letter from D. Patrick Moynihan to the President, October 13, 1975, Richard Cheney Files, Box 10, Folder President's Commission on School Integration, Gerald R. Ford Presidential Library, Ann Arbor, Michigan [hereafter GRFPL], p. 27; Finn, "On the National Institute of Education," p. 478; "National Council on Education Research (NCER), Program Committee Report and Draft Policy Resolution," July 8, 1977, American Federation of Teachers Office of the President, Box 74, Folder 74-5, Department of Health, Education, and Welfare, National Institute of Education, AFTP, p. 2.

53. "The Right to Read," American Federation of Teachers Office of the President, Box 5, Folder 5-5, Education Articles, 1963–72, AFTP, pp. 2–3; Moynihan to the President, 10/13/75, p. 14; "Education," September 8, 1976, White House Special Files, Richard Cheney Files, Box 18, Folder President Ford '76 Factbook, (2), GRFPL, p. 6.

54. John Ehrlichman Notes, n.d., White House Special Files, John Ehrlichman File, Box 6, Folder Notes of Meetings with the President 8/31/71–12/31/71 [5 of 5], RMNPP; Memorandum from Lew Engman to the President, March 6, 1972, President's Office Files, Box 88, Folder Memoranda for the President 12/17/71–2/20/72, RMNPP, pp. 2–4.

55. Memorandum from David Lissy to James Cannon et al., June 11, 1976, White House Special Files, James Cannon Files, Box 12, Folder Education, June–July 1976, GRFPL; "Congressional Breakfast Meeting," January 27, 1971, President's Office Files, Box 84, Folder Memoranda for the President, RMNPP, p. 5.

56. Irwin Unger, *These United States: The Questions of Our Past* (Upper Saddle River, N.J.: Prentice Hall, 1999), p. 744; George Tindall and David Shi, *America: A Narrative History* (New York: Norton, 1997), p. 1094; Nixon to Finch, January 30, 1969, RMNPP, p. 3; John Ehrlichman Notes, White House Special Files, John Ehrlichman File, Box 3, Folder Notes of Meetings with the President, 1/1/70–6/30/70 [1 of 5], RMNPP; John Ehrlichman Notes, January 14, 1970, Box 3, Folder Notes of Meetings with the President, 1/1/70–6/30/70 [1 of 5], RMNPP, p. 3; for discussion of Nixon's wage and price controls, see Nixon, *RN: The Memoirs of Richard Nixon*, pp. 516–22, and Stephen Ambrose, *Nixon: The Triumph of a Politician* (New York: Simon and Schuster, 1989), p. 458; telephone interview of Caspar Weinberger by author, November 4, 1997.

57. "Hearings," February 6, 1969, pp. 1–2; "ESEA Amendments of 1969: H.R. 514," *AFT Washington Newsletter*, April 1969, American Federation of Teachers Office of the President, Box 32, Folder 32-22, Legislative Department, Vol. 2, 1969–70, AFTP, p. 13; Memorandum from Arthur Burns to the President, August 18, 1969, White House Central Files, Subject file Education, Box 1, Folder EX ED 6/1/69–8/31/69, RMNPP, p. 1.

58. John Chaffee and Patricia Wagner, "Do Teachers Make a Difference?" *American Education*, May 1970, p. 1; "Urban School Crisis: The Problems and Solutions Proposed by the HEW Education Task Force," January 5, 1970, Carl Megel Collection, Box 16, Folder 16-14, Urban Education, Report of, AFTP, p. 59; Memorandum from Francis Keppel and Marian Wright Edelman to Members of the McGovern-Shriver Education Panel, October 30, 1972, American Federation of Teachers Office of the President, Box 6, Folder McGovern-Shriver Education Panel, 1972, AFTP, p. 10.

59. Finn to Morgan, October 29, 1969, RMNPP; Moynihan to the President, October 13, 1975, RMNPP, p. 13; Memorandum from Chester Finn to Edward Morgan, December 10, 1969, White House Central Files, Subject file Education, Box 1, Folder EX ED 11/21/69–12/31/69, RMNPP; Memorandum from James Cavanaugh to Kenneth Cole, January 29, 1973, White House Central Files, Subject file Education, Box 13, Folder EX ED 3 1/1/73–7/30/74, RMNPP.

60. "Goals for the Office of Education," p. 3.

61. Letter from James Allen to the President, May 5, 1970, White House Central Files, Subject file Education, Box 1, Folder EX ED 4/1/70–5/20/70, RMNPP, pp. 1–2; Letter from James Allen to the President, June 11, 1970, White House Central Files, Box 2, Folder EX ED 5/21/70–6/21/70, RMNPP, p. 1; David Rosenbaum, "Marland to Aim at New Priorities," *New York Times,* December 12, 1970, p. A17; Memorandum from Sidney Marland to the President, June 30, 1971, White House Central Files, Box 8, Folder FG 23-6, Office of Education, 1/1/71, RMNPP.

62. Richard Nixon, "Remarks Announcing the Vetoes of Two Appropriations Bills," August 11, 1970, *Public Papers of the Presidents of the United States: Richard M. Nixon, 1970* (Washington, D.C.: U.S. Government Printing Office, 1971), pp. 663–64; Richard Nixon, "Radio Address on the Federal Responsibility to Education," October 25, 1972, *Public Papers of the Presidents of the United States: Richard M. Nixon,* Book 2, *1972* (Washington, D.C.: U.S. Government Printing Office, 1974), pp. 1027–30; "Strategy for Handling Education Legislation," June 17, 1974, White House Central Files, Subject file Education, Box 8, Folder FG 23-6, Office of Education, 1/1/73, RMNPP; telephone interview of Weinberger by author, November 4, 1997.

63. Memorandum from Chester Finn to D. Patrick Moynihan, September 18, 1969, White House Central Files, Subject file Education, Folder EX ED 9/1/69–10/1/69, RMNPP; Memorandum from Edward Morgan to Kenneth Cole, November 20, 1969, White House Central Files, Subject file Education, Box 1, Folder EX ED 10/1/69–11/20/69, RMNPP; "Attention: City, Labor, and Education Editors," June 11, 1970, American Federation of Teachers Office of the President, Box 4, Folder 4-22, U.S. Commissioner of Education—Allen Jr., AFTP, p. 2.

64. Finn, "On the National Institute of Education," p. 235.

65. John Ehrlichman Notes, July 6, 1970, White House Special Files, John Ehrlichman File, Box 3, Folder Notes of Meetings with the President, 7/1/70–12/31/70 [1 of 8], RMNPP, p. 6; Memorandum from Patrick Buchanan to the President, August 11, 1970, President's Office Files, Box 81, Folder Memoranda for the President, 8/10/70–1/23/71, RMNPP, pp. 1–2.

66. Memorandum from Dana Mead to Kenneth Cole, October 4, 1971, White House Central Files, Subject file Confidential Files, 1969–74, Box 21, Folder [CF] FG 31-1, Legislative Leadership Meetings, RMNPP, p. 1; telephone interview of George Fischer by author, March 15, 1994; Memorandum from John Evans to Dwight Chapin, June 29, 1971, White House Central Files, Subject file Education, Box 10, Folder EX ED Buildings, Grounds, Facilities, RMNPP; telephone interview of Bain by author, March 25, 1994.

67. Memorandum from Charles Colson to John Dean, August 2, 1971, White House Central Files, Subject file Education, Box 10, Folder EX ED Buildings, Grounds, Facilities, RMNPP; Memorandum from W. Richard Howard to David Parker, August 4, 1971, White House Central Files, Box 10, Folder EX ED Buildings, Grounds, Facilities, RMNPP; "Broken Promises," *Time,* January 15, 1973, pp. 66–67.

68. John Ehrlichman Notes, August 5, 1970, White House Special Files, John Ehrlichman File, Box 3, Folder Notes of Meetings with the President, 7/1/70–12/31/70 [3 of 8], RMNPP; Memorandum from John Ehrlichman to Sidney Marland, October 6, 1971, White House Central Files, Subject file Education, Box 8, Folder FG 23-6, Office of Education 1/1/71–, RMNPP.

69. Letter from David Selden to Hubert Humphrey, September 1, 1971, American Federation of Teachers Office of the President, Box 7, Folder 7-15, Congressional Correspon-

dence, 1967–71 [1 of 2], AFTP; Francis Carnochan, "What Does the NEA Bill Mean to You?" *Today's Education/NEA Journal,* December 1968, p. 27; telephone interview of Fischer by author, March 15, 1994; telephone interview of Bain by author, March 25, 1994; telephone interview of Terry Herndon by author, March 14, 1994.

70. "NEA's Concerns in the New Congress," *Today's Education/NEA Journal,* January 1971, p. 33; "Statement on Education Message of President Richard M. Nixon, Adopted by the American Federation of Teachers Executive Council, Pittsburgh, PA," March 7, 1970, American Federation of Teachers Office of the President, Box 4, Folder 4-22, U.S. Commissioner of Education—Allen Jr., AFTP, p. 2; Letter from David Selden to Wilson Riles, October 28, 1969, American Federation of Teachers Office of the President, Box 6, Folder 6-42, Urban Task Force on Education [1 of 2], AFTP, pp. 1–2; "Proceedings," n.d., American Federation of Teachers Office of the President, Box 73, Folder 73-1, HEW Advisory Panel for Financing Elementary and Secondary Education, AFTP, p. 141.

71. "Statement by George D. Fischer, National Education Association President, News Conference," p. 1; "Reaction to President Nixon's Veto of Education Appropriation Bill by President Selden," August 12, 1970, American Federation of Teachers, Office of the President, Box 6, Folder 6-32, U.S. Office of Education (Harold Howe II), 1967–71 [1 of 2], AFTP; "Statement of AFL-CIO before the Senate Labor Committee in Opposition to the Nomination of Sidney P. Marland, Jr., to be United States Commissioner of Education," December 1, 1970, American Federation of Teachers Office of the President, Box 1, Folder 1-6, NEA Project Material: Jim Lerman, April 1972, AFTP, p. 2; Memorandum from David Selden to Gregory Humphrey, October 30, 1972, American Federation of Teachers Office of the President, Box 32, Folder 32-30, Legislation Department, Volume 3 [1 of 2], AFTP.

72. "Education Conference," November 16, 1971, White House Central Files, Subject file Education, Box 8, Folder FG 23-6 Office of Education, 1/1/71, RMNPP; Memorandum from Sidney Marland to John Ehrlichman, December 3, 1971, White House Central Files, Subject file Education, Folder FG 23-6 Office of Education, RMNPP; telephone interview of Weinberger by author, November 4, 1997.

73. The epigraph is from Gerald Ford, "Veto of the Education Division and Related Agencies Appropriation Act, 1976," July 25, 1975, *Public Papers of the Presidents of the United States: Gerald R. Ford, 1975* (Washington, D.C.: U.S. Government Printing Office, 1977), p. 1035.

74. Gerald R. Ford, *A Time to Heal* (New York: Harper and Row, 1979).

75. "Ford's Record on Key Issues Votes in the House, 1949–1973," *Congressional Quarterly Almanac,* 93rd Cong., 2nd sess., 1974 (Washington, D.C., 1975), pp. 913–14.

76. Memorandum from Roger Semerad to Kenneth Cole through James Cavanaugh, August 14, 1974, White House Central Files, Subject file Education, Box 1, Folder ED 8/9/74–9/30/74, GRFPL, pp. 2–4; Gerald Ford, "Statement on the Education Amendments of 1974," August 21, 1974, *Public Papers of the Presidents of the United States: Gerald R. Ford, 1974* (Washington, D.C.: U.S. Government Printing Office, 1975), pp. 35–37.

77. "Selden Hails President Ford's Decision to Sign H.R. 69," August 13, 1974, Press Release, American Federation of Teachers Office of the President, Box 81, Folder 81-18, AFTP; "For[d] Pledges Major Initiative in Federation Education Effort to 140 NEA Leaders," May 2, 1975, American Federation of Teachers Office of the President, Box 20, Folder 20-24, President Gerald Ford 1974–76, AFTP.

78. Memorandum from Caspar Weinberger to James Cavanaugh, July 17, 1975, White House Central Files, Subject file Federal Aid, Box 7, Folder FA3 6/1/75–7/24/75, GRFPL;

Ford, "Veto of the Education Division and Related Agencies Appropriation Act, 1976," p. 1035.

79. Philip Shabecoff, "Ford Vetoes School Bill as Inflationary," *New York Times*, July 26, 1975, p. A1; Richard Madden, "Senate Overrides Education Bill Veto," *New York Times*, September 11, 1975, p. L68.

80. Memorandum from David Mathews to the President, n.d., James Cannon Files, Box 37, Folder Meetings—SOTU Coordinating Group, GRFPL, pp. 4, 8, 9.

81. Memorandum from James Cannon and James Lynn to the President, January 16, 1976, Presidential Handwriting File, Box 7, Folder Federal Aid—Education, GRFPL, pp. 1–4.

82. Philip Shabecoff, "Ford to Increase Budget Request on School Funds," *New York Times*, February 17, 1976, p. A1; Memorandum from Frederick Slight to PFC Leadership, March 11, 1976, President Ford Committee Campaign Records, Box H50, Folder President Ford Committee Records, 1975–76, GRFPL, p. 6; Gerald Ford, "To the Congress of the United States," March 1, 1976, White House Central Files, Subject file Education, Box 2, Folder ED 1/1/76–4/30/76, GRFPL, pp. 1–4.

83. "Statement of Gregory A. Humphrey before the House Subcommittee on Labor-HEW Appropriations on FY 1977 Office of Education Appropriations Bill," April 8, 1976, Box 76, Folder 46-4, NEA Correspondence 1974–76, AFTP, p. 2; Memorandum from James Reichley to Richard Cheney and Jerry Jones, June 4, 1976, A. James Reichley File, Box 4, Folder National Education Association, GRFPL; Joel Havemann, "It's Not That Candidates Don't Care about the Cities—Nobody's Asking," *National Journal*, April 17, 1976, p. 518; Memorandum from Gregory Humphrey to All Concerned with Separate Education Department, January 26, 1978, American Federation of Teachers Office of the President, Box 47, Folder 47-26, Issues: Education Department, 1977–79, AFTP, p. 2.

84. Shabecoff, "Ford to Increase Budget," p. A16; Memorandum from Roger Semerad to James Cavanaugh through Paul O'Neill, August 14, 1974, White House Central Files, Subject file Education, Box 1, Folder ED 8/9/74–9/30/74, GRFPL, p. 1.

85. Letter from D. Patrick Moynihan to the President, October 13, 1975, Richard Cheney Files, Box 10, Folder Presidential Commission on School Integration, GRFPL, pp. 4, 14; "Education," September 8, 1976, Richard Cheney Files, Box 18, Folder President Ford '76 Factbook [2], GRFPL, p. 6.

86. Memorandum from David Lissy to James Cannon, April 9, 1976, James Cannon Files, Box 12, Folder Education, April–May 1976, GRFPL, pp. 1–2.

87. Finn, "On the National Institute of Education," p. 478; Memorandum from David Lissy to James Cannon, May 12, 1976, James Cannon Files, Box 12, Folder Education, April–May 1976, GRFPL, pp. 1–2; "National Council on Educational Research Program Committee Report and Draft Policy Resolution," July 8, 1977, American Federation of Teachers Office of the President, Box 74, Folder 74-5, Department of HEW: National Institute of Education, AFTP, p. 2.

88. Gerald Ford, "Remarks at Ohio State University," August 30, 1974, *Public Papers of the Presidents of the United States: Gerald R. Ford*, Book 1, 1974–75 (Washington, D.C.: U.S. Government Printing Office, 1975), p. 73.

89. Memorandum from Philip Dent, Peter Brennan, and Caspar Weinberger to the President, November 29, 1974, Robert Hartmann Files, Box 11, Folder Education and Work Initiative, GRFPL, pp. 6–9; Memorandum from Kenneth Cole to the President, January 8,

1975, White House Central Files, Subject file Education, Box 1, Folder ED 1/1/75–3/31/75, GRFPL, p. 5.

90. Cole to the President, January 8, 1975, p. 5; Memorandum from James Cannon to the President, October 17, 1975, White House Central Files, Subject file Education, Folder ED 10/7/75–10/31/75, GRFPL; telephone interview of Gerald Ford by author, January 20, 1998.

91. "For[d] Pledges Major Initiative," May 2, 1975, AFTP; Ford, "Veto of the Education Division and Related Agencies Appropriation Act, 1976," p. 1035.

92. "Statement of Carl J. Megel, Director of American Federation of Teachers, AFL-CIO, on FY 1976 Office of Education Appropriation Bill," Box 38, Folder 38-5, Legislative Department [2 of 2], AFTP, p. 1; John Mathews, "NEA President on the Role of the Teacher," July 24, 1975, American Federation of Teachers Office of the President, Box 46, Folder 46-3 NEA Correspondence, 1975–77 [3 of 4], AFTP, p. 6; Memorandum from Caspar Weinberger to the President, March 20, 1975, David Lissy Files, Box 2, Folder Busing [1], GRFPL, p. 3; "Teacher Unions Claim Strong Influence in Presidential, Other Election Victories," *Phi Delta Kappan* (January 1977): 440.

93. John Brademas, *The Politics of Education* (Norman: University of Oklahoma Press, 1987), pp. 50–51; Memorandum from Gregory Humphrey to All Concerned with Separate Education Department, AFTP; Memorandum from David Lissy to James Cannon, June 11, 1976, James Cannon Files, Box 12, Folder Education, June–July 1976, GRFPL.

94. Memorandum from Richard Hastings to Steven Kurzman, February 2, 1976, Max Friedersdorf Files, Box 6, Folder President's Meetings with House Members, February 1976, GRFPL. Sixty-five percent of Americans supported revenue sharing in 1974, and 55 percent supported it in 1975; see Havemann, "It's Not That Candidates Don't Care about the Cities," p. 518.

95. Memorandum from David Mathews to Arthur Quern, October 24, 1975, White House Central Files, Subject file Education, Box 7, Folder FA 3 Education 7/25/75–11/13/75, GRFPL, p. 3; Lissy to Cannon, April 9, 1976, GRFPL, p. 2.

96. William Brickman, "Education Developments and Issues in 1974," *Intellect*, January 1975, p. 265; "Education," GRFPL, p. 6; Brademas, *The Politics of Education*, p. 90; Memorandum from Terry O'Connell to Jerry Jones, November 22, 1975, White House Central Files, Subject file Education, Box 7, Folder FA 3 11/14/75–11/27/75, GRFPL.

97. Finn, "On the National Institute of Education," p. 227.

98. "For[d] Pledges Major Initiative," May 2, 1975, AFTP; Interview of Robert Hartmann by A. James Reichley, December 8, 1977, GRFPL, p. 3; Gerald Ford, "Address before a Joint Session of Congress Reporting on the State of the Union," January 15, 1975, *Public Papers of the Presidents of the United States: Gerald R. Ford, Book 1, 1975* (Washington, D.C.: U.S. Government Printing Office, 1977), pp. 36–47; Gerald Ford, "Address before a Joint Session of the Congress Reporting on the State of the Union," January 19, 1976, *Public Papers of the Presidents of the United States: Gerald R. Ford, Book 1, 1976–77* (Washington, D.C.: U.S. Government Printing Office, 1979), pp. 31–42.

99. The epigraph is from "Education: Two Years," January 10, 1979, White House Central Files, Subject file Education, Box ED-2, Folder ED 1/1/79–3/31/79, Jimmy Carter Presidential Library, Atlanta, Georgia [hereafter JCPL], p. 1. The Johnson quotation is from Lyndon B. Johnson, "Remarks at the University of Michigan," May 22, 1964, in *Public Papers of the Presidents of the United States: Lyndon B. Johnson, 1963–1964*, Vol. 1 (Washington, D.C.: Government Printing Office, 1964), p. 704.

242 *Notes to Pages 38–40*

100. Joel Spring, *The American School, 1642–1985* (New York: Longman, 1986), p. 316; Shabecoff, "Ford to Increase Budget Request on School Funds," p. A1.

101. Jimmy Carter, *Keeping Faith* (New York: Bantam, 1982), p. 75; Beryl A. Radin and Willis D. Hawley, *The Politics of Federal Reorganization: Creating the U.S. Department of Education* (New York: Pergamon, 1988), p. 37.

102. Allan M. West, *The National Education Association: The Power Base for Education* (New York: Free Press, 1980), p. 191; Radin and Hawley, *The Politics of Federal Reorganization*, p. 41.

103. Letter from Terry Herndon to the President, March 29, 1977, White House Central Files, Subject file Education, Box ED-1, Folder ED 1/20/77–3/31/77, JCPL; Memorandum from Joseph Califano to the President, April 8, 1977, Staff Files, Domestic Policy Staff: Eizenstat, Box 195, Folder Education, Dept. of (Separate) (4), Jimmy Carter Presidential Papers [hereafter JCPP], JCPL, p. 2; Memorandum from Elizabeth Abramowitz to Stuart Eizenstat, April 5, 1977, Staff Files, Domestic Policy Staff: Eizenstat, Box 195, Education, Dept. of (Separate) (4), JCPL, pp. 1–2.

104. Memorandum from Stuart Eizenstat to the President, April 27, 1977, Staff Files, Domestic Policy Staff: Eizenstat, Box 238, Folder National Education Association, JCPP, JCPL, p. 2; Memorandum from the Vice President to the President, May 13, 1977, Staff Files, Domestic Policy Staff: Eizenstat, Box 196, Folder Education (General) [2], JCPL.

105. Memorandum from Bert Carp to Stuart Eizenstat, June 15, 1977, Staff Files, Domestic Policy Staff: Eizenstat, Box 198, Folder Education, Dept. of (Separate) (4), JCPL, pp. 1–2.

106. Memorandum from Elizabeth Abramowitz to Stuart Eizenstat, September 19, 1977, Staff Files, Domestic Policy Staff: Eizenstat, Box 196, Folder Education (General) [2], JCPP, JCPL, pp. 1–2; Memorandum from Les Francis to Frank Moore, October 13, 1977, Chief of Staff: Jordan, Box 34, Folder Education, Dept. of, 1978, JCPL; Memorandum from Bert Carp to Stuart Eizenstat, November 23, 1977, Staff Files, Domestic Policy Staff: Eizenstat, Box 195, Folder Education, Dept. of (Separate) (4), JCPL; Memorandum from Bert Lance to Stuart Eizenstat, November 26, 1977, Staff Files, Domestic Policy Staff: Eizenstat, Box 195, Folder Education, Dept. of (Separate) (2), JCPL, pp. 1–2; Memorandum from Joseph Califano to the President, November 26, 1977, Chief of Staff: Jordan, Box 34, Folder Education, Dept. of, 1978, JCPL, 2, pp. 4–7; Memorandum from Richard Pettigrew to the President, November 28, 1977, Chief of Staff: Jordan, Box 34, Folder Education, Dept. of, 1978, JCPL, p. 1; Memorandum from Charles Schultze to the President, November 28, 1977, Chief of Staff: Jordan, Box 34, Folder Education, Dept. of, 1978, JCPL, pp. 1–2; Memorandum from James McIntyre to the President, January 7, 1978, Staff Offices, Domestic Policy Staff: Eizenstat, Box 195, Folder Education, Dept. of (Separate) [2], JCPL, pp. 1–3.

107. Memorandum from Eizenstat to the President, December 2, 1977, Staff Files, Domestic Policy Staff: Eizenstat, Box 195, Folder Education, Dept. of (Separate) [2], JCPP, JCPL, pp. 1–3; "Transcript of the President's Address Saying That the State of the Union Is Sound," *New York Times,* January 20, 1978, p. A1.

108. Marjorie Hunter, "President Proposes Education Department," *New York Times,* April 15, 1978, p. A1.

109. Memorandum from Elizabeth Abramowitz to Bert Carp, May 4, 1978, White House Central Files, Subject file Federal Government—Organizations, Box FG-236, Folder FG 999-12 1/20/77–1/20/81, JCPL, pp. 1–2.

110. McIntyre replaced Lance, who resigned on September 21, 1977; Memorandum from James McIntyre to the President, n.d., Chief of Staff: Jordan, Box 44, Folder Education—Establishing a Cabinet Department of, JCPL, pp. 4, 19, 20.

111. "An Illusion of Education Reform," *New York Times,* January 16, 1979, p. A14; Memorandum from Elizabeth Abramowitz to Stuart Eizenstat, February 13, 1979, White House Central Files, Subject file Federal Government—Organizations, Box FG 237, Folder FG 999-12 1/1/79–5/31/79, JCPL, p. 1.

112. "To the Congress of the United States," February 13, 1979, White House Central Files, Subject file Federal Government—Organizations, Box FG 237, Folder FG 999-12 1/1/79–5/31/79, JCPL, p. 1.

113. Felicity Barringer, "Lobbying Earns a Vote for Separate Department of Education," *Washington Post,* September 28, 1979, p. A6; Memorandum from Frank Moore to the President, September 25, 1979, Presidential Diary, Box PD-62, Folder 9/26/79 Backup Material, JCPL, pp. 1–3. Carter's partisanship regarding the department was not unusual; Moore would lament that the administration "made a mistake" on a number of issues "by not working more closely with the Republicans." See Interview of Frank Moore, Miller Center Interviews, Carter Presidency Project, Vol. IV, September 18–19, 1981, JCPL, p. 61. The bill would pass even though only two of the eleven wavering Republicans would vote in favor.

114. Radin and Hawley, *The Politics of Federal Reorganization,* p. 143; Spencer Rich, "Congress Passes Bill to Establish Education Department," *Washington Post,* September 28, 1979, p. A1; Marjorie Hunter, "Congress Approves Department of Education: Victory for Carter," *New York Times,* September 28, 1979, pp. A1, A20.

115. Barringer, "Lobbying Earns a Vote for Separate Department of Education," p. 6; Gene Maeroff, "U.S. Agency Set to Begin—With Serious Limitations," *New York Times,* October 30, 1979, pp. C1, C4.

116. Steven Weisman, "Carter to Name Judge to Direct Education Department," *New York Times,* November 29, 1979, p. A1.

117. John Dumbrell, *The Carter Presidency: A Re-evaluation* (New York: Manchester University Press, 1993), p. 52; Radin and Hawley, *The Politics of Federal Reorganization,* p. 41.

118. Memorandum from Hamilton Jordan to the President, n.d., Chief of Staff: Jordan, Box 34, Folder Education, Department of, 1978, JCPL, 2, pp. 13–14.

119. Joseph Califano, *Governing America* (New York: Simon and Schuster, 1981), 275; Handwritten Note from Bert Carp to Stuart Eizenstat, November 3, 1977, Staff Files, Domestic Policy Staff: Eizenstat, Box 195, Folder Education, Department of (Separate) [4], JCPL.

120. Letter from Joseph Califano to Bert Lance, February 10, 1977, Staff Offices, Domestic Policy Staff—Eizenstat, Box 212, Folder HEW, Department of [CF, O/A 48], JCPL, pp. 1, 3, 6.

121. Memorandum from Elizabeth Abramowitz to Stuart Eizenstat, April 4, 1977, Staff Offices, Domestic Policy Staff—Eizenstat, Box 196, Folder Education (General) [2], JCPL, pp. 1–3; Memorandum from Stuart Eizenstat and Elizabeth Abramowitz to the President, May 9, 1977, Staff Offices, Domestic Policy Staff—Eizenstat, Box 196, Folder Education (General) [2], pp. 1–3; Memorandum from Elizabeth Abramowitz to Stuart Eizenstat, Staff Offices, Domestic Policy Staff—Eizenstat, Box 196, Folder Education (General) [2], JCPL, p. 1.

122. Memorandum from Elizabeth Abramowitz to Stuart Eizenstat, June 28, 1977, Staff Files, Domestic Policy Staff—Eizenstat, Box 196, Folder Education [General] [2], JCPL, p. 1; Memorandum from Joseph Califano to the President, August 11, 1978, Staff Offices, Domestic Policy Staff: Eizenstat, Box 195, Folder Education, Department of (Separate) [1], JCPP, JCPL, p. 1; Memorandum from the Vice President to the President, June 30, 1977, Staff Offices, Domestic Policy Staff—Eizenstat, Box 238, Folder NEA National Education Association, JCPL, p. 7.

123. Memorandum from Elizabeth Abramowitz to Stuart Eizenstat, July 8, 1977, Staff Offices, Domestic Policy Staff: Eizenstat, Box 196, Folder Education (General) [2], JCPL, pp. 1–2.

124. Memorandum from Elizabeth Abramowitz to Jack Watson, September 1, 1977, Staff Offices, Domestic Policy Staff—Eizenstat, Box 196, Folder Education (General) [2], JCPP, JCPL, p. 1; Memorandum from Elizabeth Abramowitz to Stuart Eizenstat, September 27, 1977, Staff Offices, Domestic Policy Staff—Eizenstat, Box 196, Folder Education (General) [1], JCPP, JCPL; Memorandum for Eizenstat from Abramowitz, October 6, 1977, Staff Offices, Domestic Policy Staff: Eizenstat, Box 196, Folder Education (General) [1], JCPL.

125. Memorandum from Joseph Califano to the President, December 3, 1977, Staff Files, Domestic Policy Staff: Eizenstat, Folder Education Department of (Separate) [4], JCPL, p. 1.

126. Memorandum from Joseph Califano to the President, December 3, 1977, Staff Offices, Office of Staff Secretary: Handwriting File, Folder 12/5/77 (3), JCPL, pp. 4–5, 12, 14, 16–19, 22–23, 28, 30, 33, 36. Though impact aid began in 1950 as assistance for school districts "impacted" by military bases, it had grown to include Native American children, children of federal workers, and children living in federal housing. In 1950 it covered 512,000 children; by 1978 it reached 2.4 million. Carter would be only the latest in a series of presidents from both parties who tried and failed to curb this program's excesses; see "Enlarging a Budget Rip-off," *Time*, August 7, 1978, p. 64.

127. After the National Academy of Education opposed a national achievement test at an HEW conference on the subject in March 1978, Carter "spoke to me about testing only once again," wrote Califano in *Governing America*, pp. 295, 299.

128. "Broad Trends Affecting Educational Policy, Draft," n.d., Shirley Hufstedler Collection, Box 12, Folder FY 82–86 Planning and Budget [1], JCPL, pp. 1–3, 5, 8, 10–14.

129. "Federal Programs Fail to Promote Change," *USA Today Magazine*, December 1978, p. 11. HEW assistant secretary Mary Berry, who would succeed Boyer as Carter's commissioner of education, responded that the Rand study had included only four programs: ESEA Title III's Innovative Programs, ESEA Title VII's Bilingual Education Programs, the Vocational Education Act's Exemplary Programs section, and the Cooperative Research Act's "Right-to-Read" programs. The report "did not catch federal officials by surprise," Berry wrote; see Berry, "The Teacher and the Rand Study," *Today's Education*, April–May 1979, p. 38.

130. Memorandum from Joseph Califano to the President, February 14, 1978, White House Central Files, Subject file Federal Aid, Box FA-10, Folder FA 3 1/1/78–2/28/78, JCPP, JCPL, pp. 1, 2; Memorandum from James McIntyre and Stuart Eizenstat to the President, February 24, 1978, White House Central Files, Subject file Federal Aid, Box FA-10, Folder FA 3 1/1/78–2/28/78, JCPL, p. 1.

131. "To the Congress of the United States," February 28, 1978, JCPL, pp. 1–2.

132. Martin Tolchin, "Carter Asks 24% Rise in Education Funds, with Focus on Basics," *New York Times*, February 29, 1978, pp. A1, B14.

133. Carl D. Perkins, "Impact of PL 95-561," *Today's Education,* February 1979, p. 68; Berry, "The Teacher and the Rand Study," p. 39.

134. Perkins, "Impact of PL 95-561," p. 68.

135. Memorandum from Stuart Eizenstat and Elizabeth Abramowitz to the President, November 1, 1978, Staff Offices, Domestic Policy Staff: Eizenstat, Box 191, September 19, 1978, Folder ESEA [Elementary and Secondary Education Act] [1], JCPL, pp. 1–3.

136. "Education: Two Years," JCPL, p. 1; Memorandum from Elizabeth Abramowitz to Stuart Eizenstat, November 27, 1978, White House Central Files, Subject file Education, Box ED-2, Folder ED 8/1/78–12/31/78, JCPL, p. 2.

137. Inflation would rise from 6 percent in early 1978 to 13 percent in 1980, and the deficit would grow from $45 billion in 1978 to $60 billion in 1980; see Stephen Woolcock, "Economic Policies of the Carter Administration," in *The Carter Years: The President and Policymaking,* ed. M. Glenn Abernathy and Phil Williams (New York: St. Martin's, 1984), pp. 44–45; George Neill, "The Question Becomes: Where Will the Axe Fall?" *Phi Delta Kappan* (May 1980): 589.

138. George Neill, "Plans for Defusing the Youth Employment Time Bomb," *Phi Delta Kappan* (February 1980): 380. The bill would pass the House and the Senate committees but would die before reaching the Senate floor.

139. Steven Weisman, "Carter to Trim Budget $13 Billion and Curb Credit to Cut Inflation; Sees Need for Pain and Discipline," *New York Times*, March 15, 1980, pp. A1, A35; "Remarks of the President at the Opening Session of the 118th Annual Meeting of the NEA," July 3, 1980, Sarah Weddington Collection, Box 67, Folder Education: Department of Education, JCPL, pp. 2–3.

140. "Education: Two Years," JCPL, p. 1; telephone interview of Shirley Hufstedler by author, January 28, 1998.

141. "Transcript of the President's Address," p. 12; "Transcript of President's State of the Union Address to Joint Sessions of Congress," *New York Times*, January 24, 1979, p. A13; "Transcript of President's State of the Union Address to Joint Session of Congress," *New York Times*, January 24, 1980, p. A12; Shirley Hufstedler, "The Presidency and the Cabinet: Forming a New Cabinet Department," in *The Carter Presidency: Fourteen Intimate Perspectives of Jimmy Carter,* ed. Kenneth W. Thompson (New York: University Press of America, 1990), p. 37; Vertical Files, Cabinet Meeting Minutes, 1/24/77–12/31/80, JCPP, JCPL; Charles Jones, *Jimmy Carter and the United States Congress* (Baton Rouge: Louisiana State University Press, 1988), p. 129; Carter, *Keeping Faith*, pp. 75–76; Memorandum to Fran Voorde from Eizenstat, March 6, 1979, White House Central Files, Box ED-2, Folder ED 1/1/79–3/31/79, JCPP, JCPL.

142. Gary M. Fink, *Prelude to the Presidency* (Westport, Conn.: Greenwood, 1980), p. 166; Carter, *Keeping Faith*, p. 76; telephone interview of Hufstedler by author, January 28, 1998.

143. Carter, *Keeping Faith*, p. 76; Interview of Griffin Bell, Miller Center Interviews, Carter Presidency Project, March 23, 1988, JCPP, JCPL, p. 9; Interview of Stuart Eizenstat, Miller Center Interviews, Carter Presidency Project, January 28–29, 1982, JCPL, p. 102; telephone interview of Hufstedler by author, January 28, 1998; Exit Interview of Elizabeth Abramowitz, Carter Presidency Project, August 23, 1979, JCPL, p. 16.

144. Memorandum from James McIntyre, Stuart Eizenstat, and Frank Moore to the President, June 2, 1978, Staff Offices, Domestic Policy Staff: Eizenstat, Box 212, Folder HEW, Department of, JCPP, JCPL, pp. 1–2; Memorandum from Frank Moore to the President, June 7, 1978, Presidential Diary, Box PO-32, Folder 6/7/78 Backup Material, JCPL, p. 1.

145. Memorandum from Joseph Califano to the President, December 3, 1977, 40; Tolchin, "Carter Asks 24% Rise in Education Funds, with Focus on Basics," p. A12.

146. Califano, *Governing America,* p. 271; Donald Orlich, "Innovation and Centralization in Federal Education Policy" (condensed from *Educational Researcher*), *Education Digest* (March 1980): 13–15; David Savage, "The Federal Schoolhouse," *New Republic,* April 18, 1981, pp. 21–22.

147. Carter, *Keeping Faith,* p. 75.

## Chapter 2: School Desegregation, 1965–81

1. "Summary of Statement of Policies under Title VI of the Civil Rights Act of 1964 Respecting Desegregation of Elementary and Secondary Schools," n.d., Task Force Reports Collection, Box 27, Folder 1968 Interagency Task Force on Education, LBJPL, pp. 1–4; "Memorandum," April 23, 1965, Human Rights Collection, Box 53, Folder HU 2-5 4/1/65–9/30/65, LBJPL.

2. "Memorandum," April 23, 1965, LBJPL; Letter from Arnold Aronson to the President, May 21, 1965, Human Rights Collection, Box 53, Folder HU 2-5 4/1/65–9/30/65, LBJPL, pp. 1–2; Memorandum from Douglass Cater to the President, May 8, 1965, Human Rights Collection, Box 53, Folder HU 2-5 4/1/65–9/30/65, LBJPL.

3. Memorandum from Anthony Celebrezze to the President, July 1, 1965, Human Rights Collection, Box 53, Folder HU 4/1/65–9/30/65, LBJPL; Letter from Francis Keppel to "Dear Superintendent," August 18, 1965, Human Rights Collection, Box 53, Folder HU 4/1/65–9/30/65, LBJPL, p. 2.

4. "Integration Round Up, North and South," *Scholastic Teacher,* November 4, 1965, p. 2; Memorandum from John Gardner to Douglass Cater, January 17, 1966, Human Rights Collection, Box 53, Folder HU 2-5 10/1/65–5/15/66, LBJPL; Memorandum from Douglass Cater to Marvin Watson, February 22, 1966, Human Rights Collection, Box 53, Folder HU 2-5 10/1/65–5/15/66, LBJPL; Alexander Bickel, "Forcing Desegregation through Title VI," *New Republic,* April 9, 1966, pp. 8–9.

5. Memorandum from F. Peter Libassi to Douglas [*sic*] Cater, January 21, 1966, Human Rights Collection, Box 53, Folder HU 2-5 12/1/65–5/16/66, LBJPL, p. 3.

6. White House Referral from Paul Popple, Assistant to the President, March 26, 1966, White House Central Files, Box 246, Folder 165-4, LBJPL; "Monthly Report of the Washington Bureau," National Association for the Advancement of Colored People Papers, Library of Congress, Washington, D.C. [hereafter NAACPP], pp. 1–2; G. W. Foster, "Who Pulled the Teeth from Title VI?" *Saturday Review,* April 16, 1966, p. 88.

7. Telegram from Robert Byrd to the President, March 11, 1966, Henry Wilson Files, Box 13, Folder Wilson: Education, LBJPL, p. 1; Letter from Richard Russell, John Stennis, Sam Ervin, Allen Ellender, John Sparkman, Herman Talmadge, Willis Robertson, Everett Jordan, and Dessard Holland to the President, May 2, 1966, Human Rights Collection, Box 51, Folder HU 2-5 5/4/66–8/31/66, LBJPL, p. 5; "Elementary Education Act Expanded," *Congressional Quarterly Almanac,* 89th Cong., 2nd sess., 1966 (Washington, D.C., 1967),

p. 294; "Elementary Education Act Expanded," pp. 294–96; "Government's Plan to Deseg-regate the Suburbs," *U.S. News and World Report*, October 10, 1966, p. 76; "Education: Racial Controversy Dogs Commissioner," *Science*, October 14, 1966, pp. 242–43; Letter from Walter Jones to the President, October 5, 1966, Human Rights Collection, Box 51, Folder HU 2-5 9/1/66–1/5/67, LBJPL; "The Commissar and His Cohorts," *Library Journal*, October 15, 1966, p. 5002.

8. Memorandum from Wilbur Cohen to Douglass Cater, November 30, 1966, Human Rights Collection, Box 51, Folder HU 2-5 9/1/66–1/5/67, LBJPL.

9. Memorandum from Ralph Huitt to Michael Parker, November 28, 1966, Human Rights Collection, Box 51, Folder HU 2-5 9/1/66–1/5/67, LBJPL; Letter from John Gardner to Richard Russell, n.d., Henry Wilson Files, Box 13, Folder Wilson: Education, LBJPL; Hugh Davis Graham, *The Civil Rights Era* (New York: Oxford University Press, 1990), p. 373; "Guidelines for Integration Upheld in Court of Appeals," *Library Journal*, February 15, 1967, p. 16.

10. Letter from Douglass Cater to Robert Byrd, n.d., Human Rights Collection, Box 51, Folder HU 2-5, 5/4/66–8/31/66, LBJPL, pp. 1–2; Memorandum from Douglass Cater to Harry McPherson, July 1996, Box 51, Folder HU 2-5 5/4/66–8/31/66, LBJPL; Robert Sherill, "Guidelines to Frustration," *The Nation*, January 16, 1967, p. 73; Letter from Paul Popple to Leon Burnham, October 14, 1966, Human Rights Collection, Box 53, Folder HU 2-5 5/16/66–12/8/66, LBJPL; Sherill, "Guidelines to Frustration," p. 73.

11. Memorandum from Peter Libassi to Douglass Cater, February 2, 1967, Human Rights Collection, Box 51, Folder HU 2-5 1/6/67–2/20/67, LBJPL, p. 2; Lyndon Johnson, "Special Message to the Congress on Equal Justice," February 15, 1967, *Public Papers of the Presidents of the United States: Lyndon B. Johnson*, Book 1, *1967* (Washington, D.C.: U.S. Government Printing Office, 1968), p. 185; Letter from Lyndon Johnson to Whitney Young, January 5, 1967, Human Rights Collection, Box 51, Folder HU 2-5, 9/1/66–1/5/67, LBJPL.

12. "Ignoramuses," *Atlanta Journal*, June 22, 1967, p. B14; "Two-Year Elementary School Aid Bill Enacted," *Congressional Quarterly Almanac*, 90th Cong., 1st sess., 1967 (Washing-ton, D.C., 1967), pp. 620, 624.

13. "The President's News Conference of May 18, 1967," *Public Papers of the Presidents of the United States: Lyndon Johnson*, Book 1, *1967* (Washington, D.C.: U.S. Government Printing Office, 1968), p. 458; Memorandum from William Taylor to Harry McPherson, July 31, 1967, Human Rights Collection, Book 51, Folder HU 2-5, 7/6/67–7/31/67, LBJPL; "Two-Year Elementary School Aid Bill Enacted," p. 621; Memorandum from Peter Libassi to Douglass Cater, March 28, 1968, White House Central Files, Box 8, Folder FA 2 1/25/68–4/24/68, LBJPL, p. 1; Letter from Gary Orfield to Douglass Cater, March 31, 1968, Human Rights Collection, Box 53, Folder HU 2/5, 8/1/67, LBJPL.

14. Memorandum from Peter Libassi to John Gardner, September 9, 1997, Human Rights Collection, Box 52, Folder HU 2-5, Folder 8/1/67–9/30/67, LBJPL, pp. 1–2; Libassi to Cater, March 28, 1968, pp. 1–2.

15. Lyndon Johnson, "Special Message to the Congress on Civil Rights," January 24, 1968, *Public Papers of the Presidents of the United States*, Book 1, *1968–69* (Washington, D.C.: U.S. Government Printing Service, 1970), p. 57; Memorandum from Ruby Martin to Douglass Cater, September 13, 1968, Human Rights Collection, Box 53, Folder HU 2-5, 8/24/68, LBJPL; Memorandum from Joseph Califano to the President, October 2, 1968, Human Rights Collection, Box 53, Folder HU 2-5 8/24/68, LBJPL; "Congress Votes $186

Billion in Labor-HEW Funds," *Congressional Quarterly Almanac,* 90th Cong., 2nd sess., 1968 (Washington, D.C., 1969), p. 593.

16. "Government's Plan to Desegregate the Suburbs," pp. 76–77; Memorandum from the Vice President to the President, September 17, 1965, Human Rights Collection, Box 53, Folder HU 2-5, 4/1/65–9/30/65, LBJPL.

17. Interview of Keppel, LBJPL, p. 28.

18. Ibid.; Letter from David Seeley to Joe Frantz, March 20, 1972, attached to Interview of Keppel, LBJPL, pp. 4–5; Memorandum from the Attorney General to Lee White and Douglass Cater, December 17, 1965, Human Rights Collection, Box 53, Folder HU 2-5 10/1/65–5/15/66, LBJPL; Telephone Call from Douglass Cater to the President, October 1965, Human Rights Collection, Box 53, Folder HU 2-5 10/1/65–5/15/66, LBJPL; "Mixed Classes—Broadest Plan So Far," *U.S. News and World Report,* September 4, 1967, p. 10.

19. Memorandum from Douglass Cater to the President, October 5, 1965, Human Rights Collection, Box 53, Folder HU 2-5 10/1/65–5/15/66, pp. 1–2; Letter from the President to John Hannah, November 17, 1965, Human Rights Collection, Box 51, Folder HU 2-5 9/1/66–1/5/67, LBJPL.

20. "New Integration Targets: Northern Cities and Suburbs," *U.S. News and World Report,* July 4, 1966, pp. 47–48; Memorandum from John Gardner to Douglass Cater, August 4, 1966, Human Rights Collection, Box 51, Folder HU 2-5 5/4/66–8/31/66, LBJPL; "Monthly Report of the Washington Bureau," April 7, 1966, NAACPP, pp. 1–2; "Isolation in the Schools," n.d., NAACPP, p. 1.

21. Bruce McPherson, "Will Classrooms and Schools Built with Federal Funds Be Integrated?" *Phi Delta Kappan* (September 1966): 12.

22. "What Are Americans Receiving in Return for Their Heavy Investment in Education?" *American Education,* November 1966, pp. 24–26.

23. Ibid., p. 72; Memorandum from Samuel Halperin to Harold Howe, September 20, 1966, Henry Wilson Files, Box 13, Folder Wilson: Education, LBJPL; "Elementary Education Act Expanded," p. 287; Memorandum from Peter Libassi to Douglass Cater, February 2, 1967, Human Rights Collection, Box 51, Folder HU 2-5 1/6/67–2/20/67, LBJPL, p. 1; United States Commission on Civil Rights, "Remedies for Racial Isolation," *Education Digest* (April 1967): 1–2.

24. "Government's Plan to Desegregate the Suburbs," p. 72; Taylor to McPherson, April 12, 1967, LBJPL, pp. 1–4; "Notes on Meeting of Task Force on Education," April 14–15, 1967, Douglass Cater Files, Box 37, Folder Cater, Douglass: Material on Task Force on Education (6), LBJPL, p. 4; Memorandum from Peter Libassi to John Doar, April 28, 1967, Human Rights Collection, Box 51, Folder HU 2-5 4/6/67–7/5/67, LBJPL, p. 1.

25. Joseph Alsop, "No More Nonsense about Ghetto Education!" *New Republic,* July 22, 1967, pp. 18–23; "A Bus in Their Future?" *Newsweek,* July 3, 1967, p. 49.

26. "Shape of Things to Come in the Public Schools?" *U.S. News and World Report,* July 3, 1967, p. 52; Gerald Grant, "The Courts Take the Initiative," *Saturday Review,* July 15, 1967, p. 65; Memorandum from Douglass Cater to the President, June 30, 1967, Human Rights Collection, Box 51, Folder HU 2-5 4/6/67–7/5/67, LBJPL, p. 1.

27. Vaughn Bornet, *The Presidency of Lyndon B. Johnson* (Lawrence: University of Kansas Press, 1983), pp. 228–29; Irvin Unger, *The Best of Intentions: The Triumph and Failure of the Great Society under Kennedy, Johnson, and Nixon* (St. James, N.Y.: Brandywine, 1995), p. 288; "School Integration Is Top Educational Priority," *Scholastic Teacher,* March 28, 1968, p. 4.

28. Unger, *The Best of Intentions*, p. 236; Libassi to Doar, April 28, 1967.

29. Gary Orfield, "Congress, the President, and Anti-Busing Legislation, 1966–1974," in *School Busing: Constitutional and Political Developments*, Vol. 2, ed. Davison Douglas (New York: Garland, 1994), p. 7; Unger, *The Best of Intentions*, p. 234.

30. Memorandum from Harry McPherson to Marvin Watson, January 3, 1967, Human Rights Collection, Box 51, Folder HU 2–5, 9/1/66–1/5/67, LBJPL; Unger, *The Best of Intentions*, p. 289; Jeff Shesol, *Mutual Contempt* (New York: Norton, 1997), p. 473; Interview of Harold Sanders by Joe Frantz, March 24, 1969, Tape 2, LBJPL, p. 37; Graham, *The Civil Rights Era*, p. 174; Lyndon Johnson, *Vantage Point: Perspectives on the Presidency* (New York: Holt, Rinehart, and Winston, 1971).

31. "Shape of Things to Come in the Public Schools?" *U.S. News and World Report*, July 3, 1968, p. 52; Robert Dallek, *Flawed Giant: Lyndon Johnson and His Times, 1961–1973* (New York: Oxford University Press, 1998), p. 324.

32. For evaluations of the Great Society, see John Andrew, *Lyndon Johnson and the Great Society* (Chicago: Ivan Dee, 1998); Bornet, *The Presidency of Lyndon B. Johnson;* Paul Conkin, *Big Daddy from the Pedernales: Lyndon B. Johnson* (Boston: Twayne, 1986); Robert Divine, ed., *Exploring the Johnson Years* (Austin: University of Texas Press, 1984); Dallek, *Flawed Giant;* Eric Goldman, *The Tragedy of Lyndon Johnson* (New York: Alfred A. Knopf, 1969); Alonzo Hamby, *Liberalism and Its Challengers: F.D.R. to Reagan* (New York: Oxford University Press, 1984), and Unger, *The Best of Intentions*.

33. Garry Wills, *Nixon Agonistes* (Boston: Houghton Mifflin, 1970), pp. 244–45, 249, 251. Joan Hoff notes, however, that Nixon himself refused to acknowledge such a strategy when she interviewed him on January 26, 1983; see Hoff, *Nixon Reconsidered* (New York: Basic Books, 1994), p. 79.

34. Richard Nixon, *RN: The Memoirs of Richard Nixon* (New York: Grosset and Dunlop, 1978), p. 444; Roger Morris, *Uncertain Greatness: Henry Kissinger and American Foreign Policy* (New York: Harper and Row, 1977), p. 131; Robert Sam Anson, *Exile: The Unquiet Oblivion of Richard M. Nixon* (New York: Simon and Schuster, 1984), p. 148.

35. Hoff, *Nixon Reconsidered*, p. 74; Memorandum from Fred LaRue to Bryce Harlow, February 18, 1969, White House Central Files, Box 35, Folder [CF] HU 2-1 [Education Schooling] 1/20/69–2/28/70, RMNPP, p. 2.

36. Memorandum from Alexander Butterfield to the Attorney General and the Secretary of Health, Education, and Welfare, March 14, 1969, White House Central Files, Subject file Human Rights, Box 8, Folder HU 2-1 [Education—Schooling] 7/1/69–2/31/70, RMNPP.

37. "Statement by the Honorable Robert H. Finch, Secretary of the Department of Health, Education, and Welfare, and the Honorable John N. Mitchell, Attorney General, 3 July 1969," White House Central Files, Subject file Human Rights, Box 11, Folder [CF] HU 2-1 [Education—Schooling] 3/1/70–3/31/70, RMNPP, p. 8; "A Debt to Dixie," *Newsweek*, July 14, 1969, p. 24; "Spelling It Out in Black and White," *Newsweek*, September 22, 1969, p. 24.

38. "Up at Harry's Place," *Time*, July 11, 1969, p. 15; Tom Wicker, *One of Us: Richard M. Nixon and the American Dream* (New York: Random House, 1991), p. 493; Memorandum from Harry Dent to the President, October 30, 1969, White House Central Files, Subject file Human Rights, Box 8, Folder [EX] HU 2-1 [Education—Schooling] 7/1/69–2/31/70, RMNPP; Memorandum from Robert Finch to John Ehrlichman, January 23, 1970, White House Central Files, Subject file Human Rights, Box 9, Folder [EX] HU 2-1 [Education—Schooling] 7/1/71–9/31/71, RMNPP.

39. Memorandum from Bryce Harlow to Staff Secretary, February 21, 1970, White House Central Files, Subject file Human Rights, Box 9, Folder [EX] HU 2-1 [Education—Schooling] 7/1/71–9/31/71, RMNPP; "Nixon Administration Statement," February 11, 1970, White House Central Files, Subject file Human Rights, Box 9, Folder [EX] HU 2-1 [Education—Schooling] 7/1/71–9/31/71, RMNPP; John Osborne, "Chicken, Southern Fried," *New Republic,* February 21, 1970, pp. 13–14.

40. "Nixon on Desegregation," *U.S. News and World Report,* April 6, 1970, pp. 80–87; Memorandum from John Brown to John Ehrlichman, White House Central Files, Subject file Human Rights, Box 35, Folder [CF] HU 2-1 [Education—Schooling] 3/1/70–10/21/70 [1969–70], RMNPP.

41. Letter from Strom Thurmond to Bryce Harlow, October 21, 1969, White House Central Files, Subject file Federal Aid, Confidential Files, 1969–74, Box 11, Folder [CF] FA3 Federal Aid—Education, RMNPP; John Ehrlichman Notes, August 19, 1970, White House Special Files, John Ehrlichman Files, Box 3, Folder Notes of Meetings with the President, 7/1/70–8/31/70, RMNPP; Roy Reed, "Nixon Reassures South on Schools," *New York Times,* August 15, 1970, p. A11.

42. Memorandum from Edward Morgan to the President, September 21, 1970, President's Office Files, Box 82, Folder Memoranda for the President, 8/16/70–10/25/70, RMNPP; Archibald Cox, *The Court and the Constitution* (Boston: Houghton Mifflin, 1987), p. 264; Memorandum from H. R. Haldeman to John Ehrlichman, July 22, 1971, White House Central Files, Box 35, Folder [CF] HU 2-1 [Education—Schooling] [1971–74], RMNPP.

43. Gary Orfield, "Congress, the President, and Anti-Busing Legislation, 1966–1974," in *School Busing: Constitutional and Political Developments,* Vol. 2, ed. Davison Douglas (New York: Garland, 1994), pp. 25–29; Memorandum from Patrick Buchanan to the President, March 17, 1972, President's Office Files, Box 88, Folder Memoranda for the President, 12/17/71–2/20/72, RMNPP.

44. Orfield, "Congress, the President, and Anti-Busing Legislation, 1966–1974," p. 31; "Anti-Busing Amendments Added to Education Bill," *Congressional Quarterly Almanac,* 93rd Cong., 2nd sess., 1974 (Washington, D.C., 1975), pp. 15–16.

45. Orfield, "Congress, the President, and Anti-Busing Legislation, 1966–1974," pp. 31, 36, 37; Bernard Schwartz, *A History of the Supreme Court* (New York: Oxford University Press, 1993), p. 323; "Anti-Busing Amendments Added to Education Bill," p. 16; Memorandum from Caspar Weinberger to the President, August 5, 1974, White House Special Files, David Lissy Files, Box 4, Folder Elementary and Secondary Education Act Amendments (1974), GRFPL, p. 2.

46. Richard Nixon, *In the Arena* (New York: Simon and Schuster, 1990), pp. 105–6; Stephen Ambrose, *Nixon: The Education of a Politician, 1913–1962* (New York: Simon and Schuster, 1987), pp. 269, 434–36; Julie Nixon Eisenhower, in *Pat Nixon: The Untold Story* (New York: Kensington Publishing, 1986), p. 170. The extent of racial integration at Sidwell Friends at the time is uncertain, as the school did not keep records of the racial composition of its student body; telephone interview of Amy Fitch, Archivist, Sidwell Friends School, by author, April 29, 1997.

47. Jonathan Aitken, *Nixon: A Life* (New York: Regnery, 1993), pp. 248, 271, 324, 355–56, 375; Graham, *The Civil Rights Era,* p. 340; Herbert Parmet, *Richard Nixon and His America* (Boston: Little, Brown, 1990), pp. 266–68; Hoff, *Nixon Reconsidered,* p. 78; Robert

Brown, "Nixon's Legacy to African-Americans," n.d., RMNPL, p. 2; Interview of Kenneth Cole by James Reichley, December 21, 1978, p. 1, GRFPL; Interview of Martin Anderson by James Reichley, January 3, 1978, p. 1, GRFPL; Interview of Robert Finch by James Reichley, March 3, 1978, p. 6, GRFPL.

48. "Report of the Task Force on Education," January 3, 1969, White House Central Files, Subject file Education, Box 8, Folder FG 23-6 Office of Education, RMNPP, p. 1; "The Administration: Tenuous Balance," *Time,* July 11, 1969, p. 14.

49. John Ehrlichman Notes, September 10, 1969, White House Special Files, John Ehrlichman File, Box 3, Folder Notes of Meetings with the President, 1969, RMNPP; "Statement of Robert H. Finch, Department of Health, Education, and Welfare," October 14, 1969, White House Central Files, Subject file Human Rights, Box 11, Folder [CF] HU 2-1 [Education—Schooling] 10/1/69–12/31/69, RMNPP; Letter from Strom Thurmond to Bryce Harlow, October 21, 1969, RMNPP.

50. John Ehrlichman Notes, January 8, 1970, White House Central Files, Subject file John Ehrlichman, Box 3, Folder Notes of Meeting with the President, 1/1/70–6/30/70, RMNPP; Memorandum from Jim Keogh to the President, February 18, 1970, President's Office Files, Box 80, Folder Memoranda for the President, 1/4/70–5/31/70, RMNPP.

51. Letter to Hugh Scott, February 17, 1970, White House Central Files, Subject file Human Rights, Folder [EX] HU 2-1 [Education—Schooling] 1/1/70–2/28/70, RMNPP.

52. Memorandum from Bryce Harlow to the President, February 23, 1970, White House Central Files, Subject file Human Rights, Box 9, Folder [EX] HU 2-1 [Education—Schooling], 1/1/70–2/28/70, RMNPP, pp. 1, 3.

53. Memorandum from Patrick Buchanan to the President, February 28, 1970, White House Central Files, Subject file Human Rights, Box 11, Folder HU 2-1 [Education—Schooling], 1/1/70–2/28/70, RMNPP, pp. 1, 3; Memorandum from Robert Brown to the President, March 5, 1970, President's Office Files, Box 80, Folder Memoranda for the President, 1/4/70–5/31/70, RMNPP, p. 2.

54. "Nixon on Desegregation," pp. 80, 86.

55. "Senator Brooke on Nixon Message," p. 1; Alexander Bickel, "Realistic, Sensible (II)," *New Republic,* April 4 and 11, 1970, p. 14; Robert Semple, "President Asks for Funds for School Desegregation," *New York Times,* May 22, 1970, p. A20.

56. Memorandum from John Ehrlichman to the President, July 18, 1970, White House Central Files, Subject file Education, Box 2, Folder EX ED 6/22/70–7/31/70, RMNPP, pp. 1, 3.

57. Memorandum from Patrick Buchanan to the President, July 7, 1970, White House Central Files, Subject file Education, Box 2, Folder EX ED 6/22/70–7/31/70, RMNPP, p. 1; Memorandum from Bryce Harlow to the President, June 17, 1970, White House Central Files, Subject file Education, Box 2, Folder EX ED 5/21/70–6/21/70, RMNPP, p. 1.

58. Ehrlichman wrote on January 8, 1970, that "President favors exemption" for private schools; see John Ehrlichman Notes, White House Special Files, John Ehrlichman File, Box 3, Folder Notes on Meetings with the President, 1/1/70–6/30/70, RMNPP, p. 2. Ehrlichman wrote to Nixon on July 18 that "You will recall that you were surprised and curious that Bryce Harlow's position which [*sic*] was that option 3 should be accepted"; see Memorandum from John Ehrlichman to the President, White House Central Files, Subject file Education, Box 2, Folder EX ED 6/22/70–7/31/70, RMNPP, p. 1. Kenneth Crawford, "Thurmond Threatens," *Newsweek,* August 3, 1970, p. 25.

59. John Osborne, "Call It Desegregation," *New Republic,* January 30, 1971, p. 12.

60. Memorandum from H. R. Haldeman to the President, August 4, 1970, White House Central Files, Subject file Human Rights, Box 9, Folder [EX] HU 2-1 [Education—Schooling] 8/1/70–8/31/70, RMNPP, p. 1; John Ehrlichman, *Witness to Power* (New York: Simon and Schuster, 1982), p. 235; Keogh to the President, February 18, 1970, RMNPP, p. 3.

61. Graham, *The Civil Rights Era,* p. 565; Parmet, *Richard Nixon and His America,* p. 596; Memorandum from Patrick Buchanan to the President, March 28, 1972, President's Office Files, Box 89, Folder Memoranda for the President, 6/4/72–9/17/72, RMNPP, p. 1; Memorandum from Bryce Harlow to Peter Flanigan, May 12, 1970, White House Central Files, Subject file Human Rights, Box 9, Folder [EX] HU 2-1 [Education—Schooling] 5/1/70–5/31/70, RMNPP, p. 2.

62. Jack Rosenthal, "Major Integration Test Confronts U.S. in 1972," *New York Times,* January 19, 1972, p. A20; Alexander Bickel, "Desegregation: Where Do We Go from Here?" *New Republic,* February 7, 1970, p. 20; Memorandum from Bryce Harlow to Staff Secretary, February 21, 1970, White House Central Files, Subject file Human Rights, Box 9, Folder [EX] HU 2-1 [Education—Schooling], 1/1/70–2/28/70, RMNPP, p. 2.

63. William Raspberry, "Massive Busing: A Waste," *Washington Post,* February 26, 1972, in *School Busing: Constitutional and Political Developments,* Vol. 2, p. 67; Marjorie Hunter, "Nixon's Plan Splits Rivals: Ervin Leads Busing Attack," *New York Times,* March 18, 1972, p. A1.

64. Milton Bracker, "Nixon Optimistic on Integration," *New York Times,* October 19, 1956, p. A1. The analyses were *The Negro Family in America* (1965) by Moynihan (later Nixon's urban affairs advisor); *Equal Educational Opportunity* (1966) by Coleman; *Report of the National Advisory Commission or Civil Disorders* (1968), chaired by Governor Otto Kerner of Illinois; and "Desegregation: Where Do We Go from Here?" (1970), a *New Republic* article written by Bickel. In 1960 Nixon won 32 percent and in 1968 he won 13 percent of blacks' votes. See Hoff, *Nixon Reconsidered,* p. 78, and Parmet, *Richard Nixon and His America,* p. 631; John Ehrlichman Notes, March 19, 1970, White House Special File, John Ehrlichman File, Box 3, Folder Notes of Meetings with the President, 1/1/70–6/30/70, RMNPP.

65. Nixon, *RN: The Memoirs of Richard Nixon,* pp. 444–45.

66. "An Unfinished Task," *Time,* September 27, 1976, p. 57.

67. "Ford's Record on Key Issues Votes in the House, 1949–1973," *Congressional Quarterly Almanac,* 93rd Cong., 2nd sess., 1974 (Washington, D.C., 1975), pp. 913–14.

68. Memorandum from Roger Semerad to Kenneth Cole, August 12, 1974, White House Central Files, Subject file Education, Box 6, Folder FA 3 Education 8/9/74–8/31/74, GRFPL, p. 1; Memorandum to the President, August 15, 1974, White House Records Office Files, Box 62, Folder 8/15/74, Legislation Case Files, GRFPL.

69. "Statement by the President (on H.R. 69)," August 21, 1974, David Lissy Files, Box 4, Folder Elementary and Secondary Education Act Amendments [1974], GRFPL, p. 1.

70. Memorandum from Caspar Weinberger to the President, March 20, 1975, White House Special Files, David Lissy Files, Box 2, Folder Busing [1], GRFPL, p. 1.

71. "Transcript of the President's News Conference on Foreign and Domestic Matters," *New York Times,* October 10, 1974, p. A38; Anthony Ripley, "Ford Is Critical of Busing," *New York Times,* October 10, 1974, pp. A1, B55; Wayne King, "Federal Troops Asked for Boston," *New York Times,* October 16, 1974, p. A1; "Ford Asks Residents of Boston to Reject

Violence on Schools," *New York Times,* October 13, 1974, p. A20; John R. Greene, *The Presidency of Gerald R. Ford* (Lawrence: University of Kansas Press, 1995), p. 89.

72. "Louisville Urged to Merge Schools into County District," *New York Times,* July 24, 1974, p. A11; "Court Reaffirms Louisville Ruling," *New York Times,* December 12, 1974, p. A34; "Policy Chief Tells of Urging Cancellation of Ford Trip to Louisville," *New York Times,* October 11, 1975, p. A15.

73. "Interview with the President," August 30, 1975, White House Central Files, James Cannon Files, Box 7, Folder Busing—Presidential Statements, GRFPL, pp. 1–2.

74. "Interview with the President," pp. 1–2; "Anti-Busing Amendments Added to Education Bill," p. 455.

75. "Survey Finds Law Cited by Ford Is Unused in Most Busing Cases," *New York Times,* September 21, 1975, p. A41.

76. Philip Shabecoff, "Ford Defends His Opposition to Busing," *New York Times,* May 27, 1976, p. A24; "Remarks of the President at the Eighteenth Biennial National Federation of Republican Women's Convention, Dallas, Texas," September 13, 1975, White House Special Files, James Cannon Files, Box 7, Folder Busing—Presidential Statements, GRFPL.

77. "Meeting of 10/7/75 with President," October 8, 1975, White House Special Files, James Cannon Files, Box 5, Folder Busing, October 1975–March 1976, GRFPL; "Interview with the President," October 30, 1975, White House Special Files, James Cannon Files, Box 7, Folder Busing—Presidential Statements, GRFPL, p. 1.

78. "Minutes of the Cabinet Meeting," September 17, 1975, White House Special Files, James E. O'Connor File, Box 5, Folder 9/17/75 Cabinet Meeting Minutes, GRFPL, pp. 3–4.

79. Memorandum from Richard Parsons to James Cannon and Philip Buchen, October 23, 1975, White House Special Files, James Cannon Files, Box 5, Folder Busing, October 1975–March 1976, GRFPL, pp. 4–6.

80. Parsons to Cannon and Buchen, 6; "Chronology before November 20 Meeting," n.d., White House Special Files, Bobbie Kilberg Files, Box 15, Folder Chronology of Events, GRFPL.

81. "Chronology before November 20 Meeting," pp. 1–3.

82. Memorandum from James O'Connor to James Cannon, February 24, 1976, White House Special Files, James Cannon Files, Box 5, Folder Busing, October 1975–March 1976, GRFPL, pp. 1–3.

83. Ibid., p. 3.

84. "Remarks of the President and Question and Answer Session at the Chamber of Commerce Breakfast, Elles Hall," February 20, 1976, White House Special Files, James Cannon Files, Box 7, Folder Busing—Presidential Statements, GRFPL, pp. 1–2 (emphasis mine); "Interview with the President," February 21, 1976, White House Special Files, James Cannon Files, Box 7, Folder Busing—Presidential Statements, GRFPL, p. 2 (emphasis mine).

85. "Statement by the President," May 29, 1976, White House Special Files, James Cannon Files, Box 7, Folder Busing—Presidential Statements, GRFPL; Lesley Oelsner, "Levi, in Reversal, Won't Use Boston as Test on Busing," *New York Times,* May 30, 1976, pp. A1, A39.

86. Memorandum from Arthur Quern and Allen Moore to James Cannon, June 3, 1976, White House Special Files, James Cannon Files, Box 5, Folder Busing, June 2–9, 1976, GRFPL, p. 1.

87. "Interview with the President," May 20, 1976, White House Special Files, James Cannon Files, Box 7, Folder Busing—Presidential Statements, GRFPL, p. 4.

88. "Meeting on School Desegregation," June 1, 1976, White House Special Files, James Cannon Files, Box 6, Folder Busing—Presidential Meetings, GRFPL, pp. 3–4.

89. "Interview with the President on 'Face the Nation,'" June 5, 1976, White House Special Files, James Cannon Files, Box 7, Folder Busing—Presidential Statements, GRFPL, p. 5; Memorandum from Richard Parsons to James Cannon, June 10, 1976, White House Special Files, James Cannon Files, Box 5, Folder Busing, June 10, 1976, GRFPL, p. 1. On June 25, the Supreme Court ruled against racial discrimination in nonpublic nonsectarian schools; see Lesley Oelsner, "High Court Curbs Private Schools on Racial Barrier," *New York Times*, June 26, 1976, p. A1.

90. "President's Television Message on Busing," June 24, 1976, White House Special Files, James Cannon Files, Box 6, Folder Busing, June 24–30, 1976, GRFPL, pp. 1, 3; "Education," *President Ford 1976 Factbook*, September 9, 1976, White House Special Files, Richard Cheney Files, Box 18, Folder President Ford 1976 Factbook [2], GRFPL, p. 2.

91. Memorandum from Philip Buchen and James Cannon to the President, October 28, 1976, James Cannon Files, Box 6, Folder Busing, October 1976, GRFPL, p. 2.

92. A 1973 Gallup Poll showed that 95 percent of the public opposed busing as a means of achieving school desegregation, in Orfield, "Congress, the President, and Anti-Busing Legislation, 1966–1974," pp. 40–41; "Interview with the President on 'Face the Nation,'" p. 5.

93. "Ford's Anti-Busing Bill," *Christian Century*, July 21 and 28, 1976, p. 652.

94. "Subject: Education Appropriations Act Veto Override," September 9, 1975, White House Special Files, Ron Nessen Files, Box 118, Folder Education, GRFPL, p. 1; "Ford to Increase Budget Request on School Funds," *New York Times*, February 17, 1976, p. A1.

95. Shabecoff, "Ford Defends His Opposition to Busing," p. 24; Memorandum from Arthur Quern and Richard Parsons to James Cannon, June 22, 1976, White House Special Files, James Cannon Files, Box 5, Folder Busing, June 22, 1976, GRFPL, p. 1.

96. "Interview with the President on 'Face the Nation,'" pp. 2, 4.

97. Memorandum from James Cannon to the President, August 25, 1976, White House Special Files, David Lissy Files, Box 2, Folder Busing [5], GRFPL, p. 1; Memorandum from James Cannon to the President, September 13, 1976, White House Special Files, James Cannon Files, Box 6, Folder Busing, September 1976, GRFPL, p. 1.

98. Memorandum from Drs. Melady and Lee to Myron Kuropas, June 25, 1976, White House Special Files, Michael Duval Files, Box 27, Folder Republican Party Platform—Catholic Issues, GRFPL, p. 1; Thomas Edsall and Mary Edsall, *Chain Reaction: The Impact of Race, Rights, and Taxes on American Politics* (New York: Norton, 1991), p. 149.

99. "Meeting of 10/7/75 with the President," GRFPL; Memorandum from Edward Levi to James Cannon, March 29, 1976, White House Special Files, James Cannon Files, Box 5, Folder Busing, October 1975–March 1976, GRFPL, p. 1.

100. Memorandum from Judith Richards Hope to James Cannon through Arthur Quern, June 11, 1976, White House Special Files, James Cannon, James Cannon Files, Box 5, Folder Busing, June 11, 1976, GRFPL; Memorandum from Robert Goldwin to Ed Schmultz and James Cannon Files, Box 5, Folder Busing, June 21, 1976, GRFPL, p. 1; Letter from Diane Ravitch to Robert Goldwin, June 15, 1976, White House Special Files, James Cannon Files, Box 5, Folder Busing, June 21, 1976, GRFPL.

101. "Rosy Reporting," *Newsweek*, November 29, 1976, p. 51.

102. R. U. Denenberg and Caroline Rand Herron, "Checking Up on Desegregation," *New York Times*, October 24, 1976, p. E4.

103. J. Harvie Wilkinson, *From Brown to Bakke: The Supreme Court and School Integration, 1954–1978* (New York: Oxford University Press, 1979), p. 215. Raymond Wolters, *The Burden of Brown: Thirty Years of School Desegregation* (Knoxville, TN: University of Tennessee Press, 1979), p. 273, similarly concluded that in four of the five original *Brown v. Board of Education* school districts, desegregation had been a "failure." Ford, *A Time to Heal*, p. 412 (Ford does not mention education policy or busing in this memoir). Ford voted for the Civil Rights Act of 1964 yet spoke against busing at the Republican National Convention that year; see Greene, *The Presidency of Gerald R. Ford*, p. 88; A. James Reichley, *Conservatives in an Age of Change: The Nixon and Ford Administrations* (Washington, D.C.: The Brookings Institute, 1981), p. 279. According to a July 8, 1976, Harris Survey, 51 percent of African Americans opposed "busing children to schools outside your neighborhood to achieve racial integration"; see "Prepared Statement by Senator Bennett Johnston, The Neighborhood Schools Act," in *School Busing*, Vol. 2, ed. Douglas, p. 435; Interview of William Coleman by James Reichley, December 19, 1977, White House Special Files, A. James Reichley Files, Box 1, Folder Domestic Policy—William Coleman, GRFPL, p. 8.

104. Reichley, *Conservatives in an Age of Change*, p. 279.

105. On June 7, 1972, a group of black plaintiffs sued the City of Atlanta to require nine school systems to compose a desegregation plan for that city's schools; see "Griffin B. Bell: Hearings before the Committee of the Judiciary," January 11, 12, 13, 14, 17, 18, 19, 1977, U.S. Senate, 95th Cong., 1st sess. (Washington, D.C.: U.S. Government Printing Office, 1977), p. 406; Carter quoted in letter from Senator Joseph Biden, Senator William Roth, and Rep. Thomas Evans to President Carter, May 16, 1978, White House Central Files, Subject file Human Rights, Box HU-8, JCPL.

106. "Griffin B. Bell: Hearings," p. 406.

107. Memorandum from Kurt Schmoke to Stuart Eizenstat, February 18, 1977, Staff Office File, Domestic Policy Staff—Eizenstat, Box 183, Folder Desegregation, JCPL, pp. 1–2.

108. Letter from Joseph Califano to Warren Magnuson, May 27, 1977, Staff Office File Counsel—McKenna, Box 120, Folder Byrd Amendment 5/77–2/78 [O/A 6195], JCPL, pp. 1–2.

109. Memorandum for Margaret McKenna, June 16, 1977, Staff Office File, Counsel—McKenna, Box 120, Folder Byrd Amendment 5/77–2/78 [O/A 6195], JCPL, p. 1; Memorandum from John Harmon to Douglas Huron, June 7, 1977, Staff Office File, Counsel—McKenna, Box 120, Folder Byrd Amendment 5/77–2/78 [O/A 6195], JCPL, pp. 1, 3, 5; Memorandum from Drew Days to Douglas Huron, May 31, 1977, Staff Office Files, Counsel—McKenna, Box 120, Folder Byrd Amendment 5/77–2/78 [O/A 6195], JCPL, p. 17; Memorandum from Kurt Schmoke to Stuart Eizenstat, June 14, 1977, Staff Office File, Domestic Policy Staff—Eizenstat, Box 183, Folder Desegregation, JCPL, pp. 1–2.

110. David Rosenbaum, "New Carter Policy May Require Busing to Get School Funds," *New York Times*, June 7, 1977, pp. A1, A27.

111. Schmoke to Eizenstat, June 14, 1977, JCPL, pp. 1–2; Memorandum from Eizenstat, June 14, 1977, Staff Office File, Domestic Policy Staff—Eizenstat, Box 183, Folder Desegregation, JCPL, pp. 1–2.

112. Memorandum from Frank Moore, June 14, 1977, White House Central Files, Subject file Human Rights, Box HU-8, Folder HU 1-1 1/20/77–6/30/77, JCPL, pp. 1–2.

113. David Rosenbaum, "House Votes to Balk Carter Busing Policy," *New York Times*, June 17, 1977, pp. A1, D12; Memorandum from John Harmon to Margaret McKenna, July 15, 1977, Staff File, Counsel—McKenna, Box 120, Folder Byrd Amendment 5/77–2/78 [O/A 6195], JCPL, p. 1.

114. Letter from Arthur Flemming, Stephen Horn, Frankie Freeman, Manuel Ruiz, and Murray Saltzman to the President, July 11, 1977, White House Central Files, Subject file Human Rights, Box HU-8, Folder HU 1-1 7/1/77–12/31/77, JCPL, pp. 1–2.

115. Memorandum from Griffin Bell to the President, July 13, 1977, Staff Office Files, Domestic Policy Staff—Eizenstat, Box 183, JCPL, pp. 1–2.

116. Memorandum from Stuart Eizenstat to the President, July 19, 1977, Staff Office Files, Domestic Policy Staff—Eizenstat, Box 183, Folder Desegregation, JCPL, p. 2; Letter from Clarence Mitchell to the President, June 21, 1977, Staff Office Files, Counsel—McKenna, Box 183, JCPL, Folder Desegregation, JCPL, p. 2; Letter from Stuart Eizenstat to U.S. Commission on Civil Rights, October 3, 1977, White House Central Files, Subject file Federal Aid, Box FA-9, Folder FA 3 8/1/77–11/21/77, JCPL.

117. Jimmy Carter, "Labor-HEW Continuing Appropriations Bill," December 9, 1977, *Public Papers of the Presidents of the United States: Jimmy Carter,* Book 2, *1977* (Washington, D.C.: U.S. Government Printing Office, 1978), pp. 2087–88.

118. "Annual Report of the Executive Director," January 8, 1979, NAACP Part VI A—Administrative File, Container 17, National Association for the Advancement of Colored People Papers, Library of Congress, Washington, D.C., p. 38; Steven Roberts, "School Busing Amendment Poses Legal Problem for White House," *New York Times,* February 8, 1978, p. B2; Eliot Lichtman, "The Eagleton-Biden Amendment," n.d., Shirley Hufstedler File, Box 9, Folder FY 1981 Appropriations Hearings, JCPL, pp. 1–2.

119. "Brown v. Califano," *Federal Supplement,* July 18, 1978, Staff Office Files, Counsel—Cutler, Box 54, Folder [Busing] 7/78–12/80, JCPL, p. 838; "The Eagleton-Biden Amendment," n.d., JCPL, pp. 1, 4.

120. "Chronology of Action on Education," *Congress and the Nation,* Vol. 5, *1977–1980* (Washington, D.C.: Congressional Quarterly, 1981), p. 795; "A Civil Rights Voting Record for the Ninety-Sixth Congress, January 1979–October 1980," n.d., Staff Office Files, Domestic Policy Staff—White, Box 1, Folder Anti-Busing Amendment, JCPL, p. 1; Memorandum from Elizabeth Abramowitz and Elizabeth Zeidman, July 5, 1979, White House Central Files, Subject file Human Rights, Box HU-8, Folder HU 1-1 7/1/77–12/31/77, JCPL, p. 2.

121. Martin Tolchin, "Battle on Rights Issues Blocks Congress Adjournment," *New York Times,* December 4, 1980, p. A1; Memorandum from Frank White to Stuart Eizenstat, November 14, 1980; Staff Office Files, Domestic Policy Staff—White, Box 1, Folder Anti-Busing Amendment, JCPL; White to Eizenstat, November 14, 1980; Memorandum from Louis Martin to the President, November 18, 1980, Staff Office Files, Domestic Policy Staff—White, Box 1, Folder Anti-Busing Amendment, JCPL.

122. Jimmy Carter, "Appropriations Bill for the Departments of State, Justice, Commerce, the Judiciary, and Related Agencies," December 13, 1980, *Public Papers of the Presidents of the United States: Jimmy Carter,* Book 3, *1980–81* (Washington, D.C.: U.S. Government Printing Office, 1982), p. 2809; Letter from Louis Martin to A. C. Sutton, December 15, 1980, White House Central Files, Subject file Human Rights, Box HU-8, Folder HU 1-1 1/1/80–1/20/81, JCPL.

123. Betty Glad, *Jimmy Carter* (New York: Norton, 1980), p. 84; John Dumbrell, *The Carter Presidency: A Re-evaluation* (New York: Manchester University Press, 1993), p. 87.

124. Glad, p. 84; Dumbrell, p. 87.

125. The NAACP, American Civil Liberties Union, and Congress of Racial Equality appealed the Atlanta Plan. NAACP chief counsel Nathaniel Jones wrote in 1973 that "Press reports continue to characterize the compromise plan as an 'NAACP plan.' Such is not the case. Branch officials who participated in the formulation of that plan have been removed from office for violation of Association policy"; see "Statement of Nathaniel Jones in re Court of Appeals Decision on Atlanta's Compromise School Desegregation Plan," August 22, 1973, NAACP Part VI A—Administrative File, Container 35, NAACPP, pp. 1–2.

126. Schmoke to Eizenstat, February 18, 1977, JCPL, pp. 1–2.

127. "Cabinet Meeting Minutes," March 28, 1977, Vertical Files—Buergenthal, Thomas, through Cabinet Meeting Minutes, 10/3/77–2/7/78, no box, Folder Cabinet Meeting Minutes, 1/24/77–5/23/77, JCPL, p. 2; David Rosenbaum, "New Carter Policy May Require Busing to Get School Funds," *New York Times,* June 7, 1977, p. A27; Memorandum from Stuart Eizenstat and Louis Martin to the President, February 14, 1979, White House Central Files, Subject file Human Rights, Box HU-8, Folder HU 1-1 1/1/79–12/31/79, JCPL.

128. Joseph Califano, *Governing America* (New York: Simon and Schuster, 1981), p. 230; telephone interview of Griffin Bell by author, January 14, 1998; Exit Interview of Elizabeth Abramowitz, August 23, 1979, JCPL, p. 18.

129. Untitled, May 17, 1979, White House Central Files, Subject file Human Rights, Box HU-8, Folder HU 1-1 1/1/79–12/31/79, JCPL; Exit Interview of Abramowitz, JCPL, p. 18; "The Eagleton-Biden Amendment," JCPL, p. 1; telephone interview of Bell by author, January 14, 1998; telephone interview of Hufstedler by author, January 28, 1998.

130. Jimmy Carter, "Interview with Reporters from KNBC-TV," September 23, 1980, *Public Papers of the Presidents of the United States—Jimmy Carter,* Book 2, *1980–81* (Washington, D.C.: U.S. Government Printing Office, 1982), pp. 1890–91.

131. Carter would boast of a success rate on Capitol Hill of "seventy-five percent in 1977, seventy-eight percent in 1978, seventy-seven percent in 1979, and seventy-five percent in 1980"; see Carter, *Keeping Faith,* p. 88. Carter did not mention busing in this memoir; Memorandum from Frank White and Donald Donavan to the President, November 17, 1980, Staff Office File, Domestic Policy Staff—White, Box 1, Folder Anti-Busing Amendment, JCPL, p. 1.

## Chapter 3: Nonpublic School Aid, 1965–81

1. Lyndon Johnson, *Vantage Point: Perspectives on the Presidency* (New York: Holt, Rinehart, and Winston, 1971), p. 206; Lawrence McAndrews, "Unanswered Prayers: Church, State, and School in the Nixon Era," *U.S. Catholic Historian* (Fall 1995): 82; Lawrence McAndrews, *Broken Ground: John F. Kennedy and the Politics of Education* (New York: Garland, 1991), p. 125.

2. "Elementary Education Act Expanded," *Congressional Quarterly Almanac,* 89th Cong., 2nd sess., 1966 (Washington, D.C., 1967), pp. 291–93; McAndrews, *Broken Ground,* pp. 173–74.

3. "Elementary and Secondary Education Act Expanded," p. 295; Memorandum from Henry Wilson to Charles Roche, March 18, 1966, Henry Wilson Files, Box 13, Folder Wil-

son: Education, LBJPL, p. 1; Memorandum from Ralph Huitt to Douglass Cater and Henry Wilson, June 22, 1966, Henry Wilson Files, Box 13, Folder Education, LBJPL.

4. Memorandum from Samuel Halperin to Douglass Cater, April 13, 1966, Henry Wilson Files, Box 13, Folder Education, LBJPL; Memorandum from Harold Howe to Douglass Cater, January 23, 1967, White House Central Files, Box 246, Folder FG 165-4 9/1/65–1/24/67, LBJPL; "Elementary Education Act Expanded," p. 286.

5. "GOP Block Grant Proposal Aroused Pressure Groups," *Congressional Quarterly Almanac,* 1967 (Washington, D.C., 1968), p. 612; Albert Koob, "Where Is the ESEA Leading Catholic Education?" *Catholic School Journal* (March 1967): 48; "Educators Speak Out against Substitute to ESEA," United Press International Press Release, Irving Sprague Files, Box 1, Folder Sprague: Elementary and Secondary Education, LBJPL, p. 2.

6. Memorandum from Charles Roche to William Consedine, April 24, 1967, Irving Sprague Files, Box 1, Folder Elementary and Secondary Education, LBJPL; Memorandum from Charles Roche to Henry Wilson, May 3, 1967, Irving Sprague Files, Box 1, Folder Elementary and Secondary Education, LBJPL, p. 1; Letter from Robert Kintner to the President, May 19, 1967, White House Central Files, Box 6, Folder FA 2 4/16/67–6/24/67, LBJPL.

7. "Shortchanging Nonpublic School Pupils," *School and Society,* January 6, 1968, p. 25.

8. McAndrews, *Broken Ground,* p. 173; McAndrews, "Unanswered Prayers," p. 84; "NEA Support for Federal Aid," *School and Society,* October 12, 1968, p. 328; Interview of Sanders by Frantz, p. 37; "Trouble in the Classroom," *Time,* June 2, 1967, p. 56; Frank Largent and William May, "Swim'st Thou in Wealth," *American Education,* June 1967, p. 12.

9. "Statement of Very Rev. Msgr. James C. Donahue, Ph.D., Director, Development of Education, U.S. Catholic Conference, before the Subcommittee on Education, Committee on Labor and Public Welfare, U.S. Senate," August 10, 1967, United States Catholic Conference Departmental Committees: Education, 1967–70, Box 57, United States Catholic Conference Papers, Washington, D.C., p. 1. The diocesan school superintendents would reject a plan proposed by Msgr. Donahue to make such a commitment the schools' top priority; see Gerald Fogerty, "Catholic Schools: Their Past and Future," *America,* September 28, 1968, p. 254. "NEA Support for Federal Aid," October 12, 1968, p. 328.

10. McAndrews, "Unanswered Prayers," p. 82; "Preliminary Report of Legislative Policy Committee, Division of Elementary and Secondary Education, United States Catholic Conference," January 13, 1969, United States Catholic Conference Departmental Committees, Education, 1967–70, Box 57, USCCP, pp. 1–3.

11. "The Greeley-Rossi Report on Catholic Schools," *America,* August 6, 1966, p. 128; "Minutes, Committee on Education, United States Catholic Conference," December 14–15, 1969, Box 36, Folder Church: Church and State, Federal Aid to Education, 1968–69, USCCP.

12. "Preliminary Report of Legislative Policy Committee," USCCP, p. 5.

13. Memorandum from John Evans to the President, May 4, 1971, President's Office Files, Box 85, Folder Memoranda for the President, 5/2/71–8/15/71, RMNPP, p. 2; "Selected Quotations from President Nixon's Address of October 20, 1968, on Education," White House Central Files, Subject file Education, Box 1, Folder EX ED Beginning to 5/31/69, RMNPP, p. 1.

14. "A Fiscal Crisis," *Time,* March 28, 1969, p. 42; Murray Friedman and Peter Binzen, "Politics and Parochiaid," *New Republic,* January 23, 1971, p. 13.

15. Virgil Blum, "Tax Funds for Nonpublic Education," *America,* September 27, 1969, p. 227; "Crisis Hits Catholic Schools," p. 34.

16. John Ehrlichman Notes, January 9, 1970, White House Central Files, Subject file John Ehrlichman, Box 3, Folder Notes of Meetings with the President, 1/1/70–6/30/70, RMNPP, p. 1; John Ehrlichman Notes, February 2, 1970, White House Special Files, John Ehrlichman File, Box 3, Folder Notes of Meeting with the President, 1/1/70–6/30/70, RMNPP; Memorandum from Chester Finn to William Safire, February 3, 1970, White House Central Files, Subject file Education, Box 1, Folder EX ED 2/20/70–3/31/70, RMNPP; Memorandum from Charles Colson to the President, February 20, 1970, President's Office Files, Box 80, Folder Memoranda for the President, 1/4/70–5/31/70, RMNPP.

17. Letter from Richard Nixon to Bishop Joseph Bernardin, March 3, 1970, Box 36, Folder USCC: Folder Church: Church and State: Federal Aid to Education 1970, January–June, USCCP; Memorandum from Charles Colson to the President, March 19, 1970, President's Office Files, Box 80, Folder Memoranda for the President, 1/4/70–5/31/70, RMNPP.

18. "The Jencks Tuition Voucher Plan," *America,* June 20, 1970, pp. 644–45; Memorandum from James Robinson to Bishop Joseph Bernardin, February 11, 1971, Box 36, Folder USCC: Church: Church and State: Federal Aid to Education 1971 January–April, USCCP, pp. 1–2; Carl Megel, "Voucher Plan Opposition Growing," November 4, 1970, American Federation of Teachers Office of the President, Box 32, Folder 32-22, Legislative Department, Vol. 2, 1969–70, AFTP; Memorandum from John Ehrlichman to George Schultz and Caspar Weinberger, December 19, 1970, White House Central Files, Subject file Confidential Files, Box 11, Folder [CF] FA 3 Federal Aid Education (1969–70), RMNPP.

19. Leo Pfeffer, "The Parochiaid Decision," *Today's Education/NEA Journal,* September 1971, p. 64; Daniel Moskowitz, "Public Funds and Private Schools," *PTA Magazine* 68 (May 1974): 19; David Kucharsky, "Parochiaid Disallowed," *Christianity Today,* July 16, 1971, p. 34.

20. William Consedine, "The School Aid Decision: Preliminary Analysis," July 6, 1971, Box 57, Folder USCC: Departmental Committees: Education, USCCP, p. 3; Memorandum from James Robinson to Bishop Joseph Bernardin, July 15, 1971, Box 36, Folder USCC: Church: Church and State: Federal Aid to Education 1971, July–December, USCCP, p. 1; "A Summary Report of the Steering Committee Authorized at the Washington Conference on Nonpublic Schools," July 8, 1971, Box 57, USCC: Departmental Committees: Education, 1971, USCCP, pp. 1–3; Letter from Bishop Joseph Bernardin and Bishop William McManus to Joseph Cardinal Dearden, August 26, 1971, Box 36, Folder USCC: Church: Church and State, 1971, July–December, USCCP, p. 7.

21. Memorandum from James Robinson to Bishop Joseph Bernadin, August 4, 1971, Box 36, Folder USCC: Church: Church and State, 1971, July–December, USCCP; "Parochiaid: Drawing the Lines," *Christianity Today,* September 10, 1971, p. 43.

22. Memorandum from Bishop Joseph Bernardin and Bishop William McManus to Ad Hoc Committee on School Aid, n.d., Box 36, Folder Church: Church and State: Federal Aid to Education, USCCP, pp. 1–3; John Swomley, "Church, State, and Mr. Nixon," *Nation,* September 11, 1972, p. 168.

23. Memorandum from Lew Engman to the President, March 6, 1972, President's Office Files, Box 88, Folder Memoranda for the President, 12/17/71–2/20/72, RMNPP, pp. 1–2; Memorandum from Lew Engman to George Schultz, Peter Flanigan, and Kenneth Cole, March 29, 1972, White House Central Files, Subject file Conference Files, 1969–74, Box 11, Folder [CF] FA 3 Federal Aid—Education [1965–70], RMNPP; "Nixon: Verbal Fence-Mending," *National Review,* April 26, 1972, p. 442.

24. "Citizens' Coalition Formed to Seek Enactment of Tax Credit Legislation," CREDIT Press Release, March 27, 1972, Box 36, Folder USCC: Church: Church and State: Federal Aid to Education 1972, USCCP; Thomas Mullancy, "Tax Credits and Parochial Schools," *Commonweal*, April 27, 1973, p. 185.

25. Stanley MacFarland, "Public Aid to Nonpublic Education: An Overview of Federal Activities," February 13, 1973, American Federation of Teachers Office of the President, Box 1, Folder 1-9, Nonpublic School Tax Credit, 1972–73 [3 of 3], AFTP, p. 3; "Statement by Mr. John J. Murray, Director, Department of Nonpublic School Teachers, AFL-CIO, on H.R. 16141 before the Committee on Ways and Means, United States House of Representatives, Ninety-Second Congress, Second Session," September 6, 1972 (Washington, D.C.: U.S. Government Printing Office, 1972), p. 4; Memorandum from Robert Lynch to Most Rev. Archbishops and Bishops et al., October 3, 1972, Box 36, Folder USCC: Church: Church and State: Federal Aid to Education 1972, USCCP; "Intensive Effort Essential," CREDIT Newsletter, October 2, 1972, Box 36, Folder USCC: Church: Church and State: Federal Aid to Education, 1972, USCCP.

26. Memorandum from Lew Engman to the President, December 13, 1972, President's Office Files, Box 90, Folder Memoranda for the President, 9/24/72–1/29/73, RMNPP, p. 2; MacFarland, "Public Aid to Nonpublic Education"; "Panel Adopts Agenda for Tax Reform," *New York Times*, May 1, 1974, p. A12.

27. John Mathews, "Parochial School Funding Hit," *Washington Star News*, March 6, 1974, p. F12.

28. Carl Megel, "Department of Legislation Report," n.d., American Federation of Teachers Office of the President, Box 38, Folder 38-2, Legislative Department, 1973, AFTP, p. 2.

29. Donald Frey, "Parochiaid: Economic Tales and Realities," *Christian Century*, March 28, 1973, p. 368.

30. Friedman and Binzen, "Politics and Parochiaid," p. 13; Memorandum from Chester Finn to Robert Finch, July 2, 1969, White House Central Files, Subject file Education, Box 1, Folder EX ED 6/1/69–8/31/69, RMNPP; Mullaney, p. 185; Adam Wallinsky, "Aid to Parochial Schools," *New Republic*, October 7, 1972, p. 19; "Parochiaid: Drawing the Lines," p. 43.

31. "Supplementary Statement by S. P. Marland, Jr., Nominee, U.S. Commissioner of Education," November 19, 1970, American Federation of Teachers Office of the President, Box 3, Folder Education Department—Marland, AFTP, p. 7; Memorandum from Patrick Buchanan to John Ehrlichman, H. R. Haldeman, and Charles Colson, October 25, 1971, White House Central Files, Subject file Confidential Files, Box 26, Folder [CF] FG 273 President's Commission on School Finance [1971–74], RMNPP, p. 1; Memorandum from James Robinson to Bishop Joseph Bernardin, May 12, 1972, Box 36, Folder USCC Church: Church and State: Federal Aid to Education, USCCP, p. 2; "Summary of School Finance Paper on Aid to Nonpublic Schools," March 1972, White House Special Files, William Kendall Files, Box 9, Folder Mathews, David [2], GRFPL, p. 2.

32. "Nixon: Verbal Fence-Mending," p. 442.

33. Letter from David Selden to Kenneth Young, February 4, 1972, American Federation of Teachers Office of the President, Box 24, Folder 24-25, Legislative Department, AFL-CIO, 1976–77, AFTP; telephone interview of Weinberger by author, November 4, 1997; Minutes, USCC Committee on Education, November 2, 1971, Box 58, Folder Departmental Committees: Education 1970–73, USCCP, p. 2.

34. Memorandum from William Consedine et al. to Bishop Joseph Bernardin, February 27, 1970, Box 26, Folder USCC Church: Church and State: Federal Aid to Education, 1970 January–June, USCCP; Memorandum from Rev. Thomas Kelly to Bishop Rausch, May 17, 1972, Box 36, Folder USCC Church: Church and State: Federal Aid to Education, 1972, USCCP; "Has the Church Lost Its Soul?" *Newsweek,* October 4, 1971, p. 81.

35. "Report of the Task Force on Education," January 3, 1969, White House Central Files, Subject file Education, Box 8, Folder FG 23-6 Office of Education, RMNPP, p. 10; Bert Shamas, "Sees No U.S. Money for Parochial Schools," *New York Daily News,* December 13, 1971, p. A1; "Summary of HEW School Finance Task Force Paper on Aid to Nonpublic Schools," pp. 1–2.

36. MacFarland, "Public Aid to Nonpublic Education," pp. 2, 6, 7; Memorandum from Robert Lynch to State Catholic Conference Directors, March 15, 1973, Box 36, Folder USCC: Church: Church and State: Federal Aid to Education 1973–74, USCCP, p. 2.

37. "Has the Church Lost Its Soul?" p. 80.

38. "Hearings before the Committee on Ways and Means, House of Representatives, Ninety-Second Congress, Second Session, on H.R. 16141, Relating to Aid to Primary and Secondary Education in the Form of Tax Credits and/or Reductions," September 5, 1972 (Washington, D.C.: U.S. Government Printing Office, 1972), pp. 585–91. Other groups besides the USCC that presented similar positions at the hearings included the Advisory Committee on the Financial Crisis of the Catholic Schools in Philadelphia, Citizens for Educational Freedom, the International Organization of Catholic Alumnae, the National Catholic Education Association, and the National Council of Catholic Laity.

39. S. Francis Overlan, "Why Are Parochial Schools Closing?" *America,* September 14, 1974, pp. 111–13.

40. "The Greeley-Rossi Report on Catholic Schools," *America,* August 6, 1966, p. 128; Swomley, "Church, State, and Mr. Nixon," pp. 169–70; Ernest Bartell, "Good News and Bad for Catholic Schools," *America,* April 1, 1972, pp. 343–45; "Testimony of the American Federation of Teachers, AFL-CIO, before the Senate Committee on Finance Regarding Tax Credits for Education Expenses," n.d., American Federation of Teachers Office of the President, Box 13, Folder 13-5 Tuition Tax Credit, Legislation, 1978, AFTP; Engman to the President, March 6, 1972, p. 2.

41. "Hearings before the Committee on Ways and Means, House of Representatives, Ninety-Second Congress, Second Session, on H.R. 16141, Relating to Aid to Primary and Secondary Education in the Form of Tax Credits and/or Reductions," September 5, 1972, pp. 585–91.

42. Louis Gary and K. S. Cole, "The Politics of Aid and a Proposal for Reform," *Saturday Review,* July 22, 1972, p. 32; Kelly to Rausch, May 17, 1972, USCCP.

43. Memorandum from David Lissy to Roger Semerad, October 29, 1974, White House Central Files, Subject file Education, Box 6, Folder FA 3 Education 8/9/74–8/26/74, GRFPL, pp. 1–2; Memorandum from Roger Semerad to Jerry Jones, February 26, 1975, White House Central Files, Subject file Education, Box 6, Folder ED 2/1/75–4/10/75, GRFPL, pp. 1–2.

44. "Report of the Committee on Education," August 15, 1975, ED 89-67, Box 10, Folder 7-30 Agenda Committee on Education, 12/14–15/69, USCCP, p. 2; Lissy to Semerad, GRFPL, p. 2; Memorandum from Arthur Quern to James Cannon through James Cavanaugh, August 6, 1975, White House Special Files, David Lissy Files, Box 10, Folder Nonpublic Schools [2], GRFPL, p. 1.

45. Letter from John Cardinal Krol to Bishop Rausch, May 1975, Church: Church and State: Federal Aid to Education, Box 36, Folder Church: Church and State: Federal Aid to Education, 1975, USCCP, pp. 1–2; "Report of the Committee on Education," USCCP, p. 1.

46. Memorandum from H. Reed Saunders to Terrel Bell, July 14, 1975, David Lissy Files, Box 10, Folder Nonpublic Schools [2], GRFPL, p. 1; Memorandum from Arthur Quern to James Cannon through James Cavanaugh, July 30, 1975, White House Special Files, David Lissy Files, Box 10, Folder Nonpublic Schools [2], GRFPL, p. 2.

47. Gerald Ford, "The President's News Conference of October 9, 1974," *Public Papers of the Presidents of the United States: Gerald R. Ford, 1974* (Washington, D.C.: U.S. Government Printing Office, 1975), pp. 251–52.

48. Msgr. Olin Murdick, "A Plan of Action for Catholic School Aid," April 21, 1976, ED 89-77, Box 7, Folder "Committee on Education: Agenda," June 1976, USCCP, p. 2; Memorandum from Thomas Melady to Myron Kuropas, June 25, 1976, White House Special Files, Michael Duval Files, Box 27, Folder Republican Party Platform—Catholic Issues, GRFPL, pp. 1–2; Letter from Henry Cashen to Mike Duval, July 14, 1976, White House Special Files, Michael Duval Files, Box 27, Folder Republican Party Platform—Catholic Issues, GRFPL, p. 2.

49. Cashen to Duval, GRFPL, p. 2; "Issue: Aid to Nonpublic Schools," September 3, 1976, White House Special Files, James Cannon Files, Box 1, Folder Abortion, Meeting with Catholic Bishops, GRFPL; Cashen to Duval, pp. 1–2.

50. "Issue: Aid to Nonpublic Schools"; Cashen to Duval, GRFPL, p. 1.

51. Cashen to Duval, GRFPL, p. 1; "Issue: Aid to Nonpublic Schools," pp. 1–2.

52. Memorandum from Richard Duffy to Catholic Schools Superintendents, Diocesan Grant Programs Coordinators, and State Catholic Conference Directors of Education, August 13, 1975, Box 66, Folder Departmental Committees: Education: Federal Assistance Programs 1975–79, USCCP, pp. 1–2.

53. Saunders to Bell, GRFPL, p. 2; Quern to Cannon through Cavanaugh; "Committee on Education," January 11, 1977, USCC Departmental Committees: Education 1974–79, Box 59, Folder USCC Departmental Committees: Education 1977, USCCP, p. 1.

54. "Quality Education," n.d., James Cannon Files, Box 37, Folder Meeting—SOTU Coordinating Group, GRFPL, p. 8.

55. Murdick, "A Plan of Action for Catholic School Aid," p. 1; Memorandum from Caspar Weinberger to the President, May 14, 1975, James Cannon Files, Box 12, Folder Busing, (1), GRFPL, p. 3.

56. Murdick, "A Plan of Action for Catholic School Aid," p. 1.

57. Ibid., p. 1; "Committee on Education Meeting," June 27–30, 1976, USCC Departmental Committees: Education 1974–70, Box 59, Folder USCC Departmental Committees: Education, 1976 June–December, USCCP, p. 9.

58. Paula DiPerna, "Relief for Which Class?" *Nation,* August 19–26, 1978, 143; "Discrediting Tax Credits," *America,* April 29, 1978, p. 334.

59. *Congress and the Nation, 1977–1980* (Washington, D.C.: Congressional Quarterly, 1981), vol. 5, p. 245; "Discrediting Tax Credits," p. 335.

60. From 1964 to 1984, 40 percent of Catholic high schools and 27 percent of Catholic grade schools would close. See Jay Dolan, *The American Catholic Experience* (New York: Doubleday, 1985), p. 442.

61. "Saving Diversity by Distinctions," *America,* February 5, 1977, p. 93; "The Commit-

ment to Nonpublic Schools," *America*, April 9, 1977, p. 311; Mary Hanna, *Catholics and American Politics* (Cambridge: Harvard University Press, 1979), p. 128.

62. "A Parochial Decision," *Newsweek*, July 4, 1977, p. 50.

63. "School Tax Credits?" *Newsweek*, December 26, 1977, p. 76; "Private Schools," December 12, 1977, Staff Files, Domestic Policy Staff: Eizenstat, Box 195, Folder Education-ESEA [CF, OA, 22], JCPL, p. 4; Memorandum from Olin Murdick to Thomas Kelly, July 8, 1977, Box 37, Folder USCC: Church: Church and State: Federal Aid to Education, Tuition Tax Credits, 1973–78, USCCP; Memorandum from James Robinson to Thomas Kelly, July 13, 1977, Box 37, Folder Church: Church and State: Federal Aid to Education, Tax Credits, 1973–78, USCCP, pp. 1–2.

64. "Federal Tuition Tax Credit Legislation," October 28, 1977, Box 59, Folder Departmental Committees: Education, 1974–79, USCCP, p. 4; "School Tax Credits?" p. 76; "Tuition Tax Break May Be Unstoppable," *Washington Post*, November 4, 1977, p. B6; Letter from Msgr. Francis Barrett to Jimmy Carter, November 11, 1977, White House Central Files, Subject file Education, Box ED-3, Folder ED 7/77–12/31/77, JCPL; Letter from Rev. Patrick Farrell to "Dear Colleague," December 9, 1977, Box 37, Folder USCC Church: Church and State: Federal Aid to Education, 1973–78, USCCP, p. 1.

65. "Califano Says Parents Must Pay Private School Tuition without Federal Help," January 17, 1978, ED 89-69, Box 4, Folder Notes for Talks, USCCP; Letter from D. Patrick Moynihan to Archbishop John Quinn, February 3, 1978, Box 37, Folder USCC: Church: Church and State: Federal Aid to Education: Tax Credits, 1979, USCCP.

66. "Briefing by Califano," White House Staff Files, Box 17, Folder Education, JCPP, JCPL, pp. 9, 11, 12.

67. Telegram from J. Alan Davitt to the President, February 8, 1978, White House Central Files, Subject file Federal Aid, Box FA 12, Folder FA 3 1/1/78–7/31/78, JCPL; Memorandum from Joseph Califano to the President, February 14, 1978, White House Central Files, Subject file Federal Aid, Box FA 10, Folder FA 3 1/1/78–2/28/78, JCPL, p. 14.

68. "Shanker Raps Senate Panel on Tuition Tax Credits," February 24, 1978, White House Central Files, Subject file Federal Aid, Box FA 12, Folder FA 3 1/1/78–7/31/78, JCPL, p. 30; Memorandum from James McIntyre and Stuart Eizenstat to the President, February 24, 1978, White House Central Files, Subject file Education, Box FA 10, Folder FA 3 1/1/78–2/28/78, JCPL, p. 10.

69. "To the Congress of the United States," February 28, 1978, White House Central Files, Subject file Federal Aid, Box FA-10, Folder FA 3 1/1/78–2/28/78, JCPL, pp. 10–11.

70. Memorandum from James Robinson to Thomas Kelly, March 6, 1978, Box 37, Folder USCC Church: Church and State: Federal Aid to Education: Tax Credits 1973–78, USCCP; Telegram from D. Patrick Moynihan to Quinn, March 20, 1978, Box 37, Folder USCC Church: Church and State: Federal Aid to Education: Tax Credits, 1973–78, USCCP.

71. Ron Sarro, "Tuition Aid Backers Face an End Run," *Washington Star*, March 19, 1978, pp. A1, A10; Joseph Califano, *Governing America* (New York: Simon and Schuster, 1981), p. 305.

72. Memorandum from John Harmon to Griffin Bell, March 15, 1978, Shirley Hufstedler Collection, Box 7, Folder Tuition Tax Credit [1], JCPL, pp. 1–2.

73. Memorandum from Kelly to Members of the National Council of Catholic Bishops/United States Catholic Conference, April 13, 1978, Box 37, Folder USCC Church: Church and State: Federal Aid to Education: Tuition Tax Credits, 1979, USCCP; "Presi-

dential News Conference before the National Society of Newspaper Editors," April 11, 1978, "Weekly Compilation of Presidential Documents," Box 37, Folder USCC Church: Church and State: Federal Aid to Education: Tuition Tax Credits, 1973–78, USCCP, p. 730; Letter from Elizabeth Abramowitz to Rev. John Meyers, May 5, 1978, White House Central Files, Subject file Education, Box ED-3, Folder Ed 1/1/78–9/30/78, JCPL.

74. "Proposal for Tuition Tax Credit Campaign," February 13, 1979, Box 37, Folder USCC Church: Church and State: Federal Aid to Education: Tuition Tax Credits 1979, USCCP, p. 3; Marjorie Hunter, "House Approves Credit for Tuition by a 237–158 Vote," *New York Times,* June 2, 1978, pp. A1, B17; "Meeting with Senator Daniel P. Moynihan," June 6, 1978, Presidential Diary Collection, Box PD-32, Folder 6/7/78 Backup Material, JCPL, p. 3.

75. Letter from D. Patrick Moynihan to Archbishop John Quinn, June 6, 1978, Box 37, Folder USCC Church: Church and State: Federal Aid to Education: Tax Credits 1973–78, USCCP; "Meeting with Senator Daniel P. Moynihan," pp. 4–5.

76. Letter from Stuart Eizenstat to Bishop James Hickey, June 19, 1978, White House Central Files, Subject file Education, Box ED-2, Folder ED 6/1/78–7/31/78, JCPL; Memorandum from Thomas Kelly to Members of the NCCB, July 19, 1978, Box 37, Folder USCC Church: Church and State, Federal Aid to Education: Tax Credits, 1973–78, USCCP; Memorandum from James Robinson to Terence Cardinal Cooke, July 24, 1978, Box 37, Folder USCC: Church: Church and State, Federal Aid to Education: Tax Credits, 1973–78, USCCP; DiPerna, "Relief for Which Class?" p. 143.

77. "Telephone Call from [John Cardinal] Krol" and handwritten notes, August 2, 1978, Box 37, Folder USCC Church: Church and State, Federal Aid to Education: Tax Credits, 1973–78, USCCP; "Meeting with Senator Kaneaster Hodges," August 7, 1978, White House Central Files, Subject file Education, Box ED-2, Folder ED 8/1/78–12/31/78, JCPL; Memorandum from Thomas Kelly to Most Rev. Archbishops, August 18, 1978, Box 37, Folder USCC Church: Church and State, Federal Aid to Education: Tax Credits, 1973–78, USCCP; "Presidential News Conference," August 17, 1978, "Weekly Compilation of Presidential Documents," Box 37, Folder USCC Church: Church and State, Federal Aid to Education: Tax Credits, 1973–78, USCCP, p. 1444.

78. "Congressional Leadership Breakfast," September 25, 1978, Presidential Diary, Box PD 39, Folder 9/26/78 Backup Material, JCPL, p. 3; Califano, *Governing America,* p. 301.

79. Letter from Thomas Kelly to "Dear Congressman," October 2, 1978, Box 37, Folder USCC Church: Church and State, Federal Aid to Education: Tax Credits, 1973–78, USCCP.

80. "Proposal for Tuition Tax Credit Campaign," February 13–15, 1979, USCCP, p. 5.

81. Handwritten notes, n.d., ED 89-69, Box 4, Folder Notes for Talks, USCCP; "Major Arguments against Tuition Tax Credits by President Carter," Box 37, Folder USCC: Church: Church and State: Federal Aid to Education, Tuition Tax Credits, 1979, USCCP, pp. 1–4.

82. Memorandum from John Harmon to Griffin Bell, March 30, 1980, Shirley Hufstedler Collection, Box 7, Folder Tuition Tax Credit [1], JCPL, pp. 2–3; "Confidential Minutes of Discussion of Advisory Committee on Public Policy and Catholic Schools," September 11, 1979, Box 37, Folder USCC Church: Church and State, Federal Aid to Education: Tuition Tax Credits, 1979, USCCP, p. 2.

83. Memorandum from Msgr. Wilfrid Paradis to Thomas Kelly, July 6, 1979, Box 37, Folder USCC Church: Church and State, Federal Aid to Education: Tax Credits, 1979, USCCP, p. 1; Letter from Most Rev. Daniel Pilarczyk to Thomas Kelly, June 28, 1979, Box

37, Folder USCC Church: Church and State, Federal Aid to Education: Tuition Tax Credits, 1979, USCCP; "Confidential Minutes of Discussion of Advisory Committee on Public Policy and Catholic Schools," September 11–13, 1979, USCCP, p. 2; Wilfrid Paradis, "Testimony before Senate Committee," February 7, 1979, Box 59, Folder Departmental Committees: Education, 1974–79, USCCP, USCC, pp. 4–5; Memorandum from James Robinson to Most Rev. Archbishops, State Catholic Conference Directors, Catholic School Superintendents, and Other Interested Persons, July 24, 1979, Box 59, Folder Departmental Committees: Education 1974–79, USCCP, p. 1.

84. Letter from Bishop Edward Hughes to Thomas Kelly, March 12, 1980, Box 71, Folder USCC Departmental Committees: Education: Presidential Advisory Panel on Financing Elementary and Secondary Education 1979–80, USCCP.

85. "Cross-Cutting Analysis: Non Public Education," May 7, 1980, Shirley Hufstedler Collection, Box 12, Folder FY 1982–86 Budget and Planning Materials [2], JCPL, p. 8. PEARL refers to the National Coalition for Public Education and Religious Liberty. "The Carter Administration and Private Education," October 17, 1980, Staff Office Files, Domestic Policy Staff, Eizenstat, Box 196, Folder Education Programs, JCPL, pp. 1–4, 8; George Gallup and Jim Castelli, *The American Catholic People* (Garden City, N.Y.: Doubleday, 1987), p. 129.

86. David Anderson, "Catholics Plan Push for School Tax Credits," *Los Angeles Times*, December 13, 1980, sec. 1A, p. 23 (emphasis mine).

87. Note from "Bill" to "Dennis," April 11, 1980, Sarah Weddington Collection, Box 72, Folder Private School Children, JCPL, p. 8.

88. "Presidential News Conference before the National Society of Newspaper Editors," April 11, 1978, USCCP, p. 730; "Presidential News Conference," August 17, 1978, USCCP, p. 1444; "Remarks of the President at the Opening Session of the 118th Annual Meeting of the NEA," July 3, 1980, Sarah Weddington Collection, Box 67, Folder Education: Department of Education, JCPL, pp. 2–3; Memorandum from Stuart Eizenstat to the President and attached handwritten note by Jimmy Carter, September 28, 1978, Staff Offices— Office of Staff Secretary, Handwriting File, Box 104, Folder 9/29/78, JCPL, pp. 1–2.

89. "Presidential News Conference," August 17, 1978, USCCP, p. 1444.

90. Memorandum from Elizabeth Abramowitz to Bert Carp, May 4, 1978, White House Central Files, Subject file Federal Government—Operations, Box FG-236, Folder FG 999-12 1/20/77–1/20/81, p. 2.

91. Exit Interview of Abramowitz, JCPL, p. 15; Myron Lieberman, "Demography and the Economy Chill the AFT Convention," *Phi Delta Kappan* (September 1979): 51; Letter from Moynihan to Quinn, June 6, 1978; Letter from Robert Packwood to Wilfrid Paradis, August 29, 1978, Box 37, Folder USCC Church: Church and State, Federal Aid to Education: Tuition Tax Credits, 1973–78, USCCP.

92. Letter from Moynihan to Quinn, March 20, 1978, USCCP.

93. "Twenty-eight Senators," August 18, 1978, Box 37, Folder USCC Church: Church and State, Federal Aid to Education: Tuition Tax Credits, 1973–78, USCCP; Letter from Hughes to Kelly, March 12, 1980, p. 4.

94. "Memorandum: Archbishop Hannan," September 28, 1978, Box 37, Folder USCC Church: Church and State, Federal Aid to Education: Tuition Tax Credits, 1973–78, USCCP.

95. Letter from Moynihan to Quinn, March 20, 1978; Letter from Moynihan to Quinn, June 6, 1978; Letter from James Robinson to Terence Cardinal Cooke, June 15, 1978, Box 37,

Folder USCC Church: Church and State, Federal Aid to Education: Tuition Tax Credits, 1973–78, USCCP, pp. 1–2.

96. Memorandum from James Robinson to Thomas Kelly, April 7, 1978, Box 37, Folder USCC Church: Church and State, Federal Aid to Education: Tuition Tax Credits, 1973–78, USCCP; Memorandum from Russell Shaw to Thomas Kelly, January 16, 1979, Box 37, Folder USCC Church: Church and State, Federal Aid to Education: Tuition Tax Credits, 1979, USCCP; Hanna, p. 79; interview of Rev. Robert Cornell by author, January 6, 1997, De Pere, Wisconsin.

97. "Of Many Things," *America,* October 28, 1978, p. 1; "Characteristics of Members of 95th Congress," *Congressional Quarterly Almanac,* 95th Cong., 1st sess., 1977 (Washington, D.C., 1977), pp. 34–42; "Key Votes," *Congressional Quarterly Almanac,* 95th Cong., 2nd sess., 1978 (Washington, D.C., 1978), pp. 14C–16C; "Senate Votes," *Congressional Quarterly Almanac,* 95th Cong., 2nd sess., 1978, p. 485; *Congressional Record,* August 15, 1978, p. 26080.

98. "Feedback," *U.S. Catholic,* November 1981, p. 14.

99. "School Tax Credits Making New Converts," *Christianity Today,* September 22, 1978, pp. 37–38; Letter from Packwood to Paradis, August 29, 1978, USCCP; John Swomley, "Tuition Tax Credits: Blank Checks for Churches," *Christian Century,* May 3, 1978, p. 63.

## Chapter 4: Public School Aid, 1981–2001

1. The epigraph is from Thomas Toch, "President Charts Administration Role in Education's Electrifying Renewal," *Education Week,* May 30, 1984, p. 1.

2. Interview of Mary Hatwood Futrell by author, November 5, 1997, Washington, D.C.

3. William Pemberton, *Exit with Honor* (Armonk, N.Y.: M.E. Sharpe, 1998), p. 8; Robert Dallek, *Ronald Reagan: The Politics of Symbolism* (Cambridge: Harvard University, 1984), p. 41.

4. Transcript of "President's First News Conference on Foreign and Domestic Topics," *New York Times,* January 30, 1981, p. A10.

5. "Education," *Congressional Quarterly Almanac, 1981* (Washington, D.C., 1982), p. 268; "Cabinet Administration Staffing Memorandum" from Craig Fuller, September 18, 1981, White House Office of Records Management (WHORM), Subject file Education, Box 1, Folder ED: Education [014466–018824], Ronald Reagan Presidential Library, Simi Valley, California [hereafter RRPL], pp. 2–3; Rochelle Stanfield, "Breaking Up the Education Department—School Aid May Be the Real Target," *National Journal,* October 1981, pp. 1907–10; Terrel Bell, *The Thirteenth Man* (New York: Free Press, 1988), p. 97.

6. Memorandum from Edwin Meese to Cabinet Council on Management and Administration, January 27, 1983, Staff and Office Files: Carleson, Robert, Box 9592, Folder Education [8 of 9] CA 9592, RRPL, pp. 1–2.

7. Memorandum from "RBC," n.d., Staff and Office Files: Carleson, Robert, Box 9592, RRPL; Bell, p. 91; Edward Fiske, "Some Republicans Oppose Efforts to Abolish U.S. Education Department," *New York Times,* p. A14.

8. Ronald Reagan, "Message to the Congress Transmitting the Fiscal Year 1983 Budget," February 8, 1982, *Public Papers of the Presidents of the United States: Ronald Reagan,* Book 1, *1982* (Washington, D.C.: U.S. Government Printing Office, 1983); "Education," *Congressional Quarterly Almanac, 1982* (Washington, D.C., 1983), p. 502.

9. Bell, pp. 92, 94, 95; Memorandum from Carleson, n.d.; "Education," *Congressional*

*Quarterly Almanac, 1982*, p. 501; Donna Engelgau, "Protecting Education from Stockman's Cuts Would Be Second-Term Administration Goal, Bell Says," *Chronicle of Higher Education*, October 17, 1984, pp. 15–16.

10. John Walsh, "Budget Tailors Education to Reagan Pattern," *Science*, February 26, 1982, p. 1077.

11. Stanfield, "Breaking Up the Education Department—School Aid May Be the Real Target," p. 1907; Attachment to Memorandum from Richard Hansen to Frank Fahrenkopf, June 24, 1983, WHORM, Subject file Education, Box 5, Folder ED Education [152800-152907], RRPL, p. 2; "Education in Dire Need of New Federal Efforts," *New York Times*, June 20, 1983, p. A14.

12. Martin Tolchin, "$200 Million to Pay for School Lunches Restored by Senate," *New York Times*, March 28, 1981, p. A1; Steven Weisman, "Reagan Abandons Proposal to Pare School Nutrition," *New York Times*, September 26, 1981, p. A1.

13. Deborah Verstegen and David Clark, "The Diminution in Federal Expenditures for Education during the Reagan Administration," *Phi Delta Kappan* (October 1988): 134–35; Memorandum from Robert Carleson to Edwin Meese, May 26, 1983, Staff and Office Files: Carleson, Robert, Box 9592, Folder Education [2 of 9] CA 9592, RRPL, pp. 1–3; "Children in Need: Investment Strategies for the Educationally Disadvantaged," attached to Memorandum from Nancy Risque to Tom Griscom, November 10, 1987, WHORM, Subject file Education, Folder ED Education [518000-532499], RRPL, pp. 1–2; Terrel Bell, "Education Policy Development in the Reagan Administration," *Phi Delta Kappan* (March 1986): 39.

14. "Reagan School Aid Plan Unveiled," *New York Times*, April 30, 1981, p. A26.

15. Jack Jennings, "Will Carl Perkins' Legacy Survive Ronald Reagan's Policies?" *Phi Delta Kappan* (April 1985): 566; Thomas Eagleton, "Programs Worth Saving," *Atlantic Monthly*, July 1, 1982, p. 19; Memorandum from Robert Carleson to Edwin Harper, June 23, 1983, WHORM, Subject file Education, Box 6, Folder ED Education [156563-157999], RRPL, pp. 2–3.

16. Norm Fruchter, "The Chipping-Off-the-Old-Block Grant Strategy," *Phi Delta Kappan* (September 25, 1982): 271.

17. Edward Fiske, "Top Objectives Elude Reagan as Education Policy Evolves," *New York Times*, December 27, 1983, p. A1; Bell, *The Thirteenth Man*, p. 89.

18. Memorandum from Terrel Bell to Craig Fuller, July 6, 1981, WHORM, Subject file Education, Box 1, Folder FG 999 [018694CS], RRPL, pp. 1, 2, 4.

19. "U.S. Department of Education News," August 26, 1981, WHORM, Subject file Education, Box 1, Folder FG 999 [018694CS], RRPL, p. 1.

20. "Department Planning and Fiscal Guidance: Policy Challenges and Options: Background Paper on Exercising Leadership to Improve Equality," August 7, 1982, Douglas Holladay Files, Box 2, Folder Federal Role in Education OA 12150, RRPL, p. 1.

21. "Education," n.d., WHORM, Subject file Education, Box 26, Folder Box 26, Folder ED 003 [100000-135836], RRPL, p. l.

22. Albert Shanker, "Master Teacher: An Old and Bad Idea," *New York Times*, January 23, 1983, p. E9.

23. Memorandum from Deputy Undersecretary for Planning, Budget, and Evaluation for Addressees, March 3, 1983, Staff and Office Files: Carleson, Robert, Box 9592, Folder Education [7 of 9] OA 9592, RRPL, pp. 1–3; Memorandum from Ann Weinheimer to Jack Klenk, April 15, 1983, Douglas Holladay Files, Box 3, RRPL, pp. 3–4.

24. "Fact Sheet, National Commission on Excellence in Education," April 26, 1983, WHORM, Subject file Education, Folder ED Education [073200-073299], RRPL, pp. 1–6.

25. Bell, *The Thirteenth Man,* p. 146; Letter from Willard McGuire to Ronald Reagan, May 27, 1983, WHORM, Subject file Education, Box 4, Folder ED Education [140000-140564], RRPL, p. 1; "White House Lunch Focuses on Education," *Washington Post,* June 9, 1983, p. A7; Lawrence Feinberg, "Merit Pay Task Force Urges Test," *Washington Post,* October 11, 1983, p. A1; "Few Schools Move Quickly on Merit Pay," *Education Daily,* December 1, 1983; George Gallup, "Education Reform Supported for Years," *Richmond Times-Dispatch,* May 5, 1983, p. A6; "Americans Willing to Pay More for Quality Schools, Pollsters Say," *Education Daily,* July 26, 1983, p. 1; Memorandum from Terrel Bell to Craig Fuller, May 19, 1983, FOIA Education Issues, 1981–84, Box 1, Folder MC 143101 CA, RRPL.

26. "Presidential Remarks: Panel Discussion, Farragut High School, Knoxville, Tenn.," June 14, 1983, WHORM, Subject file Education, Box 6, Folder ED Education [156562] [1 of 3], RRPL, p. 1; David Shribman, "President, on Way West, Presses Education Drive," *New York Times,* June 30, 1983, p. A14; "Presidential Remarks: Commission on Excellence in Education Forum, Los Angeles, California," June 30, 1983, FOIA Education Issues, 1981–84, Box 1, Folder SP 781 [140590], RRPL, p. 3; "Back to School with Mr. Reagan," *Washington Post,* June 19, 1983, p. B6.

27. Steven Weisman, "Reagan Asks Drive on Unruly Pupils," *New York Times,* January 8, 1984, pp. A1, A21; Terrel Bell, "Suggested Priorities and Goals for American Education," *American Teacher,* March 1984, pp. 30–32.

28. Philip Boffey, "First Shuttle Ride by Private Citizen Goes to Teacher," August 28, 1984, *New York Times,* p. A1. The teacher, Christa McAuliffe, would die when the shuttle exploded shortly after liftoff on January 28, 1986. Memorandum from William Kristol to Rick Davis, May 9, 1986, WHORM, Subject file Education, Box 19, Folder ED Education [413126] [7 of 7], RRPL, p. 2; Douglas Holladay, Handwritten Notes, February 18, 1984, Douglas Holladay Files, Box 3, RRPL; Janet Hook, "Religious Issue Stalls Math-Science Bill," *Congressional Quarterly Weekly Report,* June 9, 1984, p. 1349; Edward Fiske, "Education Department Seeking to Alter Bilingual Efforts," *New York Times,* September 26, 1985, p. A1.

29. Dinesh D'Souza, "And Forget Today's Elites," *Wall Street Journal,* November 4, 1997, p. A22.

30. "Radio Address by the President to the Nation," June 25, 1983, Staff and Office Files: Carleson, Robert, Box 9592, Folder Education [5 of 9] O 9592, RRPL, p. 1; Draft of Letter from Ronald Reagan to Wayne Hardin, July 7, 1983, Staff and Office Files: Carleson, Robert, Box 9592, Folder Education [5 of 9], OA 9592, RRPL.

31. Memorandum from Greg Humphrey to Albert Shanker et al., February 23, 1981, AFT Office of the President, Box 74, Folder 74-7 Education, Department, 1981–83 [2 of 2], AFTP, pp. 1–2; Chester Finn, "Teacher Politics," *Commentary,* February 1983, p. 32; "National Commission Report Used to Defend Education Spending," *Education Daily,* May 4, 1983, p. 2; Shanker, "Master Teacher: An Old and Bad Idea," p. 9.

32. "White House Correspondence Tracking Worksheet" from Craig Fuller, February 14, 1981, WHORM, Subject file Education, Box 1, Folder ED Education [000001-014465], RRPL; Letter from Gregory Newell to Terry Herndon, March 2, 1981, WHORM, Subject file Education, Box 1, Folder ED Education [000001-014465], RRPL; Exchange of Letters between Ronald Reagan and Willard McGuire, May 26–27, 1983, WHORM, Subject file Education, Box 2, Folder ED Education [073300-073388], RRPL, pp. 1–2; "Reagan to Meet

Leader of Teacher Association," *New York Times,* May 29, 1983, sec. 1, p. 20; "Meeting on Education," *New York Times,* July 20, 1983, p. B8; "Meeting with Education Leaders," from Craig Fuller, July 19, 1983, WHORM, Subject file Education, Box 6, Folder ED Education [15600-15651], RRPL, p. 1; "Teacher/Pupil Ratio—Fact and Fiction," Office of Policy Development, attached to Memorandum from Craig Fuller to Fred Ryan, August 5, 1983, WHORM, Subject file Education, Box 7, Folder ED Education, RRPL, p. 3.

33. Finn, "Teacher Politics," p. 34; Myron Lieberman, "Why School Reform Isn't Working," *Forbes,* February 17, 1986, pp. 135–36; Terrel Bell, "On the Need for National Leaders to Make American Education Work," *Phi Delta Kappan* (September 1988): 10.

34. David Broder, "In Full Cry on the Education Issue," *Washington Post,* June 19, 1983, p. B7; Chester Finn, "A Bully Pulpit in the Classroom, Fine," *Wall Street Journal,* August 22, 1983, p. A18; Edward Fiske, "Top Objectives Elude Reagan as Education Policy Evolves," *New York Times,* December 27, 1983, p. B5; Fred Hechinger, "1985: A Year of Talk but Little Action," December 31, 1985, *New York Times,* p. C7.

35. Handwritten Notes on Memorandum from Bell to Fuller, July 6, 1981, p. 1; Memorandum from Edwin Harper to William Sadler, January 31, 1983, WHORM, Subject file Education, Box 3, Folder ED Education [113000-114999], RRPL, p. 1; "Education," n.d., RRPL, p. 1; Bell, "Education Policy Development in the Reagan Administration," *Phi Delta Kappan* (March 1986): 40.

36. Memorandum from Ann Weinheimer to PES Staff, June 2, 1983, Douglas Holladay Files, Box 3, Folder Master Teacher Concept (Merit Pay) [3] OA 12151, RRPL, pp. 1, 4, 5; Attachment to Memorandum from Ronald Reagan for the Heads of Executive Departments and Agencies, November 7, 1983, WHORM, Subject file Education, Box 7, Folder ED Education [16990], RRPL, p. 2.

37. Martin Tolchin, "Amendment Drive on School Prayer Loses Senate Vote," *New York Times,* March 21, 1984, p. A1; "Talking Points for the President," attached to Memorandum from William Kristol to Rick Davis, May 9, 1986, WHORM, Subject file Education, Box 19, Folder ED Education [41316] [7 of 7], RRPL, pp. 1–2; Memorandum from William Bennett to Alfred Kingon, n.d., WHORM, Subject file Education, Box 18, Folder ED Education [363098-364999], RRPL, pp. 1–2; Edward Fiske, "Reagan Agenda: Taking New Tack," *New York Times,* January 27, 1988, p. B8.

38. Memorandum from Anne Graham to David Gergen, May 3, 1983, Staff and Office Files: Bistany, Joanna, Box 7886, Folder Education OA 7886, RRPL; "New Congress Not Different Enough to Make Changes President Wants," *Phi Delta Kappan* (January 1985): 381; "Budget Cuts for K–12 not as Bad as Expected," *Phi Delta Kappan* (April 1985): 587.

39. "Education Appropriations," *Congressional Quarterly Almanac 1981–1988* (Washington, D.C., 1982–89), pp. 332, 252, 505, 422, 335, 200, 459; Steven Roberts, "House Approves Fund Increases for Ten Programs," *New York Times,* September 13, 1983, p. D27; "Evolution of Public Education Legislation," *Congressional Digest,* March 1987, pp. 69–71; David Savage, "Why Chapter 1 Hasn't Made Much Difference," *Phi Delta Kappan* (April 1987): 584; Jennings, "Will Carl Perkins' Legacy Survive Ronald Reagan's Policies?" p. 566.

40. Memorandum from Robert Sweet to Robert Carleson, May 19, 1983, WHORM, Subject file Education, Box 4, Folder ED Education [139124-139999], RRPL; Memorandum from James Coyne to Michael Deaver, June 27, 1983, FOIA Education Issues, 1981–84, Box 1, Folder SP 383 [152117], RRPL, p. 1; Memorandum from Robert Sweet to Robert Carleson, June 13, 1983, WHORM, Subject file Education, Box 4, Folder ED Education, RRPL, p. 1; Edward Fiske, "Schools Lag Despite Five-Year Effort, Bennett Says," *New York Times,*

December 27, 1983, p. A19; Bell, "Education Policy Development in the Reagan Administration," p. 40.

41. Bennett to Kingon, RRPL, pp. 1–2; "Statement by William Bennett on Fourth Annual Wall Chart of State Education Statistics," February 10, 1987, Carl Megel Papers, Box 21, Folder 21-22, Reports, 1925–87, AFTP, p. 3; "Fact Sheet on American Education: Making It Work," April 26, 1988, WHORM, Subject file Education, Box 22, Folder ED Education, RRPL, pp. 1–6.

42. "Fact Sheet on American Education: Making It Work," pp. 1–6; "Children in Need: Investment Strategies for the Educationally Disadvantaged, Committee for Economic Development," attached to Memorandum from Nancy Risque to Tom Griscom, November 10, 1982, WHORM, Subject file Education, Box 22, Folder ED Education [18000-532499], RRPL, pp. 1–2; "Education: Now the Hard Part," *Washington Post*, March 19, 1988, p. A22.

43. Memorandum from Humphrey to Shanker et al., pp. 1–2; "NEA Wants More Federal Aid," *Congressional Quarterly*, August 9, 1980, p. 2278; interview of Futrell by author, November 5, 1997; "AFT President Albert Shanker Proposes the Creation of a National Teacher Examination for New Teachers, National Press Club," January 29, 1985, AFT Office of the President, no box, no folder, AFTP, p. 1; Gene Maeroff, "Big Teacher Union Is Willing to Discuss Merit Pay Plans," *New York Times*, June 30, 1983, p. A14.

44. Gallup, "Education Reform Supported for Years," p. 6. According to a Gallup Poll, the number of parents with children in public schools who cited discipline as their major concern fell from 29 percent in 1983 to 23 percent in 1984; see "Education Agenda," attached to Memorandum from Jan McMinn to Richard Darman, August 23, 1984, WHORM, Subject file Education, Box 14, Folder ED Education [262000-262999], RRPL, p. 8. Republican pollster Robert Teeter and Democratic pollster Peter Hart agreed that Americans "are willing to pay higher taxes if they can be assured that the quality of public education will improve"; see "Americans Willing to Pay More for Quality Schools, Pollsters Say," *Education Daily*, July 26, 1983, p. 1; Tolchin, p. 1.

45. State officials were less sympathetic toward the block grants, however; see "State and Local Officials Disagree about Chapter 2," *Phi Delta Kappan* (January 1985): 382. John Jennings, "Working in Mysterious Ways: The Federal Government in Education," *Phi Delta Kappan* (January 1989): 63–64.

46. Bell, "Education Policy Development in the Reagan Administration," p. 35. Finn distinguished between a "federal" and a "national" effort in education; see "A Bully Pulpit in the Classroom, Fine," p. 18.

47. George Bush, "Remarks at a Reception for Participants in the National Endowment for the Humanities Teacher-Scholar Program: March 2, 1989," *Public Papers of the Presidents of the United States: George Bush*, Book 1, 1989 (Washington, D.C.: U.S. Government Printing Office, 1990) p. 167.

48. Susan Chira, "Long Fight for Local Support Hampers Bush on Education," *New York Times*, June 30, 1992, pp. A1, A25.

49. George Bush, "Address on Administration Goals before a Joint Session of Congress, February 9, 1989," *Public Papers of the Presidents of the United States: George Bush*, Book 1, 1989 (Washington, D.C.: U.S. Government Printing Office, 1990), p. 76.

50. David Mervin, *George Bush and the Guardianship Presidency* (New York: St. Martin's, 1998), pp. 44, 226.

51. Steven Roberts, "Education Pledge Renewed by Bush," *New York Times*, January 19,

1989, p. B9; George Bush, "Address on Administration Goals before a Joint Session of Congress, February 9, 1989," *Public Papers of the Presidents of the United States: George Bush,* Book 1, *1989* (Washington, D.C.: U.S. Government Printing Office, 1990), p. 76; Letter from Roger Porter to William Goodling, April 4, 1989, WHORM, Subject file Education, Box 2, Folder ED Education [021200-029999] [3], George Bush Presidential Library, College Station, Texas [hereafter GBPL], pp. 1–3; "President Transmits 'Educational Excellence Act of 1989 to Hill," *White House Wire,* April 5, 1989, WHORM, Subject file Education, Box 2, Folder ED Education [021200-029999] [2], GBPL; Maureen Dowd, "President Unveils School Proposal," *New York Times,* April 6, 1989, p. A24; Julie Johnson, "So Far, Educators Give Bush No Passing Grade," *New York Times,* April 26, 1989, p. B8.

52. Julie Johnson, "Nation's Schools Termed Stagnant in Federal Report," *New York Times,* May 4, 1989, p. B14; Edward Fiske, "Concerns Raised on School Quality," *New York Times,* June 6, 1989, p. A19; Letter from Jonathan Wilson and James Oglesby to Charles Kolb, April 21, 1989, WHORM, Subject file Education, Box 2, Folder ED Education [030000-039999] [1], GBPL.

53. "Bush's Education Proposals Unfulfilled," *Congressional Quarterly Almanac,* 1990 (Washington, D.C., 1991), pp. 610–15; Memorandum from Roger Porter to the President, February 12, 1990, WHORM, Subject file Education, Folder ED Education [112500-115999] [2], GBPL.

54. "Bush's Education Proposals Unfulfilled," pp. 610–15; Letter from William Goodling to George Bush, September 13, 1990, WHORM, Subject file Education, Box 18, Folder ED Education [172000-176999] [1], GBPL.

55. Memorandum from Richard Thornburgh to Domestic Policy Council, Secretary of Defense, Secretary of Agriculture, Secretary of Labor and the Director of the Office of National Drug Control Policy, June 1, 1989, Bush Presidential Records, Domestic Policy Council, Subject file Education, Box 8, Folder America 2000 [OA/ID 04793] [3 of 3], GBPL; Fiske, "Concerns Raised on School Quality," p. 19.

56. Letter from Terry Sanford to George Bush, June 8, 1989, WHORM, Subject file Education, Box 2, Folder ED Education [040000-059999] [1], GBPL, pp. 1–6.

57. E. J. Dionne, "President Stresses Schools and Drugs in His Courting of Governors," *New York Times,* July 31, 1989, p. A14.

58. Julie Johnson, "Bush Will Back National Goals on Education," *New York Times,* September 24, 1989, p. A24.

59. The other times were Theodore Roosevelt's Conference on Conservation and Franklin Roosevelt's Conference on the Depression; "Talking Points, Meeting with NEA," n.d., WHORM, Subject file Education, Box 7, Folder ED Education [077000-079499] [3], GBPL, pp. 1–2; Edward Fiske, "Meeting on Education Starts Today in Virginia," *New York Times,* September 27, 1989, p. B8; "The President's Education Summit with Governors," September 27–28, 1989, Bush Presidential Records, Domestic Policy Council, Subject file Education, Box 8, Folder ED Education 2000 [OA/ID 4793] [2 of 3], GBPL, pp. 1–5.

60. Deidre Carmody, "Teachers Praise Bush's Effort to Set a New Education Agenda," *New York Times,* September 30, 1989, p. A9; Bernard Weinraub, "Hope and Dissent Blend in Education Conference," *New York Times,* September 28, 1989, p. B13; Edward Fiske, "Lessons," *New York Times,* October 4, 1989, p. B8; "In the Spotlight, AFT Shines at Bush's Education Summit," *Action,* October 13, 1989, Carl Megel Collection, Box 20, Folder 20-1, Executive Council Minutes, AFTP, p. 1; Letter from Roger Porter to William Goodling, November 8, 1989, WHORM, Subject file Education, Box 13, Folder ED Education

[116000-122999] [1], GBPL; Bernard Weinraub, "Bennett Chastised for Comments on Pap," *New York Times,* September 30, 1989, p. A9.

61. George Bush, "Address before a Joint Session of the Congress on the State of the Union," January 31, 1990, *Public Papers of the Presidents of the United States: George Bush,* Book 1, *1990* (Washington, D.C.: U.S. Government Printing Office, 1991), p. 131.

62. David Broder, "Losing the Future in the Schools," *Washington Post,* January 17, 1990, p. A21; Anthony Flint, "Educators Say Bush Is Short on Specifics," *Boston Globe,* February 2, 1990, pp. A1, A8; Susan Tifft, "Reading, Writing, and Rhetoric," *Time,* February 12, 1990, p. 54; Michael Hinds, "Cutting the Dropout Rate: High Goal but Low Hopes," *New York Times,* February 17, 1990, p. A1; Marshal Ingwerson, "Bush Effort to Set Goals for Education Earns Praise," *Christian Science Monitor,* February 6, 1990, p. A1.

63. Kenneth Cooper, "Tests of U.S. Students Show Little Progress," *Washington Post,* January 10, 1990, pp. A1, A5; "U.S. Is Said to Lag in School Spending," *New York Times,* January 16, 1990, p. A23.

64. Cooper, "Tests of U.S. Students Show Little Progress," p. 5; John Hood, "Education: Money Isn't Everything," *Wall Street Journal,* February 9, 1990, p. A10; Ingwerson, "Bush Effort to Set Goals for Education Earns Praise," p. 1.

65. "Joint Statement of the President and Governors," July 31, 1990, WHORM, Subject file Education, Folder ED Education [162000-167999] [1], GBPL; Scott Jaschik, "Governors and White House Form a Panel to Track the Progress of Education Reform," *New York Times,* August 8, 1990, pp. 1–2.

66. Memorandum from Roger Porter to John Sununu, December 17, 1990, WHORM, Subject file Education, Folder ED Education [200000-201999] [1], GBPL, pp. 1–2; "Measuring Progress toward the National Education Goals," *National Education Goals Report,* Volume 2, Bush Presidential Records, Office of Policy Development, Johannes Kuttner File, Box 14, Folder National Education Goals: The National Education Goals Report [OA/ID 08372], GBPL, pp. 1–2.

67. Memorandum from Charles Kolb to Roger Porter, February 13, 1991, WHORM, Subject file Education, Box 22, Folder ED Education [210400-215999] [2], GBPL, pp. 1–2; Letter from Roger Porter to Thad Cochran, March 12, 1991, WHORM, Subject file Education, Box 25, Folder ED Education [245000-248999] [2], GBPL, p. 1.

68. Memorandum from Roger Porter to George Bush and handwritten notes from Bush, WHORM, Subject file Education, Box 22, Folder ED Education [220000-225999] [1], GBPL, pp. 1–5.

69. Maureen Dowd, "Cavazos Quits as Education Chief amid Pressure from White House," *New York Times,* December 13, 1990, p. A1.

70. William Celis, "Educator Who Fulfills a Vision," *New York Times,* December 18, 1990, p. B14; Karen DeWitt, "A Tennessean's View on Education," *New York Times,* December 24, 1990, p. A9.

71. Jill Zuckerman, "Elbowing Democrats Aside, Bush Unveils School Plan," *New York Times,* April 20, 1991, pp. 983–86.

72. "White House Fact Sheet on the President's Education Strategy," April 18, 1991, *Public Papers of the Presidents of the United States: George Bush,* Book 1, *1991* (Washington, D.C.: U.S. Government Printing Office, 1992), pp. 399–403.

73. Memorandum from Lamar Alexander to the President, March 29, 1991, WHORM, Subject file Education, Box 23, Folder ED Education [230000-232999] [2], GBPL, pp. 1–2.

74. Memorandum from Charles Kolb to Roger Porter, April 10, 1991, WHORM, Subject file Education, Box 25, Folder ED Education [245000-246999] [1], pp. 1–4.

75. "America 2000: An Education Strategy Sourcebook," n.d., WHORM Alpha File, Box 6, Folder Bush Presidential Records Office of Cabinet Affairs, GBPL, pp. 29–33.

76. "Thirty Experts on School Reform Critique Bush America 2000 Strategy," *Congressional Quarterly Weekly Report,* July 23, 1991, p. 1; Memorandum from Roger Porter to the President, April 19, 1991, Bush Presidential Records, Office of Policy [OA/ID 05162], GBPL.

77. Memorandum from Ede Holiday to the President, May 8, 1991, WHORM, Subject file Education, Box 23, Folder ED Education [236000-238999] [2], GBPL, pp. 1–3.

78. White House News Summary, May 23, 1991, Bush Presidential Records, Office of Policy Department, Doreen Torgerson File, Box 11, Folder America 2000 Kickoff 4/18/91 [OA/ID 05162], GBPL, p. B2.

79. "Remarks by the President to the National Education Goals Panel Meeting," June 3, 1991, WHORM, Subject file Education, Box 25, Folder ED Education [243000-244999] [1], GBPL, pp. 1–3; "Other Education Bills Considered in 1991," *Congressional Quarterly Almanac,* 1991 (Washington, D.C., 1992), pp. 380–81; "Remarks by the President in Announcement of the New American Schools Development Corporation Board," July 8, 1991, Bush Presidential Records, Office of Legislative Affairs, Linda Tarplin File, Box 12, Folder Education Issues: America 2000 [OA/ID 8457] [2 of 2], GBPL, p. 2; "Signing Ceremony for H.R. 751," July 25, 1991, WHORM, Subject file Education, Box 27, Folder ED Education [258000-261999], GBPL.

80. Karen DeWitt, "Alexander Takes Education Plan to Nation," *New York Times,* August 14, 1991, p. A17; Andrew Rosenthal, "Bush Stresses Schools, and Critics Turn Up Heat," *New York Times,* September 4, 1991, p. B8; "America 2000: First-Year Accomplishments," April 16, 1992, Bush Presidential Records, Office of Intergovernmental Affairs, Jim Snyder File, Box 9, Folder America 2000 [OA/ID 07179], GBPL, p. 2.

81. Mary Jordan, "Alexander Says Education Unlikely to Be Issue; Clinton Campaign Demurs," *Washington Post,* April 9, 1992, p. A13; "President Bush Sets Historic Partnership and New Education Agenda," *America 2000,* U.S. Department of Education, November 23, 1992, Bush Presidential Records, Office of Policy Development, Gina Willis subject file, Box 13, Folder America 2000 Newsletters [OA/ID 08176], GBPL, p. 1.

82. "Educating Rita," *National Review,* May 13, 1991, p. 17; Memorandum from Jonathan Levey to Roger Porter, November 5, 1991, WHORM, Subject file Education, Box 32, ED [288500-290999] [2], GBPL, pp. 1–2; interview of Mary Hatwood Futrell by author, November 5, 1997, Washington, D.C.; Kenneth Cooper, "School Groups Urge Congress to Hold Off Administration Plan for Voluntary National Tests," June 12, 1991, p. A21.

83. "Conservatives Should Be Wary of Bush's Education Bill," *Human Events,* July 27, 1991, p. 1; Memorandum from Roger Porter to Clayton Yeutter, May 17, 1992, WHORM, Subject file Education, Box 33, Folder ED Education [325000-366452] [3], GBPL, p. 2; "The Part-Time Education President," *New York Times,* April 24, 1992, p. A34; Karen DeWitt, "Brought to You by Exxon—School Reform," *New York Times,* July 21, 1991, p. E4.

84. "White House Statement on Federal Budget Amendments for the Education Reform Strategy," June 7, 1991, *Public Papers of the Presidents of the United States: George Bush,* Book 1, *1991* (Washington, D.C.: U.S. Government Printing Office, 1992), p. 625; Julie Miller and Mark Pitsch, "Bush and Kennedy Set Stage for Federal Debate," *Education Week,* May 29, 1991, pp. 4–5.

85. "Hill Counters President's Education Plan," *Congressional Quarterly Almanac,* 1991 (Washington, D.C., 1992), p. 380; Memorandum from Frederick McClure to Philip Brady, November 23, 1991, WHORM, Subject file Education, Box 32, Folder ED Education [291000–295999] [1], GBPL, p. 1.

86. "Scorned School Bill Dies in Senate," *Congressional Quarterly Almanac,* 1992 (Washington, D.C., 1993), pp. 455–61.

87. "Press Briefing by Secretary of Education Lamar Alexander, Mr. Paul O'Neill, Governor of Colorado Roy Romer, and Governor of South Carolina Carroll Campbell," April 18, 1991, WHORM Alpha File, Box 6, Folder Office of Cabinet Affairs, Michael P. Jackson File, America 2000 [OA/ID 06382], GBPL, p. 7; telephone interview of Roger Porter by author, November 26, 1997; interview of Futrell by author, November 5, 1997; telephone interview of Lamar Alexander by author, January 28, 1998.

88. "House Passes Administration's Mental Health and Elementary Education Bill, Defeats GOP Recommittal Move on School Bill," *Congressional Quarterly Almanac,* 1967 (Washington, D.C., 1968), p. 29-H; Herbert Parmet, *George Bush: The Life of a Lone Star Yankee* (New York: Simon and Schuster, 1997), p. 94; "The Education President," *New Republic,* May 9, 1988, p. 1; Chester Finn, "Education: The Dud of Campaign '88," *American Spectator,* November 1988, p. 38.

89. Memorandum from Roger Porter to the President, September 12, 1989, WHORM, Subject file Education, Box 7, Folder ED Education [060000–062999] [4], GBPL, p. 3; Memorandum from Rae Nelson to Roger Porter, November 25, 1989, Bush Presidential Records, Office of Policy Department, Gina Willis File, Box 13, Folder National Education Goals Panel—State of the Union, Goals Document [OA/ID 08302], GBPL, p. 3; Memorandum from Charles Kolb to Roger Porter, March 4, 1991, WHORM, Subject file Education, Box 22, Folder ED Education [216000–219999] [1], GBPL, pp. 1–4; George Bush, "The Bush Strategy for Excellence in Education," *Phi Delta Kappan* (October 1988): 114; Rosenthal, "Bush Stresses Schools, and Critics Turn Up Heat," p. 8; "Bush Says School Children Watch Too Much TV," *New York Times,* p. B10.

90. "AFT Background Paper on National Standards and Assessments," n.d., Carl Megel Collection, Box 20, Folder 20-1, Executive Council Minutes, AFTP, p. 1; "National Education Goals: A Second Report to the Nation's Governors," 1992, WHORM, Subject file Education, Folder ED Education [210400], pp. 25–45.

91. Edward Fiske, "Lessons," *New York Times,* October 4, 1989, p. B5; Kenneth Cooper, "National Standards at Core of Strategy," *Washington Post,* April 19, 1991, p. A1.

92. Susan Chira, "Rivals Agree on Need for National School Standards but Differ on Role," *New York Times,* October 23, 1992, p. A22; Karen DeWitt, "First Report Card Issued on U.S. Education Goals," *New York Times,* October 1, 1991, p. A18; Memorandum from Mary Farrell to Roger Porter, August 9, 1991, Bush Presidential Records, Office of Policy Development, Rae Nelson File, Box 13, Folder America 2000, Track II Draft Speech (M. Farrell) [OA/ID 08235], GBPL, p. 3; D. Patrick Moynihan, "Education Goals and Political Plans," *Public Interest* (Winter 1991): 47; Memorandum from Roger Porter to the President, September 16, 1989, WHORM, Subject file Education, Box 7, Folder ED Education [077000–079499] [3], GBPL, pp. 1–6.

93. Denis Doyle, "America 2000," *Phi Delta Kappan* (November 1991): 185; "School Haze," *New Republic,* December 16, 1991, pp. 7–8.

94. Doyle, "America 2000," p. 185; Fiske, "Lessons," p. 8.

95. "Press Briefing by Secretary of Education Lamar Alexander et al.," p. 10; "Fact Sheet:

President Bush's Plan for Education Reform," April 30, 1992, WHORM, Subject file Education, Box 36, Folder ED Education [325000-366452] [2], GBPL; telephone interview of Roger Porter by author, November 26, 1997; telephone interview of Lamar Alexander by author, January 28, 1998.

96. Memorandum from Lamar Alexander to the President, April 19, 1991, WHORM, Subject file Education, Box 26, Folder ED Education [250000-251299], GBPL, p. 1; "Press Briefing by Secretary of Education Lamar Alexander, et al.," p. 9; Memorandum from Lamar Alexander to the President, February 3, 1991, Bush Presidential Records, Office of Policy Department, Randolph Beales File, Box 13, Folder America 2000 Development and Alexander Transition Team Materials [OA/ID 07959], GBPL, p. 4.

97. Susan Chira, "Schools Plan: Big Goals, Little Money," *New York Times*, February 2, 1990, p. A19.

98. Memorandum from Charles Kolb to Roger Porter, June 25, 1990, WHORM, Subject file Education, Box 16, Folder ED Education [135000-161999] [9], GBPL; Susan Chira, "Long Fight for Local Support Hampers Bush on Education," *New York Times*, June 30, 1992, p. A1.

99. Charles Tiefer, *The Semi-Sovereign Presidency: The Bush Administration's Strategy for Governing without Congress* (Boulder, Colo.: Westview, 1994), p. 115; telephone interview of Alexander by author, January 28, 1998.

100. Chira, "Long Fight for Local Support Hampers Bush on Education," p. A25; Tiefer, *The Semi-Sovereign Presidency,* p. 16.

101. The epigraph is from William Clinton, "1997 State of the Union Address," *Vital Speeches of the Day*, March 1, 1997, p. 290.

102. Bill Clinton and Al Gore, *Putting People First* (New York: Random House, 1992), p. 86.

103. William Clinton, "Remarks and a Question-and-Answer Session on the Economic Program in Chillicothe, Ohio," February 19, 1993, *Public Papers of the Presidents of the United States: William J. Clinton*, Book 1, *1993* (Washington, D.C.: U.S. Government Printing Office, 1994), p. 137.

104. Michael Kelly, *Bill Clinton: Politician* (Broomall, Pa.: Chelsea House, 1998), p. 21.

105. Ibid., pp. 50–51.

106. Charles Allen and Jonathan Portis, *The Comeback Kid: The Life and Career of Bill Clinton* (Secaucus, N.J.: Birch Lane, 1992), pp. 83, 96.

107. Ibid., pp. 97–98. A June 1984 poll showed 65.5 percent of Arkansans in favor of state teacher testing and 61.5 percent in favor of national teacher testing (ibid., p. 100).

108. Ibid., pp. 109–10; Clinton and Gore, *Putting People First,* pp. 85–86.

109. Jonathan Kozol, *Savage Inequalities: Children in America's Schools* (New York: Crown, 1991); Jonathan Kozol, "Let's 'Throw' Money at the Pentagon and Allocate It to Education," *Education Digest* (January 1993): 10–11; Thomas Sowell, *Inside American Education: The Decline, the Deception, the Dogmas* (New York: Free Press, 1993), p. 3.

110. Chris Pipho, "Fiscal Gridlock," *Phi Delta Kappan* (February 1993): 430–31; William Celis, "U.S. School Program Criticized Anew," *New York Times*, February 23, 1993, p. A1.

111. William Clinton, "The President's Radio Address," April 1, 1995, *Public Papers of the Presidents of the United States: William J. Clinton*, Book 1, *1995* (Washington, D.C.: U.S. Government Printing Office, 1996), pp. 440–41.

112. "Congress Looks to Chapter One Rewrite," *Congressional Quarterly Almanac*, 103rd Cong., 1st sess., 1993 (Washington, D.C., 1994), pp. 407–8; Clifford Krauss, "Clinton Aims

to Redirect School Aid to the Poor from Wealthy Districts," *New York Times,* September 15, 1993, p. B15; William Celis, "Educators Find a Lot to Like in a Little Increase," *New York Times,* April 14, 1993, p. B9.

113. Gwen Ifill, "Clinton Admits Big Changes in Budget Plan as Needed," *New York Times,* June 2, 1993, p. A14; Thomas Toch and Andrea Wright, "Public Schooling's Opportunity Gap," *U.S. News and World Report,* August 2, 1993, p. 45; Stephanie A. Forest, "True or False: More Money Buys Better Schools," *Business Week,* August 2, 1993, pp. 62–63.

114. David Hoff, "GAO Documents Persistent School Inequities," *Education Week,* March 4, 1998, pp. 20–22; "Clinton's Chapter One Formula Runs Aground in House," *Congressional Quarterly Weekly Report,* January 15, 1994, pp. 1–3. The GAO study "Rural Children, Increasing Poverty Rates Pose Educational Challenges" found that 80 percent of those schools no longer eligible for Chapter One monies under the Clinton plan were in rural counties; see Lynn Schnalberg, "Chapter One Funding Would Hurt Rural Schools the Most, GAO Finds," *Education Week,* January 26, 1994, p. 17.

115. "Clinton's Chapter One Formula," pp. 1–3.

116. Mark Pitsch, "Picture Mixed for Education, Clinton Team," *Education Week,* January 26, 1994, pp. 1–2; Michael Barone, "Setting School Standards Quietly," *U.S. News and World Report,* February 14, 1994, p. 28.

117. "Lawmakers Renew and Revamp 1965 Education Act," *Congressional Quarterly Almanac,* 103rd Cong., 2nd sess., 1994 (Washington, D.C., 1995), pp. 383–86.

118. Ibid.

119. Ibid., p. 389.

120. William Clinton, Remarks to the National Governors Association Summit in Palisades, New York, March 27, 1996, *Public Papers of the Presidents of the United States: William J. Clinton,* Book 1, *1996* (Washington, D.C.: U.S. Government Printing Office, 1997), p. 513.

121. William Celis, "Schools to Get Wide License on Spending Federal Money under New Education Law," *New York Times,* October 19, 1994, p. B11.

122. Gail Chaddock, "Point Man on Education," *Christian Science Monitor,* May 19, 1998, p. B1; Clinton, "Remarks to the National Governors Association," p. 516.

123. Garry Wills, "The War between the States . . . and Washington," *New York Times Magazine,* July 5, 1998, p. 26; Jacob Weisberg, "The Governor-President," *New York Times Magazine,* January 17, 1999, pp. 31–32.

124. "Federal Elementary and Secondary Education Programs," *Congressional Digest,* January 1994, p. 11; Susan Chira, "Clinton to Offer Plan for Change in U.S. Schools," *New York Times,* April 21, 1993, p. K1; "House Advances Education Reform Bill," *Congressional Quarterly Almanac,* 103rd Cong., 1st sess., 1993 (Washington, D.C., 1994), p. 405.

125. William Clinton, "Remarks to the AFL-CIO Convention in New York City," October 23, 1995, *Public Papers of the Presidents of the United States: William J. Clinton,* Book 2, *1995* (Washington, D.C.: U.S. Government Printing Office, 1996), p. 1669; Diane Ravitch, "Clinton's Math: More Get Less," *New York Times,* May 26, 1993, p. A21; Charles Kolb, "Return of the Education Blob," Box 189, Chester Finn Papers, Hoover Institution on War, Revolution, and Peace, Stanford, Calif., p. 2; Svi Shapiro, "Clinton and Education: Policies without Meaning," *Tikuun* (May/June 1994): 20; "House Advances Education Reform Bill," p. 405.

126. Barone, "Setting School Standards Quietly," p. 28; "House Advances Education Reform Bill," p. 406.

127. Peter Cookson, "Goals 2000: Framework for the New Educational Federalism," *Teachers College Record,* Spring 1995, p. 405; Anne Lewis, "Of Rhetoric and Standards," *Phi Delta Kappan* (January 1996): 332.

128. "In Appearance before House Committee, Education Secretary Opens Fight for His Department's Survival," *Department of Education Newsletter,* January 16, 1995, Box 189, CFP, p. 1; Diane Ravitch, "A Big No to Education Reform," *Forbes,* September 9, 1996, p. 65; "Goals 2000 Legislation and Related Items," Department of Education http://www.ed.gov/G2K/index.html (accessed January 8, 2006). The history standards invited criticism for their perceived emphasis on the new social history (which studies women and minorities) at the expense of traditional political history (which studies white male elites). Clinton, "Remarks to the National Governors Association," p. 513; Alison Mitchell, "Clinton Urges State Action on Education," *New York Times,* March 28, 1996, p. B10.

129. Jay Campbell, Clyde M. Reese, Christine O'Sullivan and John A. Dossey, *NAEP 1994 Trends in Academic Progress* (Washington, D.C.: National Center for Education Statistics, 1996), p. iv; "Nation Lags in Its Drive to Meet Education Goals, Report Finds," *New York Times,* November 19, 1996, p. A17.

130. William Clinton, "1997 State of the Union Address: The Bold New World of the Twenty-First Century," *Vital Speeches of the Day,* March 1, 1997, p. 291. The exams would be based on two existing tests, the NAEP and the Third International Mathematics and Science Study (TIMSS); see James Bennet, "President, Citing Education as a Top Priority of Second Term, Asks for a 'Call to Action,' " *New York Times,* February 5, 1997, pp. A1, A19.

131. William Clinton, "Remarks to the California Democratic Party in Sacramento," April 8, 1995, *Public Papers of the Presidents of the United States: William J. Clinton,* Book 1, 1995 (Washington, D.C.: U.S. Government Printing Office, 1996), p. 501. When Clinton finally signed the fiscal 1996 omnibus spending bill, however, he had cut education spending by 5.9 percent over the previous year's budget; see "GOP Steps Lightly in Response to Clinton's Proposals," *Congressional Quarterly Weekly Report,* February 15, 1997, p. 427. Jackie Koszczuk, "The Gloves Are On as Republicans Fight for Small Victories," *Congressional Quarterly Almanac,* 105th Cong., 1st sess., 1997 (Washington, D.C., 1998), p. 2154.

132. "Testing Plan Nearly Sinks Labor Bill," *Congressional Quarterly Almanac,* 105th Cong., 1st sess., 1997 (Washington, D.C., 1998), pp. 9–50, 9–53, 9–57.

133. Ibid.

134. David Broder, "Teachers Learning," *Washington Post,* November 9, 1997, p. C9; William Honan, "SAT Math Scores Improve but Verbal Results Stay Flat," *New York Times,* August 27, 1997, p. A12; Debra Viadero, "U.S. Seniors Near Bottom in World Test," *Education Week,* March 4, 1998, p. 1.

135. John Donahue, "Anyone for National Tests?" *America,* April 11, 1998, p. 9; Tamara Henry, "Vote Spells Trouble for National School Test," *USA Today,* February 9, 1998, p. B8; Kerry White, "Governors Press for Funding Freedom in Washington," *Education Week,* March 4, 1998, p. 1.

136. Tamara Henry, "Efforts to Improve School Standards Come at a Price," *USA Today,* July 14, 1998, p. A1; Carey Goldberg, "Massachusetts Retreats on Threshold for Teacher Test, Flunking Nearly Sixty Percent," *New York Times,* p. A11; Tamara Henry, "U.S. Losing Ground in the Race toward Education Equality," *USA Today,* November 24, 1998, p. D10; "Teacher Quality, not Standards Important," *Green Bay Press-Gazette,* November 27, 1998,

p. A7; William Honan, "Nearly Fifth of Teachers Say They Feel Unqualified," *New York Times*, January 29, 1999, p. A10.

137. William Clinton, "State of the Union 1999: Looking Towards the New Millennium," *Vital Speeches of the Day*, February 1, 1999, p. 227.

138. Todd Purham, "President Urges Educators to Fight Truancy," *New York Times*, July 4, 1996, p. B6.

139. Tamara Henry, "Nineties See Boom in School Enrollment," *USA Today*, July 2, 1999, p. A1; "Poll Shows Dole to Be a Major Republican Contender," *Green Bay Press-Gazette*, January 13, 1999, p. A4; Interview of Jay Johnson by author, November 6, 1997, Washington, D.C.

140. William Clinton, "Remarks to the Community at Abraham Lincoln Middle School in Selma," September 5, 1995, *Public Papers of the Presidents of the United States: William J. Clinton*, Book 2, *1995* (Washington, D.C.: U.S. Government Printing Office, 1996), p. 1306; Chuck Raasch, "Most Are Optimistic about Education," *Green Bay Press-Gazette*, December 29, 1997, p. A4; interview of Gerald Tirozzi by author, November 5, 1997, Washington, D.C.

141. Peter Applebome, "Yelling at the Little Red Menace," *New York Times*, September 14, 1997, p. D1; Ethan Bronner, "Teachers Pursuing Quality Control," *New York Times*, July 20, 1998, p. A13; Steven Greenhouse, "Teachers' Leader Seeks New Path," *New York Times*, July 4, 1998, p. A7; Romesh Ratsenar, "The Bite on Teachers," *Time*, July 20, 1998, pp. 23–24.

142. George O'Brien and Charles Peters, "Why the Right May Be Right," *Washington Monthly*, April 1997, p. 28; George Will, "Let's Play Twenty Questions," *Newsweek*, March 15, 1999, p. 86; James Dao, "Congress Passes Flexible School-Money Bill," *New York Times*, April 22, 1999, p. A26.

143. Tamar Lewin, "Patchwork of School Financing Schemes Offers Few Answers and Much Conflict," *New York Times*, April 8, 1998, p. C24; Wills, "The War between the States . . . and Washington," p. 28.

144. Nina Shokrai Rees, "The Real Divide Over Education," *New York Times*, October 8, 1998, p. A31; Ethan Bronner, "Congress Provides $1.2 Billion for Hiring Teachers Nationwide," *New York Times*, October 16, 1998, p. A17; Chester Finn and Michael Petrilli, "Washington versus School Reform," *Public Interest* (Fall 1998): 55.

145. Finn and Petrilli, "Washington versus School Reform," p. 55; Chester Finn, "Gentleman's C for the GOP," *Weekly Standard*, July 19, 1999, p. 20.

146. Henry, "Nineties See Boom in School Enrollment," p. 1; Raasch, "Most Are Optimistic about Education," p. 4; Ratsenar, "The Bite on Teachers," p. 69. The poll was by *USA Today* in Mona Charen, "Polls Showing That Republicans Finally Are Being Vindicated," *Green Bay Press-Gazette*, p. A14.

147. Joe Williams, "Teachers Reject Union Merger," *Milwaukee Journal-Sentinel*, July 6, 1998, pp. A1, A7; O'Brien and Peters, "Why the Right May Be Right," p. 29.

148. Michael Catanzaro, "Gorton Amendment to Cut Education Department and Terminate Goals 2000 Clears Senate," *Human Events*, September 26, 1997, p. 5.

149. Chester Finn, "Blindspots on the Right," *National Review*, September 25, 1995, p. 68; Irwin Molotsky, "Clinton Aid Plan in Partisan Grinder," *New York Times*, July 7, 1999, p. A21.

150. William Clinton, "Remarks to the National Education Association," July 6, 1995, *Public Papers of the Presidents of the United States: William J. Clinton*, Book 2, *1995* (Washington, D.C.: U.S. Government Printing Office, 1996), p. 1060; William Clinton, "Remarks

on Vetoing Budget Reconciliation Legislation," December 6, 1995, *Public Papers of the Presidents of the United States: William J. Clinton,* Book 2, *1995* (Washington, D.C.: U.S. Government Printing Office, 1996), p. 1851.

151. Interview of Tirozzi by author, November 5, 1997; "Excerpts: These Are Good Times for America," *USA Today,* January 28, 1998, p. A8.

## Chapter 5: School Desegregation, 1981–2001

1. Ronald Reagan, *An American Life* (New York: Pocket Books, 1990), p. 163.

2. Thomas Edsall and Mary Edsall, *Chain Reaction: The Impact of Race, Rights and Taxes on American Politics* (New York: W. W. Norton, 1991), p. 89.

3. Herman Schwartz, *Packing the Courts: The Conservative Campaign to Rewrite the Constitution* (New York: Charles Scribner and Sons, 1988), p. 182.

4. A 1979 George Washington University study concluded that only 3.2 percent more white students and only 8.8 percent more minority students had been bused after desegregation than before, but a National Opinion Research Center study the same year found only 12.3 percent of minority parents in favor of busing children from one district to another; see Gwendolyn Mikell Remy and Bert Mogin, "The Brown Decision Twenty-five Years Later: Indicators of Desegregation and Equal Educational Opportunity," May 17, 1979, Stephen Galenbach Files, Box 1, Folder Busing [3 of 3] OA 11313, RRPL, p. 7. "Busing," January 31, 1980, Richard Hauser Files, Box 1, Folder Busing/Desegregation [1 of 2] OA 10311, RRPL, p. 1.

5. Donald Doane, "Why So Many Say Busing Is a Failure," *U.S. News and World Report,* December 8, 1980, p. 59.

6. "Briefing Notes: The Chicago Plan," June 16, 1982, WHORM, Subject file Human Rights, Box 2, Folder HU 089000-090999, RRPL, pp. 1–2; "Summary of Initial Considerations: Pupil Assignment for Chicago School Desegregation," H-G-H Associates, Spring, Tex., March 12, 1981, Office of the White House Intergovernmental Affairs Files, Folder Chicago Busing [1 of 2] OA 7874, RRPL, p. 6; Letter from Roger McAuliffe to Ronald Reagan, April 9, 1981, attached to Memorandum from Henry Wilson to Fred Fielding, May 5, 1981, WHORM, Subject file Judicial-Legal Matters, Box 1, Folder JL 002 (Civil Matters)—128726, RRPL; Memorandum from Richard Williamson to Martin Anderson and Michael Uhlmann, March 27, 1981, Office of the White House Intergovernmental Affairs Files, Box 4, Folder Chicago Busing [1 of 2] OA 7874, RRPL; Nathaniel Shephard, "Justice Department Assails Chicago Integration Plan," *New York Times,* July 22, 1981, p. A12; Memorandum from David Waller to Richard Hauser, July 21, 1981, Richard Hauser Files, Box 1, Folder Busing/Desegregation [1 of 2] OA 10311, RRPL.

7. Letter from Mark White to Ronald Reagan, May 6, 1981, WHORM, Subject file Human Rights, Box 1, Folder HU 011-01600-024999, RRPL, p. 1; "Powell Rejects Texas Plea," *New York Times,* July 22, 1981, p. A12. Reynolds claimed that the administration submitted two plans, one voluntary, based primarily on magnet schools, and the second compulsory, including busing: "The court rejected all plans before it and devised its own plan"; see Memorandum from W. Bradford Reynolds to Richard Hauser, September 8, 1981, Richard Hauser Files, Box 1, Folder Busing/Desegregation [2 of 2] Texas School Desegregation Case, RRPL, pp. 1–3. Letter from Kenneth Eikenberry to Lyn Nofziger, August 4, 1981, attached to Memorandum from Nofziger to Edwin Meese et al., August 24, 1981, Fred Fielding Files, Box 17, Folder Busing, RRPL, pp. 1–7.

8. "The St. Louis Voluntary School Desegregation Case," attached to Memorandum from D. Edward Wilson to Fred Fielding, May 5, 1981, WHORM, Subject file Judicial-Legal Matters, Box 1, Folder JL 002 (Civil Matters)—128726, RRPL pp. 1–3; Letter from Barbara Mueller to Ronald Reagan, May 29, 1981, WHORM, Subject file Human Rights, Box 1, Folder HU 011-025000-029999, RRPL; Memorandum from James Medas to Richard Williamson, May 5, 1981, WHORM, Subject file Human Rights, Box 1, Folder HU 011-01600-024999, RRPL.

9. Statement by William French Smith, May 6, 1981, attached to Memorandum from Diane Lozano to Elizabeth Dole, May 29, 1981, Elizabeth Dole Files, Box 1, Folder Busing OA 9591, RRPL, p. 1.

10. Raymond Wolters, *Right Turn: William Bradford Reynolds, the Reagan Administration, and Black Civil Rights* (New Brunswick, N.J.: Transaction, 1996), pp. 382–83; Letter from W. Bradford Reynolds to Morton Blackwell, September 24, 1981, Michael Luttig Files, Box 1, Folder School Desegregation Testimony, OA 10021, RRPL, pp. 2, 4.

11. Letter from Dan Seale to Ronald Reagan, October 1, 1981, attached to Memorandum from Neal Hammerstrom to Nancy Kennedy, October 6, 1981, WHORM, Subject file Human Rights, Box 1, Folder HU 011-050000-053799, RRPL.

12. Letter from Edwin Meese to Donna Pope, February 22, 1982, WHORM, Subject file Human Rights, Box 1, Folder HU 011-06000-062999, RRPL; "Senate OK's Stiff Anti-Busing Bill," *Human Events,* March 13, 1982, pp. 7–9; Letter from William French Smith to Peter Rodino, May 6, 1982, WHORM, Subject file Human Rights, Box 1, Folder HU 011-088000-088999, RRPL, pp. 3, 5; Memorandum from Morton Blackwell to Elizabeth Dole, July 22, 1982, Elizabeth Dole Files, Box 1, Folder Busing OA 6412, RRPL, pp. 1–2.

13. Blackwell to Dole, July 22, 1982, RRPL, p. 2; Letter from Arthur Flemming to Ronald Reagan, February 12, 1982, WHORM, Subject file Human Rights, Box 1, Folder HU 011-06000-06299, RRPL, pp. 10, 17; Wolters, *Right Turn,* p. 381. The Senate had delayed confirmation of the three others whom Reagan had appointed to replace Mary Frances Berry and Blandina Cardenas Ramirez, chosen by Carter, and Rabbi Murray Saltzman, selected by Ford; see Robert Pear, "Rights Unit Affirms Support of Court-Ordered Busing," *New York Times,* October 13, 1982, p. A18. Never in the twenty-four-year history of the commission had a new president fired the chairman; see Laurence Barrett, *Gambling with History: Ronald Reagan in the White House* (Garden City, N.Y.: Doubleday, 1983), p. 423.

14. Wolters, *Right Turn,* pp. 368–69; Letter from W. Bradford Reynolds to Millicent Fenwick, September 30, 1982, WHORM, Subject file Human Rights, Box 2, Folder HU 100583-107549, RRPL, pp. 1–2; Letter from Millicent Fenwick to Ronald Reagan, September 30, 1982, WHORM, Subject file Human Rights, Box 2, Folder HU 100583-101549, RRPL, pp. 1–2; Mary Thornton, "U.S. Weighs New Rebuff to Busing," *Washington Post,* September 28, 1982, p. A1; Memorandum from Michael Uhlmann and Kevin Hopkins to Larry Speakes, October 14, 1982, WHORM, Subject file Human Rights, Box 2, Folder HU 011-100583-107549, RRPL, pp. 1, 3.

15. Norman Amaker, *Civil Rights and the Reagan Administration* (Washington, D.C.: Urban Institute Press, 1988), p. 41; Caroline Rand Herron, Michael Wright, and Carlyle C. Douglas, "Judge Approves St. Louis Busing," *New York Times,* July 10, 1983, p. E4; Dan Balz, "Busing School Inadvertently Draws Praise," *Washington Post,* May 20, 1983, p. A2; Memorandum from Stephen Galebach to Kenneth Cribb, July 6, 1983, White House Office of Intergovernmental Affairs, Box 4, Folder Education Policy Meeting BA 11849, RRPL, pp. 1–2; William French Smith, "Yes, We Do Enforce Civil Rights Laws," *Washington Post,* July

10, 1983, p. C26; Mary Thornton, "Civil Rights Chief Says He's Unchanged," *Washington Post*, July 11, 1983, p. A9.

16. Wolters, *Right Turn*, pp. 372, 387; "Desegregation Funds Veto," *Congressional Quarterly Almanac*, 98th Cong., 1st sess., 1983 (Washington, D.C., 1984), p. 35E; Amaker, *Civil Rights and the Reagan Administration*, p. 38; Letter from Lyn Nofziger to Michael Deaver, September 22, 1983, WHORM, Subject file Human Rights, Box 3, Folder HU 011-168000-179999, RRPL; Amaker, *Civil Rights and the Reagan Administration*, p. 48; Letter from Joyce Haws to Ronald Reagan, March 19, 1984, WHORM, Subject file Human Rights, Box 3, Folder HU 011-204000-215999, RRPL.

17. Wilbur Edel, *The Reagan Presidency: An Actor's Finest Performance* (New York: Hippocrene, 1992), p. 133.

18. Telephone interview of William Bradford Reynolds by author, July 8, 1999; David O'Brien, "The Reagan Judges: His Most Enduring Legacy," in *The Reagan Legacy: Promise and Performance*, ed. Charles Jones (Chatham, N.J.: Chatham House, 1988), p. 66; Amaker, *Civil Rights and the Reagan Administration*, p. 38.

19. Wolters, *Right Turn*, pp. 11–12.

20. Ibid., pp. 444, 12.

21. "President Praises Enriched School Program," *New York Times*, January 21, 1988, p. A20.

22. Steven Shull, *A Kinder, Gentler Racism: The Reagan-Bush Civil Rights Legacy* (New York: M. E. Sharpe, 1993), pp. 226, 205; David Savage, *Turning Right: The Making of the Rehnquist Supreme Court* (New York: Wiley and Sons), 1992, p. 365; "Resolutions of the Seventy-Sixth Annual National Convention, 23–27 June, 1985," *Crisis* (May 1986): 22; "The Conservative Political Action Committee Conference," February 19, 1987, *Major Policy Statements of the Attorney General: Edwin Meese III, 1985–1988* (Washington, D.C.: U.S. Government Printing Office, 1989), pp. 178–85; telephone interview of Edwin Meese by author, June 23, 1999.

23. Walter Murphy, "Reagan's Judicial Strategy," in *Looking Back on the Reagan Presidency*, ed. Larry Berman (Baltimore: Johns Hopkins University Press, 1990), p. 210; O'Brien, "The Reagan Judges: His Most Enduring Legacy," pp. 60, 83; Gary Orfield and Susan Eaton, *Dismantling Desegregation* (New York: New Press, 1997), p. 336.

24. William French Smith, *Law and Justice in the Reagan Administration* (Stanford, Calif.: Hoover Institution Press, 1991), p. 94; Wolters, *Right Turn*, pp. 374–75, 400; Rolf Blank, "The Effect of Magnet Schools on the Quality of Education in Urban School Districts," *Phi Delta Kappan* (December 1984): 270; Finis Welch and Audrey Light, "New Evidence on School Desegregation," *Report of the United States Civil Rights Commission* (June 1987): v.

25. Wolters, *Right Turn*, pp. 375, 393–94; Orfield and Eaton, *Dismantling Desegregation*, p. 331.

26. Lou Cannon, *President Reagan: The Role of a Lifetime* (New York: Simon and Schuster, 1991), pp. 519–20; Lena Williams, "Reagan Meets with Blacks on Education Cuts," *New York Times*, February 26, 1987, p. A15; "A Matter of Politics and Linguistics," *New York Times*, August 25, 1981, p. B7; "The Reagan Record," White House Office of Public Affairs, 1988, RRPP, RRPL, p. 19; Shull, *A Kinder, Gentler Racism*, p. 217.

27. Telephone interview of Meese by author, June 23, 1999; telephone interview of Reynolds by author, July 8, 1999.

28. TRB, "Pandora's Box," *New Republic* 199 (November 14, 1988): 4, 45.

29. David Mervin, *George Bush and the Guardianship Presidency* (New York: St. Martin's, 1998), p. 219; Charles Henry, "What Can We Expect from the New President?" *Crisis* (December 1988): 15.

30. Letter from David Armor to Roger Porter, February 14, 1989, WHORM, Subject file Education, Box 13, Folder ED Education [116000-122999] (1), GBPL, p. 1; David Armor, "After Busing: Education and Choice," *Current* (October 14–20, 1989): 14; Letter from James Turner to Rebecca Amerson, December 19, 1989, Freedom of Information Act Request, Box 2, WHORM Alpha File, Folder WHORM Alpha File: Bush Presidential Records [OA15525] (2 of 4), GBPL, p. 2.

31. Memorandum from Doreen Torgerson to Charles Kolb, September 17, 1990, FOIA Request, Box 11, Folder Bush Presidential Records, Office of Policy Development, GBPL, p. 1.

32. Ruth Marcus, "Justices Question Extent of Responsibility on School Busing," *Washington Post*, October 3, 1990, p. A16.

33. Ibid.; Joan Beck, "Court Will Decide If Busing Must Go on Forever," *Chicago Tribune*, October 4, 1990, p. A23.

34. Linda Chavez and Bonnie Erbe, "Busing an Ineffective Remedy for Education Imbalance," *Dallas Times Herald*, October 5, 1990, p. A17; Beck, "Court Will Decide If Busing Must Go on Forever," p. 23; William Raspberry, "Another Look at Busing," *Washington Post*, October 5, 1990, p. A25; William Murchison, "Down This Road Before," *Washington Times*, October 4, 1990, p. G1.

35. Chavez and Erbe, "Busing an Ineffective Remedy for Education Imbalance," p. 17.

36. Ann Kornhauser, "Starr Seeks Strict Tests for Schools," *Legal Times*, October 1, 1990, p. 2; Ruth Marcus, "School Desegregation: Do Obligations Remain?" *Washington Post*, September 28, 1990, p. A1.

37. Linda Greenhouse, "Justices Rule Mandatory Busing May Go, Even If Races Stay Apart," *New York Times*, January 17, 1991, p. A1; "Excerpts from Court Decision," *New York Times*, January 17, 1991, p. B7. Since the case began before his ascension to the Court, Justice David Souter did not participate in the decision.

38. Mark Whitman, *The Irony of Desegregation Law, 1955–1995* (Princeton, N.J.: Markus Wiener, 1998), p. 310.

39. Amy Stuart Wells, "Asking What Students Have Done or Can Do to Help Desegregation," *New York Times*, January 16, 1991, p. A1; Benjamin Hooks, "Publisher's Foreword," *Crisis* (October 1991): 3.

40. "Strong Support for Goals and Bush Strategy," August 22, 1991, WHORM, Subject file Education, Box 28, Folder ED Education [267000-268999] [2], GBPL, p. 4.

41. Orfield and Eaton, *Dismantling Desegregation*, p. 22.

42. Kornhauser, "Starr Seeks Strict Tests for Schools," p. 2; Greenhouse, "Justices Rule Mandatory Busing May Go, Even If Races Stay Apart," p. B7.

43. Letter from Roger Porter to William Goodling, April 4, 1989, WHORM, Subject file Education, Box 2, Folder ED Education [021200-029999], GBPL, p. 1; House Republican Research Committee Empowerment Task Force, "Choice in Education and School Desegregation," March 1990, attached to letter from Stephen Bartlett to George Bush, May 2, 1990, WHORM, Subject file Education, Box 15, Folder ED Education [135000-161999], GBPL, p. 1; Memorandum from Torgerson to Kolb, GBPL.

44. Telephone interview of Roger Porter by author, November 26, 1997; telephone interview of Lamar Alexander by author, January 28, 1998.

45. George Bush, "Remarks at the United Negro College Fund Dinner in New York, New York," March 9, 1989, *Public Papers of the Presidents of the United States: George Bush, Book 1, 1989* (Washington, D.C.: U.S. Government Printing Office, 1990), p. 202. The riots erupted after the acquittal of white police officers accused of brutality toward defendant Rodney King. The retrial of the case under federal civil rights statutes would result in the conviction of the officers.

46. William Clinton, "Remarks at the NAACP Legal Defense and Educational Fund Dinner," May 16, 1994, *Public Papers of the Presidents of the United States: William J. Clinton, Book 1, 1994* (Washington, D.C.: U.S. Government Printing Office, 1995), p. 933.

47. William Clinton, "Commencement Address at the University of California, San Diego, in La Jolla, California," June 14, 1997, *Public Papers of the Presidents of the United States: William J. Clinton, Book 1, 1997* (Washington, D.C.: U.S. Government Printing Office, 1998), p. 739.

48. "Excerpts from President's Comments on School Desegregation," *New York Times,* September 26, 1997, p. A14.

49. William Celis, "An Impatient Advocate Stirs Up the Education Department's Rights Office," *New York Times,* August 3, 1994, p. B6.

50. William Clinton, "Remarks to a Town Meeting, Cranston, Rhode Island," May 9, 1994, *Public Papers of the Presidents of the United States: William J. Clinton, Book 1, 1994* (Washington, D.C.: U.S. Government Printing Office, 1995), p. 881.

51. William Celis, "Kansas City's Widely Debated Desegregation Experiment Reaches the Supreme Court," *New York Times,* January 11, 1995, p. B7; Mark Whitman, *The Irony of Desegregation Law, 1955–1999* (Princeton, N.J.: Markus Weiner, 1998), pp. 315–17.

52. William Celis, "Study Finds Rising Concentration of Black and Hispanic Students," *New York Times,* p. A1.

53. Kenneth Clark, "Unfinished Business: The Toll of Psychic Violence," *Newsweek,* January 11, 1993, p. 38; Roger Wilkins, "The 'Brown' Decision: Forty Years Later," *America,* July 17, 1993, pp. 4–5; Ellis Cose, "The Realities of Black and White," *Newsweek,* April 29, 1996, p. 38; James Kumen, "Integration Forever?" *Time,* July 21, 1997, p. 39. Mfume defended busing but added, "There has been too much focus on busing as the only remedy to segregated schools"; see Paul Ruffins, "Whatever Happened to Integration?" *Black Issues in Higher Education,* January 7, 1999, p. 18. Pam Belluck, "Deal Struck for Ending Busing Ban in St. Louis," *New York Times,* January 8, 1999, p. A10.

54. James Traub, "Can Separate Be Equal?" *Harper's* (June 1994): 40; interview of Tirozzi by author, November 5, 1997; "News in Brief," *Christian Science Monitor,* January 8, 1999, p. A24; "Excerpts from President's Comments," p. 14.

55. William Clinton, "Remarks Prior to a Meeting with the President's Advisory Board on Race and an Exchange with Reporters," June 13, 1997, *Public Papers of the Presidents of the United States: William J. Clinton, Book 1, 1997* (Washington, D.C.: U.S. Government Printing Office, 1998), p. 732; David Maraniss, *The Clinton Enigma* (New York: Simon and Schuster, 1998), pp. 17–18; Paul Greenberg, *No Surprises* (Washington, D.C.: Brassey's, 1996), p. 18; Sidney Blumenthal, *The Clinton Wars* (New York: Farrar, Straus, and Giroux, 2003), p. 274.

56. John Hope Franklin, "Talking, Not Shouting about Race," *New York Times,* September 19, 1998, p. A7.

57. Steven Holmes, "Race Advisory Panel Gives Report to Clinton," *New York Times,* September 19, 1998, p. A7.

58. Clinton, "Commencement Address," p. 737; "Moving Forward, but Still Behind," *Newsweek,* June 7, 1999, pp. 32–33.

59. "Moving Forward," pp. 32–33.

60. Clinton, "Remarks to a Town Meeting," p. 881; "School Busing: An Era in Decline," *Christian Science Monitor,* February 2, 1999, p. A1; Del Stover, "Segregation Makes a Comeback," *Education Digest* (February 1995): 50; Kumen, "Integration Forever?" pp. 39–40.

61. Joe Williams, "Segregation Coming Back in State's Schools," *Milwaukee Journal-Sentinel,* June 13, 1999, p. B1; Tamar Jacoby, "Beyond Busing," *Wall Street Journal,* July 21, 1999, p. A22.

62. "A Change of Course in Boston," *New York Times,* July 17, 1999, p. A24.

## Chapter 6: Nonpublic School Aid, 1981–2001

1. "Saving Diversity by Distinctions," *America,* February 5, 1977, p. 93; George Gallup and Jim Castelli, *The American Catholic People* (Garden City, N.Y.: Doubleday, 1987), p. 128; Memorandum from Bishop Thomas Kelly to Most Rev. Archbishop, August 18, 1978, Box 37, Folder USCC: Church: Church and State: Federal Aid to Education, Tax Credits, 1973–78, USCCP; Bob Watson and Jack Hales, "Tuition Tax Credits High on Reagan List," *Cincinnati Enquirer,* October 21, 1980, p. A1; Gallup and Castelli, *The American Catholic People,* p. 129; Steven Roberts, "Senate Approves Increase in Limit on Federal Debt," *New York Times,* November 17, 1983, p. A1.

2. Memorandum from Rev. Thomas Gallagher to Catholic School Superintendents, November 19, 1980, Box 70, Folder USCC: Departmental Committees: Education: Tax Credits, USCCP, p. 1; "Tuition Tax Credits: Now or Never," *America,* December 13, 1980, pp. 380–81; "Packwood Introduces Tuition Tax Credits," February 24, 1981, Box 70, Folder U.S. Departmental Committees: Education: Tax Credits, 1981 January–June, USCCP.

3. Thomas Edsall, "Reagan Win May Be Far Reaching," *Washington Post,* August 13, 1981, p. A2; Memorandum from Msgr. Thomas Leonard to Bishop Thomas Kelly, August 21, 1981, Box 70, Folder USCC Departmental Committees: Education Tax Credits, 1981 July–August, USCCP; Memorandum from Bishop Thomas Kelly to All Ordinary and Auxiliary Bishops, Box 70, Folder USCC: Departmental Committees: Education Tax Credits, 1981 September–December, USCCP; Telegram from President Ronald Reagan to the Chief Administrators of Catholic Education, October 16, 1981, Box 70, Folder USCC: Departmental Committees: Education Tax Credits, 1981 September–December, USCCP, pp. 1–2.

4. Owen Ullman, "Tuition Credit," November 15, 1981, Box 70, Folder USCC: Departmental Committees: Education Tax Credits, 1981 September–December, USCCP; "Advisory Panel on Financing Elementary and Secondary Education, Annual Report," December 1981, AFT Office of the President, Box 23, Folder Dept. HEW, Advisory Panel, Dec. 1981, AFTP, p. 2; Steven Weisman, "Reagan to Offer a Plan to Provide Tuition Tax Credit," *New York Times,* April 13, 1982, p. D28.

5. Howell Raines, "Reagan Asks Tuition Tax Credit," *New York Times,* April 16, 1978, p. A15; Albert Menendez, "Reagan Tuition Tax Credit Plan Faces Uncertain Future," *Church and State,* June 1982, p. 6; "Status Report on Tuition Tax Credit Campaign," May 17, 1982, Box ED 89-38, Folder Draft Proposal, Tuition Tax Credit Campaign, USCCP, p. 2; Memorandum from Frank Monahan to Msgr. Daniel Hoye, July 2, 1982, Box: ED 89-59, Folder Advisory Committee on Public Policy and Catholic Schools, 1981–82, USCCP, p. 1.

6. Monahan to Hoye, July 2, 1982, USCCP, pp. 3–4.

7. "Tuition Tax Credit Update," August 9, 1982, Box 70, Folder USCC Departmental Committees: Education: Tax Credits, 1982 July–August, USCCP; Memorandum from Msgr. Edward Spiers to Members, Committee for Private Education, October 5, 1982, Box 70, Folder USCC Departmental Committees: Education: Tax Credits, 1982 September–December, USCCP, pp. 1–2.

8. "Minutes, Committee on Public Policy and Catholic Schools," January 19, 1983, Box ED 89-59, Folder Public Policy, 9/8/83, USCCP, p. 1; Ronald Reagan, "Address before a Joint Session of the Congress on the State of the Union," July 25, 1983, *Public Papers of the Presidents of the United States: Ronald Reagan*, Book 1, *1983* (Washington, D.C.: U.S. Government Printing Office, 1984), p. 106; Ronald Reagan, "Message to the Congress Transmitting the Fiscal Year 1984 Budget," January 31, 1983, *Public Papers of the Presidents of the United States: Ronald Reagan*, Book 1, *1983*, p. 145; Memorandum from Judy Barnacke to Tuition Tax Credit Petition Drive Coordinators et al., March 18, 1983, AFT Office of the President, Box 64, Folder 64–16, AFTP, p. 1; Juan Williams, "White House Pushes for Tuition Tax Credit," *Washington Post*, March 5, 1983, p. A5.

9. Letter from President Ronald Reagan to "Your Excellency," March 1, 1983, Box 70, Folder USCC Departmental Committees, Education: Tax Credits, 1983 January–April, USCCP; Williams, "White House Pushes for Tuition Tax Credit," p. A5; Barnacke to Tuition Tax Credit Petition Drive Coordinators, AFTP, p. 1.

10. Thomas Brandt, "White House Uses Rider to Save Tuition Credit," *Washington Times*, June 3, 1983, p. A3; Memorandum from Edward Anthony to Msgr. Daniel Hoye, June 9, 1983, Box 70, Folder USCC Departmental Committees: Education: Tax Credits, 1983 May–July, USCCP, p. 2.

11. Edwin Dorn and Mary Frances Berry, "Tax Credits for Tuition Address the Wrong Issue," *Los Angeles Times*, July 13, 1983, in *Congressional Record*, July 28, 1983, p. E382.

12. Memorandum from J. Stephen O'Brien to the Executive Staff, July 25, 1983, Box ED 89-59, Folder *Mueller v. Allen*, 1983, USCCP.

13. Felicity Barringer, "Inside the Education Department," *Washington Post*, October 25, 1983, p. A17.

14. Memorandum from Frank Monahan to Msgr. Daniel Hoye, November 21, 1983, Box 70, Folder USCC: Departmental Committees: Education: Tax Credits, 1983 November–December, USCCP.

15. "Minutes of the Tuition Credit Advisory Committees," December 19, 1983, Box 70, Folder USCC: Departmental Committees: Education: Tax Credits, 1983 November–December, USCCP, pp. 1–3.

16. Carol Innerst, "Contenders Outline Education Goals," *Washington Post*, September 14, 1984, p. A4; Ronald Reagan, "Address before a Joint Session of Congress on the State of the Union," February 6, 1985, *Public Papers of the Presidents of the United States: Ronald Reagan*, Book 1, *1985* (Washington, D.C.: U.S. Government Printing Office, 1988), p. 132; Memorandum from Robert W. Sweet to John A. Svahn, August 12, 1985, WHORM, Subject file Education, Box 17, Folder ED Education [358500-360162], RRPL, p. 1; Ronald Reagan, "Message to the Congress on America's Agenda for the Future," *Public Papers of the Presidents of the United States: Ronald Reagan*, Book 1, *1986* (Washington, D.C.: U.S. Government Printing Office, 1988), p. 153; Ronald Reagan, "America's Economic Bill of Rights," July 3, 1987, *Public Papers of the Presidents of the United States: Ronald Reagan*, Book 1, *1987* (Washington, D.C.: U.S. Government Printing Office, 1988), p. 745; "The Rea-

gan Record on Education," September 1, 1988, WHORM, Subject file Education, Box 24, Folder ED Education [606422-614918], RRPL, p. 12; William Bennett, "Education Reform and the 1988 Election, Address at the National Press Club," September 8, 1987, FOIA Education Issues 1981–84 File, Folder FG 026 Dept. of Education [582480], RRPL, p. 15; Ronald Reagan, "1988 Legislative and Administrative Message: A Union of Individuals," January 25, 1988, *Public Papers of the Presidents of the United States: Ronald Reagan*, Book 1, *1988* (Washington, D.C.: U.S. Government Printing Office, 1990), p. 108.

17. Steven Weisman, "President Accepts Blame in Dispute on Tax Exemption," *New York Times,* January 20, 1982, pp. A1, A21; Linda Greenhouse, "High Court Bans Tax Exemptions for Schools with Racial Barriers," *New York Times,* May 25, 1983, pp. A1, A22.

18. "Tuition Tax Credit Update," USCCP; Memorandum from Msgr. Spiers to Virgil Dechant, September 1, 1982, Box 70, Folder USCC: Departmental Committees: Tax Credits, 1982 September–December, pp. 1–4; Charles Babcock, "Tuition Tax Credit Action Blocked by Democrats," *Washington Post,* August 12, 1982, p. A8; Charles Babcock, "Bias Issue Delays Tuition Tax Credit Bill," *Washington Post,* August 24, 1982, p. A2; Memorandum from Frank Monahan to Msgr. Daniel Hoye, October 26, 1982, Box 70, Folder USCC: Departmental Committees: Education Tax Credits, 1982 September–December, USCCP, pp. 1–8.

19. Memorandum from Frank Monahan to Msgr. Daniel Hoye, October 25, 1983, Box 71, Folder USCC: Departmental Committees: Education: Tax Credits, 1983 August–October, USCCP; Memorandum from Msgr. Daniel Hoye to Executive Committee, October 31, 1983, Box 71, Folder USCC: Departmental Committees: Education: Tax Credits, 1983 August–October, USCCP, pp. 1–2.

20. Memorandum from Sr. Renee Oliver to CEF Board Members and Leaders, August 17, 1982, Box 70, USCC: Departmental Committees: Education, 1982 July–August, USCCP, pp. 2–3; Babcock, "Bias Issue Delays Tuition Tax Credit Bill," p. 2; Letter from Marilyn Lundy to Rev. Daniel Pilarczyk, July 4, 1981, Box 70, Folder USCC: Departmental Committees: Education: Tax Credits, 1981 July–August, USCCP.

21. Memorandum from Rev. Thomas Gallagher to Msgr. Daniel Hoye, October 6, 1983, Box 70, Folder USCC: Departmental Committees: Education: Tax Credits, 1983 August–October, USCCP, pp. 1–2; "Minutes of the Federal Assistance Advisory Commission Meeting," October 17, 1981, Box 70, Folder USCC: Departmental Committees: Education Tax Credits, 1981 September–December, USCCP, pp. 2–3.

22. Menendez, "Reagan Tuition Tax Credit Plan Faces Uncertain Future," p. 6; John Donahue, "Public School Teachers' Targets," *America,* August 28, 1982, p. 86; "AFT Gearing Up for Election Push," *Education USA,* July 12, 1982, p. 361; "Just Entering Politics, NEA Says," *Education USA,* July 12, 1982, p. 361; "Politics, Job Issues Dominate NEA, AFT Annual Meetings," *Education USA,* June 30, 1982, p. 1; Karen Cook, "Stalemate," *Forbes,* August 16, 1982, p. 93; Memorandum from Rev. Thomas Gallagher to Msgr. Daniel Hoye, March 10, 1983, Box ED 89-38, Folder USCC and Tuition Tax Credits, USCCP; Interview of Robert Packwood by author, November 4, 1997, Washington, D.C.

23. Letter from Rev. Virgil Blum to Archbishop John Roach, January 16, 1981, Box 70, Folder USCC Departmental Committees: Education: Tax Credits, 1981 January–June, USCCP, pp. 2–3; Letter from Moynihan to Kelly, July 17, 1981, USCCP, p. 4; Memorandum from Richard Duffy to Rev. Thomas Gallagher, James Robinson, Frank Monahan, and John Liekwig, March 22, 1983, Box 60, Folder USCC: Departmental Committees: Education: Tax Credits, 1983, USCCP, p. 1; Alice in Potomac Land, "Selling (Out) Reagan Policy," *Washington Post,* August 9, 1983, p. A3.

24. In 1981, Congress and the Reagan administration agreed to expand Title (now Chapter) II to fund nonpublic school children not only through public agencies but through programs contracted by these agencies to other public or nonpublic organizations; see Memorandum from Frank Monahan to Members of the Committee on Public Policy and Catholic Schools, the Federal Advisory Commission, and other Interested Persons, August 3, 1981, Box 70, USCC: Departmental Committees: Education: Tax Credits, 1981 July–August, USCCP, pp. 1–2. The USCC's Federal Assistance Advisory Commission pronounced the resulting Education Consolidation and Improvement Act of 1981 to be "everything we wanted"; see "Minutes of the Federal Assistance Advisory Commissions Meeting," October 17, 1981, Box 70, Folder USCC: Departmental Committees: Education: Tax Credits, 1981 September–December, USCCP, p. 11. "Major Recommendations of National Commission on Excellence in Education," Staff and Office Files: Carleson, Robert, Box 9592, Folder Education [6 of 9] OA 9592, RRPL. After Reagan presented his "Equal Education Opportunity Act of 1983" to voucherize Chapter One of the ESEA, the USCC's Rev. Thomas Gallagher wrote, "We have a series of concerns/questions about the proposal, including whether the vouchers could pay for nonpublic school tuition as well as services. Until those concerns are satisfied, we cannot voice an opinion pro or con"; see Memorandum from Rev. Thomas Gallagher to Msgr. Daniel Hoye, March 29, 1983, Box ED 89-59, Folder Public Policy 9/8/83, USCCP. Calling the voucher initiative a "neat political ploy," Richard Duffy accurately predicted that the USCC's Office of Government Liaison "is of the opinion that the chances of this legislation being enacted are virtually nonexistent"; see Memorandum from Duffy to Gallagher, Robinson, Monahan, and Liekweg, March 22, 1983, USCCP, pp. 1–2.

25. "Meet the Press," May 29, 1983, AFT Office of the President, Box 82, Folder June—Miscellaneous, 1983, AFTP, p. 9; Ronald Reagan, "Interview with a Group of Senior Executives and Staff Members of the *Wall Street Journal*," February 7, 1985, *Public Papers of the Presidents of the United States: Ronald Reagan*, Book 1, 1985, p. 141.

26. Bob Schieffer and Gary Paul Gates, *The Acting President* (New York: E. F. Dutton, 1989), p. 88; Memorandum from Frank Monahan to Msgr. Thomas Leonard, James Robinson, and Rev. Thomas Gallagher, April 6, 1981, Box 70, Folder USCC: Departmental Committees: Education: Tax Credits, USCCP, pp. 1–2; Garry Wills, *Reagan's America: Innocents at Home* (Garden City, N.Y.: Doubleday, 1987), p. 345; Monahan to Hoye, October 26, 1982, USCCP, p. 1; Robert Dallek, *Ronald Reagan: The Politics of Symbolism* (Cambridge: Harvard University, 1984), p. 123; "Minutes, Committee on Public Policy and Catholic Schools," Education: Tax Credits, December 1982, Box 70, Folder Departmental Committees: Tax Credits, 1981 September–December, USCCP, p. 1.

27. Alonzo Hamby, *Liberalism and Its Challengers: From F.D.R. to Bush* (New York: Oxford University Press, 1992), p. 361; Schieffer and Gates, *The Acting President*, p. 85; Memorandum from Edward Anthony to Msgr. Daniel Hoye, June 9, 1983, Box ED 89-38, Folder USCC Office of the General Secretary, USCCP, p. 2; Alice in Potomac Land, "Selling (Out) Reagan Policy," p. 3; Memorandum from Rev. Thomas Gallagher to James Robinson, September 16, 1983, Box 71, Folder USCC: Departmental Committees: Education: Tax Credits, 1983 August–October, USCCP.

28. William Raspberry, "Trouble for Tuition Credits," *Washington Post*, May 18, 1981, p. A15; Letter from Moynihan to Kelly, July 17, 1981, USCCP, p. 1; Memorandum from James Robinson to Terence Cardinal Cooke, January 25, 1982, Box 70, Folder USCC: Departmental Committees: Education Tax Credits, 1982 January–June, USCCP, pp. 1–2; Steven

Roberts, "Lawmakers Doubt Fast Passage of Tuition Credit," *New York Times,* April 16, 1982, p. A15; Menendez, "Reagan Tuition Tax Credit Plan Faces Uncertain Future," p. 10.

29. "Minutes of the Tuition Tax Credit Advisory Committees," pp. 1–2; "Savaging the Schools," *New Republic,* May 5, 1982, pp. 7–8.

30. Edward Fiske, "Lessons," *New York Times,* January 11, 1989, p. B5.

31. Warren Brookes, "Demise of the Education Presidency," *Washington Times,* April 7, 1989, p. F1; Letter from Lauro Cavazos to Kenneth Brown and Roslyn Cooperman, March 21, 1989, WHORM, Subject file Education, Box 1, Folder ED Education [900378-900577], GBPL, p. 1; "Bush Rejects Tax Break for Private School Cost," *New York Times,* March 30, 1989, p. A20.

32. "President Submits Educational Excellence Act of 1989 to Hill," *White House Wire,* April 5, 1989, WHORM, Subject file Education, Box 2, Folder ED Education [020000-021199] [2], GBPL, p. 1; Letter from Lauro Cavazos to the President, May 16, 1989, WHORM, Subject file Education, Box 2, Folder Education [030000-039999] [1], GBPL, p. 2; Julie Johnson, "Administration Makes Choice a Top School Priority," *New York Times,* May 20, 1989, p. A33.

33. "Meeting with Key Catholic Lay Leaders," Talking Points, March 27, 1989, WHORM, Subject file Religious Matters, Box 2, Folder RM Religious Matters, RM 031 [003529-290843], GBPL; Letter from Rev. Robert Lynch to John Sununu, April 10, 1989, WHORM, Subject file Finance, Box 42, Folder FI Finance [005-03] [1], GBPL; Letter from Sr. Anne Leonard to George Bush, May 16, 1989, Bush Presidential Records Office of Policy Development, William Roper subject file, Folder Tuition Tax Credits, GBPL.

34. Letter from William Roper to Rev. Edward Lynch, April 21, 1989, Bush Presidential Records, Office of Policy Development, William Roper subject file, Box 11, Folder Tuition Tax Credits, GBPL; Letter from Lynch to Roper, May 23, 1989, Bush Presidential Records, Office of Policy Development, William Roper subject file, Box 11, Folder Tuition Tax Credits, GBPL; Carol Innerst, "Private School Advocates Want 'Choice' Vow Kept," *Washington Times,* June 10, 1989, p. A3. Bush wrote in the margin of the *Washington Times* story on the meeting, "Is this [McNamee] who came in here?" in WHORM, Subject file Education, Box 33, Folder ED Education [296000-299999] [4], GPBL.

35. Telegram from Manya Unger to George Bush, March 30, 1989, WHORM, Subject file Finance, Box 42, Folder FI Finance [005-03] [1], March 30, 1989, GBPL, pp. 1–2; Julie Johnson, "Administration Makes Choice a Top School Priority," *New York Times,* May 20, 1989, p. L33; Memorandum from Roger Porter to the President, April 23, 1989, WHORM, Subject file Education, Box 15, Folder ED Education [135000-161999] [1], GBPL, pp. 1–2; Letter from William Goodling to George Bush, September 14, 1989, WHORM, Subject file Education, Box 7, Folder ED Education [069000-076999], GBPL.

36. Letter from Mae Duggan to Roger Porter, September 20, 1989, WHORM, Subject file Education, Box 7, Folder ED Education [069000-076999] [14], GBPL; interview of Robert Packwood by author, November 4, 1989, Washington, D.C.; Memorandum from Rae Nelson to Roger Porter, November 25, 1989, WHORM, Subject file Education, Box 11, Folder ED Education [095000-103199] [4], GBPL.

37. Letter from Lauro Cavazos to George Bush, December 20, 1989, WHORM, Subject file Education, Folder ED Education [103200-112499] [4], GBPL; "Bush's Education Proposals Unfulfilled," *Congressional Quarterly Almanac* 1990 (Washington, D.C., 1991), p. 610; Letter from George Bush to Polly Williams, September 15, 1990, Bush Presidential Records, Office of Policy Development, Box 12, Folder Doreen Torgerson File, Milwaukee

Vouchers [OA/ID 05164], GBPL; Letter from Roger Porter to Pierre DuPont, November 13, 1990, WHORM, Subject file Education, Box 24, Folder ED Education [238400-238999] [3], GBPL, pp. 1–2; Letter from Jack Klenk to Sr. Anita Henning, February 4, 1991, WHORM Alpha File, Box 3, Folder Henning [OA 15981] [1 of 2], GBPL, pp. 1–2.

38. Memorandum from Rev. Charles O'Malley to Senior Officers, August 22, 1990, WHORM, Subject file Education, Box 1, Folder ED Education [005894-089827], GBPL, p. 1; Jeanne Allen, "Nine Phoney Assertions about School Choice," *Heritage Foundation Backgrounder,* September 13, 1990, p. 1; interview of Roger Porter by author, November 26, 1997; Memorandum from Roger Porter to the President, March 21, 1991, WHORM, Subject file Education, Box 22, Folder ED Education [200000-225999] [1], GBPL, p. 3.

39. "Remarks by the President at Presentation of National Education Strategy," April 18, 1991, Bush Presidential Records, Office of Policy Development, Charles E. M. Kolb subject file, Box 12, Folder Johannes Kuttner, America 2000 [OA/ID 06978] [1 of 2], GBPL, p. 3; Letter from Roger Porter to Paul Mecklenburg, April 15, 1991, WHORM Alpha File, Box 4, Folder Meckl [OA 16295] GBPL; Letter from Rev. Daniel Pilarczyk to Roger Porter, May 8, 1991, WHORM, Subject file Education, Box 23, Folder ED Education [236000-238399] [2], GBPL, pp. 1–2; "Statement by the Institute of Public Affairs of the Union of Orthodox Jewish Congregations of America," April 26, 1991, WHORM, Subject file Education, Box 23, Folder ED Education [233000-235999] (1), GBPL.

40. Albert Shanker, "Incentives and Reforms," August 1991, Office of the President, no box, no folder, AFTP, p. 2; Keith Geiger, "Choosing Universal Excellence," *Education Week,* May 22, 1991, p. 48.

41. Memorandum from Roger Porter to John Sununu, May 23, 1989, WHORM, Subject file Judicial-Legal Matters, Box 57, Folder JL 004-03 Judicial-Legal Matters [055173-070442], GBPL; Sam Allis, "Can Catholic Schools Do It Better?" *Time,* May 27, 1991, pp. 48–49; George Bush, "Remarks at the Presidential Open Forum on Educational Choice in Philadelphia, Pennsylvania," July 21, 1992, *Public Papers of the Presidents of the United States: George Bush,* Book 1, *1992–93* (Washington, D.C.: U.S. Government Printing Office 1993), p. 1147.

42. George Bush, "Presidential Remarks: Christian Schools, Anaheim, CA," November 19, 1991, WHORM, Subject file Education, Box 32, Folder ED Education [288000-288499] [2], GBPL, pp. 1, 4.

43. "Press Briefing with Secretary Lamar Alexander and Governors William O'Neill, Roy Romer, and Carroll Campbell," April 18, 1991, Bush Presidential Records, Office of Policy Development, Doreen Torgerson file, Box 11, Folder America 2000 Kickoff 4/18/91 [OA/ID 05162], GBPL, p. 1; telephone interview of Porter by author, November 26, 1997.

44. Letter from Bartlett to Bush, GBPL; David Armor, "After Busing: Education and Choice," *Current* (October 14–20, 1989): 26, 29.

45. Handwritten notes by Charles Kolb and Memorandum from Doreen Torgerson to Charles Kolb, in September 1990, Bush Presidential Records, Office of Policy Development, Doreen Torgerson, Desegregation [OS/ID 05164]; George Bush, "Question and Answer Session in Paducah, Kentucky," October 27, 1992, *Public Papers of the Presidents of the United States: George Bush,* Book 2, *1992,* p. 2022.

46. Memorandum from Charles Kolb to Roger Porter, September 28, 1990, WHORM, Subject file Education, Folder ED Education [177000-179999] [3], GBPL, p. 1; Letter from George Bush to William Goodling, February 22, 1991, WHORM, Subject file Education, Folder ED Education [220000-225999], GBPL; Jeanne Allen and Michael McLaughlin,

"Assessing the Bush Education Proposal," *Heritage Foundation Issues Bulletin,* June 28, 1991, p. 3; "The Polly Williams Backlash," *Wall Street Journal,* June 14, 1990, p. A14.

47. Memorandum from Mary Farrell to Roger Porter, August 22, 1991, WHORM, Subject file Education, Box 28, Folder ED Education [267000-268999], GBPL, p. 4; Memorandum from Lamar Alexander to George Bush, June 7, 1991, WHORM, Subject file Education, Box 26, Folder ED Education [253000-257999] [2], GBPL.

48. Adam Clymer, "For the Education Plan, A Rare Rosy Forecast," *New York Times,* April 17, 1991, p. A19; Julie Miller, "House Panel's Vote Marks Sea Change on the Choice Issue," *Education Week,* November 6, 1991, p. 137.

49. "Scorned School Bill Dies in Senate," pp. 455–61.

50. Letter from George Bush to Congress and attachment, June 17, 1972, WHORM, Subject file Education, Box 36, Folder ED Education [325000-366452] [3], GBPL, p. 1.

51. "President Bush Sets Historic Partnership and New Education Agenda," *America 2000 Newsletter,* U.S. Department of Education, November 23, 1992, Bush Presidential Records, Office of Policy Development, Charles E. M. Kolb subject file, Alexander, Lamar—Strategy [OA/IS 06827] [1 of 4], GBPL, p. 1; George Bush, "Presidential Remarks: G.I. Bill for Kids," June 25, 1992, WHORM, Subject file Federal Aid, Folder FA 003 Education [329506-334845], GBPL, p. 9.

52. "House Panel's Vote Marks Sea Change on the Choice Issue," p. 137; "Domestic Policy Meeting," December 19, 1991, Bush Presidential Records, Office of Policy Development, Charles E. M. Kolb subject file, Alexander, Lamar—Strategy [OA/ID 06827] [1 of 4], GBPL.

53. George Bush, "Question and Answer Session in Grand Rapids," October 29, 1992, *Public Papers of the Presidents of the United States: George Bush,* Book 1, 1992–93 (Washington, D.C.: U.S. Government Printing Office, 1993), p. 2083.

54. Bush, "Remarks at the Presidential Open Forum on Educational Choice in Philadelphia, Pennsylvania," July 21, 1992, p. 1147.

55. Karen DeWitt, "New Education Chief Stresses Commitment," *New York Times,* March 19, 1991, p. A21; William McGurn, "Lamar's Choice," *National Review,* August 26, 1991, pp. 20–21; Mark Pitsch, "Kearns Vows to Turn E.D. Around as He did Xerox," *Education Week,* June 5, 1991, p. 1; John J. Miller, "Opting Out," *New Republic,* November 30, 1992, p. 13.

56. Clifford Kraus, "Senate Rejects Bush Plan to Aid the Poor Who Use Private Schools," *New York Times,* January 24, 1992, p. A15; Paul Taylor, "Milwaukee's Controversial Private School Choice Plan Off to Shaky Start," *Washington Post,* May 25, 1991, p. A3.

57. George Bush, "Question and Answer Session in Grand Rapids," p. 2082; Susan Chira, "Clinton to Offer Plan for Change in U.S. Schools," *New York Times,* April 21, 1993, pp. K1, K8.

58. Charles Tiefer, *The Semi-Sovereign Presidency: The Bush Administration's Strategy for Governing without Congress* (Boulder, Colo.: Westview, 1994), p. 16; Bush, "Remarks at the Presidential Open Forum on Educational Choice in Philadelphia, Pennsylvania," July 21, 1992, p. 1148.

59. Thomas Friedman, "Clintons Pick Private School in Capital for Their Daughter," *New York Times,* January 6, 1993, p. A14.

60. Ibid.

61. William Clinton, "Remarks to the AFL-CIO Convention in San Francisco, California," October 4, 1993, *Public Papers of the Presidents of the United States: William J. Clinton,* Book 2, 1993 (Washington, D.C.: U.S. Government Printing Service, 1994), p. 1672.

62. Linda Greenhouse, "Justices Allow Religious Groups After Hours Use of Public Schools," *New York Times,* June 8, 1993, pp. A1, A23.

63. Linda Greenhouse, "Court Says Government May Pay for Interpreter in Religious School," *New York Times,* June 19, 1993, pp. A1, A8.

64. Winnifred Sullivan, "The USCC and the Rebbe," *Commonweal,* May 20, 1994, pp. 6–7; Frank Kemerer and Kimi Lynn King, "Are School Vouchers Constitutional?" *Phi Delta Kappan* (December 1995): 309.

65. Kemerer and King, "Are School Vouchers Constitutional?" p. 311.

66. "Voters in California Reject Proposal on School Vouchers," *New York Times,* November 3, 1993, p. A24; Linda Greenhouse, "High Court Bars School District Created to Benefit Hasidic Jews," *New York Times,* June 28, 1994, p. D21. Within days of this decision, however, the New York legislature passed new legislation drafted by Democratic governor Mario Cuomo that the state supreme court upheld the following year as "religiously neutral, accommodating the Hasidic residents of the village of Kiryas Joel without singling them for favorable treatment"; see Joseph Berger, "Court Affirms Public School for Hasidim," *New York Times,* March 9, 1995, p. D21.

67. Kemerer and King, "Are School Vouchers Constitutional?" pp. 309–10; "House Passes High School Job-Training Bill," *Congressional Quarterly Almanac,* 103rd Cong., 1st sess., 1994 (Washington, D.C., 1995), p. 398; Thomas Content, "School Choice Is Alive," *Green Bay Press-Gazette,* November 12, 1994, p. A1.

68. "Labor-HHS Bill in Limbo at Year's End," *Congressional Quarterly Almanac,* 104th Cong., 1st sess., 1995 (Washington, D.C., 1996), pp. 11–57; John Leo, "Choice Words for Teacher Unions," *U.S. News and World Report,* March 11, 1996, p. 17.

69. Sharon Brooks Hodge, "School Choice Works, Parents Say," *Headway,* October 1996, pp. 22–23.

70. Thomas Toch and Warren Cohen, "Why Vouchers Won't Work," *U.S. News and World Report,* October 7, 1996, p. 66; Alex Molnar, Walter Farrell, James Johnson, and Marty Sapp, "Research, Politics, and the School Choice Agenda," *Phi Delta Kappan* (November 1996): 241–42.

71. Toch and Cohen, "Why Vouchers Won't Work," p. 66; "Presidential Debate in Hartford, Connecticut," October 6, 1996, *Public Papers of the Presidents of the United States: William J. Clinton,* Book 2, *1996* (Washington, D.C.: U.S. Government Printing Office, 1998), pp. 1771–72.

72. "Presidential Debate in Hartford, Connecticut," pp. 1771–72.

73. "The President's News Conference," December 13, 1996, *Public Papers of the Presidents of the United States: William J. Clinton,* Book 2, *1996* (Washington, D.C.: U.S. Government Printing Office, 1998), p. 2204.

74. Krista Kafer and Jonathan Butcher, "How Members of Congress Practice School Choice," *Heritage Foundation,* http://www.heritage.org/Research/Education/BG1684.cfm (accessed December 23, 2005); Elizabeth Shogren and Janet Hook, "Clinton Wins Uncertain School Voucher Victory," *Milwaukee Journal-Sentinel,* October 1, 1997, p. A1.

75. "Study Finds Pupils Are Helped by Program," *Milwaukee Journal-Sentinel,* October 16, 1997, p. A16; Shokrai, "How Members of Congress Practice School Choice," p. 4; Clarence Page, "Vouchers and Other School Aids Are for the Lucky Few," *Chicago Tribune,* October 29, 1997, sec. 1, p. 13.

76. "Clinton Promotes Charter Schools," *Education Week,* October 1, 1997, p. 24.

77. Tamar Lewin, "School Voucher Study Finds Satisfaction," *Milwaukee Journal-Sentinel,* September 18, 1997, p. A12; "Public vs. Private," *U.S. News and World Report,* November 23, 1998, p. 5.

78. George Will, "In 1998, It's Liberals Who Block Schoolhouse Door," *Milwaukee Journal-Sentinel,* November 30, 1998, p. A8; Robert Coles, "Wisconsin's Historic Decision," *America,* August 29–September 5, 1998, p. 5; Scott Hildebrand, "Private-School Choice Unlikely to Be Expanded," *Green Bay Press-Gazette,* p. A2.

79. Tamara Henry, "Majority Backs Public Money for Private Schools," *USA Today,* August 26, 1998, p. D1; "Vouchers," National Education Association Center for the Advancement of Public Education, http://www.nea.org./vouchers/index.html (accessed January 8, 2006); Pam Belluck, "Federal Judge Revises Order, Allowing Vouchers for Now," *New York Times,* August 27, 1999, p. A1.

80. Clarence Page, "Resistance to School Vouchers by African-Americans Is Starting to Change," *Chicago Tribune,* June 2, 1999, sec. 1, p. 13.

81. Neil Lewis, "School Vouchers Survive as Justices Sidestep a Debate," *New York Times,* November 10, 1998, p. A19; Alan Borsuk, "Wall Dividing Church and State Under Renovation," *Milwaukee Journal-Sentinel,* July 5, 1998, p. A14.

82. Joe Nathan, "Heat and Light in the Charter School Movement," *Phi Delta Kappan* (March 1998): 505; "NEA Charter Schools Take Initiative," *NEA Today* (April 1998): 21; William Raspberry, "How Can We Help Public Schools Heal Themselves?" *Milwaukee Journal-Sentinel,* June 27, 1998, p. A12.

83. Page, "Resistance to School Vouchers by African-Americans Is Starting to Change," p. 13.

84. Borsuk, "Wall Dividing Church and State Under Renovation," p. 14.

85. Steven Greenhouse, "Teachers' Leader Seeks New Path," *New York Times,* July 4, 1998, p. A7; Joe Williams, "Teacher Union Chief Assails School Choice," *Milwaukee Journal-Sentinel,* July 4, 1999, p. A1; "Lessons Cleveland Can Teach," *Economist,* November 29, 1997, p. 30; Joe Williams, "NEA Gave Money to Anti-Voucher Group," *Milwaukee Journal-Sentinel,* July 5, 1999, pp. B1, B7.

86. John Miller, "Opting Out," *New Republic,* November 30, 1992, p. 13; "Other Education-Related Bills," *Congressional Quarterly Almanac,* 105th Cong., 1st sess., 1997 (Washington, D.C., 1998), pp. 7–8.

87. Michael Hinds, "Schools and Churches Close, Angering Catholics," *New York Times,* July 5, 1993, p. A6; Edd Doerr, "Vouchers and Educational Equity," *Humanist* (July/August 1977): 32.

88. Joe Williams, "For MPS, School Choice Comes Down to Dollars," *Milwaukee Journal-Sentinel,* October 26, 1998, p. A10; Joetta Sack, "Voucher Debate Plays Out in the Capitol's Shadow," *Education Week,* April 22, 1998, p. 25.

## Conclusion

1. John Jennings, "Title I: A Success," *Education Week,* January 26, 2001, p. 30.

2. Maris Vinovskis, "Do Federal Compensatory Programs Really Work?" *American Journal of Education* 107 (May 1999): 202; Michael Puma, Nancy Karucit, and Michael Vaden-Kiernan, *Prospects: Student Outcomes Final Report,* United States Department of Education (Washington, D.C.: Planning and Evaluation Service, 1997), p. 1.

3. Diane Ravitch, "The Search for Order and the Rejection of Conformity," in *Learning from the Past,* ed. Diane Ravitch and Maris Vinovskis (Baltimore: Johns Hopkins University Press, 1995), pp. 181, 183; *Mapping Out the National Assessment of Title I: The Interim Report, 1996,* August 7, 2001, http://www.ed.gov/pubs/NatAssess/sec2.html (accessed September 30, 2001), p. 3.

4. *No Excuses: Lessons from Twenty-One High-Performing, High-Poverty Schools* (Washington, D.C.: Heritage Foundation, 2000), p. 1; Mary Marklen, "Math Scores: Optimism Rises as SAT Hits Thirty-Year High," *USA Today,* August 30, 2000, p. A1.

5. Richard Rothstein, "In Standardized Tests, Standards Vary," *New York Times,* July 18, 2001, p. A18; Susan Ohanian, "Goals 2000: What's in a Name?" *Phi Delta Kappan,* January 2000, p. 351.

6. David Hoff, "Goals Push for 2000 Falls Short," *Education Week,* December 8, 1999, pp. 1–2.

7. Gregory Cizek, *Unintended Consequences of High-Stakes Testing,* Education News Organization, n.d., http://www.educationnews.org/in_defense_of_testing_series_uni .htm (accessed January 8, 2006), p. 6.

8. Jennifer Hochschild, *The New American Dilemma* (New Haven: Yale University Press, 1984), p. 177; Susan Eaton and Gary Orfield, *Dismantling Desegregation* (Cambridge: Harvard University Press, 1996), p. 22; Joseph Watras, *Politics, Race, and the Schools: Racial Integration, 1954–1974* (New York: Garland), p. xviii.

9. Christine Rossell, *The Carrot or the Stick for School Desegreation Policy: Magnet Schools or Forced Busing?* (Philadelphia: Temple University Press, 1990), p. 187; David Armor, *Forced Justice* (New York: Oxford University Press, 1995), p. 223.

10. Rossell, *The Carrot or the Stick for School Desegreation Policy,* p. xiii; Amy Stuart Wells and Robert Crain, *Stepping Over the Colored Line* (New Haven: Yale University Press, 1997), p. 335.

11. Jeffrey Rosen, "The Lost Promise of School Integration," *New York Times,* April 2, 2000, sec. 4, p. 5.

12. Diana Schemo, "U.S. Schools Turn More Segregated, A Study Finds," *New York Times,* July 20, 2001, p. A12.

13. Nina Shrokrai Rees, *School Choice 2000: What's Happening in The States* (Washington, D.C.: Heritage Foundation, 2001), pp. xxi–xxii; Jodi Wilgore, "Two Florida Schools Become Testing Ground for Vouchers," *New York Times,* March 14, 2000, p. A18; Tamara Henry, "Alliance Promotes Vouchers," *USA Today,* May 7, 2001, p. D1.

14. William Howell, Patrick Wolf, Paul Peterson, and David Campbell, "The Effect of School Vouchers on Student Achievement: A Response to Critics," Program on Education Policy and Governance, Harvard University, n.d., p. 1; Diana Schemo, "Voucher Threat Incites Schools to Improve, Florida Study Says," *New York Times,* February 16, 2001, p. A14; Sam Schulhofer-Wohl, "MPS Gains Are Linked to Vouchers," *Milwaukee Journal-Sentinel,* April 24, 2001, p. A1.

15. Howell, Wolf, Peterson, and Campbell, "The Effect of School Vouchers on Student Achievement," pp. 1–2; Schemo, "Voucher Threat," p. 14; Schulhofer-Wohl, "MPS Gains Are Linked to Vouchers," p. 10.

16. Tamara Henry, "Poll: Vouchers Lose Support, but Public Schools Gain," *USA Today,* August 23, 2001, p. A1; Richard Rothstein, "Yes, Vouchers Are Dead, and Alternatives Are Flawed," *New York Times,* June 20, 2001, p. A14.

17. Henry, "Poll: Vouchers Lose Support," p. 1.

18. Charles Lane, "Court Upholds School Vouchers," *Washington Post*, June 28, 2002, pp. A1, A11.

19. Joseph Michalak, "Father of Invention," *New York Times Magazine*, November 3, 1991, sec. 4A, p. 15.

20. Chester Finn, "Reflections on 'The Disassembly of the Federal Educational Role,'" *Education and Urban Society* (May 1983): 291; Letter from Chester Finn to William Bennett, February 3, 1988, Box 105, Chester Finn Papers, Hoover Institution on War, Revolution, and Peace, Stanford University, Stanford, Calif.; Letter from Chester Finn to Lauro Cavazos, September 21, 1989, Box 105, Chester Finn Papers, Hoover Institution on War, Revolution, and Peace.

21. Fowler writes that "Charles Peters founded neoliberalism in 1969 when he started his political magazine *The Washington Monthly*. A former member of the Kennedy Administration, Peters had become disillusioned with what he called traditional liberalism. . . . Neoliberals had decided to retain liberal ends while rethinking their means to those ends"; see Frances Fowler, "The Neoliberal Value Shift and Its Implications for Federal Education Policy under Clinton," *Educational Administration Quarterly* (February 1995): 38–61.

22. Telephone interview of Robert Wood by author, November 26, 1997. Michael Harrington's *The Other America* (New York: Macmillan, 1962) helped make "poverty" a regular part of the political lexicon, and Kenneth Auletta's *The Underclass* (New York: Overlook Press, 1982) was an eloquent plea to remember the poor. Arianna Huffington, "Black Voters Look Past Rhetoric," *Chicago Sun-Times*, August 27, 1999, p. A51. For a historical perspective on U.S. federal approaches to the underprivileged, see Theda Skocpol, *Social Policy in the United States* (Princeton, N.J.: Princeton University Press, 1995).

23. The No Child Left Behind Act of 2001, the latest five-year extension of the ESEA, increased ESEA spending by $8 billion and mandated annual testing of third through eighth-graders. After it passed the House, 381–41, and the Senate, 87 to 10, President Bush signed it on January 8, 2002; see Helen DeWar, "Landmark Education Legislation Gets Final Approval in Congress," *Washington Post*, December 19, 2001, p. A1.

24. A December 1999 Associated Press poll identified education as the nation's "top issue," followed by Social Security/Medicare, the economy, and the nation's moral values; see Paul Leavitt, "Report: Budget for 2000 Will Touch Both Surpluses," *USA Today*, December 2, 1999, p. A10. Not only had the nation failed to achieve any of the eight Bush-Clinton educational goals by the end of 1999, but the National Education Goals Panel conceded as much, recommending that "Goals 2000" become "America's Education Goals" in the coming year; see Richard Rothstein, "'Goals 2000' Scorecard: Failure Pitches a Shutout," *New York Times*, December 22, 1999, p. A22.

# INDEX

LAWRENCE J. MCANDREWS received his doctorate in history from Georgetown University. He is currently Professor of History at St. Norbert College in DePere, Wisconsin, where he has won several awards for his teaching and scholarship. Dr. McAndrews is the author of the book *Broken Ground: John F. Kennedy and the Politics of Education* as well as numerous articles in a variety of books and journals.

The University of Illinois Press
is a founding member of the
Association of American University Presses.

———————————————————————

Composed in 10.5/13 Adobe Minion
with Minion display
by BookComp, Inc.
Manufactured by Thomson-Shore, Inc.

University of Illinois Press
1325 South Oak Street
Champaign, IL 61820-6903
www.press.uillinois.edu